Cracking the Coconut

Cracking the Coconut

CLASSIC THAI

HOME COOKING

Su-Mei Yu

William Morrow
An Imprint of HarperCollinsPublishers

FIRST EDITION
Designed by Ralph Fowler
Printed on acid-free paper

Library of Congress Cataloging-in-Publication Data has
been applied for.

ISBN 0-688-16542-7

02 03 04 QW 10 9 8 7 6 5 4

To my father,

Yu Hung Been,

and

my mother,

Yu Li Kwei Chi

Contents

Acknowledgments

Four years ago at the Symposium for Professional Food Writers at the Greenbrier in West Virginia, my longtime friend Antonia Allegra revived the seed for this book, which had been gestating in the depths of my mind for many years. Many hands helped nurture this seed into a blooming plant, beginning with Sarah Jane Freymann, my agent, who believed in its potential so strongly she was able to convince Justin Schwartz at William Morrow to take a chance on an exotic, unique book concept from an unknown author. Lois Stanton, my true and faithful friend, tested every recipe in her basic American kitchen equipped with an electric stove and limited counter space. Her husband, Doctor Bill, consumed and critiqued our results night after night. Amy Albert and Nikki Symington read and edited the manuscript with loving criticism, striving for clarity in cooking methods and engaging stories. Brenda Baker read through the whole book one more time. My companion, Italo Scanga, stood by me as I wrote from early dawn to late into the night. My daughter, Angela Goding, cheered me on whenever I was overwhelmed with the task.

This book would not have been possible without Raoul Marquis, my longtime companion, whose untimely death left a void in my life. It was Raoul who first recognized my love of cooking and desire to write about it. He made it possible for me to do both. But my reverence for food, cooking, and eating began with my mother, Yu Li Kwei Chi, whose passion for the art of cooking remains unequaled in my life.

Finally, my annual culinary trips to Thailand would have been less adventurous if not for my brother, Dr. Kim Pao Yu, who staked out the marvelous places to eat. He also introduced me to his friends Bob Halliday and Suthon Sukphisit, whose knowledge about, and zeal for, Thai food are unsurpassed. Vithi Panichphant, my childhood friend, delighted me with the exotic side of Thai cooking and taught me the importance of history and tradition. Through them, I made new friends who shared their stories, recipes, techniques, and culinary secrets with me. I hope to honor all of them and the heritage of Thai cooking with this book.

Introduction

During the past fifteen years, I have journeyed back to Thailand each year in search of my heritage and the "ancient ones" who still remember and cook the food of the past. In my quest to taste and understand the evolution of this complex and delectable cuisine, I have haunted homes, villages, markets, restaurants, libraries, and old and new bookstores. While tracking down the history of Thai food and traditional recipes, I've acquired some ancient funeral books, which are now among my most precious possessions. From a Thai tradition that began with the reign of King Mongkut, Rama the Fourth (1851–1868), recipes were included in funeral books if the deceased loved cooking or eating. Copies of the books would be given as a commemoration to friends and families at funerals. These books mirror the Thai love of cooking and honor the relationship and continuity between food and the life of an individual, a family, and society.

More than a simple recipe book, this is a book about the history of Thai cooking and the people and customs that shaped it. For the past and the present are strung together like a priceless pearl necklace, with the cultural, artistic, social, and religious influences shaping and molding the pearls of each era. Together with ingenious leaders who had the vision to embrace new and foreign ways, common people transformed their simple fare into an acclaimed culinary art.

This book is my gift to those who have discovered Thai food and share my love for it. Their passion has cultivated a continuing appreciation of this amazing cuisine. Among these are people who want to learn to cook real Thai food. This book is for them, for their use and enjoyment.

Finally, this is a book of celebration, in the tradition of the Thai people of long ago who not only practiced the art of cooking and eating with zeal, but wrote poetry to honor their wondrous ritual.

When I was a little girl, my mother used to gather my brother, sister, and me together to tell us stories. This was the way she taught us to grow up to become "people with culture and manners." She always started each story in the same way, saying, "Back in our old home, we did . . ." Her approach to teaching us about food was the same.

Although my mother was an exceptional cook who entertained dignitaries and friends alike in our humble home, she never allowed us to help her in the kitchen. Instead, she took us to the markets, allowed us to watch her as she cooked, and told us endless stories about the food. A simple dish had countless legends behind it, and an ordinary ingredient held hidden secrets that only the wise ones could uncover. This was how her children grew infatuated with food. Through her example, we are all lovers of food and dedicated cooks.

My lessons came from others as well. Growing up away from home in a Thai boarding school, I was surrounded by friends whose families also had great cooks. Through my friends, I had the chance to see, learn about, and taste new dishes. Their families taught me as my mother did, never allowing me to cook, but telling stories that always began "In the ancient time, we used to . . ."

It is an odd way to learn to cook, yet this was the old way. And for me, it seems that cooking, eating, talking, and thinking about food has been a life-long avocation. Until I began to cook, I didn't know that it would come as naturally to me as breathing. It's as if I had been preparing all my life for that moment, when the words of wisdom from my mother, cooks I'd observed, and old friends would come flooding back to me. Even now, they're always looking over my shoulder, ready to help and watching to make certain I have it right.

After thirty-five years, I have come of age. Now, it's time for me to pass along the ancient

tradition. Instead of simply telling the stories, I have chosen to write them, not only to teach, but also to preserve knowledge that might otherwise be lost to future generations. It's my debt and homage to the ancient ones.

I began to cook Thai food out of necessity, when I came to the United States at the age of fifteen. Living and going to school in a small town in Kentucky, I grew homesick for familiar dishes. I had to make do with just a few seasonings, like cayenne, garlic, and scallions. During my college years, I cooked with only an electric skillet on the bathroom counter in my dormitory room.

Today, I cook as if I am in Thailand. My pantry and garden overflow with Thai ingredients. The outdoor kitchen resembles the Thai kitchens of my childhood and is equipped with only my mother's mortar and pestle, a skillet, a saucepan, knives, and a couple of butane stoves. With these few simple tools, I have taught many students to cook the traditional Thai way, and something more important as well: a new way of being. To the Thai people, cooking is not a chore that can be hurried through and completed in fifteen minutes, nor is food prepared to be gulped down in twenty seconds. The Thai way is gracious and joyful, giving and taking great pleasure in all the simple acts of living.

With this book, I want to dispel the notion that cooking Thai food is difficult and mysterious. To me, cooking and eating are sensual experiences. Each time I crack open a coconut and my hands touch the hard, rough shell, the visual surprise of uncovering the contrasting pristine inner white meat delights me. I love the feel of the smooth silken flesh as I begin to extract it for milking and get a whiff of the sweet faint aroma from the juices. The slow and rhythmic pounding of fresh and dried herbs and spices and the scents of the wonderful perfumes relax and renew my spirits. When I finally begin to cook, I'm almost mesmerized, watching the vibrant colors of the ingredients as they change and emerge. By the time the dish is ready, I am drunk with desire. And with my first bite, I am rewarded with a flood of spectacular flavors and textures.

To me, teaching someone how to cook Thai food is like teaching someone to dance. It takes practice to be a graceful dancer. Each step must be patiently learned and tried. When mastered, each step brings new pleasure. Then, finally, all the steps flow into a dance, a rhythm that is so natural and exhilarating you cannot wait to begin again.

The Basics of Thai Cooking

When my parents immigrated to America twenty years ago, the one thing from my home in Thailand I asked to have was my mother's mortar and pestle. It was the first thing she had bought for her kitchen when she emigrated from China to Thailand fifty years before. This small carved granite tool, worn and smooth from years of use, lay for a long time in my kitchen cabinet, an anachronism among my electric appliances. For years I kept it for sentimental reasons, savoring the memories of my mother's fabulous meals. I didn't know how to use it properly, nor was I interested in learning. It was a souvenir of a time past.

I cooked familiar Thai meals from memory, using new Western inventions. With the push of a button, things swirled and blended like magic. In no time at all, I could cook food that was tasty and that, to my surprise, friends thought marvelous. I was encouraged by my success and rave reviews. But I knew my food could be better and more authentic. I longed to taste the exquisite meals of my childhood again.

So I went home to Thailand to eat and learn to cook like my mother. There, caught up in the spirit of the Thai people and their romance with cooking and eating, I reconnected with the essence of Thai food and one of the important lessons of my childhood. I recognized, like my mother before me, that cooking is not a chore, but a creative process, a gift we give to ourselves and those we love.

Today I have mastered the use of my mother's mortar and pestle. It is out of the cabinet and on my countertop, my constant cooking companion, a reminder that cooking, especially Thai cooking, is meant to be a celebration of life.

Most Americans prefer to go to Thai restaurants rather than cook Thai food at home. As an owner of a Thai restaurant, I am glad they come and like my food. But Thai food tastes better—and is meant to be—prepared and served at home. To the Thais, refined and gracious dining is a way of life, a way of being and sharing.

Unfortunately, Americans believe that Thai cooking is too hard and takes too long, and that the ingredients are too exotic and difficult to find. My response is: If you think food from your favorite Thai restaurant is great, you will love preparing and eating the recipes in this book. There is no comparison between restaurant Thai cooking and an authentic, fresh, home-prepared meal. In this book, I am going to introduce you to, and teach you how to prepare, the incomparable culinary wonders of authentic Thai foods. I will take you step by step through shopping, preparation, and serving. You will be amazed at how easy, convenient, and adaptable Thai cooking is to your lifestyle.

This first chapter will guide you through Thai cooking, starting with explanations on how to use and where to purchase the cooking equipment you will need. Here you will learn traditional and modern cooking techniques, and how to buy, plan, organize, prepare, and store ingredients for last-minute cooking. I won't promise you "quick and easy," but I do promise you less time than you ever thought you'd need.

The wonders and mysteries of Thai food's exquisite flavors are the ingredients. Learning where to buy and how to use them and how to substitute available ingredients for traditional or seasonal ingredients will give you the foundation on which to build a lasting, intimate, and enjoyable relationship with Thai home cooking. You are about to embark on an adventure, an experience with satisfaction guaranteed through hundreds of years of loving perfection in humble Thai kitchens.

The Thai Neighbor's Kitchen

The road to authentic Thai cooking begins with the cooking tools Thai use.

As a child in Bangkok, I thought the kitchen was the most fascinating place to be. I spent hours watching my mother and the servants of our wealthy neighbors chop, grind, mix, blend, steam, and fry. For a small child, the kitchen offered a ringside seat to a magic show.

On my street, the homes were tiny row houses, jumbled and squeezed together like sardines in a can. But there was one exception. It was the home of a wealthy Thai family. Behind a huge gate and forbidding walls, the great house sat surrounded by massive, aging trees and immense grounds rich with lush landscaping

and a pond. This fine home was a constant source of wonder and mystery.

Occasionally a friend and I were invited to visit the family and explore the large teak buildings, verandahs with shiny ceramic roofs that surrounded the house, and the magnificent gardens and pond. The family lived in a large structure that was connected to a smaller building by a bridge over the pond. The smaller building was the kitchen. It was always dark inside, even in the daytime. I remember how amazed I was to discover that a kitchen could have walls, and a roof, no less! Quite a contrast to the cement slab behind our house that served as my family's kitchen. Despite the fact that the kitchen seemed more like a house than a place to cook, it was sparsely furnished with simple cooking utensils just like my mother's. Pots and pans were piled neatly on the floor in one corner. Mortars and pestles of different sizes were prominently displayed along one wall. Against

another wall sat a big wooden cupboard used to store perishable ingredients, leftovers, and seasonings. The cupboard stood on legs resting in porcelain bowls filled with water, to discourage climbing insects. Bowls and baskets overflowing with garlic, chiles, and other herbs and spices were stacked against another wall.

Several brick braziers reclined on the floor beneath the only window. There was a wooden crate containing charcoal sticks, and outside the door stood a large terra-cotta jar for storing water. That was it—the extent of the kitchen's contents. The family owned a small refrigerator, a rare possession in Thailand in the early 1950s, but it was kept in the dining room of the main house.

In the kitchen, women servants squatted on the floor or sat on tiny stools as they washed meat and vegetables or dishes. All the slicing, chopping, grinding, pounding, and cooking was done on the wooden floor. There were open spaces between the floorboards, and you could peek through the cracks and see the water in the pond below. The cook usually had a baited hook dangling into the pond hoping to catch a big old catfish that appeared whenever the used water was poured though the gaps between the boards.

Like all Thai cooks at that time, the cook went to the market every day. A teenage servant helped her cut, slice, chop, mince, grind, and puree the food. Whenever the young girl's pestle hit the mortar in an uneven way, the cook berated her. "You will never find a husband!" she would say. You see, the signature of a great Thai cook is the way the pestle hits the mortar in an even, musical rhythm. It's a courting song for unmarried girls that takes years of practice—and innumerable scoldings—to perfect.

One day the cook lit the charcoal brazier

and black smoke saturated the dark, poorly ventilated kitchen, sending all of us outdoors, gasping for air. When she was ready to stir-fry, the cook moved the brazier outside so as not to suffocate from the smoke and heavy-scented spices. This experience made me appreciate my family's outdoor kitchen—the humble uncovered cement slab—even though, during the monsoons, my mother would get soaking wet cooking under an umbrella in the downpour. Like my mother, I prefer to cook outdoors in the open air, whenever the weather permits, that is.

The Modern Thai Kitchen

Today high-rise condominiums and Western-style homes are rapidly replacing traditional Thai architecture. City homes have indoor kitchens equipped with fancy electric or gas ranges, microwaves, and hot and cold running water. Many rural families still use and prefer the outdoors for cooking. Urban people no longer squat or sit outdoors, however, but stand and work at convenient counters, with roofs over their heads and everything needed for cooking at their fingertips.

Thais are fascinated with Western kitchen equipment and the latest gadgets. Department stores sell all types of modern kitchenware, all of which promise to produce quick and perfect meals. Even for the wealthy modern Thai, the lifestyle has changed. The servants who once did all the cooking have been replaced by new mechanical inventions.

An open-mindedness in regard to foreign ways and willingness to try new things is one of the best qualities of the Thai people. Ready acceptance of such innovations has made adaptation of traditional Thai recipes easy for them and for Western cooks. But, for Thais and Westerners alike to cook authentic Thai food, it is necessary to use traditional methods. The simple equipment used for generations still proves to be the best way to capture the unique and original textures, aromas, and flavors of Thai food. That is why the mortar and pestle still rules in all Thai kitchens, and why you will need one of your own.

A stone mortar and pestle from Thailand with a 2-cup capacity can be purchased in Asian supermarkets. Although many Thai cookbooks written for Americans recommend using a blender or food processor, there is no substitute for pounding herbs and spices with a mortar and pestle. There are many new ways to modernize the preparation of Thai food without compromising the taste. But this traditional method is

the only way to make pastes that release the aromatic oils from the herbs and spices to produce the rich Thai flavors and perfumes. Advocates of the blender and food processor for grinding herbs and spices reason that these machines save time and labor. They may be more convenient, but they alter the taste and texture of herbs and spices. The art of pounding and grinding to make a paste using a mortar and pestle is not difficult; it just takes practice.

You can cook real Thai food with only a few other "must have" pieces of equipment. These include a good-quality food processor with a steel blade; a Chinese cleaver; a 12-inch skillet; a 6- or 8-quart pasta cooker with a steamer insert and a glass lid, which is a more versatile replacement for the traditional Chinese or Thai bamboo steamer; and an electric rice cooker, a newer invention that makes cooking rice a dream.

The following is a list of everything you will need to turn your kitchen into a modern Thai kitchen, your first step to becoming an accomplished Thai cook. Most of these items are available in stores that specialize in cooking equipment; if not, they can be purchased in Asian markets.

KNIVES: An 8- or 10-inch chef's knife, a 3-inch paring knife, and a Chinese cleaver. A Chinese cleaver has an oblong blade and is heavier and wider than other cleavers; one is needed to cut bones. It can be found in Asian markets and in some cookware stores too. You will also need good-quality knives that feel well balanced and comfortable in your hand. Keep them sharpened.

CHOPPING BOARD: The best chopping boards are made of hardwood, such as maple. Buy one that is at least 16 by 21 inches. Because a wood board yields and gives to pressure, it is better for your knives than acrylic.

VEGETABLE GRATER AND PEELER: The Japanese vegetable grater called a Benriner has a flat

To season a new steel wok, wash it lightly with soap and very warm water. Let dry. Coat the inside lightly with vegetable oil and place in a 300°F oven for 1 hour. Remove and cool completely. After using, wash the wok with soap and hot water, using a sponge so as not to scratch the surface. Dry thoroughly and apply a light coat of oil on the surface. Repeat the process for several months, until a black coating covers the surface.

oblong plastic frame with interchangeable blades and different sizes of graters and shredders. Available in Asian markets, it is the best buy for your money. Good sharp vegetable peelers are indispensable, inexpensive, and available in any supermarket.

GRINDER, FOOD PROCESSOR, AND MORTAR AND PESTLE: An electric coffee bean grinder is wonderful for grinding roasted dried spices—use it only for spices. A heavy-duty food processor is useful for making coconut cream; the bowl should hold at least a quart. As mentioned above, a Thai-style stone mortar and pestle is a must. These are different from the small marble ones sold in gourmet cook shops, which cannot be substituted. They can be purchased in most Asian markets or by mail order (see page 313). Buy a mortar that is at least 7 inches in diameter and carved from a solid piece of stone with a wide 2-cup-capacity bowl. The pestle is also carved from stone. A ceramic urn-shaped mortar with a wooden pestle is not a necessity but is useful when making a dish like green papaya salad or grinding dried roasted chiles. It is fairly inexpensive. You may want to splurge and buy both.

POTS, PANS, SKILLETS, AND WOK: Invest in good-quality, heavy-duty cooking equipment. You will need a 2-quart saucepan with a tight-fitting lid, a 4-quart saucepan with a tight-fitting lid, a 6- to 8-quart pasta pot with steamer insert and glass lid, a 7-inch skillet, a 12-inch skillet, and a well-seasoned 12-inch steel flat-bottomed wok with a lid.

Note that all of these recipes were tested using nonstick cookware. Be sure to buy high-quality nonstick pans. The nonstick coating on lesser-quality pans may begin to flake off under the stress of high heat.

STRAINER, PADDLE, AND SPOON: A long-handled wooden or metal spoon and paddle, slotted spoon, and fine-mesh strainer are essential for stirring, mixing, and straining.

Preparation the Easy Thai Way

Traditional Thai cooking methods relied on heat from charcoal burned in a brick brazier (a stove made from brick and shaped like a bucket or a flowerpot). Charcoal, however, was expensive. Village people could rarely afford it and instead used dried leaves and kindling from nearby woods or forests. Dry-roasting, slow-cooking, and steaming were the most commonly used methods, because they require less fuel. Slow-cooking over low heat was the preferred method for a very practical reason. Busy farm women could do other chores while food cooked. Also, cooking was done in terra-cotta vessels, which could crack over more intense heat. Meats such as pork, chicken, or wild game were tough and slow-cooking helped tenderize them.

Not until the late 1800s, when Chinese metalworkers began manufacturing them for sale, did metal woks and pots begin to replace terra-cotta. Even though European traders and Chinese settlers were importing metal pots and pans for their own use since the 1600s, few

Thais could afford them. But it was the Royal Court of King Chulalongkhorn that led the way in institutionalizing the metal woks that revolutionized Thai cooking. The king adored cooking and eating. He fell in love with the steel wok, and made it part of the royal kitchen. The people followed his lead, quickly catching onto the endless possibilities available to a creative cook, freed from worrying about the heat of cooking cracking the pots.

The key to Thai cooking is a combination of flavors and textures with enticing aromas and a pleasing appearance. Mincing and pounding release the oils and scents of herbs and spices. Until eating utensils were introduced, Thai people ate mostly with their hands. That's why even today most ingredients are cut into bite-sized pieces convenient for picking up with fingers. Cutting meats and vegetables into smaller pieces helped them absorb seasonings, enhancing flavor. Liquids like soup were scooped with sea or coconut shells carved into spoons.

For modern Thai cooks, like traditional cooks, the ritual of food preparation begins with pounding herbs and spices into a paste. To lessen

mincing, and pounding. I will show you short-cuts to quicken the process. And time-saving techniques for preparing ingredients either ahead of time or in stages. The same seasoning pastes are used in many different recipes and can be made ahead in large quantities without affecting their flavor. Understanding how and why Thais cook the way they do, as well as organization and planning, is the key to success and makes the last-minute cooking that produces the unique Thai tastes easy.

Following are basic explanations of Thai cooking techniques and methods; directions are given in greater detail in chapters dealing with specific ingredients or recipes. Consider this a primer—an introduction and your ringside seat to the magic show.

Tumm

GRINDING, POUNDING, AND PUREEING

GRINDING

Grinding is used to turn dry-roasted spices into powder. Roasting spices brings out their aroma and is common in Thai recipes. Large quantities of spices can be roasted, ground, and stored in an airtight glass jar at room temperature for future use.

THE THAI WAY: Place a tablespoon or two of the roasted spice in a mortar. Place the mortar on a pot holder or damp kitchen towel to prevent it from "dancing" on the counter. Use one hand to cradle and brace the side of the mortar to steady it, and hold the narrow end of the pestle firmly in your other hand. Make hard circular motions around the inside of the mortar, pressing and grinding the roasted spice grains or seeds against the stone until they turn to powder.

the work and time, each ingredient is finely minced or ground before pounding. Once made, the paste is set aside. If there is to be a curry included in the menu, coconut milk is made from fresh coconuts and set aside. Next a soup broth is prepared and set to simmer as meat and vegetables are washed, sliced, or chopped into bite-sized pieces. Lastly, ingredients for garnishes are washed and cut, and additional condiments are made and set aside. Everything is arranged and grouped in sequence for last-minute cooking. Rice is always cooked just before serving. Final cooking and assembly is quick, and all the dishes are served at once with the steaming-hot rice.

In our busy world, even when cooking is done for pleasure, time is a major consideration. Let me assure you that Thai cooking does not have to involve endless hours of chopping,

To clean the mortar and pestle, pour a mixture of 1 cup distilled vinegar and water into the mortar and set the pestle in it. Let soak for an hour or so, then drain and rinse with cold water. After grinding chiles, clean the mortar and pestle with lime and sea salt.

THE WESTERN WAY: Put several spoonfuls of the roasted spice into an electric coffee grinder you keep exclusively for grinding spices. Cover tightly and grind for a couple of minutes, then turn off the grinder and let the powder settle for a minute or two before opening the lid so the pungent fragrance doesn't cause you to sneeze or irritate your eyes.

Clean the grinder by putting 2 to 3 tablespoons of sugar in it and grind for a couple of seconds. Discard the sugar and wipe clean with a paper towel.

POUNDING AND PUREEING

The most important technique in Thai cooking, pounding with a pestle in a mortar produces a well-blended and smooth paste. Minced herbs and spices are added one at a time, each new ingredient only after the previous one is blended and pounded into the paste. There is a precise order for adding ingredients, specified in each recipe.

Start with the sea salt and garlic, pounded into a paste, then follow with fresh chiles or dried chiles that have been soaked in warm water and minced. Next comes the roasted spice powder. Fibrous herbs like lemongrass and kaffir lime zest or leaves follow. Finally, juicy aromatics like shallots are added, and all the ingredients are bound together with a binder such as shrimp or soybean paste.

Traditional Thai cooks pound while squatting or sitting on the floor, hunched over the mortar to allow them to put their body weight into the process. You don't need to squat, but do find a comfortable way to give you the leverage you need.

As a beginner, you will find that it takes you about 30 minutes to make a fine paste of a large quantity of ingredients. Most Thai cooks take their time pounding, taking breaks to ease the tension on the back and hand.

Select a work table or counter that is waist-high. Place a damp dish towel or a pot holder under the mortar. Have the finely minced fresh ingredients and roasted spice powder for the paste ready in separate bowls. With one hand, cradle and brace the side of the mortar and use your other hand to hold the pestle firmly at the narrow top, where it is easy to grasp. Strike the pestle straight down, then up and down again repeatedly into the center of the mortar, working in an even rhythm. Do not pound in a circular motion, as if you were stirring—doing so is not only laborious and hard on your back, but will produce a coarse and lumpy paste. Turn and rotate the mortar frequently as you pound.

As you add each new ingredient to the paste, stir the mixture with a spoon before pounding it. Scrape the paste into the center of the mortar when it creeps up the side. If the mortar becomes too full, remove the paste and then pound the remaining ingredients in the proper sequence. Before adding the shrimp or soybean binder, put the paste you removed back into the mortar and mix well, then pound all the ingredients together. Set aside, or place in a jar with a tight-fitting lid and refrigerate. Clean the mortar and pestle with the distilled vinegar and water mixture mentioned above, or lime and sea salt if there were chiles in the paste.

Pow
DRY-ROASTING

Dry-roasting is the process of roasting dried spices, chiles, and raw or cooked rice in a shallow pan or skillet without oil or liquid. Dry-roasting cooks the surface of these ingredients and turns them golden brown, producing a smoky and very slightly burnt flavor.

To dry-roast, use a 7- or 8-inch shallow saucepan or skillet. Add a tablespoon or two of the spices called for in the recipe, or, if roasting chiles, rice, coconut, seeds, or nuts, enough to make a single layer in the pan, leaving plenty of room for the ingredients to be shaken around. Cook over high heat, sliding the pan constantly back and forth over the burner, for 1 minute, then lower the heat to medium. Roast for several more minutes, or until you can smell the aroma of the ingredients and they turn brown. Remove from the heat and transfer to a plate to cool completely. Store in a tightly sealed jar at room temperature.

Keang
SLOW-COOKING

In Western cooking, this method is referred to as stewing or braising. The Thai word *keang* came from the Mon, the people who originally inhabited the countries now known as Thailand, Burma, and Cambodia. *Keang* means "to boil" and typically identifies soups. *Keang pet* indicates a spicy soup or curry (see page 216). The traditional terra-cotta pots used to make *keang* produced a richly flavored broth. Chinese ceramic medicine pots, or the Mexican ceramic pots called *cazuelas*, can be used as modern substitutes. To avoid cracking the pot, cover and boil slowly and gently over medium-low heat. A stainless steel pot or large saucepan

will also do the job. Slow boiling is the secret of *keang*.

Bring the liquid (broth or water) to a rapid boil. Lower the heat, add the pounded herbs and spices, and mix well. Cover the pot and let the broth simmer slowly over medium-low heat for 20 minutes before adding the meat or poultry. If the meat is tough, cover and cook over medium-low heat for about 1 hour, or until the meat is tender. If you are preparing the soup ahead, remove it from the heat to cool completely, then transfer to a tightly sealed container and refrigerate. When ready to serve, bring the soup to a slow boil in a covered pot. Don't add the vegetables until just before serving the soup.

Neung
STEAMING

Steaming originated in China, where special bamboo steamers are used. The Chinese steamer consists of deep round bamboo trays with latticework bottoms stacked one on top of the other and covered with a tightly woven bamboo lid. The food is placed inside the trays, which are lined with wet muslin or fresh leaves, and set into a metal wok filled with enough water to just touch the bottom of the steamer. The water is brought to a boil, sending steam through the stacked trays; when the food reaches the same temperature as the steam, it is cooked.

You can steam meat, seafood, poultry, vegetables, or wrapped bundles such as Soft Sweet Sticky Rice Bundles (page 58) in a 6- to 8-quart pasta pot with a shallow steamer basket insert and a lid. Fill the pot halfway with water. Place a Pyrex pie plate inside the steamer basket insert and place the seasoned ingredients in the pie plate. Bring the water to a boil, put the steamer basket insert with the pie plate in the pot, cover, and steam over medium-high heat until the food is cooked.

To steam sticky rice, fill the pasta pot halfway with water. Line the steamer basket insert with fresh corn husks, dried corn husks softened in water, or fresh banana leaves. Place the presoaked sticky rice on top of the husks or leaves, place the steamer basket insert into the pot, cover, and steam over high heat for 2 to 3 minutes. Lower the heat to medium and steam for 20 minutes, or until the rice is cooked.

Padd

STIR-FRY

With the introduction of the steel wok, the Thais learned from the Chinese how to stir-fry. Using very high heat and an extremely hot pan, this quick and easy technique produces crisp and delicious food. A Western-style stove is not designed for using a wok. The stove does not generate enough heat for a wok set onto a wok ring. Stir-frying in a 12-inch skillet, so that the pan bottom is sitting directly on top of the burner, is a superior method. A flat-bottomed steel wok also works well. Because stir-fry dishes are cooked at the last minute, other dishes for the meal that are slow-cooked or steamed must be prepared first and kept warm. At a Thai meal, all the various dishes are served together.

For stir-frying, it is essential that all ingredients are prepared, measured, and arranged in the sequence that they will be added to the wok or skillet. Vegetables should be preminced, prechopped, presliced, or prediced. Vegetable stems, florets, and root vegetables should be separated from leafy vegetables or leaves of vegetables. Dried spices or herbs should be roasted and ground, fresh spices and herbs minced or pureed. Meat, poultry, or seafood should be trimmed (or peeled, as with shrimp), sliced, or diced. Measure separately and set aside the oil and other liquids to be added. Have the serving plate or platter at hand as well as the garnish.

Arrange everything in the order to be added to the skillet, beginning with the oil, herbs, and spices, followed by the meat, poultry, or seafood and water or wine. Next come stemmed and firm vegetables, which take longer to cook, and then the leafy vegetables. Seasonings and garnishes are last.

To cook, heat the skillet or wok over very high heat for 2 to 3 minutes. Test the temperature by placing your hand 2 to 3 inches above the pan; when you can feel the heat, it is time to add the oil. Within seconds, the oil will begin to smoke. Add any minced fresh spices and stir quickly with a paddle or spatula to prevent burning. Add the meat, poultry, or seafood and stir-fry until completely cooked. If the pan is dry and the ingredients are sticking, sprinkle on a bit of water or add a tablespoon of wine and continue to stir-fry, lifting and tossing the ingredients. Once the meat or seafood is cooked, add the firm and stemmed vegetables and stir and cook until their color brightens. Add the leafy vegetables and stir until the leaves wilt, then add the seasonings. Stir and mix well. Transfer to a serving platter and add the final garnish. Serve immediately. The whole procedure should take you no more than 6 to 7 minutes!

Neur, Moo, Gai, Ped
BEEF, PORK, CHICKEN, DUCK

Thais are not big meat eaters. Historically, they were foragers who gathered their foods from the forests, fields, rivers, and sea. Their main staple was rice, supplemented with wild or cultivated greens, insects, worms, small birds, fowl eggs, fish, and wild pigs or other wild animals. Meat was a luxury and reserved mostly for special religious ceremonies, when animals such as chickens, ducks, or pigs were slaughtered as an offering. Even then, a small amount of meat went a long way.

Beef was considered taboo for most Thais. The water buffalo was considered sacred, the people's partner who toiled with them in the rice fields. Only if it had been injured was a water buffalo slaughtered for food. Over time, however, exposure to a wider variety of meats, as well as prosperity and the greater availability of meat, has changed the Thai diet. Today meat is no longer an expensive luxury reserved for special occasions, but is common to everyday meals, though still in smaller amounts than in Western diets. So, when cooking these recipes, if you like more meat, you can double the portions.

Thais like to eat meat and poultry on the bone, which is why for these recipes, you need a heavy Chinese cleaver for cutting up bone-in meat and poultry. They also like to eat the cooked fat and skin.

Most Thais buy freshly killed or live poultry at markets. Traditional Thai markets are noisy and smelly. Straw cages display live pigeons, ducks, and chickens for sale, and market stalls feature slabs of fresh meats or whole birds hanging on hooks. Thais like to select their game and poultry while still alive. After they make their selection, it is either slaughtered on the spot or taken home alive, to be slaughtered later.

The following section will acquaint you with the ways Thai cooks prepare meat and poultry for cooking.

SLICING

The Thais slice meat and poultry on a diagonal. Thick slices are for soups or curries, and thin slices for stir-fries and salads. Slightly frozen meat is easier to slice. Always use a sharp knife and slice across the grain of the meat. Begin by rinsing and drying the meat thoroughly. Slice off unwanted fat and skin. A simple technique is to use the hand that is not holding the knife as a guide to sizing and cutting the slices. Curl your fingers under while holding or stabilizing the meat with your fingers and palm. Place the middle knuckles at approximately the place where you want to make the slice. Rest the knife against the knuckles to make a clean and precise slice through the meat. Inch the hand holding the meat backward away from where the slice is made and repeat the process. This makes even slices and speeds up the process. Slice lengthwise along the grain into 1- to 1½-inch-wide pieces. Slice crosswise across the grain into bite-sized pieces: larger ones (1 to 1½ inches) for curries or soups, paper-thin (¼ inch) for stir-fries or salads. Even slices ensure even cooking.

In general, allow 6 to 7 chunks per person for curry or soup, and 8 to 10 slices for a stir-fry; double the amount if you like a lot of meat. If preparing ahead, wrap the sliced meat in heavy-duty plastic wrap in individual portions, label, and freeze. To use, thaw overnight in the refrigerator.

CHOPPING MEAT WITH BONES

Thai people love meat attached to bones, especially the marrow inside and the gelatinous texture of cooked tendons.

THE THAI WAY: Place a chopping board on a waist-high counter or work table. To prevent the board from skidding, place a damp towel under the board. Place the meat in the center of the chopping board. Gauge where and how many pieces you want to chop. Grasping the cleaver firmly, relax and breathe as you raise the cleaver up to shoulder height. Keep your other hand up in the air or behind your back, out of the cleaver's path, and with one hard blow, bring down the cleaver, cutting through the meat and bone.

THE WESTERN WAY: The easy alternative to chopping the bones is to make friends with a butcher and have the meat cut at the market. Store the precut meat in the refrigerator for immediate use or freeze for future use.

Pla, Pla Meug, Goong, Hoi
FISH, SQUID, SHRIMP, AND OTHER SHELLFISH

In Thai cooking, "fresh is always better than frozen." And for seafood, it's the Golden Rule.

Before buying fish, unless it is still alive, insist on smelling and touching it. It should feel firm and have a faint smell of the water where it once lived; it should not smell fishy. The skin should likewise be firm and not slimy; the eyes clear, not cloudy; and the gills red, not brown.

Thais love strong-flavored fish with firm flesh and high oil content, such as mackerel (*pla thu*), white pomfret (*pla jara met*), snapper (*pla kaphong*), catfish (*pla duk*), and serpent head (*pla chont*). Whole fish are grilled, deep-fried, or steamed. Fillets or steaks are sliced into thin ribbons for stir-fries, into chunks with or without bones for soups or curries. Unlike Westerners, Thais are not too concerned about fishbones. On the contrary, they feel that the bones add extra flavor, and they believe it is only natural to expect bones with fish (they simply spit them out).

Whole fish are sold in Asian markets either killed or kept alive in water tanks. The seller will clean and scale the fish for you. He will also chop or fillet it any way you like. This service is available in many American supermarkets with seafood sections. It's always best to start with a whole fresh fish.

FISH FILLETS

Rub your fingertips across the fish fillet to check for tiny bones, and remove any with tweezers. Sprinkle with salt and let sit in a strainer in the sink for 10 minutes. Rinse several times with cool water and pat dry. Slice diagonally across the fillet into ¼-inch-wide strips for a stir-fry, 2-inch strips for a soup or curry. Refrigerate until ready to cook.

SQUID

The squid sold in the market have been frozen and thawed. They taste fine if they have not sat

> To get rid of any fishy smell, rub your hands with sea salt and lemon. (Use the lemon rind to clean the sink after cleaning shrimp.) My mother's secret for fresh-tasting, crispy-textured cooked shrimp is to immediately reverse the temperature from cold storage to cooking with intense high heat.

for more than a day. Always touch and smell before buying. Squid should feel fairly firm, not slimy, and have a fresh, not fishy, smell. Squid may be grilled, deep-fried, steamed, or added to soup. Before cooking, it must be cleaned as described below. Some fish markets sell already cleaned squid. It costs a bit more, but it may be more convenient for you.

CLEANING SQUID: Pull out the tentacles. Cut off and discard the thick end including the eyes and save the rest. Starting from the opening of the body sac, rub and peel off the thin dark purple membrane. Reach inside the sac and pull out the guts. Lightly rub the sac inside and out with salt and set aside for 5 to 10 minutes, then rinse off the salt with cool water. Pat dry and store the sac and tentacles in a Ziploc bag in the refrigerator until ready to use. Cleaned squid will keep overnight.

STUFFING SQUID: Finely chop the tentacles. Combine the chopped tentacles with the stuffing ingredients called for in the recipe. Stuff the sac three-quarters full, to allow space for the stuffing to expand during cooking. Secure the opening of the sac with toothpicks. Stuffed squid is grilled, deep-fried, steamed, or added to soups.

SLICING SQUID: Slit the squid's sac by inserting a knife in the opening (where the tentacles were) and slice open lengthwise. Place the squid with the inner flesh up. With a sharp knife, make shallow pencil-thin long parallel lines on the surface; do not cut all the way through. Score the squid in the other direction until the surface is covered with tiny squares, then slice into four pieces. When cooked, the squares will curl up. The tentacles need to be cooked longer than squid sliced like this.

SHRIMP AND OTHER SHELLFISH

Buy shellfish alive, with tightly closed shells. Take time to smell each one. Good shellfish smell lightly of the sea, while bad ones exude a strong unpleasant odor. Scrub each shell clean with a stiff brush. Put the shellfish in a bowl of fresh water and refrigerate. It will live overnight. Dry well before cooking.

Live fresh shrimp are hard to find, but are sometimes available in water tanks in Asian markets. Once you have tasted them, it is hard to eat frozen shrimp. When buying shrimp, use the same guidelines as for buying squid. Shrimp are cooked with or without shells, whole or sliced for soups and stir-fries.

SHRIMP IN THE SHELL: To cook shrimp with the shell on, make a lengthwise slit down the back and remove the dark vein inside.

PEELED (SHELLED) SHRIMP: Peel off the shell, including the tail. Run a knife down the back of the shrimp and remove the dark vein. Massage the shrimp with a bit of salt and let stand for 5 to 10 minutes, then rinse with cool water and pat dry with paper towels. Peeled shrimp are left whole, sliced in half lengthwise down the back, or sliced crosswise into chunks for stir-fries and soups. For shrimp balls, peeled shrimp can be minced in a food processor with the steel blade. Peeled shrimp can be stored in a Ziploc bag in the refrigerator overnight.

Pakk Sodd
VEGETABLES

Over centuries of foraging for food, the Thais have gained a reverence for seasonal vegetables. Vegetables were viewed as a special gift of nature, possessing spiritual and healing values. Instead of visiting the doctor or the pharmacy, Thais have traditionally gone to the vegetable garden or market to cure their ailments and prevent illness. Believed to maintain equilibrium and harmony among the four basic human elements—earth, water, wind, and fire—vegetables prepared appropriately and in the right combinations ensured a healthy life. Seasonal vegetables were nature's prescription for staying healthy and guarding against sickness during changes in the weather.

Seasonal plants including vegetables and herbs are divided into five major groups: tender shoots and leaves, roots, flowers, pod-containing seeds, and fruits. They are further classified according to their primary taste: astringent, sweet, alcoholic, bitter, buttery, refreshing, salty, sour, and piquant.

Harvested at their peak, seasonal vegetables are highly sought after by Thai people. Cooks always know which market has the best and freshest vegetables. The so-called wet markets in northern Thailand sell fresh vegetables, fruits, and meat. Famous for their beautiful straw mushrooms, snow peas, yard-long green and purple beans, and tender young bamboo shoots, the markets sell an abundance of nature's seasonal gifts that are such an important part of Thai culture. On weekends, planeloads of city folks from Bangkok fly to the city of Chiang Mai just to shop at wet markets. The term *wet market* comes from the large amounts of water sprayed on the fresh produce to keep it crisp and prevent wilting: The continuous spraying ends up getting the ground and everything else wet.

Eating the best of the season is serious business in Thailand. Fresh vegetables almost guarantee a meal will be exceptionally delicious, and it is not unusual for a cook to build a menu around freshly picked or chosen vegetables.

Traditional Thai cooks believe that vegetables torn or separated by hand taste better than those sliced with a knife. You can do it either way. Usually vegetables are prepared just before cooking, but for a complicated menu, you may want to prepare them ahead. Following are descriptions of vegetables used in the recipes in this book, along with how and where to buy them and how to prepare, use, and store them.

LEAFY VEGETABLES
Pakk Gadd, Pakk Kom, Pakk Gadd Jean, Pakk Boog

Mustard Greens, Spinach, Napa Cabbage, Swamp Spinach

These leafy vegetables are valued for the crispness and texture they bring to dishes. Some produce a bitter flavor and some add a tender fresh taste. All parts of these vegetables are used, but each part is used separately and to produce a different result. Thais enjoy leafy vegetables for their vibrant green and yellow-green colors, resulting in a dish that boasts freshness of color as well as of taste.

To prepare leafy greens, pull off the leaves

until you reach the heart. Rinse the leaves well in cool water. Slice off the hard stems from the soft leaves and set the leaves aside. Stack a few stems at a time together and slice across on the diagonal into pieces about 1½ inches wide. Slice the heart of the vegetable in the same way. To store for future use, wrap the sliced stems and hearts gently in paper towels to avoid bruising, since it would cause the vegetables to spoil, place in a plastic bag, and refrigerate.

Take a handful of leaves at a time and slice or tear them crosswise. Set them aside or wrap them in paper towels and place them in a separate bag and refrigerate. (It is important to keep the leaves and hard stems separated, since the latter take longer to cook.)

Swamp spinach, or water morning glory (*pakk boog*), which is actually an herb, grows in moist areas near rivers and canals. It has long, slender, hollow green stems and thin ovate green leaves with pointed tips. In the summer, Asian markets sell swamp spinach in large bundles. Only the leaves and the tips of the stems are eaten. They are crunchy and a bit chewy, and they retain their shape even after long cooking.

Hua Ka-Lum Pee
Cabbage

Cabbage is eaten raw as an accompaniment to chile sauces or cooked in stir-fries and soups. The most commonly used variety is white cabbage. Cabbage is either finely sliced or cut into squares, depending upon the recipe. If preparing cabbage in advance, store it in a plastic bag in the refrigerator. It will keep for a week.

SLICING: To finely slice cabbage, cut the head in half from the top to the stem. Cut out and discard the hard inner core. Place each half cut side down on the chopping board and slice crosswise into thin strips.

CUTTING INTO SQUARES: After cutting the cabbage in half and removing the hard core, put it cut side down on the board and slice crosswise into 1-inch-wide strips. Keeping the sliced pieces together, cut across into 1-inch squares.

Gai Lan
Chinese Broccoli

This leafy dark green broccoli has thin 10- to 12-inch-long stalks with clusters of tiny green and white blossoms and dark green leaves on long stems. It turns bright green when cooked and is valued for its crunchy, chewy texture and sweet, slightly bitter taste.

To prepare Chinese broccoli, pull off the individual stems from each stalk until nothing is left but the flowers. Peel the hard, fibrous layer from the stalk with a vegetable peeler or small paring knife. Snap off the flowers. Wash the stems and leaves well and dry thoroughly. Slice the stalks on the diagonal about ½ inch wide.

Slice the leaves across in half. To store, refrigerate wrapped in paper towels in plastic bags, keeping the stalks and flowers separate from the leaves.

Geun Chai
Chinese Celery

Resembling Italian parsley, with long, thin, porous stalks like regular celery, Chinese celery is sold in large bundles. It is extremely aromatic and favored by Thai cooks primarily for this reason. Usually the stalks and stems are used and the leaves discarded.

To prepare Chinese celery, wash it well, then remove and discard the leaves. Dry the stalks and stems thoroughly, wrap in paper towels, and store in a plastic bag in the refrigerator until needed.

Slice the celery only when ready to use. Holding the stalks in a bundle, slice crosswise into very fine thin pieces for garnish. Or, for adding to stir-fries, slice into longer pieces, about 1 inch.

VEGETABLES WITH FLORETS
Bok-Ka-Li
Broccoli

Broccoli is new to Thai cooking, hence the Thai name is a variation of the Western word for it. Broccoli has been added to the list of favored Thai ingredients because of its shape and vibrant color, as well as its taste.

To prepare broccoli, use a small paring knife to peel off the hard outer layer from the stalks. Slice each stalk across on the diagonal into $1/2$-inch slices until you reach the florets, then slice the florets lengthwise to separate them. Start cooking the florets first, then the stems.

Pakk Ka-Lum Dok
Cauliflower

Thai cooks love cauliflower's shape and its crispy, crunchy texture. It is used for stir-fries and curry dishes.

Prepare cauliflower by separating the florets and discarding the core. Then slice the florets lengthwise into bite-sized pieces. Make thinner slices for stir-fries, larger ones for soup.

ROOT, BULB, AND SHOOT VEGETABLES
Nor-Mai
Bamboo Shoots

Roots, bulbs, and shoots are popular with both the old and new generations of Thai cooks. Bamboo is one of Thailand's indigenous plants, along with the coconut and the banana. The bamboo plant plays many roles in Thai life beyond cooking. The hollow tube of the bamboo stalk is used as a container for roasting sweet sticky rice, to capture its refreshing scent. The shoot is used in a variety of ways in cooking.

Bamboo shoots are harvested at different stages and seasons to provide different flavors and textures. The canned bamboo shoots found in most supermarkets can be substituted for fresh bamboo shoots in the recipes. However, there is a difference and fresh is best.

FRESH BAMBOO SHOOTS: Fresh bamboo shoots are a real treat. The meat is crunchy and nutty, with a slightly sweet flavor. Fresh bamboo shoots are available here in Asian markets in early spring. The brownish shoots are about 9 to 10 inches long, iridescent, and covered with almost invisible hairs that feel like paper.

To prepare fresh bamboo shoots, use a paring knife to remove the outer rough peel until you reach the off-white inner section, which will no longer feel papery. Rinse, then blanch in boiling water for 10 to 15 minutes, drain, and rinse again in cool water. Cool completely before refrigerating in a Ziploc plastic bag; the bamboo shoots will keep for up to a week. When ready to use, slice the shoots into thin rounds, matchsticks, or chunks for soup, curries, and stir-fries, or mince for stuffings.

CANNED BAMBOO SHOOTS: Canned bamboo shoots preserved in brine come whole or sliced in a variety of ways. Because manufacturers are not required to print the canning date, there is no way to tell how long the shoots have been sitting on the shelf. Before using, inspect the shoots carefully; yellow spots on the surface indicate they have been in the can too long. However, since it is likely that you will find shoots with these unpleasant spots, just slice them off and rinse the shoots well with cool water. Massage with sea salt and set the bamboo shoots in a colander in the sink to drain for 10 minutes. Rinse once again with cool water. Canned bamboo shoots taste slightly sour and are not as crunchy as fresh bamboo shoots.

Kea-Rod

Carrots

Carrots, like broccoli, are a new Western addition to Thai cooking, hence their Thai name is a Thai variation of the English. Carrots are used for their color as well as their sweet taste and crunchy texture.

To prepare carrots for soup or curry, peel and slice into 1-inch chunks. For a stir-fry, slice paper-thin, about 1/10 inch thick, on a diagonal. For matchsticks, stack several long thin slices at a time and cut lengthwise.

Hua Chai Poh

Daikon

A member of the radish-turnip family, sometimes called the Asian radish, daikon is a long ivory-white cylindrical vegetable about 12 to 14 inches in length and 3 inches in diameter. In Asian markets, it is often sold broken into smaller pieces. Unlike the Japanese, who like raw daikon for its peppery, refreshing, crunchy texture, Thais seldom eat it uncooked. Cooked daikon remains crunchy but turns sweet and readily absorbs all the other flavors in a dish. Buy daikon that is heavy and firm to the touch. The thin peel should be smooth, not wrinkled.

Grated daikon is used by vegetarians to add texture and bind other vegetables together for fillings; it may also be shaped into balls for deep-frying. Thais believe that daikon cools the body, helps blood circulation, and assists in digestion.

To use, peel off the outer layer and grate the daikon. Add a couple of pinches of sea salt and toss gently. Let sit for a few minutes. Rinse with cool water and squeeze dry before combining with the other ingredients called for in the recipe. Unsalted grated daikon is a wonderful tenderizer for seafood. For soups, peel off the outer layer and slice across into thin slices or slice into matchsticks.

Munn Gew

Jícama

You will find jícama, looking like a very large turnip wrapped in a brown paper bag, among the potato and onion bins in the produce section. A good jícama should feel very heavy when you pick it up. The brown skin should be smooth and free of any moldy spots. The flesh is crunchy, crispy, and sweet. Some describe its flavor as a cross between apple and potato.

To prepare jícama, use a small paring knife to peel off the outer skin and slice off the

Cut into thin circular slices and soak in cold water until you are ready to use. For salads and stir-fries, lotus root must be boiled in hot water for 10 minutes. For soups, it can be added directly to the broth. It will turn the broth slightly pink and sweeten it as well. Sliced lotus root can also be deep-fried into chips like potato chips. Slice paper-thin and dry the slices well before adding to the hot oil. The beautiful natural lacy pattern adds a festive touch to any dish.

Hua Hom
Onion

The onion is the one of the most ancient vegetables used by Thai cooks. It is used both as a seasoning and for its cooling flavor. It is also valued for its crispy texture and often added for a touch of elegance to a dish. Thai onions resemble the common yellow onion, but they are small, more pungent, and have a sweet-peppery flavor. To use, slice into chunks or long thin slices for soups, curries, and stir-fries. Finely sliced onion is used for stir-fries and salads.

CHUNKS: Slice off the roots and peel the onion. Stand it root side down on the chopping board and cut in half. Place cut side down on the chopping board and cut crosswise into 1-inch pieces. Keeping the sliced onion together, cut crosswise into 1-inch chunks.

THIN SLICES: Cut the peeled onion in half. Place cut side down on the chopping board. Cut either crosswise or lengthwise into 1/8- to 1/4-inch slices.

FINELY SLICED: Follow the directions for thin slices, but cut crosswise into paper-thin slices.

Hoy Kew
Water Chestnut

The water chestnuts with which most Americans are familiar come in cans, packed in water and either whole or sliced. The canning process

fibrous outer surface until you reach the translucent white flesh. Refrigerated in a plastic bag, peeled and trimmed jícama will keep for about a week. To use, slice jícama into thin matchsticks for salads or stir-fries.

Raag Bua
Lotus Roots

Fresh lotus roots are about 7 to 9 inches long and 2 inches in diameter and grow in connective links that look like sausages. Light beige-pink with paper-thin skin, a fresh lotus root should feel heavy, indicating that the flesh is replete with liquid. In contrast, older dried lotus roots feel hollow. Lotus root is carried by some specialty and organic markets and available in Asian markets.

To use, peel off the outer skin with a small paring knife. The inner pulp will appear porous, like a sponge. The root is crunchy, but as you slice across it, the pieces may be sticky with sap.

removes most of the flavor but retains texture. Canned water chestnuts should be used for adding texture to stir-fry dishes or, minced, in stuffings.

Fresh water chestnuts, available in Asian markets, are crunchy, crispy, and sweet. The small, shiny, black round nuggets are the size of a medium radish. Select those that are rounded, not caved-in, and without yellow spots. They should feel as hard as rocks. Even with careful picking, you may end up with a few bad ones. Peel off the outer skin with a small paring knife and soak the water chestnuts in water, refrigerated, until you are ready to use. Slice into paper-thin slices or into tiny matchsticks.

DOK
FLOWERS

Thais love the delicate, soft textures and sweet musty aromas flowers can add to a dish. Flowers, like banana blossoms, pea blossoms, squash blossoms, or rose petals, add interest and surprise to both appearance and taste. Flowers are eaten raw, or in salad.

Dok Pratani, Hua-Plee, Klouy-Plee
Banana Blossom

This elongated dark burgundy blossom is approximately 5 inches long and 3 inches wide at the base. It is sold wrapped in plastic in Asian markets. When you remove the outer petals, you will discover a roll of tiny baby bananas. To reach the inner white blossom core that is used in recipes, you need to remove both the tough fibrous burgundy petals and the tiny bananas. When you do so, you will get a dark sap on your hands—to remove the stains, wash your hands with lemon juice. Have a bowl of water with sliced lemon on hand in which to place the inner blossoms. Refrigerate until ready to use.

To serve, quarter banana blossoms lengthwise and dip in lemon juice to prevent them from turning brown. The individual petals can be removed and eaten raw with noodle dishes or minced and added to a salad.

THUA
LEGUMES

Legumes, such as beans and peas, are eaten raw, partially cooked, added to stir-fries and curries, or stuffed and deep-fried to accompany chile waters (see "Chile Water: The Crown Jewel," page 179) and spicy soups. Beans come in all shapes and colors. All add texture and visual appeal to a dish. Beans commonly used in Thai cooking include long beans, snap beans, and wing beans.

Most of the beans used in the recipes in this book are familiar and can be purchased in

supermarkets. Look for the more exotic varieties in Asian markets. Always buy the freshest of the season, not the canned or frozen varieties. Store them wrapped in plastic in the vegetable bin of the refrigerator. They should last a week.

Thua Keuw

Long Beans, or Yard-Long Beans

These thin long beans are sold in bunches. The most common ones are dark green, although there are light green and deep purple varieties. They all taste pretty much the same. Slice them into 1- to 2-inch lengths for stir-fries or curries, or parboil for salads. Thinly sliced circles are used in fried rice or added to salads.

Thua Keuw

Snap Beans

Snap beans come in shades of green, yellow, and purple. Once cooked, they taste more or less the same. The purple, somewhat disappointingly, will turn green. Snap beans are eaten raw or parboiled and cut into 2-inch lengths for soups or thin slivers for stir-fries.

Thua Pluu

Wing Beans or Asparagus Peas

These odd-looking beans are the same length as snap beans, but the smooth outer surface has frilly edges like wings, and the cross section when sliced is a triangle instead of an oval. To use, cut into paper-thin slices for salads or longer ones for soup. If the beans are to be used for salad, blanch in boiling water with a couple of pinches of salt for a few seconds and rinse in cold water several times, until they are completely cold.

VEGETABLE-FRUITS

There are some fruits, those that typically grow on vines, that the Thais, like Westerners, consider and use as vegetables. These include cucumbers, eggplant, melons, okra, squash, and tomato. Cucumbers, okra, and tomatoes are used as garnish, eaten raw, and, together with eggplant, melons, and squash, are prized for their soft pulpy-to-crispy textures when cooked. In addition to absorbing and balancing flavors, these fruits are believed to be an antidote to the summer heat.

Wrapped in paper towels, eggplants, melons, okra, and squash will keep in the refrigerator's vegetable bin for a couple of weeks. Sliced ingredients should be wrapped in plastic and refrigerated. Keep tomatoes in a basket at room temperature until sliced. Refrigerating tomatoes will keep them from spoiling as quickly, but it will also alter the taste.

Teang Kua

Cucumber

Thai people are partial to the small pickling cucumber, which is half the size of a regular cucumber. The skin is rough and bumpy. These are found in most produce markets. The cucumber is refreshing and adds a touch of crispy texture to a dish. When cooked, it absorbs and blends with other flavors, a wonderful soft and delicate addition to the dish.

There are three ways of preparing cucumbers, large or small. Peel and cut lengthwise in half. Scoop out the seeds using the handle of the vegetable peeler or a teaspoon. For salads, lay cut side down on the chopping board and cut into paper-thin diagonal slices. For stir-fries, slice diagonally into ⅛-inch slices. For soups, leave the peeled cucumber whole and slice across into 3-inch sections. Scoop out the seeds from these pieces with a small spoon or vegetable peeler. Fill it with a meat stuffing as directed in the recipe and add to the soup.

Mah-Kheua

Eggplant

Thai cooking uses several sizes of eggplants, believed by some to be native to Southeast Asia, China, and India. The small and miniature varieties of eggplant are favored by the Thais.

MAH-KHEUA PRUANG (A BUNCH OF BABY EGG-PLANTS): Tiny green miniature eggplants the size of large peas are clustered together like grapes. They are firm and hard with dense flesh that is packed with seeds. When cooked, the soft slippery texture can add contrast to a dish. The bitter flesh both blends with and absorbs other flavors. These fresh eggplants are available occasionally in the summer months in Asian markets. To prepare them, remove the eggplants from the stems. They are typically added to a curry, 10 to 15 minutes before serving so they are completely cooked but not falling apart. Fresh peas can be substituted.

MAH-KHEUA PROH (SMALL EGGPLANT): Available in Asian markets, these eggplants are the size of golf balls. They are white with a green pattern, pure white, or pale or deep purple. They are quite firm. To use, remove the stems and quarter them. Add to curries or serve raw with chile water.

MAH-KHEUA (LONG PURPLE, GREEN, AND JAPAN-ESE EGGPLANT): The Japanese eggplant, which actually originated in the Middle East, is used in many Thai dishes similar to Middle Eastern dishes such as stuffed eggplants or grilled eggplant salad. These long thin eggplants, about 10 inches in length and 1 to 1¼ inches in diameter, are available in produce and Asian markets. Whole eggplants are steamed, then peeled and sliced for salad. After slicing, salt the eggplant with sea salt and drain in a colander for about 10 minutes; this is necessary to extract the bitter flavor and soften the texture. Rinse off the salt and pat dry before using. For stir-fries, slice diagonally into thin slices. For soups or curries, slice diagonally into 1-inch pieces.

For stuffing, start at the pointed end of the eggplant and make a ¾-inch diagonal cut deep into the flesh, leaving the slice attached to the eggplant. Make an equal cut next to it, but this time slice the piece from the eggplant. The first cut forms a pouch for stuffing. Repeat the process with the remaining eggplant. Salt the eggplant pieces, rinse with cold water, and dry completely before stuffing. The eggplant can be prepared a day ahead and refrigerated; it will discolor, but this will not affect the taste.

Taeng

Melon

Many varieties of summer and cool-season melons are used in Thai cooking. They are valued for their neutral quality, readily absorbing other flavors. They are believed to cool one's system. When shopping in Asian markets, be adventurous and buy any melon that intrigues you. Try lots of them—you will find some you cannot live without.

MA-RAH JEEN (BITTER MELON): Looking like a bumpy malformed cucumber, this pale to dark green melon should feel firm to the touch. Darker green ones that feel heavy taste less bitter. Unlike other types of melon, bitter melon does not have to be peeled, but it must be treated with salt to lessen the bitterness. For stir-fries, slice the melon lengthwise in half. Scoop out the seeds with a spoon. Put cut side down on the chopping block and slice into diagonal paper-thin slices. Salt the slices generously and leave in a colander over the sink for 10 to 15 minutes. Wash well with cool water and pat dry. For soups, slice the melon into 2-inch-long chunks. Scoop out the seeds. After salting and draining, stuff the centers with a meat filling as directed in the recipe. Add to the soup and cook for 15 minutes, or until the melon is soft but not

falling apart. Keeping the soup covered while cooking the melon helps lessen the bitterness.

TAENG (WAX GOURD OR FUZZY MELON): These come in a variety of shapes. Some are stubby, while others look like long fuzzy cucumbers. The skin is light green, the flesh pale green, almost white, with soft seeds like those of cucumbers. Peel and slice into 1-inch squares for soups or stir-fries. Cooked, it stays intact, but is soft like soaked bread.

Bua Liem
Chinese Okra or Angled Luffa

This odd vegetable looks just like overgrown okra with sharp, hard ridges on its pale green skin. The flesh is white and spongy with soft white seeds. Pick one that is long and slender and not too bloated—when you squeeze it, it should give a bit but not feel mushy. Chinese okra is found in Asian markets. To use, peel with a small paring knife. Cut into 1-inch chunks for stir-fries or soups.

Luk Kajerb
Okra

Okra is favored in Thai cooking for its squishy texture. It is eaten raw, grilled, or in stir-fries and soups. Beyond its raw and crispy, or cooked and mushy, texture, okra absorbs other flavors, embracing them with its slippery and soft flesh. Okra can be purchased in most supermarkets. Slice tiny okra into thin diagonal slices for stir-fries. Whole ones can be grilled on bamboo skewers and eaten with a spicy chile water.

Fuk
Squash

A typical Thai garden will have squash similar to summer squash growing among the beans and cucumbers. With its vibrant color and meaty texture squash is used to add a sweet taste to main dishes and desserts. Summer squashes are available in most markets.

JAPANESE SQUASH OR KABOCHA: Much like a pumpkin in shape and about 6 to 8 inches in diameter, this squash is dark green with yellow spots and faint green lines. The skin is very hard and tough, and the squash should feel heavy and compact. The firm bright yellow to orange flesh surrounding the seeds is about ¾ inch thick. Use a sharp vegetable peeler or a small paring knife to peel off the skin. With a chef's knife, cut the squash in half. Remove the seeds with a tablespoon. Slice into 1-inch chunks for soup or long paper-thin slices, to be dipped in batter, for deep-frying.

Ma-Kheau Tedd

Tomato

The tomato came to Thailand from the Americas via the Europeans. It is very popular and used for much the same purposes as in Western cooking. In addition, tomatoes are added to soups or stir-fries for their sweet-fruity taste and vibrant color. Thais favor tomatoes that are acidic and filled with seeds. Small cherry tomatoes are sliced in half or left whole for salads or soups. Larger tomatoes are sliced for salads or added to stir-fries and soups.

Pun Rah Mai

FRUITS

Fruits were used as flavorings and seasonings in Thailand long before sugar and vinegar. Fruits give Thai dishes their own unique sweet and sour flavors. Like vegetables, seasonal fruits are believed to offer balance and nutrients the body needs during climatic changes and to promote a healthy and harmonious disposition.

Fruits such as mango, papaya, orange, lime, and pineapple are prized for their sharp flavor

and intense aroma. Thais love dishes that are sensual and full of surprises. The perfect Thai dish engages all the senses. It not only boasts a variety of distinctive flavors and textures, but is visually colorful and topped off with an aroma that pleases and excites the sense of smell. The following fruits are typically eaten fresh or added to salads, and sometimes used for cooking as seasoning. They have zestful distinct tastes, nice for contrast and important for the contribution they make to the final presentation.

Store ripe mango, papaya, pineapple, and star fruit in a basket at room temperature. Once they've been sliced, wrap securely in plastic and refrigerate.

Mah-Muen

Mango

Green, or unripened, mango is used for salads. The tender young leaves are eaten raw with chile water. Tightly closed fresh blossoms are added to spicy soups. Fresh mangoes are found in most markets and the green fruit is available in Asian markets.

When choosing a green mango, pick a firm one with a dark green, almost blue skin. It should feel heavy in the palm of your hand. For salads, peel with a vegetable peeler, then coarsely grate on a box grater or slice off the flesh and shred in a food processor with a large-holed grating blade.

Ma-Rah Gor

Papaya

Both green and ripe papayas are used in Thai dishes. The seeds are also used as a tenderizer when marinating meat. Green papaya is grated for salads or sliced paper-thin for spicy soups. Green papaya is sold here in Asian markets. It is called Mexican papaya and is twice as big as the familiar Hawaiian papaya; it is similar to the papaya grown in Thailand.

Shredding green papaya is done with a cleaver. This method gives the fruit a texture that absorbs the seasonings during the pounding process. The shredded pieces are eaten with a sticky rice ball in the same way a tortilla is used in Mexican food. For a green papaya salad, peel the fruit with a vegetable peeler. Drape a dish towel over the palm of one hand and put the peeled papaya on top, then with a knife or cleaver, lightly chop the surface randomly. Cut thin slices from the chopped surface; you will get uneven but fine shredded strands. Save the remaining papaya for spicy soup.

Like the green Mexican papaya, ripened Mexican papayas are more fleshy and sweeter than Hawaiian papayas. Ripe papayas are peeled and sliced into bite-sized chunks for salads.

Subparod

Pineapple

Fresh ripe pineapple is eaten raw in salads, as an accompaniment to noodle dishes, and in spicy soups. When buying a pineapple, examine it for bruises and mold. It should feel heavy. Pull off a leaf close to the core. If the pineapple is ripe, it will come off easily. Turn it upside down and smell the bottom. Good ripe pineapples smell sweet and fruity.

To prepare a fresh pineapple the Thai way, cover the chopping board with newspaper, for easy cleanup. Set the pineapple on top of the newspaper. To peel away the hard outer skin, hold the leafy part of the pineapple with one hand and slice lengthwise down the fruit with a chef's knife, removing the skin all around. You will notice that the pineapple has "eyes" set in a perfect diagonal pattern. With a paring knife, cut a triangular wedge out of the pineapple to remove the eyes: When you finish, the pineapple should look as if it has a swirl of ribbons around it. Slice off the bottom and top. Wrap the skin, top and bottom, and the eyes in the newspaper and discard.

Immerse the pineapple in a bowl of cool water with a pinch of sea salt (this is believed to sweeten the pineapple). Rinse again in cool water, put in a sealed plastic bag, and refrigerate until needed. To prepare pineapple slices or

> Canned pineapple only looks like pineapple: It has been stripped of its natural gifts, taste and aroma. Often it is artificially sweetened. However, if you need to use the canned variety, which I recommend only in an emergency, buy pineapple in its natural juice.

chunks, first quarter the pineapple lengthwise and cut out the hard inner core. Slice each quarter into chunks for soup, thin slices for stir-fries, or fine slices for salad.

Mah Feung

Star Fruit

Star fruit gets its name from the fact that it looks like a star when sliced crosswise. The fruits are yellowish-green in color, about 3 to 4 inches in diameter, and 6 inches long. Also called carambola, star fruit is available in most specialty markets as well as Asian markets. The green and slightly unripe ones are sour, acidic, but slightly sweet. They are sliced into matchsticks and added to noodles and salads. Ripe star fruit is sweeter and is eaten raw with salt and a squeeze of lime juice. The slices are a beautiful garnish for salads.

Rice
THE SOUL OF
THAI COOKING

From rice grains to polished kernels

From polished kernels to cooked rice

From cooked rice to rice crust

From rice crust to rice crackers

Mother cook knows all

Even rice crackers are irresistible

**Translated from *Mae Khloa Hoa Paa*
(*Head Cook from the Forest*),
between 1868 and 1900**

Think of rice as bread! Just as bread is a Western staple used and served many ways with every meal, rice is the staple of Thailand, the one food served at every meal. You wouldn't serve just any bread with a spectacular gourmet meal. You would carefully choose one to complement the wonderful dishes you have taken time to prepare. It tastes delicious by itself and even better with a meal. You probably agree that fresh bread is best. Homemade is better. The same is true of rice.

Rice can be a meal in itself. Rice absorbs sauces and tempers sharp, intense flavors like the heat of chiles. It provides texture and enhances other foods. Rice fills and satisfies. A meal in Thailand is not a meal without rice.

Kao is the Thai word for rice. All Thai dishes except *ah haun wung,* or snacks, are meant to accompany rice. The term *gupp kao,* meaning "with rice," describes the other dishes that are created specifically to be eaten with rice.

Rice was the earliest food cultivated and eaten by Thai people. Long before the arrival of the immigrants who founded the nation eventually known as Thailand, the Mon people inhabited the area. It was the Mon, the indigenous inhabitants, who developed the sophisticated method of wet-rice cultivation. They were the first to domesticate rice and with it created the potential to grow abundant, consistent quantities by using irrigation systems that stored rain during the monsoon season to sustain the rice field.

Gordon Luce, an eminent Southeast Asian historian, considers the Mon's seemingly humble development of rice cultivation to be one of mankind's great economic contributions, influencing the course of world history. Because of the Mon discovery of rice cultivation, rice eventually became the economic foundation and primary export of Southeast Asia. From rice grew civilizations. Great advances in religion, philosophy, art, music, literature, and laws flowed from these civilizations, and, along with rice, were adapted and integrated into other cultures and societies.

During the sixth century, groups of people migrated south from China, following the Menam River into Southeast Asia, and settled in a region inhabited by the Mon people. The Chinese record encountering the Mon people as early as A.D. 550. These industrious new settlers adopted rice as their staple, copied and perfected the Mon methods of growing large quantities of rice, and entered into trade with other countries.

Arab and Indian merchants soon began purchasing rice and, eventually, sugar as commodities, exchanges for spices, silk, cotton, and precious gems. Rice opened frontiers, brought good fortune, and carried information and ideas from one culture to another.

Just as rice nurtured civilization, it brought destruction. As a precious commodity valued not only by the people of Southeast Asia, but by other countries as well, rice represented power and wealth. As such, it was also the root of warfare. History is rife with attempts, both failed and successful, to dominate the rice-growing territories and people who cultivated it.

Its worldwide influence as a force of history aside, rice was and continues to be more than just food to the Thai people. As the foundation on which self-sustaining and self-supporting communities were built, rice and rice growing has shaped the country's social structure, cultural expression, and religious beliefs. Rice gave life and became a way of life still practiced in rural Thailand.

As the single source of existence, rice was scared and treated with great reverence. Traditional Thai people believed that rice was alive with a humanlike spirit. They identified with rice and found many human similarities. Rice needs to be nurtured and cared for to grow and mature, just like a child. The cycle of rice cultivation, from germinating the rice grains into rice saplings to planting to harvesting the ripened grains, reflects human life from birth to death, and rebirth.

Rice is used symbolically in the Thai language to connote the human condition. For example, rice is synonymous with wealth and well-being. When one is poor and destitute, Thais describe the condition as "not having any rice to eat." The Rice Angel, *Phra Mae Phsot*, watches over people who appreciate rice and punishes those who waste it. In times past, Thais were very superstitious and would never throw leftover rice away. To even consider feeding leftover rice to animals was enough to anger the Rice Angel. Instead, leftover rice was dry-roasted and stored in bamboo tubes or banana leaves for farmers or hunters to eat in the field.

Rice was offered as alms to Buddhist monks, who dried leftover rice into sheets and gave or sold it back to the people. Such rice was considered blessed rice and highly prized. Ancient recipes include ingenious ways of turning leftover rice into snacks and desserts. Unfortunately, these old recipes have disappeared, lost to later generations of Thais.

Selecting and Storing Rice

Thailand is one of the world's biggest exporters of rice. However, there are many varieties grown all over the world, covering a wide range of quality. For Thai cooking, it's the quality of rice that counts. With good-quality rice, you are halfway to a perfect Thai meal.

Long-grain rice is considered to be the finest quality, and it is the most expensive. Rice labeled "Thai jasmine" rice is best. Jasmine rice is an aromatic rice grown in Thailand. When cooked, it exudes a distinct sweet floral scent. Jasmine rice is rare, in that the cooked grains are tender, fluffy, and moist, yet at the same time each singular grain remains intact, preserving the integrity and consistency of the rice. It does not dissolve into a sticky, gummy mass.

Basmati rice from India, also a long-grain aromatic rice, can be substituted for Thai rice. However, it doesn't possess the perfume of jasmine rice and the grains cook to a drier and chewier texture.

If you cannot find imported jasmine or basmati rice, or California basmati rice, you can substitute long-grain American-grown rice. Buy rice that is in a clear package, allowing you to inspect for quality. Look for grains that are whole, not broken or chipped. The color should be pearly white and the rice free of stones or dirt. Avoid packages that look old or are covered with a film of flour dust—old rice can turn into rice flour. When you open the package, the rice should not smell musty.

Rice from Thailand comes in one-, five-, twenty-five-, and fifty-pound bags. The larger quantities are sold in either burlap sacks or white plastic bags. Generally, any busy Asian market with a rapid turnover of merchandise will have high-quality rice. Sometimes the label will say "new rice." Don't be fooled: "New" is not necessarily fresh or high quality. You can only be certain it is truly "new" if you happen to be in Thailand during the harvest season in June, November, or December. In regions where rice is grown and in Bangkok, the capital, traditional open markets display rices with different names and by grades. Only a connoisseur can tell the difference.

Rice grown in the central part of Thailand is excellent. Because the soil has more clay, it produces rice grains that are moist when cooked. Rice grown in arid northeastern Thailand, where the soil is sandy, has harder grains and will cook drier and firmer. Rice from this area is preferred by vendors because the cooked grains remain firm and have a longer shelf life.

The region between central and northeastern Thailand, where the soil is a combination of both clay and sand, produces most of the rice sold in Thailand and exported to world markets. This is where jasmine rice is grown. Newly harvested rice from this region is prized for its soft, velvety, delicate texture. It is used to make Thai desserts. When properly aged, jasmine rice makes excellent steamed rice.

The best-quality rice is harvested during December, when the weather is cool and dry. The rice grains ripen slowly and perfectly. The harsh tropical heat of other months causes the rice grains to ripen prematurely, while rice ripening in the rainy or monsoon seasons is prone to develop mold on the husk.

Rice should be aged for a year after harvesting before being sold. The new rice sold in America has actually been aged at least a year. Aging produces the most reliable cooking results. Authentic newly harvested rice is delicate and difficult to cook, except by experts. The exact amount of water used in cooking newly harvested rice is very difficult to gauge. It requires much less water than aged rice and tends to become wet and soggy when too much water is used. To cook newly harvested rice, the rule is to start with less water than you think you need. Once it is partially cooked but the top layer is still dry, add only a tiny bit more water. With its wonderful aroma, newly harvested rice is a rare treat. It is sensuous, teases the palate, and feels pleasing in the mouth.

Thai farmers told me that traditional hand-processed rice, which is light brown in color, tastes very different from factory-processed rice. I had the opportunity to witness the traditional harvesting and rice processing on one of my trips to Thailand when I volunteered to work with farmers during the harvest. My job was

simple: As the workers cut off handfuls of rice stalks, I would hit the stalks against the rim of a large bamboo basket. This shook loose the grains, causing them to fall neatly into the basket. The stalks were left in the fields to dry and later piled into large mounds for hay. The grains were bagged in large burlap sacks and taken to the farmer's home. There women took turns pounding the grains in a large wooden mortar. Their first duty was to separate enough grains from the husks to be cooked for a harvest celebration that evening.

Rice processing machines came to Thailand in the late 1800s and completely revolutionized rice growing. Small industries owned by Chinese immigrants took over the work of processing rice from the farmers. Machines quickly stripped the husk from the grain, leaving only the pearly white aleurone layer, or cuticle, around the grain. Sometimes a cornstarch powder is used in the final polishing process. When it first appeared, machine-processed rice was considered more refined and it became the rage among those who could afford it. Today, this is the rice most Thais eat.

The farmers were right, however, when they told me that hand-processed rice is far more flavorful and has a special and exquisite aroma. Sadly, few Thais know what they are missing and what has been lost with modern techniques.

In general, distinguishing characteristics of Thai rice are elongated, not round, grains and a pearly white color. Another long-grain rice is sticky, or glutinous, rice. Do not mistake long-grain Thai jasmine sticky rice for the round short-grain glutinous Japanese rice. Thai sticky rice is whiter, while Japanese sticky rice grain has a pearly sheen. When cooked, the grains of Thai sticky rice remain whole yet tender; Japanese sticky rice breaks down and congeals.

Few Thais eat brown rice. Hand-polished

rice is pounded to remove both the husk and brown bran, until the white rice grain is exposed. Brown rice is considered to be unpolished rice, even though it is very nutritious. Thais judge brown rice to be inferior, unrefined, and coarse. It was once fed only to prisoners. Thais have always preferred *kao seway,* or "beautiful rice," or at least until recently, when the younger generation and vegetarians, influenced by the Western ideas about healthful eating, became converts to brown rice. Restaurants appealing to foreigners sometimes have brown rice on the menu. I'll stick to my *kao seway.* With its

soft, delicate, and slightly chewy texture and scented aroma, it is the perfect accompaniment to Thai dishes.

If you love rice and eat it more than once a week, it pays to buy a big bag. I buy a ten-pound bag and open it at the top just wide enough to scoop out the rice I need. To seal the bag, I use a large plastic potato chip clip. This protects the rice from insects. A few Kaffir lime leaves inside the bag also help to discourage bugs. Store rice in small bags the same way. If you want to keep rice in a smaller container, a glass jar with a tight lid or a plastic Ziploc bag is best.

Cooking Rice

When I was a little girl, my Thai neighbor cooked rice in a terra-cotta pot shaped like a spittoon. Not only was the pot different from the metal pot my mother used to boil rice, but the way my neighbor cooked rice, stirring the grains in the pot and then pouring out the water, was strange. The process fascinated me so much that discovering and trying the many ways rice is cooked has become an obsession in my adult life. I could write an entire book about cooking rice.

There are several typical ways to cook rice. Many traditional ways are no longer practiced in Thailand. Cooking rice in a terra-cotta pot, for example, has all but disappeared. I was, however, fortunate to taste hand-polished rice cooked this way during a recent trip to a small village in the central part of Thailand. In addition to a marvelously soft texture, the rice had a wonderful earthy fragrance.

Bronze skillets were once used to cook rice for Buddhist monks. Large iron wok-like skillets, as big as a washtub, were used to boil large quantities of rice for parties. Cooking rice this

way left a thin brown sheet of rice on the bottom of the skillet. This method is still prized by the Thais. It is not easy to cook a perfect pot of rice and yet retain a thin layer of hardened rice at the bottom. The rice sheet is left to cool, then dried completely in the sun; later it is deep-fried in oil, making delicate rice crackers.

The traditional Mon way of cooking rice preserves the grain's firm texture, and it is still practiced in the seaside resorts of Petchburi and Hua Hin in Central Thailand. Each year, during the height of the hot season of March and April, and before the arrival of the monsoons, several of my friends journey in search of this particular rice dish, which is called *kao chair,* or soaked rice. The process involves rinsing partially cooked rice in cold water several times. The rice is then sifted through a thin piece of cotton, dried, and perfumed with jasmine incense.

The way we cook rice today is referred to by

the Thai as "Canton-style cooked rice," named after the city of Canton in South China. In the West, the result of this process is often referred to as "steamed rice." The reality is that the rice is initially boiled, then steamed. The water is absorbed into the grains during boiling, then the pot is covered, allowing the remaining moisture to turn to steam, gently softening the rice grains and finishing the cooking process.

In an old Thai recipe book, I read instructions on how to fix partially cooked rice. There was a great tip, suggesting that salted water be added as the rice is slowly cooked again. According to Harold McGee, food scientist and author of *On Food and Cooking,* salt slows the cooking process, allowing the uncooked portions of the rice to cook while preventing the cooked rice from burning.

The Thai people have cooked and eaten rice for hundreds of years. Even so, some have not perfected its cooking! So don't be discouraged if you don't have perfect rice the first time. You always can fix it, or simply start over again.

NINE GOLDEN RULES FOR PERFECT COOKED RICE

1. Use top-quality rice, such as Thai jasmine or Indian or California basmati.

2. Use a heavy-duty pot, preferably nonstick, with a tight-fitting lid, to ensure even cooking.

3. Wash the rice three times. This is an old ritual that is believed to evoke magic. For practical reasons, rice needs to be washed.

One never knows how it was processed and packaged before being sold. Rinse the rice three times by swirling it in a pot of tap water and then draining off the water. Some say washing rice strips away vitamins and other minerals. Actually, these were removed during processing and polishing. Washing won't hurt the rice. In fact, it helps to remove the excess starch used during processing and polishing, making the cooked rice grains less sticky and gummy.

4. Use bottled or filtered water to cook rice, especially if your tap water has an off taste.

5. Use equal amounts of rice and water for perfect fluffy rice. The traditional rule was to add only enough water to come up to your middle knuckle as you lay your hand gently on top of the rice. This is still the method I prefer. For newly harvested rice, use less water. For old rice, use more.

6. Start cooking over medium-high heat, and once the water starts to boil rapidly, lower the heat to medium, uncover, and cook until the water evaporates completely, small steam holes appear on the surface of the rice and the pot looks dry.

7. Cover the pot and turn the heat to low. Continue to cook for 10 minutes. No peeking or stirring!

8. Remove the rice from the heat and stir with a wooden spoon.

9. Let the rice rest for 10 minutes before serving.

To Store and Reheat Cooked Rice

Cooked rice can be kept in the refrigerator for up to a week in a container with a tight-fitting lid. Simply reheat the amount you want to eat by one of these three methods:

Microwave method: Put the rice into a microwave-proof container. Break up the rice clumps. Cover with a paper towel, plastic wrap, or waxed paper and cook the rice on high power for 2 to 3 minutes. If necessary, stir the rice, re-cover, and cook for 1 minute more.

Rice cooker method: Reheating rice in a rice cooker is just as easy as using the microwave. Place the rice in the pot. Add 1 to 2 tablespoons of water. Break up the rice clumps. Cover with the lid. Push the button on the rice cooker. It will take 5 to 7 minutes to reheat. When the timer sounds, it is ready.

Stovetop method: Place the rice in a heavy saucepan. Add 1 to 2 tablespoons of water and break up the rice clumps. Cover and cook over low heat for 7 to 10 minutes, or until warm throughout.

Covered Saucepan Method

Makes 4 to 6 servings

A four-quart heavy saucepan with a tight-fitting lid will do the job here. Cooking will take 20 to 25 minutes.

2 cups long-grain rice, preferably Thai jasmine or Indian or California basmati, rinsed well (see page 36)
2 cups (approximately) bottled or filtered water

Put the rice in the saucepan. Put one hand on top of the rice. Pour enough water over your hand and the rice to reach the middle knuckle of your middle finger.

Bring to a rapid boil over high heat. Lower the heat to medium and continue cooking, uncovered, until the water disappears and the steam has created holes in the surface of the rice, 7 to 10 minutes. Turn the heat to low, cover the pan, and cook the rice for another 10 to 12 minutes, or until the top layer is moist and the rice grains are tender and have lost their sheen. If some grains remain shiny, add 1 to 2 tablespoons of water and continue to cook for a minute or two.

Cover and cook, without stirring, for another 10 minutes, or until the rice is uniform in color. Stir the rice lightly with a fork. It should separate easily. Fluff the rice several times with a wooden spoon. Remove from the heat, cover, and let the rice rest for 10 minutes before serving.

Electric Rice Cooker Method

I love my electric rice cooker, and you'll find one in nearly every Thai household. It frees you up to do other tasks and is just about fool-proof. Rice cookers have a timer that goes off when the rice is finished cooking. Unless you live alone and never have company for dinner, buy one with a 6-cup capacity.

Follow the instructions above, but instead of worrying about the heat, or covering and uncovering the pot, push the button on the rice cooker and go do something else while the rice cooks. It will take 15 to 20 minutes. When it is done, the timer will sound. Stir the rice with a wooden spoon, cover, and let it rest for 10 minutes.

Other Methods of Cooking Rice

It is told that the Thai king Narai (1656–1688) was extremely fond of Persian cooking. The king commanded his Persian appointed officials to share their daily meals with him, and palace banquets were cooked by Persian cooks to please the king. Thais adapted various foreign ways of cooking rice, particularly from the Persians, Ceylonese, and Chinese, using other liquids instead of water. The following recipes use coconut cream or chicken broth, changing the flavor and adding texture and aroma.

Kao Mun
RICE COOKED WITH COCONUT CREAM

Makes 4 servings

Kao mun is a fragrant and old-fashioned dish served with Spicy Green Papaya Salad (page 160) and Grilled Chicken (page 162). Some traditional recipes add pandanus leaves to intensify the perfume, but if none are available, almond extract will do.

Follow the instructions on cooking rice with the Covered Saucepan Method (see page 37). When the liquid has disappeared and the steam has created holes in the rice, lay the pandanus leaf, if using, on top of the rice, cover, and finish cooking the rice. Remove the pandanus leaf, fluff the rice, cover, and let it rest for 10 minutes before serving. If using almond extract instead of the pandanus leaf, stir it in just before removing the rice from the heat.

2 cups long-grain rice, preferably Thai jasmine or Indian or California basmati rice, rinsed well
About 1 cup Fresh Unsweetened Coconut Cream (page 69)
About 1 cup Fresh Unsweetened Coconut Milk (page 69)
Fine sea salt
1 pandanus leaf (see page 135), cut into 2-inch lengths, or 2 to 3 drops almond extract

Kao Mun Gai
CHICKEN RICE

Makes 4 servings

**For the dipping sauce
(makes ¾ cup)**

5 to 6 fresh bird chiles or 3 to 4
serrano chiles, thinly sliced

1 tablespoon salted bean sauce or
bean paste (see Cook's Notes)

2 tablespoons soy sauce

1 tablespoon dark corn syrup or
molasses

1 tablespoon rice vinegar or cider
vinegar

For the garnishes

1 cucumber

Several sprigs cilantro

4 to 6 scallions, trimmed

For the chicken

One 3-pound chicken, fat left intact,
rinsed and thoroughly dried

2 to 3 teaspoons fine sea salt (no
more than 1 tablespoon)

12 cloves garlic, or more, unpeeled,
lightly crushed

2½ cups (approximately) bottled or
filtered water

3 cups long-grain rice, preferably
Thai jasmine or Indian or
California basmati, rinsed well

Kao (rice), *mun* (oil), and *gai* (chicken)—or chicken rice—is a popular dish of Hainan, an island off South China. It was brought to Thailand by Chinese immigrant workers, who married there and taught their Thai brides to cook the Chinese way. Today throughout Thailand, street vendors selling this popular dish are testament to these settlers' die-hard habits.

Chicken with some fat is needed for this dish. The fat and liquid resulting from the steamed chicken are added to the rice for cooking, giving it a rich flavor. The recipe also includes a spicy dipping sauce for the chicken.

Make the dipping sauce by mixing the ingredients together in a small bowl. Set aside. Or, to store, put the sauce in a jar with a tight-fitting lid and refrigerate.

To prepare the cucumber, peel it and cut it lengthwise in half. Scoop out the seeds. Slice the cucumber into thin half-moon slices.

Rub the chicken cavity with sea salt and insert the garlic cloves. Put the chicken in a 9-inch Pyrex pie plate. Select a 6-quart pasta pot with a steamer basket insert that's big enough to hold the pie plate and fill the pot with water to come up to 1 inch under the steamer insert. Place the pie plate with the chicken in the steamer basket, insert the steamer basket into the pot, and cover tightly. Place the pot over high heat. When the water boils, lower the heat to medium-low and steam for 50 minutes, or until the chicken is cooked through. Check for doneness by piercing the fold between the thigh and leg—the juices should be clear, not pink. Halfway through the cooking time, check the water level; if it is reduced to less than one third of the original amount, add 2 cups hot water.

Drain the liquid from the chicken by tipping the steamer basket with the pie plate and cooked chicken over a bowl. Remove the garlic cloves from the chicken, add them to the bowl, and set aside. Return the steamer basket with the chicken to the pot, cover, and keep warm until ready to serve.

Measure the liquid from the chicken, then add enough bottled water to make 3 cups. Add the rice, stirring with a wooden spoon. Transfer to a 4-quart saucepan. Bring to a rapid boil, then lower the heat to medium. When the water has evaporated and the steam has created holes in the rice, turn the heat to low, cover the pan, and cook over low heat for 10 to 12 minutes, or until the rice is soft, fluffy, and no longer shiny. If there are some grains that are not completely cooked, add 1 to 2 table-spoons of water, cover the pan, and continue cooking over low heat for about another 10 minutes. Stir gently with a wooden spoon. Remove from the heat, cover the pan, and let the rice rest for 10 minutes before serving.

To serve, remove the chicken meat from the bones and cut into bite-sized pieces. Spoon the rice onto individual plates. Arrange the chicken on top of the rice. Garnish with the sliced cucumber, cilantro sprigs, and scallions. Serve the dipping sauce in a bowl, so guests can spoon the sauce onto the chicken pieces and rice.

Cook's Notes

Bean sauce is made with whole beans fermented with salt, sugar, and rice powder. Bean paste is pureed fermented beans with salt. Both are available in most Asian markets.

The dipping sauce can be made a day or so ahead of time and will in fact taste better, as the chile has time to pickle in the soy sauce and vinegar.

You can prepare the garnishes ahead, wrap them in paper towels, seal them in a plastic bag, and refrigerate. The chicken can also be steamed hours before serving. Save the cooked garlic and liquid together in a container. When ready to serve, if the chicken is cold, you can steam it once more, or serve it cold with the hot steamed rice: The contrast in the temperature between the steaming-hot rice and the cold chicken adds a marvelous sensation. Street ven-dors in Thailand often serve chicken rice this way.

Kao Suratan

SULTAN'S RICE

One 3-pound chicken, fat trimmed,
rinsed and thoroughly dried
4 cups bottled or filtered water
1/2 teaspoon saffron threads or
1/2 teaspoon turmeric powder
3 tablespoons unsalted butter
3 cups long-grain rice, preferably
Thai jasmine or Indian or
California basmati, rinsed well
1 cup Fresh Unsweetened Coconut
Cream (page 69) or heavy cream
1/4 teaspoon freshly grated nutmeg
1/4 teaspoon ground mace
3 whole cloves, dry-roasted (see
page 13) and finely ground
1 1/2 teaspoons sea salt

As early as the seventh century, seafarers from Srivijava (present-day Sumatra) traveled the globe, trading spices from Southeast Asia with India and China. They were like bees pollinating the cuisine everywhere they went. This is the way many cooking techniques using spices such as cinnamon from China and cloves, nutmeg, and mace from Jakarta, formerly Batavia, were introduced to the Thai people.

Since both Srivijava and Batavia had been converted to Islam by the Arab merchants, their rulers were called the Sultans. Initially, only the Thai Royal Court and wealthy Thais were able to afford to use these spices. This recipe, using a pilaf-type technique, was adapted by the Thais and named after the Sultan, in honor of the priceless spices used in the dish.

Put the chicken in a stockpot, add the bottled water and saffron, and bring to a rapid boil. Turn the heat to medium-low, cover the pot, and cook for about 1 hour, or until the chicken is thoroughly cooked. Check for doneness by piercing the fold between the thigh and leg: The juices should be clear, not pink.

Remove the pot from the heat and remove the chicken from the broth. Remove the chicken from the bones, tearing the meat into long bite-sized pieces. Discard the bones and skin, cover the meat, and set aside. Strain the broth, measure out 2 cups into a small saucepan, and bring it to a boil. Reduce the heat and keep at a simmer.

Place the butter in a 12-inch heavy skillet over medium heat. When the butter begins to melt, add the rice and cook, stirring frequently so the rice grains don't burn, for about 15 minutes, or until the rice turns golden. Add the simmering broth to the pan. Mix well, add the coconut cream, and mix until well incorporated. Add the nutmeg, mace, cloves, and sea salt, stirring well. Continue to cook, uncovered, until the liquid disappears, leaving steam holes all over the surface of the rice, 10 to 15 minutes. Turn the heat to low, cover with a tight-fitting lid, and cook for another 10 minutes, or until the rice grains are soft and separate easily. Stir with a wooden spoon and scrape the bottom of the pot. It may be brown from the butter and coconut cream; this is fine. Cover and cook over low heat for another 10 minutes. Remove the pan from the heat. Stir in the chicken and serve.

Cook's Notes

You can prepare the chicken up to a day ahead. Strain the broth and refrigerate the broth and chicken separately. Reheat the chicken before using. Leftover broth can be stored in a glass jar or Ziploc plastic bags and refrigerated or frozen for later use for other recipes, such as Hot-Sour Shrimp Soup (page 165).

Kao Buri

CITY RICE

One 3-pound chicken, rinsed and
   thoroughly dried
4 cups bottled or filtered water
1½ teaspoons sea salt
3 cups long-grain rice, preferably
   Thai jasmine or Indian or
   California basmati, rinsed well
3 tablespoons vegetable oil
¼ teaspoon ground cardamom
3 bay leaves
3 whole cloves, dry-roasted (see
   page 13) and ground
¼ teaspoon ground cinnamon
¼ teaspoon freshly grated nutmeg
¼ teaspoon ground mace
¼ teaspoon turmeric powder
1½ cups golden raisins
½ cup cilantro leaves, chopped
3 to 4 fresh bird chiles or 4 to 5
   serrano chiles, seeded if desired
   and minced
½ cup sweet pickled ginger (see
   page 140)

This southern Thai rice dish reflects the influence of the Arab traders, who visited China as early as A.D. 758. Records of Marco Polo's journey in 1292 noted their presence all over Batavia (now Jakarta). Thailand, located between the Arab-Chinese trade routes, was settled by Arab people long before Thailand was established as a nation, known in 1283 as Siam. Thais love blending aromatic spices; that, along with their partiality to sweet flavors, probably prompted them to adopt this dish as their own.

Place the chicken in a stockpot, add the bottled water and 1 teaspoon of the sea salt, and bring to a boil. Lower the heat to medium-low, cover, and let the chicken simmer for about 1 hour, or until it is cooked thoroughly. Check for doneness by piercing the fold between the thigh and leg. The juices should be clear, not pink. Transfer the chicken to a plate; cover loosely with a dish towel and let cool. Cover the chicken broth and keep warm on the stove over very low heat.

When the chicken is cool enough to handle, remove the meat from the bones and cut it into bite-sized pieces. Set aside 3 cups for this dish and reserve the remainder.

Cook the rice following the instructions for the Covered Saucepan Method (page 37), substituting the hot chicken broth for water.

While the rice sits, heat the oil in a 12-inch skillet over medium-low heat. Add the cardamom, bay leaves, cloves, cinnamon, nutmeg, mace, and turmeric and stir for a minute, or until the mixture becomes aromatic. Stir in about 3 cups of the chicken and the remaining ½ teaspoon salt, mixing well. Raise the heat to medium and stir in the rice and raisins. Transfer the mixture to a platter and sprinkle the chopped cilantro over the top. Serve with the minced chiles and sweet pickled ginger in small bowls.

Cook's Notes

Sweet pickled ginger—pale pink, paper-thin slices pickled in sugar and vinegar—is used as a garnish for sushi. It can be bought in Asian supermarkets and is sometimes stocked in the deli or ethnic food section of the supermarket, with other Asian specialties.

Since making the broth takes about 1 hour, it may be convenient to make it in advance. Strain the broth, remove the chicken from the bones, and refrigerate the broth and chicken separately. Bring the cooked chicken to room temperature and heat the broth prior to cooking.

All the spices can be roasted and pounded ahead and stored in a glass jar.

The fresh chiles can either be seeded or not, depending on your preference for spiciness.

Yumm Kao
RICE SALAD

For the dressing

½ cup salt-packed anchovies (see
    Cook's Notes)
1½ cups water
1 cup palm sugar or packed light
    brown sugar
3 stalks lemongrass, green parts and
    hard outer layers removed,
    lightly pounded (page 133)
One 1-inch chunk galangal or 2-inch
    chunk fresh ginger, peeled and
    lightly pounded
3 to 4 large shallots, unpeeled,
    lightly pounded
6 kaffir lime leaves, torn, or zest of
    2 limes

For the rice salad

4 cups cooked long-grain rice,
    preferably Thai jasmine or Indian
    or California basmati (see pages
    37 and 38), at room temperature
1 cup green beans, parboiled in
    4 cups water and 1 teaspoon sea
    salt, rinsed, patted dry, and
    thinly sliced
½ cup thinly sliced (crosswise)
    Belgian endive
½ cup arugula cut crosswise into
    thin strands
1 cup fresh bean sprouts
1 green mango, coarsely grated, or
    1 Granny Smith apple, coarsely
    grated and tossed with
    1 teaspoon fresh lemon juice
3 stalks lemongrass, green parts and
    hard outer layers removed, thinly
    sliced

(continued)

Yumm kao is a great way to use leftover rice. During the hot, dry tropical season from February to May, the air in Thailand feels like a furnace. People retreat into their cool dark homes and snack on delicate dishes such as this rice salad. *Yumm kao* is an ancient remedy for keeping cool when the temperature soars. Aromatic leaves such as sour orange leaf, kaffir lime, and jasmine are known for their medicinal benefits, including the ability to cool the body.

In southern Thailand, where this dish originated, the dressing is made from a salty and sweet syrup called *namm muu doo,* which is bottled and sold in markets. The major ingredient in the dressing is a salted dried fish called *pla inntaree,* or mackerel, boiled with herbs and palm sugar. In this recipe, I have substituted salted anchovies for the *pla inntaree.* As you prepare the dressing, you may think it is the strangest thing you've ever made, but proceed: You'll be rewarded with an explosion of texture and an unexpected combination of tastes. The original recipe also calls for powdered dried shrimp, for which I substitute dried smoked fish.

For the dressing, place the anchovies and water in a saucepan. Bring to a rapid boil and cook for 3 minutes, or until the anchovies begin to fall apart. Add the palm sugar, lemongrass, galangal, shallots, and kaffir lime leaves and boil for 20 minutes, or until the liquid begins to caramelize and becomes syrupy. Turn off the heat and let the dressing sit for 10 minutes. Strain, discarding the solids. You should have about ½ cup of thick salty-sweet syrup.

To assemble the salad, put the dressing in a small bowl and set it in the center of a large platter. Arrange mounds of the cooked rice (mold it in custard cups and invert onto the platter), along with mounds of green beans, endive, arugula, bean sprouts, and green mango on the platter. Wedge mounds of the lemongrass, dried smoked fish, and coconut flakes between the rice and vegetables.

Sprinkle the kaffir lime leaves and orange zest on top of the rice. Put the dried chile powder in a tiny bowl at one end of the platter and arrange the lime wedges all around.

At serving time, this salad makes a beautiful and dramatic presentation: Pour the dressing over all the ingredients on the platter, add the amount of chile powder you want, and squeeze the lime wedges all over the entire dish. Mix well and taste for balance of piquant-salty-sweet-sour taste. Enjoy.

Cook's Notes

Salt-packed anchovies are available in Italian markets. To use, wash off the salt and dry thoroughly on paper towels. Smoked fish is available in the deli section of supermarkets, fish markets, or gourmet food shops.

Most of the preparation for the salad can be done in stages, or several days in advance, so it is only a matter of assembling it at the last minute. The dressing can be stored in a glass jar with a lid in the refrigerator for up to 1 week. You can prepare the vegetables and fruits—except the apple, if using, which should be grated close to serving time, as it will discolor—in advance. Wrap each separately in paper towels and store in Ziploc bags in the refrigerator. The roasted coconut flakes can also be stored in a plastic bag in the refrigerator for several weeks. Mince the dried smoked fish ahead and store in a plastic bag until ready to use. The rice can be cooked in advance, or you can use leftover cooked rice that has been brought to room temperature before being added to the salad.

1 cup finely minced dried smoked fish, such as tuna, salmon, or trout

1 cup Roasted Fresh Grated Coconut Flakes (page 71)

4 kaffir lime leaves, sliced into long thin strands, or grated zest of 1 lime

1 tablespoon grated orange zest (preferably bitter or blood orange)

1 to 2 tablespoons Roasted Dried Chile Powder (page 91) or cayenne

1 to 2 limes, sliced into wedges

Kao Padd

STIR-FRIED RICE

Makes 4 servings

For the garnishes and condiments

4 to 5 fresh bird chiles or 2 to 3
  serrano chiles, finely chopped
2 tablespoons fish sauce (*namm pla*)
4 scallions
3 to 4 sprigs cilantro, finely chopped
1 cucumber, peeled, sliced
  lengthwise in half, seeded, and
  thinly sliced on the diagonal
1 to 2 limes or lemons, sliced into
  wedges

For the rice

5 tablespoons vegetable oil
1 clove garlic, minced
½ medium yellow onion, chopped
2 to 3 thin slivers fresh ginger, minced
½ cup each of your choice of
  vegetables, such as fresh or
  frozen corn, peas, diced red or
  green bell pepper, and diced
  green beans (1½ cups in all)
4 to 6 ounces each of your choice of
  precooked or leftover ham,
  turkey, chicken, pork, beef,
  crabmeat, or shrimp, cut into
  bite-sized pieces (1 cup in all)
½ teaspoon sea salt
½ teaspoon freshly ground white
  pepper
2 tablespoons ketchup
2 tablespoons soy sauce
4 cups cooked long-grain rice,
  preferably Thai jasmine or
  Indian or California basmati (see
  pages 37 and 38), at room
  temperature, clumps broken up
  with a fork
2 to 3 tablespoons water, as needed
1 large egg

One of my favorite foods is *kao padd,* stir-fried rice, made with whatever leftover cooked meat or vegetables I have in the refrigerator. The secret ingredient is ketchup, which was originated by the Chinese. Thais love the sweet-and-sour taste and the reddish color it adds to the rice. Preparing ahead is the key to a successful stir-fry. Arrange the ingredients in the order in which they are to be added to the pan; stir-frying is a very fast method, so once you start, you cannot stop until the dish is done.

In a small bowl, make the sauce by combining the chiles with the fish sauce. Set aside. Mince the whites and light green parts of 1 scallion, leaving the other 3 whole for garnish. Combine the minced scallion and the cilantro in another small bowl. Unless serving right away, wrap all the condiments and garnishes in plastic and set aside.

Heat a 12-inch nonstick heavy skillet or flat-bottomed wok over high heat. If when you put your hand 2 to 3 inches above the pan you feel the heat, the pan is hot enough to begin cooking. Add 3 tablespoons of the oil. As soon as the oil begins to smoke, about 1 minute, add the garlic, stirring with a spatula to avoid burning. Quickly add the onion and continue to cook, stirring. As soon as the onion becomes translucent, about 1 minute, add the ginger and continue stirring for 30 seconds. Add the vegetables, continuing to stir for 1 to 2 minutes. Add the meat, then the sea salt, pepper, ketchup, and soy sauce and stir for another minute. Add the rice and continue stirring to heat and combine well. If it sticks to the pan, sprinkle a bit of water onto the rice, a little at a time.

When everything is well mixed, push the mixture to one side of the pan, and add the remaining 2 tablespoons oil to the cleared space. Crack the egg over the oil and scramble it lightly. When the egg starts to solidify, pile the rice mixture on top and mix well.

Transfer the rice to a serving platter and sprinkle with the chopped scallion and cilantro. Arrange the whole or sliced scallions, cucumber slices, and lime wedges around the sides of the platter. Serve with the chile and fish sauce in a small bowl.

Kao Pun

ROASTED RICE POWDER

Use *kao pun*, roasted rice powder, to add texture to meat salads. It's the secret ingredient in Beef Salad (page 259), *laab,* or minced meat, and *Laab* with Roast Duck (page 250). A tablespoon added to soup will thicken and flavor it. This powder keeps for a month in an airtight glass jar.

To dry-roast the rice grains, place the rice in a 10-inch skillet over medium-high heat. Roast for 10 to 15 minutes, shaking the skillet frequently and stirring with a wooden spoon to ensure even cooking. If the rice grains begin to roast unevenly or too quickly, lower the heat. When all the rice grains are golden, transfer them to a bowl to cool.

Grind the rice with a mortar and pestle, adding a couple of tablespoons of roasted rice to the mortar at a time and pressing the pestle onto the rice grains against the mortar in a continuous circular motion until the grains turn almost to powder. Don't worry if the grains aren't completely and evenly ground; the result should resemble coarse cornmeal.

You can also grind the powder with a coffee or spice grinder. To do so, add 1 to 2 tablespoons of roasted rice grains to the grinder at a time and pulse and grind until the rice resembles coarse cornmeal.

¼ cup long-grain rice, preferably Thai jasmine or Indian or California basmati

Kao Neuw

STICKY, OR GLUTINOUS, RICE

Makes 4 to 5 servings

2 cups long-grain Thai jasmine
sticky rice

While the people from central and southern Thailand eat regular long-grain rice, the northern and northeastern Thais eat another type of long-grain rice, known as *kao neuw,* or sticky rice. *Kao neuw* grains adhere to each other and are easily shaped into balls. The Laotians also share this custom.

Sticky rice is soaked in cool water overnight before cooking. Unlike the boil-steam method for regular long-grain rice, sticky rice is steamed in a strange contraption. The bottom of this unorthodox-looking steamer is an aluminum pot shaped like a spittoon, while the top is a bamboo basket, resembling a conical hat with the edges curved into two high pointed corners. Once the water in the lower pot begins to boil, the soaked rice is added to the bamboo basket. The rice closest to the heat begins to cook first and, because the rice sticks together, after several minutes, the rice in the basket can be flipped over and cooked. The top layer goes to the bottom and the bottom comes to the top.

Sticky rice is chewy and tastes buttery and nutty. Cooked sticky rice is traditionally kept in, and served from, a beautiful bamboo woven basket, where it stays moist and warm for a long time. Farmers in the fields lunch on sticky rice with dried meat. Because sticky rice is eaten only with the hands, a strict etiquette of washing before a meal is practiced.

To eat, each person takes a handful of sticky rice from the container and breaks off a small amount, kneading it into a ball. He or she then dips this small ball of rice into the sauce or uses it to scoop up pieces of vegetable or meat.

Thai people believe that sticky rice makes them mellow. Therefore, it is common to rest after eating sticky rice. One should avoid eating sticky rice and consuming cold liquids at the same time—it is believed that cold liquids will solidify the already sticky rice, making digestion difficult. The people of Central Thailand, who seldom eat sticky rice, believe that those who eat sticky rice tend to be lazy!

COOKING STICKY RICE IN A TRADITIONAL THAI POT

The spittoon-shaped pot and bamboo basket shaped like a conical hat made especially for cooking sticky rice are available in most Asian markets. They are very inexpensive. The pot doubles as an attractive flower vase and the basket makes a great strainer or sieve. In addition to the pot and the basket, you'll need a Pyrex or stainless steel pie plate or a lid from another pot to use as a cover.

Rinse the rice 3 times, then fill a bowl with cool water and let the rice soak overnight. (If you would like to try a shortcut, soak the rice in very warm water. When the water is cool, the rice will be soft. The water will turn murky and the rice grains slightly slimy; rinse once more in cool water. The shortcut rice may not be as soft and sticky as that soaked overnight.) It takes at least 5 to 6 hours for the rice to slowly expand and soften. Test to see if the rice is adequately soaked and ready for steaming by pressing a grain lightly with your fingernails. The grain should break easily.

Fill the pot about one-third full of water and bring it to a boil. Meanwhile, place the bamboo steamer basket in the sink, pour the rice and soaking water into the basket, and drain thoroughly. Put the basket on top of the pot. Cover the pot with a pie plate or lid and let the rice steam for about 10 minutes as the water continues to boil.

Using hot pads or tongs, remove the pie plate. Take hold of the two high-pointed corners of the bamboo basket and, holding them at waist level, lightly shake the basket to loosen the rice, then toss the rice to flip it over, as if you were flipping a pancake, so the rice at the bottom goes to the top and vice versa. Return the basket to the pot, cover, and let the rice steam for another 10 minutes, or until the grains look glossy and somewhat translucent and stick together. To make absolutely certain the rice is thoroughly steamed, cook a bit longer than the time suggested; while sticky rice cannot be overcooked, it can be undercooked. Transfer to a serving bowl or basket and keep covered until ready to serve; serve hot.

(continued)

COOKING STICKY RICE IN A PASTA POT

Line the steamer basket insert of the pot with fresh corn husks or soaked dried corn husks (used as Mexican tamale wrappers). Spray the corn husks with vegetable oil spray to prevent sticking. Spread the soaked rice evenly over the husks.

Fill the pot with water to come to just under the steamer basket insert. Put the steamer basket insert into the pot, cover, and bring to a boil over medium-high heat. Steam the rice for at least 20 minutes, or longer. Transfer the rice to a serving bowl when ready to serve. Cover the rice with some corn husks to keep it moist and warm.

REHEATING STICKY RICE

Divide the leftover cooked rice into small serving portions, wrap in plastic, and refrigerate. The rice will keep well for 2 to 3 days. The easiest and best way to reheat the sticky rice is by microwave. Warm the wrapped sticky rice in the plastic it was stored in on high power for 1 to 2 minutes, or until hot. To reheat by steaming, unwrap the sticky rice and follow the method outlined in Cooking Sticky Rice in a Pasta Pot (above).

Kao Neuw Kati

SWEET STICKY RICE DESSERT

Makes 6 servings

In the early 1950s, a beautiful vendor sold sweet sticky rice dessert with mango at Bang Rak, a market in Bangkok. She had graceful fingers and long painted fingernails, which she used to scrap the warm sticky rice onto banana leaves. The men lined up just to look at her. She fluttered her long false eyelashes while spooning sweet rich coconut syrup over the bowls of sticky rice, and men swooned. One day she disappeared and was replaced by an old woman. Both the wait and lines of men shortened immediately. Rumor spread around the market that the general-dictator of Thailand had summoned her to his home to become his mistress.

After you've prepared the rice, make the sauce syrup: Combine the sugar, palm sugar, pandanus leaves, if using, and the coconut milk in a 2-quart saucepan. Heat over medium-low heat, stirring occasionally, until the sugar is dissolved. Without increasing the heat, allow the coconut cream to come to a gentle boil, and boil and thicken for 5 to 6 minutes. Remove the saucepan from the heat. Cover to keep warm. Leave the pandanus leaves in the syrup until you are ready to make the syrup for topping, or, if you are using extract, add it now.

To make the topping syrup, if you are using pandanus leaves, pull them out of the sauce syrup and place them in a 2-quart saucepan. Add the sugar, salt, and coconut cream. Heat over low to medium-low heat until the sugar and salt dissolve; do not let the coconut cream boil, or it will curdle. Let the syrup simmer slowly until it thickens, 7 to 10 minutes. Remove the saucepan from the heat. Leave the pandanus leaves in the syrup until ready to be used. Or, if you are using extract instead, add it now and stir well. Pour the mixture into a medium bowl and set aside.

To make the sticky rice dessert, put the hot rice in a large mixing bowl. Pour the warm sauce syrup over the rice, mixing well with a wooden spoon. The mixture will be soupy. Cover tightly with clear plastic wrap and let the rice absorb the syrup for about 10 minutes, then stir the rice mixture again with the wooden spoon. Cover tightly with plastic wrap again and let it rest for another 10 minutes.

2 cups long-grain Thai jasmine sticky rice, cooked (see page 50), and kept hot in the steamer

For the sauce syrup

1/2 cup granulated sugar

2 tablespoons palm sugar or light brown sugar

2 to 3 long strips pandanus leaves (see page 135) or 1 to 2 drops orange or almond extract

1 cup Fresh Unsweetened Coconut Milk (page 69)

For the topping syrup

2 to 3 long strips pandanus leaves (reserved from sauce syrup) or 1 to 2 drops orange or almond extract

1/4 cup granulated sugar

1 teaspoon sea salt

1 cup Fresh Unsweetened Coconut Cream (page 69)

(continued)

To shape the rice for serving, dip your hands in a bowl of cool water and shake off excess droplets. Scoop a handful of rice at a time from the bowl and mold it into an oval shape. Or shape the rice by using a rubber spatula to scoop up a mound of rice onto a large oval wooden spoon, shape it with the spoon, and transfer the mound to a serving platter. The rice may stick to the spatula, so dip it in cold water and shake off excess droplets before scooping more rice.

Put the rice on a serving platter or individual plates. Spoon the thickened coconut syrup topping over the rice. Garnish with sliced fruits (see below) and serve.

Cook's Notes

Both syrups can be made a couple of days ahead and refrigerated. Bring each syrup to a simmer over medium-low heat before using.

Leftover sweet sticky rice will keep for 2 to 3 days in the refrigerator. Divide the rice into small portions, wrap in plastic wrap, and refrigerate. To reheat, microwave single portions of rice one at a time on high for 1 to 2 minutes; or wrap the rice in softened dried corn husks and steam until the rice is soft and warm.

Accompaniments

Traditionally, sticky rice is served with slices of ripe mango. For a contemporary variation, try soft fruits with sweet and tart flavors, such as sliced peaches, pears, or kiwifruit. Fresh strawberries and raspberries make a dramatic contrast in both presentation and taste.

Variation

Wrapped and Grilled Sticky Rice: Grilling not only nicely reheats sticky rice, but allows you to wrap it in a variety of leaves to perfume it and add interesting aromas. Fresh banana leaves, fresh corn husks, and dried corn husks are all used in Thailand to wrap both cooked jasmine rice and cooked sticky rice for grilling. Grilling transforms the rice into an entirely new dish. Grill the rice packets over a medium-hot fire for 7 to 10 minutes.

Banana leaves: Wash banana leaves with soap and water; rinse and dry thoroughly. Cut away and discard the hard stems and cut the leaves into 10-inch squares. Fan both sides of each leaf over a low gas flame over the stove or place directly on top of an electric burner for a couple of seconds to soften; do not burn.

Layer two leaves together, with the dull side facing up. Spoon 2 to 3 tablespoons of sticky rice into the center. Fold the leaves over lengthwise, making an oblong bundle. Fold the sides over the rice and secure each end with toothpicks. Brush with water before grilling.

Fresh corn husks: Layer 2 to 3 clean husks together. Put 2 to 3 tablespoons of sticky rice in the center. Fold the long sides of the husks over the rice. Tie each end with a torn corn husk strand or secure with toothpicks. Brush with water before grilling.

Dried corn husks: Soak dried corn husks in water for at least 10 minutes, or until pliable. Assemble as for fresh corn husks.

Bha Jung

CHINESE-STYLE STICKY RICE BUNDLES

Makes 6 servings

For the seasoning sauce

1 teaspoon Thai white peppercorns
   or other white peppercorns
3 cloves garlic, minced
1 teaspoon sea salt
1 tablespoon soy sauce
2 tablespoons molasses
1 teaspoon Roasted Dried Chile
   Powder (page 91) or cayenne
1 tablespoon sesame oil

For the sticky rice

1 cup shelled raw peanuts (with
   skins left on)
¼ cup dried lily blossoms or dried
   wood ear mushrooms
¼ cup dried shiitake mushrooms
Sea salt
12 dried corn husks, soaked in
   warm water until softened, or
   fresh corn husks
Vegetable oil spray
2 cups long-grain Thai jasmine
   sticky rice, soaked overnight in
   cool water
½ white onion, coarsely chopped
1 stalk celery, thinly sliced
3 Chinese dried sweet pork or
   chicken sausages, thinly sliced on
   the diagonal (optional)
½ cup sweet pickled ginger (see
   page 140)

This savory dish originated in southern China; sticky rice is wrapped in bamboo leaves and steamed. Several years ago, while visiting Thailand, I went to a vegetarian restaurant in the northern province of Chiang Mai operated by Thai Buddhist nuns. Nothing on the menu cost more than five *baht,* which is less than a penny in American currency. Among my favorites was *bha jung,* which they served unwrapped on a large tray. What made their *bha jung* special was the freshly harvested peanuts that had been boiled until soft but still crunchy. The southern Chinese also vary their *bha jung* by adding sweet Chinese sausages. Both versions are wonderful. Here, I have left the meat optional. I recommend serving *bha jung* with sweet pickled sliced ginger.

Dry-roast the peppercorns in a 10-inch skillet over medium heat for 5 to 7 minutes, or until they are fragrant. Remove from the heat and cool completely.

Transfer the roasted peppercorns to a coffee or spice grinder and grind to a fine powder. Let the powder settle for a minute before opening the lid. Transfer to a mortar, add the garlic, and pound to a paste. Add the sea salt and continue to pound until the paste is smooth. Transfer to a small mixing bowl. Add the soy sauce, molasses, chile powder, and sesame oil, mix well, and set aside.

In a small saucepan, cover the peanuts with water, bring to a boil gently for 1 hour, or until soft. Drain the peanuts in a strainer and rinse several times with cool water. Put the boiled peanuts in a mixing bowl and cover with cool water. Rub the peanuts, a handful at a time, between the palms of your hands in the water to loosen the skins, peel off, and discard the skins. Transfer the peanuts to a bowl, pat dry, and set aside.

Place the dried lily blossoms (or wood ear mushrooms) and shiitake mushrooms in separate bowls. Add enough hot water to cover them. Let cool completely, then drain, rinse the softened lily blossoms several times in cool water, squeeze out the excess water, and set aside. Remove the hard stems from the mushrooms, then rinse several times in cool water. Massage the caps thoroughly with 1 teaspoon salt and let them sit for 5 to 10 minutes. Rinse in cool water and squeeze out the excess.

Gather the mushrooms into a tight bundle and slice into long, thin strands. Set aside.

Choose a pasta pot with a steamer basket insert. Fill the pot with water to just below the insert, cover, and bring to a boil over high heat.

Meanwhile, line the steamer basket insert with 6 of the softened corn husks and spray with vegetable oil. Put the soaked sticky rice in a large mixing bowl. Add the onion, celery, peanuts, lily blossoms, and mushrooms and mix well with a wooden spoon. Pour the seasoning sauce over the rice and vegetables, add the sausage slices, if using, and mix well. Transfer the mixture to the steamer insert spreading it evenly. Cover with the remaining 6 corn husks.

When the water comes to a rolling boil, carefully insert the steamer basket in the pot, cover tightly, and steam the rice for 35 to 40 minutes, or until completely cooked. Transfer the *bha jung* to a serving bowl and cover with corn husks to keep it moist and hot.

When ready to serve, remove the corn husks, spoon the *bha jung* onto individual plates, and garnish the side of each serving with sweet pickled ginger.

Variation

Instead of spreading the rice in a lined steamer, wrap 2 to 3 tablespoons of the rice mixture in a couple of fresh or softened dried corn husks, following the instructions on page 55. Steam 6 to 7 bundles at a time for 35 to 40 minutes. They are great for picnics or to take for lunch.

Kao Thom Padd
SOFT SWEET STICKY RICE BUNDLES

Makes 20 bundles

2 cups long-grain Thai jasmine
   sticky rice
1 teaspoon baking soda
¼ cup dried black beans
3 cups Fresh Unsweetened Coconut
   Cream (page 169)
1 cup sugar
½ teaspoon sea salt
3 ripe bananas, peeled and
   quartered lengthwise
2 packages banana leaves (see page
   135), washed and dried, cut into
   forty 7- by 9-inch pieces
Forty 12-inch pieces kitchen twine

Kao thom means "boiled, or soft, rice" and *padd* means "stir to cook." *Kao thom padd* is also called *kao thom mud,* meaning "boiled soft rice that is tied." The ingredients are few and consist of traditional and common Thai staples. Believed to be food of the ancient foragers, because it is easy to make and to carry on long trips, it is commonly used as a religious offering.

The significance of *kao thom padd* comes from a legend about the villagers who journeyed to visit the Lord Buddha. *Kao thom padd* was their main sustenance on their long trip, and when they arrived, it was all they had to present to the Lord Buddha. From that time on, it has been given as an offering at religious ceremonies.

The traditional way of making *kao thom padd* is by stirring soaked sticky rice with coconut cream and sugar in a skillet until it is partially cooked. The mixture is spread on either banana or sugarcane leaves, cooked black beans are sprinkled on top of the rice, a wedge of banana is placed in the center, and the banana leaves are wrapped into a bundle. The bundles are then tied together in twos with banana twine, from the ribs of the leaves, and steamed. The cooked rice is soft and silky and tastes like creamy rice pudding. This recipe follows the ancient way of making *kao thom padd*.

Soak the sticky rice with the baking soda in water for at least 5 hours, or overnight.

Rinse the rice in several changes of cool water and drain. Set aside.

Bring a small pot of water to the boil. Meanwhile, dry-roast the black beans in a small skillet over medium heat for 3 to 4 minutes, or until very shiny. Transfer to a bowl and cover with boiling water. Let the beans sit for 30 minutes.

Drain the beans and put in a small saucepan; cover with water. Boil for 10 minutes, or until softened and cooked. Drain the cooked beans in a strainer in the sink and rinse in several changes of cool water. Drain well, transfer to a small bowl, and set aside.

Combine the coconut cream, sugar, and sea salt in a 12-inch skillet and heat over high heat for 3 minutes, or until the mixture begins to bubble. Add the soaked sticky rice and stir to mix. Lower the heat to medium-high and cook, stirring occasionally, for 6 minutes, or until the rice grains turn shiny and sticky and the liquid has a consistency like pudding. Remove from the heat and let sit until the rice is cool enough to touch and the liquid has been absorbed by the rice.

Fan both sides of each banana leaf over a gas flame or directly over a burner on medium heat for 1 to 2 seconds to soften. Stack 2 banana leaves together on the work surface with the dull side up. Place them so the grains of the leaves run the same direction and are horizontal. Place 3 tablespoons of the rice mixture in the center and spread to flatten it lengthwise into an oval. Sprinkle 6 to 7 cooked beans on top of the rice and place a piece of banana in the center of the rice. Pick the edge of the banana leaves closest to you, join it with the opposite edge of the leaves, and fold them over until the fold touches the filling. Fold the sides over to meet in the center to form a bundle. Set aside and make another bundle. Join two bundles together, folded sides facing one another, and tie the ends together with the twine. Repeat with the remaining leaves and filling ingredients.

Fill a steamer pot that has a steamer basket insert halfway with water. Arrange the banana bundles in the steamer basket, then place in the steamer, cover, and cook over medium-high heat for 20 to 25 minutes. Unwrap the bundles and serve warm or at room temperature.

Cook's Note

Cooked *kao thom padd* can be frozen for a month. To reheat, steam according to the instructions above for 6 to 7 minutes, or microwave 1 to 2 bundles at a time on high power for 3 minutes.

Kao Neuw Kao Poud

SWEET STICKY RICE AND CORN DESSERT

Makes 6 servings

1 ear young sweet corn, husked
1 cup Fresh Grated Coconut Flakes
   (page 71)
2 tablespoons sesame seeds, dry-
   roasted (see page 13)
2 cups long-grain Thai jasmine
   sticky rice, cooked (see page 50)
   and kept hot in the steamer
¾ cup sugar
Pinch of sea salt
Fresh mint leaves for garnish

If you have never had corn for dessert, you're in for a treat—the taste and texture of this easy dessert will make it a family favorite. When sweet corn is available, make this dish and serve it warm or at room temperature, with vanilla or coconut ice cream. Place one large scoop of the dessert and a scoop of ice cream on each plate. Garnish with fresh mint leaves.

Fill a medium saucepan with water, bring it to a boil, and add the corn. Let it boil for 1 minute, or until the color of the corn brightens. Drain the corn, let it sit in cold water until cool, drain, and pat dry.

Holding the pointed end of the corn, stand it up on a large dinner plate and slice off the kernels. Transfer them to a large mixing bowl, add the coconut flakes and roasted sesame seeds, and mix well. Add the hot cooked rice and mix in the sugar and sea salt. Cover with plastic wrap and let rest for 10 minutes before serving, garnished with mint leaves.

Kao Tung

RICE CRACKERS

Kao tung make wonderful snacks or accompaniments with dipping sauces (see pages 100 and 146). Make these rice crackers in stages, since drying them can take days in the sun or several hours in the oven. Once the crackers are completely dry, they'll keep for months. Store in a Ziploc bag.

To shape and dry the rice crackers, take a tablespoon of rice and roll it into a ball, then flatten it between the palms of your hands so that you have a disk that is about 2 inches in diameter and ¼ inch thick. Put it on a wire rack and repeat with the remaining rice. Dry in the sun for a couple of days until hardened and dried, or place the disks on baking sheets and bake them slowly at 200°F for 2 to 3 hours, until completely dry. For either method, flip the rice crackers over occasionally to ensure even drying.

To deep-fry the rice crackers, heat the vegetable oil in a 12-inch skillet over medium-high heat to between 325° and 350°F. (You can also test for readiness by dipping the tip of a wooden spoon into the oil; if tiny bubbles begin forming around it, the oil is ready.) Carefully drop 6 to 7 rice crackers into the hot oil (do not crowd them) and fry until they are crispy and golden, turning them regularly to ensure even browning, 1 to 2 minutes. Transfer to paper towels to drain. When cool, serve or store, sealed tightly. Fried crackers keep for about a week.

3 cups cooked sticky rice (see page 50)
4 cups vegetable oil

Ghin Kao

EAT RICE, OR LET'S EAT

The Thai words for "let's eat" are *ghin kao*, which translated literally mean "eat rice." This gives you some idea of how important rice is in Thai cooking. Thais consider rice to be the most nutritious part of the meal, but, eaten alone, it can be bland and lacking in zest. Adding *gupp kao*—which means "with rice"—makes eating rice more interesting.

Gupp kao are highly seasoned and served in small quantities. Thai is one of the few cuisines that encourage the diner to add and flavor *gupp kao* to his or her liking by providing small bowls of chile paste, chiles marinated in fish sauce and lime juice, and other condiments. When it is time to eat, diners gather around with their individual plates of rice, then spoon on small amounts of the various dishes and flavorings.

The skill of a great cook is measured not only by the ability to cook, but also by whether the meal has balanced flavors, textures, and enticing aromas and looks appetizing and inviting. In a traditional Thai menu, every dish stands distinctively on its own, at the same time balancing the other dishes. The ideal menu includes five dishes with varied amounts of liquid or sauce in each dish. Desserts follow, one with sauce and another dry. Fresh fruits are served last.

Cooking a traditional Thai meal takes time, but you can create one or just part of one with the *gupp kao* recipes in the next chapters. Or serve rice as part of your own creative menu including meat, poultry, fish or shellfish, vegeta-bles, stew, or soup. In the beginning, as you learn, your meals can center on one or two Thai dishes instead of a full traditional Thai menu. Learn to balance the menu by following Thai menu logic: rice, potato, or bread; a soup (lightly or highly seasoned) or curry; a vegetable dish; salad; and a meat, fish, or shellfish dish.

Here are the elements and principles on which a traditional Thai menu is built:

TOMM—LITERALLY "TO BOIL": Essentially soup based on water or a broth made from meat, poultry, fish, or shellfish, seasoned with pounded herbs and spices, and with meat or vegetables, or both. It can be subtle, salty, or a combination of salty, sour, and peppery.

KEANG—SOUP: Soup or stew made with coconut cream. *Keang* is usually a peppery soup made with meat, poultry, fish, or shellfish, but *keang* sometimes refers to soups that are neither spicy nor peppery. *Keang jeurn* is a bland soup.

PADD—STIR-FRY WITH A MODERATE AMOUNT OF LIQUID: Meat, poultry, fish, shellfish, and/or vegetables are cooked with seasonings that complement other dishes in the menu. *Yumm*, or salad, is interchangeable with *padd*. Thai salads are a mixture of cold meat, poultry, fish or shellfish and vegetables and fruits. Whether it's *padd* or *yumm*, this course adds a touch of surprise and contrast to the menu.

KREANG KANG—SIDE DISHES OR ACCOMPANIMENTS: These include grilled, roasted, steamed or fried meat or fish and raw or lightly cooked vegetables and fruits to enhance the flavors and textures of *keang*.

NAMM PRIKK—CHILE WATER OR CHILE SAUCE, OR *NAMM JIMM*, DIPPING SAUCES: These round out a Thai meal and are very pungent. Both are used in very small amounts as condiments to accompany *kreang kang* and to complement the rest of the meal. Made with other herbs and spices as well as chiles pounded with or without meat, fish, or shellfish. When coconut cream is added, the name of the sauce changes to *lon*.

Coconut

THE SPIRIT OF THAI COOKING

Spirited cook
Zealous eater
Savory seasoned
Ambrosia

Translated from *Mae Khloa Hoa Paa*
(*Head Cook from the Forest*),
between 1868 and 1900

Coconut is to the Thais what butter, cream, and oil are to Western cooks. Whereas rice is revered and believed to have a soul like a human being, the coconut tree has a spirit that anchors, protects, and secures the land. Coconut is more than food to the Thai people. I was reminded of this when I took a boat ride across the Chao Phra Ya River from Thailand's present-day capital city, Bangkok, to where the old capital, Dhonburi, is located.

Upon entering through one of its major docks, Tah Pak Glate, I wandered through a lively market selling everything from traditional homemade snacks to knockoff Calvin Klein blue jeans. I was drawn by the water and hired a man with a small motorboat to take me for a ride on the *klong,* or rivers. The boatman maneuvered through a crush of boat traffic and river taxis jammed with local folks and tourists. After a while, he made a sharp turn away from the traffic, to an area where both sides of the river glittered with Buddhist temples, ornate Chinese temples, and towering mosques. The high-rise buildings disappeared, replaced by lovely old wooden houses with their porches perched over the river.

After another turn into a small river named Klong Phra Adom, the silence was so complete that the only sounds were the engine of the motorboat and an occasional bird. An old man with a plastic fishing line waved and smiled, clutching his wooden sampan as the waves of our boat rocked his tiny boat. On both sides of the river, wooden houses built on stilts above the water sat erect among scattered banana groves and coconut palms heavy with fruits.

It was near dusk and people were bathing in the river, getting ready for supper. Smoke rose from the backs of the houses and the aroma of fried garlic and curry filled the air. As we came near a house with a thatched palm leaf roof surrounded by a coconut grove, I noticed several naked children clinging to the thick trunk of one of the trees. They shimmied to the treetop, where they hung, seemingly frozen in midair, silhouetted in a horizon of coconut trees that stretched endlessly along the river. Then, one by one, the children dove into the chocolate-colored water.

The scene brought back memories of an art class I had taken as a student in Thailand. Our art teacher had us copy his drawing of a typical Thai home: a wooden shanty on stilts with a thatched roof of palm leaves. Next to the house, a coconut palm, heavy with coconuts, leaned close. I loved the picture. However, as a city kid, I'd never lived in or even seen such a house. My boat ride on the river that late afternoon reminded me of that picture and confirmed a vision of the "real" Thailand I had cherished in my imagination for so many years.

Much of Thailand has changed. It has become noisy, busy, overbuilt, and treeless, like modern countries everywhere, but in the past for the Thai people, and for many today, a home without a coconut palm is not a true home.

Romancing the Coconut

In the diary of King Ramkamhaeng of Sokothai (1275–1317), the creator of the Thai written language, there is a record of the plants and trees that grew in his garden, including banana, tamarind, mango, coconut, and sugar palm. These plants were taken from the wild and domesticated along the rice fields. The farmers grew fruit trees, particularly coconut and sugar palm, to shore up the earthen dikes between the rice paddies.

Besides being the anchor to the land, the fruit of the coconut tree, next to rice, is the country's most important crop. The Thais use every part of the coconut tree. Even the green husks have a use as fertilizer and as natural containers for other plants. Orchids especially thrive in the porous fibers of the coconut husks, because they retain moisture and air. Hard coconut shells are dried and sanded into bowls, spoons, ladles, or hair ornaments. Old and dried-out coconuts are often used as floats by young children learning to swim. The palm fronds make thatch roofs and palm trunks are dried and carved into dishes and pestles.

With its tropical climate, Thailand is the perfect environment for coconut trees. As a result, they are bountiful, growing in every region of the country. In southern Thailand, where coconut was once the primary commercial product, monkeys were trained to harvest the crops. Tender young green coconuts are now picked for the juice and meat. Workers carefully hack off the top with a machete, without spilling even one drop of juice. The jelly-like fruit, barely formed inside the husk, is both refreshingly sweet and tender. When slightly frozen, the juice turns to ice, and it is like a sorbet—a nectar of the gods.

Sometimes the soft green husk of the coconut is peeled off, exposing the white round interior. The whole coconut is then roasted in smoldering hot ashes and refrigerated until ice-cold. This process changes the taste of the juice and the meat, intensifying the sweetness and giving the flesh a slightly nutty taste. Nothing can quench the thirst that comes with tropical heat like the juice from a fresh green coconut.

Coconut cream is the essential cooking oil in Thailand. Used traditionally to sauté pounded herbs and spices before adding meat and vegetables, coconut oil is essential to the Thai way of stir-frying. Coconut flesh is grated, shredded, roasted, milked, and simply eaten raw. Coconut cream, easily extracted, enriches, thickens, sweetens, and flavors a dish. The cream and milk from one coconut can make a sumptuous meal for an average family.

The convenience and availability of coconut cream made it the essential source of fat in the traditional Thai diet. Animal fat was a luxury. In the past, pigs were seldom killed and then only for religious rituals or celebrations; occasionally wild pigs were caught and provided an extravagant addition to the otherwise simple diet of the common people. And, unlike coconut cream, animal fat spoiled quickly in the tropical heat, making it difficult to keep for any length of time.

During the reign of King Narai (1656–1688), a Greek named Phalkan became the first foreigner appointed as king's advisor. Phalkan's wife, who was half Japanese and half Portuguese, excelled in the art of making coconut cream desserts. These sweets so pleased the king that he created a special position, recognizing her talent. She became a member of his Royal Court, teaching the women how to use coconut cream and milk in place of butter and cream in the European tradition, thus creating a whole new repertoire of Thai sweets and dishes.

Coconut harvested in its prime, when the meat is thick and full of flavor, can command premium prices. In a Bangkok Sunday market, proprietors proudly display coconuts perfectly split in half, revealing pure white meat almost an inch thick. Just one is enough to make a big batch of desserts or a large pot of curry. The mature coconuts familiar to Americans are harvested when the outer fibers have turned tough and brown. The porous fibers are sawed off and loose strands pulled away, leaving the inner hard rounded shells. Thai cooks are champs at smoothing the hairy surface of a mature coconut with a machete. After piercing the eyes at the top of the coconut, they drain the juice and reserve it for a pickling liquid or coconut vinegar.

The coconut is then cracked open at the center, forming two perfect bowls. The firm white flesh is grated on a special coconut grater called a "rabbit" or a "cat." Ancient carvers shaped these tiny stools into animal shapes or, sometimes, a crawling child with a jagged metal blade attached provocatively to the child's bottom. The cook sits on the stool holding the halved coconut facing the metal grater. Starting from the outer rim and working toward the inner center, he or she grates the coconut evenly and so fine that it resembles powder. The quality of grated coconut distinguishes great cooks from mediocre ones. In today's markets, entrepreneurs use noisy machines to spew out mounds of freshly grated coconut meat with the outer thin brown skin still attached. Depending on the dish, coconut is grated to different consistencies. Different gradations are used for milking, roasting, and garnishing. The grated coconut is squeezed by hand to extract the purest and thickest cream, which is reserved for garnishes. The grated coconut is then mixed with warm water and massaged repeatedly, producing different consistencies of milk. Each grade of thickness is used at various stages of cooking and for different types of flavoring.

Leftover coconut flakes are never discarded. They are roasted as crispy toppings for salads, used as a condiment for snacks, or mixed with sugar and flour to make marvelous macaroons.

A particularly exotic way of using the brown hard coconut shells is to roast and grind them into a fine powder, and use it as coloring for a Thai dessert made with rice flour, sugar, coconut cream, and lime water. This floury, pasty dessert, *kanum peuk poon*, is a cross between a pudding and steamed custard and is black in color. It is cut into squares or more elaborate decorative shapes. Fresh coconut, grated into long white strands, is used as a garnish on top, adding a dramatic color contrast that Thais greatly appreciate. It is one of my favorite desserts.

Cracking the Coconut

Learning to crack open a coconut is essential to becoming a Thai cook. You may find the thought scary. However, with your first attempt, you will discover how easy and fun cracking coconuts can be. I had to learn how to crack my first one out of necessity when I first came to America as a fifteen-year-old student. Now I find it most therapeutic to come home and whack open a few coconuts, especially after a hard day at the restaurant. Grating coconut into a snowy mound and milking, massaging, and squeezing the meat into thick cream for cooking is very soothing and satisfying.

Before supermarkets began to carry canned unsweetened coconut cream and milk, I had to work with the raw ingredient. After several years

of experimenting, I developed an easy method, using the oven, a food processor, a hammer, a screwdriver, and a potato ricer! This may sound like a major surgical procedure, but in fact, it's a breeze. You will only need an hour or less of your time for coconut therapy, which can be more helpful—and more delicious—than visiting a counselor after a hard day!

Furthermore, there is no comparison between the taste and aroma of fresh coconut cream and the canned variety. The only thing beneficial about canned coconut cream is convenience. When you plan ahead, making your own coconut cream and milk is simple and worth the effort. The grated coconut can be frozen and the fresh cream and milk refrigerated for a week or frozen for up to a month.

I always crack more than one coconut at a time. If I am going to do all the work of processing fresh coconuts, I might as well do more than I need and store some of the results, making the best use of my time. One coconut will yield 1 cup of thick cream and 3 cups of milk with the same consistency as 2% milk. One coconut will make enough milk and cream for a pot of curry to serve six people; it will also do nicely for a large quantity of salad dressing or sweet sticky rice with coconut cream.

If you follow my example, though, cracking open a bunch of coconuts at a time and extracting the meat, puree the meat from only one coconut at a time in the food processor.

Tools to Crack a Coconut

You will need a heavy-duty food processor (this investment will pay off), heavy hammer, dish towel, Phillips and small flat-head screwdrivers, fine-mesh strainer or potato ricer or bouillon strainer, large bowl with spout for pouring, three large mixing bowls, and a metal spoon.

How to Crack a Coconut

Choose a good coconut: It should feel heavy. Shake it and listen for a sloshing sound. Look at the three indentations, or "eyes," on top of the coconut. They should be of uniform dark brown color. The husk should be clean and dry, and not moldy.

Before you crack the outer shell, if you wish to reserve the liquid or to avoid being squirted with juice, place a Phillips screwdriver in one of the three eyes and hit it with a hammer to punch a hole. Repeat the process on another eye. Drain off the liquid and save in the refrigerator for drinking or for pickling juice.

Put the coconut on the center rack of a pre-heated 375°F oven. Bake it for 20 minutes. Remove the coconut and let it cool to room temperature. Lay the coconut on a hard cement surface, strike a couple of good blows with a hammer, and crack open the coconut. Break into four or five manageable pieces. Holding a piece of shattered coconut with a dish towel, extract the coconut meat from the shell with a flat-head screwdriver. It should come off easily. Use a vegetable peeler to remove the outer dark skin from the white meat. You can store the coconut meat in a sealed plastic bag in the freezer for weeks.

Cook's Note

Save the outer shells and use as starter for charcoal when grilling. The dark skins can be dried and saved for smoking meat. Place them directly on the charcoal briquettes when grilling or smoking meat.

Fresh Unsweetened Coconut Cream and Milk

Fresh unsweetened coconut cream and milk are called for in many of these recipes. After peeling the dark skins off the chunks of white meat, cut the meat into 1- to 2-inch chunks and place them in a heavy-duty food processor fitted with the steel blade. (If the coconut meat has been frozen, thaw it completely before slicing and grinding.) Grind for 30 to 60 seconds. Pause to scrape down the sides of the processor bowl; then pulse and blend until the meat turns to pulp. Add 1 cup warm water and process for 30 seconds. Transfer the coconut meat and liquid to a large mixing bowl, preferably one with a spout for pouring. "Milk" the coconut—that is, massage and squeeze the meat at least eighty-nine times. This is a Thai ritual believed to produce a rich and creamy coconut milk. It works!

Place a fine-mesh strainer, potato ricer, or bouillon strainer over another large mixing bowl. Pour the coconut cream and meat into the strainer, then press firmly to extract the liquid from the pulp. Refrigerate the liquid for at least an hour. The thick cream will coagulate on top, leaving the whey, or milk, in the bottom of the bowl. Skim off the thick cream into a Ziploc bag or plastic container and refrigerate or freeze.

Meanwhile, put the coconut pulp back into the first mixing bowl. Pour 3 cups of warm water over the pulp, and massage and squeeze the coconut meat another eighty-nine times. Strain the liquid into another bowl, as before, and refrigerate the liquid for at least an hour, giving the thick cream time to rise to the top.

Skim off the cream and combine with the thick cream extracted from the first milking. Pour the thin whey into a separate glass or plastic container and refrigerate until ready to use.

Cook's Note

More cream that can be used as cooking oil can be extracted from the thin whey after the second milking. Boil the milk gently in a large saucepan for 5 to 7 minutes. When the cream rises to the surface, skim it off and use as cooking oil to stir-fry chile or spice pastes. The thin milk can be used for a broth to cook and tenderize meat.

Unsweetened Canned Coconut Cream

The 16-ounce cans of coconut cream from Thailand, often labeled as coconut milk, contain coconut cream thickened with flour. In recent years, most of the large coconut groves have disappeared. This is partly because scenic Koh Samui, a tiny island off southern Thailand, historically famous for its coconuts, cut down its coconut groves to make room for tourists. Today, coconuts used to make canned coconut cream in Thailand actually come from the islands of Fiji and Samoa.

Using canned coconut cream and milk is like using canned milk and should be reserved for an emergency. Canned coconut cream and milk may give the impression of being rich and luscious, but all it really does is thicken more quickly because of the added flour. Also because of the flour, the oil separates only slightly, so curry made with canned coconut lacks the colorful sheen given by a real coconut cream, unless cooking oil is used initially to cook the curry paste. Authentic Thai dishes both savory and sweet, such as curries, salad dressings, soups, and desserts, are made with fresh coconut cream and milk. The sauce will be thinner than one made with the canned product, not as sweet or as condensed, with exquisite taste and heavenly aroma. The result is dishes that taste far better than anything you will find in most Thai restaurants.

If you must use canned coconut cream, keep in mind that not all brands are the same. I recommend two labels from Thailand: Chao Koh and Mae Ploy. Both are made with good-quality coconuts and I have never encountered bad cream from either company. They are available in Asian markets and large supermarkets. Lesser brands may sometimes exude a musty smell, indicating spoiled coconut. If you find one, return it immediately and get your money back!

Do not shake the coconut cream before opening the can. When you open the can, the liquid should be pure white and very thick, like clotted cream. Take a whiff: It should be fragrant. The thick cream is on the top; the remaining thin liquid is the coconut whey, or milk. The different thicknesses are used at various stages of cooking. Leftover canned coconut cream should be transferred to a glass jar with a tight-fitting lid or sealed plastic container. It will keep in the refrigerator for about a week and frozen for a month.

Recently, Americans have become conscious of the high cholesterol content of coconut cream. Consequently, gourmet food and specialty stores have started selling "lite" canned coconut cream, which is thin and watered down. (Ironically, it is more expensive than the regular condensed version.) Despite the people's daily intake of coconut cream, Thailand has a low incidence of heart ailments. However, if you have dietary concerns, I suggest you use a smaller amount of regular canned coconut cream and dilute it with water. Even better, make your own fresh coconut cream and milk.

Fresh Grated Coconut Flakes

Fresh coconut flakes add texture to a dish. After extracting the cream and milk from the flakes, do not discard the pulp. Place it in a plastic bag and freeze; it will keep for a month. Thaw to room temperature before using it for cooking. It can also be dry-roasted for toppings or to make desserts and cookies such as macaroons.

Roasted Fresh Grated Coconut Flakes

Roasted fresh grated coconut flakes add a smoky-buttery flavor to a dish. Place 1 cup of grated coconut at a time in a large skillet over medium heat, shaking the pan and stirring until evenly browned. Cool completely before transferring to a jar with a tight lid or a sealed plastic bag. Roasted grated coconut will keep in the refrigerator for a couple of months.

Roasted Fresh Coconut Matchsticks

Coconut matchsticks add texture to many Thai snack and salad recipes. They are good as toppings for desserts such as custards and ice cream and, like roasted grated coconut flakes, they keep for a long time in the refrigerator.

To make coconut matchsticks, after removing the dark outer skin, use the vegetable peeler to slice the coconut meat across the grain into wide paper-thin ribbons. Stack several ribbons and slice them crosswise into very thin matchsticks. Roast 1 cup of the matchsticks at a time in a large skillet over medium heat, shaking the pan and stirring until evenly browned. Cool completely before transferring to a jar with a tight lid or a sealed plastic bag. Toasted coconut matchsticks will keep in the refrigerator for a couple of months.

Miang Kati

CHEWY COCONUT SNACK

Makes 4 to 6 servings

1 cup vegetable oil

8 shallots, thinly sliced

A pinch plus 1 teaspoon sea salt

¾ cup (4 ounces) unsalted peanuts, dry-roasted (see page 13) and coarsely ground

¾ cup sugar

2 cups Roasted Fresh Grated Coconut Flakes (page 71)

20 to 24 sorrel or spinach leaves, stems discarded, rinsed and dried

1 cup Fresh Unsweetened Coconut Cream (page 69)

The word *miang* refers to a betel-nut bundle or fermented leaf bundle, both chewed by traditional Thai people as a stimulant. This recipe acquired the name *miang* because it is shaped like a bundle. It is a rich and decadent snack from E-Sann, a northeastern region of Thailand, made from bitter greens wrapped into tiny cone shapes, with *kati,* or pure creamy coconut sauce, drizzled over the top by each diner. In place of the native greens, I substitute tender sorrel or spinach leaves. *Miang kati* can be served with afternoon tea or as a picnic snack.

Put the vegetable oil in a 10-inch skillet over medium-low heat. Separate the shallots into individual rings and add them to the oil. Fry the shallots slowly, stirring occasionally, and adding the pinch of sea salt, until golden brown. With a slotted spoon, transfer to a plate lined with paper towels. Set aside to cool.

Drain all but 1 tablespoon of the oil from the skillet (save the rest for another use, if desired). Cook the ground peanuts, stirring, in the oil with the sugar and the remaining 1 teaspoon sea salt, until the peanuts are coated with the mixture. Add the fried shallots and roasted coconut flakes and transfer to a serving bowl.

Arrange the sorrel leaves on a serving platter. Place the bowl of peanut and coconut filling in the center, with the coconut cream in a separate bowl. Roll each leaf into a cone, spoon in some filling, and drizzle coconut cream on top.

Cook's Notes

This is a snack that requires quick last-minute assembly, but all of the ingredients can be made ahead and stored for a week. Fresh coconut cream and grated coconut flakes will keep in the refrigerator. Crispy shallots and roasted peanuts will stay fresh in sealed plastic bags or glass jars with tight-fitting lids at room temperature. Thoroughly dry cleaned sorrel or spinach leaves will keep well in the refrigerator if wrapped in paper towels and stored in a plastic bag.

Keang Kati Pla Heang

COCONUT CREAM SOUP WITH DRIED FISH

Makes 4 servings

The traditional Thai recipe for this soup combines fresh coconut cream with tender sour tamarind shoots. Here, I substitute sorrel leaves and whole kumquats for the tamarind shoots, since they are not available in America. The result has the same delicate and subtle taste.

In a 4-quart saucepan, combine the coconut cream and coconut milk and bring to a boil over high heat. Lower the heat to medium-high and add the sorrel leaves. When the mixture begins to boil again, add the galangal, shallots, chiles, Big Four Paste, and fish sauce and stir to mix. Lower the heat to medium and cook for 10 minutes, then add the mushrooms. Cook for 20 minutes, or until the mushrooms are tender. Add the whitefish and kumquats and cook for 10 minutes. Serve hot.

1 cup Fresh Unsweetened Coconut Cream (page 69)
3 cups Fresh Unsweetened Coconut Milk (page 69)
½ pound sorrel leaves, coarsely chopped (about 4 cups)
One ¼-inch chunk galangal or ½-inch chunk fresh ginger, slivered and slightly crushed
6 shallots, peeled
7 to 8 fresh bird chiles or 5 to 6 serrano chiles, lightly crushed
1 tablespoon Big Four Paste (page 86)
2 tablespoons fish sauce (*namm pla*)
½ pound fresh oyster mushrooms, thinly sliced (2 cups)
½ pound smoked whitefish, skinned, boned, and cut into chunks
6 kumquats, unpeeled, thinly sliced and seeded

Tomm Gai Kaa Onn

CHICKEN COCONUT CREAM SOUP

Makes 6 servings

One 4-inch piece young galangal or
   5-inch piece fresh young ginger,
   thinly sliced (1 cup)

9 cloves garlic, minced

15 sprigs cilantro stems with roots,
   minced (¼ cup), plus 4 sprigs
   cilantro

4 stalks lemongrass, green parts
   and hard outer layers removed,
   2 stalks minced, 2 stalks sliced
   into 3-inch lengths and lightly
   crushed

1 teaspoon Thai white peppercorns,
   dry-roasted (see page 13) and
   finely ground

3 shallots, minced

4 cups Fresh Unsweetened Coconut
   Cream and Milk (combined to
   make consistency of whole milk;
   page 69)

One 3-pound chicken, rinsed,
   thoroughly dried, and chopped
   into bite-sized pieces

7 kaffir lime leaves, hard center
   stems removed, or zest of 2 limes

½ teaspoon sea salt

3 tablespoons fish sauce (namm pla)

7 fresh bird chiles or 5 to 6 serrano
   chiles

1 to 2 limes, sliced into wedges

This northern Thai soup resembles a traditional Laotian coconut soup, but its decadent and richly flavored broth is made entirely of coconut cream and milk, a far cry from the Laotians' simple fare without any coconut cream. My doctor swears by this soup for curing head colds. We serve it at Saffron during the winter months to keep our customers healthy.

For a mild soup, omit the fresh bird chiles entirely. The seven bird chiles called for will make a medium-spicy soup. Add fresh shiitake or canned straw mushrooms for a delicious variation.

Patience is the key in making this soup. Use medium heat to bring the broth to a gentle boil, and add each ingredient only after the broth begins to bubble again. After 30 to 45 minutes, the coconut cream will have curdled somewhat, while the chicken pieces will be moist and tender. Lime juice, the final touch, is added to the soup just before serving to balance the sweet-creamy flavors. It will curdle the soup, which is fine.

Using a mortar and pestle, pound half of the galangal with the garlic into a paste. One at a time, add the cilantro stems and roots, minced lemongrass, ground peppercorns, and shallots in sequence, adding each new ingredient only after the previous one is pureed and incorporated into a fine paste. (Follow the directions for pounding on page 11.) Set aside, or transfer to a jar with a tight-fitting lid and refrigerate.

In a 4-quart saucepan, bring the coconut cream and milk to a gentle boil over medium heat. Do not overheat or it will curdle. Add the galangal paste and stir well, then add the chicken and bring to a boil. Add the kaffir lime leaves, lemongrass stalks, sea salt, fish sauce, the remaining galangal, and the chiles, cover, and simmer over medium-low heat for about 45 minutes, until the chicken is completely cooked.

Transfer to a serving bowl, garnish with the cilantro sprigs, and serve with the lime wedges.

Kao Neuw Nong Kao

STICKY RICE FROM NONG KAO

Makes 6 servings

Snack vendors in Thailand who specialize in sweet sticky rice offer a variety of rices as well as toppings. Besides unadorned plain sweet sticky rice, there are such choices as wild sticky rice, deep black burgundy in color; sweet sticky rice with corn; green sticky rice colored with pandanus leaves; and *kao neuw* from Nong Kao, sweet sticky rice with grated fresh coconut and roasted sesame seeds. Toppings include sweetened fresh coconut cream, coconut custard, and a mixture of dried shrimp, sugar, coconut flakes, and shredded kaffir lime leaves—sounds outrageous, but it is really delicious!

After making fresh coconut cream and milk (page 69), you can use the leftover grated coconut for this recipe. Serve as an afternoon snack with tea or as a dessert.

In a large mixing bowl, combine the warm sticky rice with the grated coconut. Transfer the mixture to an 8-inch Pyrex pie plate and place in the steamer basket insert for a pasta pot. Fill the pasta pot halfway with water and bring to a boil. Insert the steamer basket insert, cover, and let steam for 10 minutes. Remove from the heat.

In a large mixing bowl, combine the roasted sesame seeds, sugar, and salt. Add the steamed sticky rice mixture; stir well to combine. Cover tightly with plastic wrap and let it sit for 10 minutes.

To serve, pack the sticky rice into custard cups or ramekins to shape, then invert each onto an individual serving plate. Serve with the mango slices.

2 cups cooked Sticky Rice (page 50), kept warm
2 cups Fresh Grated Coconut Flakes (page 71)
2 ounces (about ½ cup) sesame seeds, dry-roasted (see page 13)
½ cup sugar
½ teaspoon sea salt
2 cups sliced mangoes or peaches (about 2 mangoes or 4 peaches)

See Da Ram Dong

THE FAITHFUL SEE DA

3 large ripe but firm bananas,
  peeled
1 cup Fresh Unsweetened Coconut
  Cream (page 69)
¼ cup sugar
2 tablespoons orange flower water
  or 1 teaspoon orange extract
1 quart vanilla ice cream
Fresh mint leaves for garnish

The name of this dish is based upon an episode in the *Ramakein,* the Thai version of *Ramayana,* a Hindu epic. See Da was the wife of Phra Ram, the hero of *Ramakein.* Captured by the Monkey King, she remained true—*ram dong*—and invincible against the Monkey King's attempted seduction. The banana and the coconut cream, both white, are symbols of purity, representing See Da's faithfulness and purity.

Slice each banana crosswise in half, then slice both pieces lengthwise in half and slice each piece lengthwise in half to yield 8 slices. Layer the banana slices in an 8-inch Pyrex pie plate.

In a medium bowl, mix the coconut cream, sugar, and orange flower water. Pour the mixture over the bananas. Fill a pasta pot that has a steamer basket insert halfway with water and bring the water to a boil. Set the pie plate inside the steamer basket insert, place it in the pasta pot, cover, and steam for 3 minutes, or until the bananas soften. Remove the steamer basket insert and let the bananas cool until they are just slightly warm, or cool to room temperature.

To serve, arrange 4 banana slices on each dessert plate, put a scoop of vanilla ice cream next to them, spoon the sauce over both, garnish with mint leaves, and serve.

Subparod Geuw
PINEAPPLE CRYSTAL

Makes 6 servings

The best pineapple is said to come from Prungburi, in the central plain of Thailand. The fruits are large with pale yellow flesh, extremely sweet, acidic, and crunchy. The literal translation of the name of this dessert, "pineapple crystal," refers to the process of cooking fresh fruit in a heavy sugar syrup, or *namm tann geuw*—sugar like crystal. The traditional way of serving adds ice chips, or *roy geuw,* translated as "floating crystal," to the pineapple and syrup. This recipe is strikingly similar to one I found in an English cookbook from the eighteenth century, the earliest recipe in English using pineapple.

1 small pineapple, peeled and eyes removed (see page 28)
¾ cup sugar
¾ cup water
2 tablespoons orange or rose water or 1 teaspoon orange extract
1 cup Fresh Unsweetened Coconut Cream (page 69), plus
2 tablespoons for topping
Crushed ice or 1 quart vanilla ice cream
Mint sprigs for garnish

Slice the pineapple across into 8 to 10 rounds a little less than ½ inch thick. Remove the hard inner core with an apple corer.

In a 12-inch skillet, combine the sugar, water, and orange water, bring to a boil over high heat, and cook for 3 minutes, or until thickened. Add the pineapple slices (it is all right to layer the slices if necessary), return to a boil, and cook turning the pineapple slices to ensure they cook evenly, for 5 minutes, or until soft. Add the 1 cup of coconut cream to the skillet, stirring gently with a wooden spoon so as not to tear the pineapple slices, and cook for another 2 minutes. Transfer the pineapple slices to a bowl and pour the sauce over the top. Set aside to cool completely, then cover and refrigerate to chill before serving.

There are two ways to serve this dish: The first is to place 1 to 2 pineapple rings in each individual dessert bowl. Add 2 tablespoons of crushed ice to each bowl. Spoon the sauce over the slices, and top with the remaining coconut cream. Garnish with mint sprigs. The second way is to place a pineapple ring in the center of each individual dessert plate, add a scoop of ice cream, and drizzle the sauce over the ice cream. Spoon the remaining coconut cream on top and garnish with sprigs of mint.

Cook's Notes

The pineapple can be refrigerated for several days. The coconut cream may curdle in the cold, but microwaving it for 10 to 20 seconds or allowing it to sit until it reaches room temperature will solve the problem.

Kanum Bah-Bin

THAI COCONUT MACAROONS

Makes 6 dozen macaroons

½ cup glutinous or sticky rice flour
¼ cup arrowroot or cornstarch
1 large egg, lightly beaten
1 cup sugar
1 teaspoon almond extract
1 tablespoon vegetable oil
3 cups Fresh Grated Coconut Flakes
   (page 71), plus more if needed
Vegetable oil spray

Thai macaroons are an imitation of a Western dessert. Because ovens are not found in traditional Thai kitchens, these Thai macaroons are grilled, not baked. They look like pancakes and have a soft, chewy texture.

You can make them by grating fresh coconut or using leftover grated coconut from making coconut cream.

In a medium mixing bowl, combine the rice flour with the arrowroot. In another medium bowl, beat the egg. Add the sugar, almond extract, and oil and combine. Add the flour mixture in 2 to 3 additions, mixing well. Add the coconut flakes and stir until the mixture resembles thick cooked oatmeal. If the batter is runny, add a bit more grated coconut.

Heat a skillet or a pancake griddle over high heat. Coat it with vegetable spray. When the oil begins to smoke, scoop up the batter with a small ice cream scoop or a soupspoon onto the hot skillet: Each portion should be about the size of a silver dollar. Brown on each side for 2 to 3 minutes, or until cooked through, lowering the heat if necessary, to avoid burning. Transfer the macaroons to a wire rack to cool. Do not stack them, or they will turn soggy. Repeat with the remaining batter, oiling the skillet between each batch. Cool the macaroons completely before storing in sealed plastic bags.

I-Thim Mah Plow

LOIS STANTON'S COCONUT GRANITA

Makes 6 to 8 servings

As we worked on this book, Lois, my friend and recipe tester, found herself with cups and cups of coconut milk invading her refrigerator. She developed this delicious way to use up the leftovers. It reminded me of old-fashioned Thai coconut ice cream.

Ice cream was first introduced to the Thai Royal Court in 1903. Years before, during the reign of Rama the Fourth, King Mongkut (1851–1868) had had blocks of ice shipped regularly from Singapore to the Royal Court for his private use. Sawdust, rice husks, and burlap sacks were used to cover the ice, preventing it from melting during transport to Thailand. *I-thim,* or ice cream, became fashionable in the Royal Court during the reign of King Mongkut's son, King Chula-longkhorn.

It was not until the 1950s that street vendors began selling *i-thim* and it became a common dessert. The ice cream is kept in an ice cream maker the vendor carries, along with extra ice and salt. He must churn it frequently to prevent it from melting in the hot sun. Like Lois's granita, the ice cream is light, delicate, and garnished with coarsely ground roasted peanuts.

1 cup sugar
1 cup water
4 cups Fresh Unsweetened Coconut Milk (page 69)
1/2 to 1 teaspoon almond extract
2 ounces unsalted peanuts, dry-roasted (see page 13) and coarsely ground (about 1/2 cup), for topping

In a medium saucepan, combine the sugar and water, mixing thoroughly. Bring to a boil over high heat and boil for 3 to 4 minutes, until the sugar has dissolved. Transfer to a large mixing bowl and cool thoroughly.

Add the coconut milk and almond extract to the sugar syrup, mixing well to combine. Pour into a 9- by 13-inch cake pan or plastic container and place in the freezer. After an hour, ice crystals will start to form around the edges of the container. Use a fork to break up the ice crystals, and continue to freeze, mixing and scraping with a fork every 30 to 45 minutes, until the mixture turns to ice shavings. The granita can be made and kept in the freezer for weeks.

To serve, use a fork or ice cream scoop to shave off the layers of the frozen block. If the granita is too hard to scrape, leave it out at room temperature until it starts to melt, or break it up into pieces and pulse it in a food processor. Serve in small bowls and garnish with the crushed peanuts.

The Big Four Seasonings

THE ESSENCE OF THAI COOKING

Frivolous woman
Flashy makeup
Clumsy cook
Disastrous kitchen

Translated from *Mae Khloa Hoa Paa*
(Head Cook from the Forest),
between 1868 and 1900

Regardless of the individual recipe or the complexity of the ingredients, what gives Thai cuisine its distinct flavors are the basic seasonings, which I call the "Big Four Seasonings." They are: salt, garlic, cilantro (or fresh coriander) root, and Thai peppercorns. If rice is the soul and the coconut the heart of Thai cooking, the Big Four Seasonings are the spirit, the zest, and the aroma: the special essence that is the foundation of Thai food and makes for Thai eminence in the world of cooking. Chiles and fish sauce highlight, accentuate, and round out a dish. Like the Big Four Seasonings, the supporting cast of chiles and fish sauce have their origins in ancient times.

My friend Vithi Panichphant, a Thai social and cultural historian, is a world traveler and connoisseur of fine foods. Knowing how much I love Thai food, he never fails to add some unusual culinary surprises to my visits. Each year when I return to Thailand, I look forward to going to Chiang Mai for a visit with Vithi and his family, and then a drive to his ancestral home in Lam Pung to visit his aunt. We start our day early, no matter how late we were up the night before, to check out the village market before going to his aunt's for breakfast.

Our trip to the market is always a taster's adventure. A dirt field flattened by years of use, the market features myriad food vendors in their wooden stalls, furnished with tables and chairs. Legions of fruit and vegetable sellers squat happily on woven mats in front of their merchandise. These neatly stacked displays offer the homegrown and wild herbs and spices that are found cooking in the pots of the food vendors. By the time we visit the last stall in the last part of the market, I am not only stuffed, but feel I have been on an archaeological expedition. However, we have only begun eating.

When we arrive at Vithi's aunt's, we're always greeted with her small dining room table brimming with bowls and plates of glistering spicy soup, mounds of crispy-fried tiny fish, thin strips of grilled pork flattened and pressed between bamboo sticks, biscuit-sized fried sweet bread dough encrusted with specks of sesame seeds, and a beautiful bamboo woven basket filled with steaming sticky rice. From the center of the table, a white porcelain bowl containing a dull brownish green liquid beckons us with the sharp, harsh, fermented bouquet of fiery-hot chile water. Seated facing the entrance to the house, Vithi's aunt beams at us. Vithi acts as if he hasn't eaten for days and enthusiastically sits down to the breakfast his aunt has prepared.

The dishes Vithi prefers, even for breakfast, are the "soul food" of Thailand. The rice he rel-

ishes is grown and harvested by a sharecropper on the family's estate. The fermented fish is made by his aunt with fish from the nearby river. The wild greens are bought fresh from the local market. And the herbs, spices, and chiles are homegrown in a small garden in the backyard.

Despite his worldly sophistication and vast knowledge of food, Vithi claims that nothing is better than Thai food, with its robust variety of flavors and contrasting array of aromas created by the Big Four Seasonings, combined with chiles and fish sauce. His partiality to this simple food speaks of his Thai heritage, and the powerful relationship between the Thai people and their food.

According to Mom Radjawong (Lord) Kirit Pramode, a prominent Thai historian and food connoisseur, for centuries the basic Thai seasoning was simply a bit of salt, fermented fish or beans, Thai peppercorns, and wild onion, pounded together and diluted with water. Salt, or *glurh,* an ingredient we take for granted today, was once a scarce and valued commodity. Without salt, food lacks essence. Salt is the primary ingredient in fermented fish and fish sauce.

Throughout its history, the Kingdom of Siam always protected its important cities. These were predominantly those lining the Gulf of Siam, prized for supplying salt as well as access to the sea trade. Commoners bartered for salt from the sea or the earth, depending on where they lived. Precious salt crystals weren't used just for seasoning, but also to preserve meat, fish, and vegetables in the harsh tropical climate. Even today, for the peasants, when there's nothing else to eat, salt with rice is what keeps them from starving.

The dominant taste of traditional Thai food is saltiness, combined with a tingling sensation from Thai peppercorns and their inviting aroma. Onions add complexity and depth to the flavors.

Fish and vegetables add variety and another layer of intricate taste. The chewy texture but bland taste of rice balances and completes the meal. In ancient times, *namm prikk thai,* Thai pepper chile paste, or seasoning paste, consisted only of *glurh* (salt), *hom* (wild onion), and *prikk Thai* (Thai peppercorns), diluted with *pla-rah,* or fermented fish. From this humble formula comes a magic potion. A droplet on a spoonful of rice awakens the appetite. Diluted with water, it becomes a spicy soup. Used as a marinade to season meat or fish, 'it dresses up the dish and gives it a new identity. This seasoning paste was and still is the basis for all Thai dishes.

The evolution of Thai food as we know it today was a slow process, with foreign influences contributing to the elegant and complex indigenous cuisine. There's controversy regarding the role of the chile in Thai cooking, beginning with the date it was introduced. Much credit is given to the Portuguese, the first Europeans to arrive in Siam, in 1511, for introducing the chiles, or *capsicum.* Yet Simon de la Lourbere, an "Envoy Extraordinary from France" from 1687 to 1688, wrote in his diary, *Historical Relations of the Kingdom of Siam,* that Thai food consisted of "simply rice, fish, a sauce—plain, a little water with some spices, garlic, Chibols, or some sweet herb, as Baulm."

While the use of chiles was slowly being incorporated into Thai cooking, it would be another two centuries before the chile became a major ingredient. When chiles were first used, they were seeded to remove the heat. Until the twentieth century, in fact, Thai dishes were more subtle and mildly seasoned than they are today. While Westerners often refer to these fiery spicy chiles as Thai chiles, the Thais do not. They identify chiles by shape, color, or a name honoring the place where they are grown. The crown of Thai seasoning belongs not to chiles,

but to *prikk thai,* that ancient but venerable seasoning: Thai peppercorns. Chiles did not replace Thai peppercorns, but came to be used in combination with these and other spices.

Like chiles, fish sauce is a latecomer to Thai cuisine, replacing the use of fermented fish. While northern and northeastern Thais have continued to rely on fermented fish, fish sauce gained favor throughout the rest of the country because of its versatility and less intense flavor and aroma. A spoonful of fish sauce makes a world of difference, turning an ordinary dish into a zestful one. However, all Thai cooks continue to use fermented fish, albeit sparingly, when a strong fishy taste is the dominant flavor desired.

The other major ingredients—garlic and cilantro—gradually gained favor with the Thais because of their ability to enhance and heighten other favorite flavors. Garlic, *ka-tiem,* is believed to have originated in China. Its penetrating aroma and piquant taste blend and combine perfectly with traditional Thai herbs and spices.

The use of cilantro roots, or *rugg phakk chee,* was borrowed from southern Chinese cooking. Today, cilantro roots have pretty much disappeared from the Chinese repertoire of recipes, but remain a staple of Thai seasoning. Thai cooking wouldn't be what it is without this intensely aromatic root. Cilantro root is used not so much for its taste, which is bitter and sharp, but for the musty and earthy perfume it adds to a dish.

Shallots, *hom,* eventually replaced wild onion, as Thai cooks admire its mild, slightly bitter and metallic aftertaste. However, garlic is usually preferred to shallots for its flavor, rich aroma, and healthful benefits. Thais believe the more garlic used, the better the health, while shallots need to be used in moderation, as they may cause an adverse effect.

Mastering the use of the Big Four Seasonings is the key to understanding the delicate balancing act of flavors that is Thai food. They are the seasoning paste for marinades and stir-fries, an addition to soups, and a foundation for most curry pastes.

The Big Four Seasonings

Glurh
SALT

There are two kinds of salt from Thailand. One is harvested from the sea, the other mined from the earth. They are very different in taste. Sea salt excites an intense reaction from the saliva glands with its saltiness, while earth salt has a metallic taste. Both are coarser than regular American salt. Salts from different regions of Thailand have their own distinct flavors. For example, salt harvested from the Gulf of Thailand tastes less salty than what is harvested from the Andaman Sea.

A variety of salts is available in supermarkets and specialty stores, including French sea salt, kosher salt, and Italian sea salt. I recommend them instead of regular table salt. Always taste before using. I keep various salts in labeled bowls and leave them on the counter in place of a saltshaker.

Ka-Tiem
GARLIC

Thai garlic cloves are much smaller and more aromatic than those grown in other countries. Garlic is highly prized for its subtle peppery and gentle flavoring. Its pungent flavor is believed to cure coughs, skin rashes, and fainting spells and to cleanse the blood. Commonly added to salt, garlic is used in the pounded spice pastes that are so important in Thai cooking because it both helps break down other ingredients and enhances other flavors.

Thai cooks prefer to use mature garlic for making pastes and young tender garlic for stir-fries. The green shoots sometimes found in mature garlic cloves are not a problem. Simply peel off the skin, pound the clove slightly, and remove the green shoot; use the garlic for making a spice paste. Mature garlic is richer in flavor and aroma than young garlic. Sometimes the peel may be left on a slightly pounded clove for extra flavor. Tender young garlic, available in early spring, is best thinly sliced for stir-fries, added to salads, or roasted for salad dressing.

Store garlic cloves in a basket out of direct sunlight. Garlic can be prepared the traditional Thai way or the Western way.

THE THAI WAY: To prepare garlic the Thai way, place 2 to 3 cloves on a chopping board. Smash the cloves hard, using the flat surface of a cleaver. Peel the cloves and slice lengthwise. Remove any green sprouts. Slice lengthwise into very thin slivers, moving from the hard stem to the pointed end, then slice across the slivers into tiny pieces. Discard the hard stem. Gather the garlic into a mound, then chop until finely minced. Wrap in plastic or put in a jar with a tight-fitting lid and refrigerate up to a week. The garlic may discolor, but this won't affect the taste.

THE WESTERN WAY: To prepare garlic the Western way, fit the food processor with the metal blade. Turn the food processor on and then drop the peeled garlic cloves through the feed tube. Process for 1 to 2 minutes, until the garlic is finely minced.

Prikk Thai
THAI WHITE PEPPERCORNS

White peppercorns have had the outer and inner coatings and rough surfaces of the dried mature fruit of the black peppercorn removed. The dried fruit, or "berries," are soaked, then the outer layers are rubbed off and the peppercorns are ground to smooth the surface. White peppercorns, which may be white, yellow, or gray with a few specks of black, are therefore less intense than black peppercorns. They leave a glowing warm sensation after the initial pungent flavor has dissipated. The Thai variety of white peppercorn is grayish white and is more flavorful than other white peppercorns sold in supermarkets; it is available in most Asian markets. White peppercorns packaged in Thailand tend to be less expensive than other types, but do need to be cleaned—before roasting, pick out any debris. Peppercorns keep well in a sealed Ziploc bag or a jar with a tight-fitting lid at room temperature for months.

To make Thai peppercorn powder, in a medium skillet, roast at least ¼ cup white peppercorns over medium-high heat for 3 to 4 minutes, or until the peppercorns exude a wonderful aroma. Slide the skillet back and forth on the burner to prevent the peppercorns from burning and to ensure even roasting. Cool completely before grinding to a powder in an electric spice or coffee grinder. Stored in a jar with a tight-fitting lid at room temperature, it will keep for a couple of months.

Rugg Pakk Chee
CILANTRO ROOTS

Cilantro, or fresh coriander, root is used by Thai cooks for its aroma; it's strong, and a little goes a long way. The root's fibrous texture is used to bind the other ingredients in making seasoning pastes. Cilantro is believed to enhance the appetite, soothe the digestive system, clear phlegm, break a fever, and cure fainting spells. Since it is usually a matter of sheer luck to find cilantro with roots intact in American supermarkets, I adapt the ingredients in the Big Four Paste to maintain the right balance, using cilantro stems in combination with roasted coriander seeds. (Of course, with this variation, the Big Four actually has five ingredients.)

To prepare cilantro roots for pounding, hold the cilantro by the stems and clean the roots with a vegetable brush. Cut the roots from the stems and set the stems, with leaves attached, aside. Place the roots in the center of the chopping board. Using the flat side of a cleaver, smash them several times, then gather the roots together, slice crosswise into short pieces, and mince. To store, wrap the minced roots in plastic wrap or place in a jar with a tight-fitting lid and refrigerate. They will keep for at least a week. Whole cilantro roots can be frozen, well wrapped, for a couple of months.

Glurh, Ka-Tiem, Prikk Thai, Rugg Pakk Chee

THE BIG FOUR PASTE

Makes ¾ cup

1 tablespoon coriander seeds
2 tablespoons Thai white
   peppercorns
1 teaspoon sea salt
12 to 15 cloves garlic, minced
   (½ cup)
1 cup minced cilantro stems and
   roots

The Big Four Paste, which can be made ahead and refrigerated for a month, is extremely versatile. For pungency, this ancient recipe relies on white peppercorns, which are gentler and more subtle than chiles. First you smell the wonderful aroma from the roasted peppercorns, then, as you eat, you experience a gentle rush of warmth that lingers. For a less pungent paste, decrease the peppercorns to 2 teaspoons and the coriander seeds to 1 teaspoon. If you are concerned about salt, you can leave it out, though I wouldn't advise it. Here, salt helps preserve the paste as well as bring out its flavor.

TO PREPARE WITH A MORTAR AND PESTLE

Heat a 7-inch skillet over medium-high heat. Add the coriander seeds and dry-roast, sliding the skillet back and forth over the burner, until the seeds are fragrant, about 3 minutes. Transfer the seeds to a small bowl to cool and repeat with the peppercorns. When cool, grind the coriander seeds and peppercorns separately in an electric spice or coffee grinder and transfer to separate bowls.

Place a mortar on top of a damp towel on the kitchen counter, preferably waist-high. Add the sea salt and garlic to the mortar and pound them together by holding the pestle securely in the center of your palm and pounding straight up and down into the center of the mortar. Use a spoon or spatula to scrape the ingredients from the sides into the center of the mortar as needed, and pound until a paste forms. Add the cilantro roots and stems and pound to a smooth paste. Add the ground coriander and peppercorn powders and pound and blend until the paste is smooth. Transfer the paste to a jar, seal, and refrigerate.

TO PREPARE WITH A FOOD PROCESSOR

Roast and grind the coriander seeds and peppercorns as above. Fit the food processor with the steel blade. Add the sea salt, garlic, and cilantro roots and stems and pulse until finely minced, scraping down the side of the bowl frequently. Add the ground spices and process to a paste. Transfer to a jar, seal, and refrigerate.

Cook's Note

The paste made in the food processor will be coarser than paste made using the mortar and pestle.

Using the Big Four Paste

For Grilling: Coat 1 pound meat, fish, or shellfish with the juice of 1 lemon and 1 tablespoon olive oil; rub generously with 1 teaspoon Big Four Paste. Cover and refrigerate for an hour. Grill, leaving steaks and other meats and fish whole or threading chunks on skewers.

For Deep-Frying: Add 1 tablespoon minced fresh ginger to 1 teaspoon Big Four Paste and rub the mixture onto 1 pound meat or fish, sliced into chunks, or shellfish. Coat the meat or fish with a batter (see page 150) and fry in very hot vegetable oil. Serve with Fresh Chiles with Fish Sauce (page 93).

For Roast Chicken or Turkey: For chicken, rub a 3-pound bird with 2 tablespoons olive oil and the juice of 1 lemon, then massage 1 tablespoon Big Four Paste all over the bird, under its skin, and in the cavity. Place in a plastic bag, seal tightly, and refrigerate overnight. For a 16-pound turkey, use 1 cup olive oil, the juice of 2 lemons, and ¾ cup Big Four Paste.

For Stir-Fries: Use 1 tablespoon Big Four Paste for each ¼ to ½ pound meat, fish, or shellfish and 2 to 3 cups sliced vegetables. Or use the same amount for stir-frying 2 cups noodles, adding ¼ to ½ pound each sliced meat, fish, and shellfish and 1 cup sliced vegetables. Add the Big Four Paste at the beginning of stir-frying, after you've added the oil to a hot skillet.

For Meatballs for Soup, Curry, or Noodles: Add 1 tablespoon Big Four Paste per each pound ground meat mixture and shape into meatballs. Add to the boiling broth. Meatballs can also be grilled.

For Meat Loaf: Add 1 tablespoon Big Four Paste for each pound of ground meat, mixing it in with the other ingredients.

The Supporting Cast: Prikk and Namm Pla

CHILES AND FISH SAUCE

Thais use chiles not only for their spicy heat, but also for their fragrance. Eating Thai dishes prepared with chiles need not be a contest to see who will survive. Selecting chiles for Thai recipes is often an experiment, because the kinds of chiles available in American markets are not the same as those grown in Thailand. Even if the chiles are of the same variety, different growing conditions—the soil, water, and amount of sun—alter the taste. Instead of searching for the sameness, go for variety. Several factors, however, should be considered in choosing chiles: color, size, spiciness or heat, aroma, and flavor.

The color of a chile will remain the same whether it is pounded or left whole for cooking. Thais are particular that their dishes have a pleasing color. The brilliant red, yellow, or orange of chiles makes a dish appetizing, and a curry paste made using green chiles combined with chile leaves results in a rich green sauce.

Larger chiles have more moisture in their flesh than smaller ones. When chiles are to be pounded in a paste, large chiles with thicker flesh should be added at the end, or the paste will splash dangerously during the pounding. When a paste made with thick fleshy chiles is used for curry, it takes longer to cook the paste because more time is needed for the liquid to evaporate and the sauce to thicken.

Chiles' spicy stinging sensation comes from the inner membrane where fine strands of placenta are attached to the seeds inside. *Prikk kee nuu,* or *prikk kun nuu* (also known as "rat droppings" chile), is a tiny chile slightly less than half an inch long, which has paper-thin flesh and is packed solid with seeds. It is similar to the *chiltepín, chilipiquín,* or bird chile and is the hottest of all Thai chiles. I find the sensation of eating these chiles pleasingly painful for a short period, followed by a floral aroma like a cool, fresh wind on a hot dry day. The habanero chile, used by Mexican cooks and claimed to be the hottest chile of all, isn't used by the Thais. The habanero produces a burning sensation that will knock you out, and if the bite doesn't do you in, the unpleasant musty aroma of these chiles will.

Although most of us are attracted to the fiery sensation created by chiles, the aroma and flavor of chiles are equally important. A fresh chile has a faint aroma that becomes intense when it is sliced. So potent is the fragrance of hot chiles that traditional Thai cooks believe that a couple of whole red chiles stored with fresh coconut keep the coconut from spoiling. Chiles with a floral or smoky aroma and taste are better matched for Thai food. These are typically chiles with bittersweet flavors that heighten the sensation of heat, thus enhancing the flavor experience yet gentling the rush of pain to a lingering pleasure.

Prikk Sodd
FRESH CHILES

Fresh chiles should be firm to the touch and glossy or shiny. Older slightly shriveled chiles can still be used, though their flavor will be different. They are best used for dry-roasting or grilling. Thai cooks suggest storing fresh chiles by wrapping them in newspaper and refrigerating. Thai cooks believe that soaking chiles in lime or other fruit juice before slicing and pounding reduces the heat and eliminates the burning sensation.

To cut a chile into slivers, holding the chile firmly by the stem on a chopping board, using a paring knife, make a cut lengthwise down one side of the chile. Put the sliced chile in a bowl of lemon or lime juice and water and fan the chile in the water to remove the seeds, then return the chile to the cutting board. Thinly slice lengthwise into slivers.

To mince a chile, follow the instructions above, then gather the chile slivers together and thinly slice across.

After working with chiles, rub your hands well with sliced lemon or lime and salt. Use the lemon or lime to clean the chopping board too, as well as the sink. (Rubbing alcohol also works well to remove the stinging heat of chiles.) Avoid touching your eyes while working with chiles.

The following fresh chiles are available in most American supermarkets:

NEW MEXICO OR ANAHEIM (SOMETIMES LABELED CALIFORNIA): A red or green slender pod, about 5 to 6 inches long. It has thick flesh with a nice floral aroma and a slightly sweet flavor. The hotness varies depending on growing conditions. It is a good substitute for *prikk numm*, used to make Chile Water (page 179).

DE ÁRBOL: Related to the cayenne pepper, sometimes known as "finger pepper" because of its shape. It is similar to what are called Thai chiles in American and Asian supermarkets. These chiles are red, orange, or green, about 2 inches long, and firm. The hotness varies according to the thickness of the flesh and the amount of seeds. The flavor is bitter with a smoky and floral aroma. Red de árbol chiles make wonderful chile paste.

CHILTEPÍN OR *CHILIPIQUÍN:* Sometimes called "bird," "bird droppings," or "mosquito" chile,

because of its small size. It is similar in size and pungency to the Thai chile called *prikk kee nuu* (or "rat droppings" chiles). Sold red or green, these chiles are about ½ inch long and extremely spicy, with thin flesh filled with seeds. They have an earthy, smoky, and floral aroma and a piquant to bitter-metallic flavor. Both the red and green add a zing to chile pastes.

POBLANO: About 4 to 5 inches long, a dark blackish green color, with a wider top tapering to a pointed end. It is mild with thick flesh and a sweet flavor and is good for making chile paste for green sweet curry (see page 220).

JALAPEÑO: Both red and green are available, with a broad range of acidic and spicy flavor. About 2 inches long, with thick flesh and a fair amount of seeds, they have a floral aroma and sweet taste.

SERRANO: Perhaps the chile that is most often found in supermarkets, with a slender red or green pod, about 2 inches long, and medium-hot to fiery flavor. The flesh is rather thin with a fair amount of seeds. The aroma is both floral and smoky, while the flavor is bitter-sweet. It is ideal for Thai cooking, and it makes a good substitute for fresh bird chiles.

Prikk Heang
DRIED CHILES

The shelves of supermarkets all over America have blossomed with a variety of dried chiles because of the popularity of a variety of ethnic cuisines that use these chiles. Most are packaged in clear cellophane. Look for chiles that are shiny, mold-free, and whole, not broken. I keep dried chiles in sealed Ziploc bags in the freezer for months.

To prepare dried chiles for paste, soften them by soaking in hot water for about 30 minutes. Drain and cover again with cool water. Slice a lime or lemon, squeeze the juice into the bowl, and add the slices. Let sit for 10 minutes. Lift out the chiles, squeeze out the excess water, slit each chile lengthwise in half, and return to the bowl of water. Fan the pods back and forth in the water until all the seeds fall out. Pinch off the hard stems and dry the pods well with paper towels.

The seemingly repetitive method of softening dried chiles by soaking, then drying them again, is truly an example of Thai logic. This process lessens the heat as well as softens the texture, making the chiles more pliable for slicing and for pounding into paste. When deep-fried, twice-dried chiles are crisper and lighter. Traditional Thai cooks dry the soaked chiles in the sun for several hours before using them. Drying on a cookie sheet in a 150°F oven for an hour also works well.

After softening, whole dried chiles can be wrapped in paper towels, sealed in a plastic Ziploc bag, and then stored in the refrigerator for several days. To mince presoaked chiles for chile paste, slice each chile into long thin slivers, then slice the slivers crosswise into tiny pieces. Stored in a jar with a tight-fitting lid, the sliced chiles will keep for up to a week in the refrigerator.

The dried chiles listed below are categorized and used according to color, flavor, and spiciness.

COLOR AND FLAVOR

NEW MEXICO OR ANAHEIM (SOMETIMES LABELED CALIFORNIA): Large dark red pods that are about 6 inches long and have a pleasant smoky flavor. They are mild if the seeds are removed, and make beautiful roasted chiles in oil (see page 94).

PASILLA: Resembling a smaller version of the New Mexico chile, about 3 to 4 inches long, deep red in color, with a smoky, nutty, slightly musty flavor. They are only mildly spicy if the seeds are removed.

SPICINESS

CHILTEPÍN OR CHILIPIQUÍN: Very tiny pods slightly less than half an inch long. Very spicy, with a pleasant smoky flavor. They add an extra punch to chile paste.

DE ÁRBOL: Very hot chiles if the seeds are left intact, with a marvelous musty, smoky flavor. They are commonly available in supermarkets or through mail-order catalogues and make spicy chile pastes with a beautiful red hue.

JAPONÉS: Bright red, with slender long pods about 3 inches long, aromatic and peppery whether used with or without seeds. They are also commonly found in supermarkets and can be used interchangeably with de árbol chiles.

Crispy Dried Chiles

Crispy dried chiles can be used as garnishes or accompaniments. To prepare them, put the chiles on a sheet of aluminum foil and drizzle with a tablespoon of olive oil. Tightly seal the chiles and put the foil pouch in a toaster oven at 375°F for 10 to 15 minutes. The chiles will turn black and crispy. Cool before storing in a jar at room temperature.

Another way is to cook them in a skillet with or without 2 to 3 tablespoons of vegetable oil, according to the particular recipe.

Prikk Pow Poun

ROASTED DRIED CHILE POWDER

Makes about ½ cup

This condiment graces the Thai table with the explicit purpose of encouraging the diner to season according to his or her individual taste. It is also used in making salad dressing. Roasted dried chile powder is a strong mixture, so before starting to prepare the chiles, turn on the exhaust fan in your kitchen, or work in a well-ventilated place. Afterward, boil 1 cup of vinegar and 4 cups of water in a saucepan for at least 30 minutes to clean the air. Wash all equipment thoroughly with detergent and/or vinegar or lime juice with salt and water.

In a 12-inch skillet, dry-roast the dried chiles over medium heat, shaking the skillet or tossing and stirring with a wooden spatula to ensure even heating, until blackened. To cut down the fumes, add a pinch of sea salt to the skillet. Transfer to a plate to cool completely.

Fit a food processor with the steel blade, add the chiles, and process until they turn to powder. Let the powder settle in the machine for a minute or two; even so, when you remove the food processor lid, do so at arm's length, and do not inhale the powder. Carefully transfer the powder to a glass jar, seal with a tight-fitting lid, and store at room temperature for up to a year. Remember that the chile powder will be slightly salty, so add salt accordingly in recipes.

1 cup dried de árbol or Japonés chiles, for mild to medium-spicy powder, or 1 cup dried *chiltepín* chiles for an extremely spicy powder, stems removed
Sea salt

Prikk Todd Poun

CRISPY DRIED CHILE POWDER

Makes about ½ cup

1 cup dried de árbol or Japonés
  chiles, stems removed
1 lime or lemon
2 to 3 cups vegetable oil
Sea salt

This is another variation of chile powder used both as a condiment and as seasoning. Because the chiles are deep-fried, this chile powder is richer than the one on page 91, with a buttery taste. This makes a mild chile powder; for a very spicy powder, skip the soaking step and do not remove the seeds.

Put the dried chiles in a medium mixing bowl, cover with hot water, and let stand for 1 hour, or until the chiles are softened.

Pour off the water and cover the chiles with cool water. Slice the lime and squeeze the juice into the bowl of chiles, then add the slices. Let sit for 10 minutes. Take a handful of chiles at a time from the water and put them on a chopping board. Split each lengthwise with a paring knife and return to the bowl of water. Fan the chiles back and forth in the water until the seeds are dislodged. Dry thoroughly with paper towels. Place the chiles on a cookie sheet in the sun for a day or in a 150°F oven for an hour until dried.

In a 12-inch skillet, heat at least 1 inch of oil over high heat to 300° to 325°F. (You can also test for readiness by dipping the tip of a wooden spoon into the oil; if tiny bubbles begin to form around the spoon, the oil is ready for frying.) Lower the heat to medium, add the chiles and a pinch of sea salt, and stir and toss the chiles in the oil with a wooden spoon until blackened. Remove the chiles from the oil with a strainer and drain on paper towels. Cool completely. Repeat with the remaining chiles.

Fit a food processor with the steel blade. Add the crispy fried chiles and process until the chiles turn into powder, approximately 1 minute. Let the powder settle in the bowl for a minute or so before removing the lid and transferring the chile powder to a glass jar with a tight-fitting lid. Store at room temperature for up to 6 months.

Prikk Namm Pla
FRESH CHILES WITH FISH SAUCE

Makes about ½ cup

This classic condiment is served with any Thai meal that includes noodles. It keeps in a glass jar with a tight-fitting lid in the refrigerator for 3 to 4 days. Without the lime juice, the chiles and fish sauce may be served with other main dishes, including soups, curries, salads, and stir-fries.

Mix all the ingredients together. Serve in a small deep bowl.

7 to 8 fresh bird chiles or
    4 to 5 serrano chiles, minced
¼ cup fish sauce (*namm pla*)
Juice of ½ lime (optional)

Prikk Namm Som
FRESH CHILES IN VINEGAR

Makes about 1 cup

This condiment is always served with noodles. It will keep for a week tightly sealed in the refrigerator. The taste will change over time, as the vinegar will take on more of the spicy heat from the chiles.

Mix all the ingredients together. Serve in a small deep bowl.

20 fresh bird chiles or
    10 to 12 serrano chiles, thinly
    sliced crosswise
½ cup rice or cider vinegar
1 teaspoon sea salt

Namm Prikk Pow
ROASTED CHILES IN OIL

Makes about 1 cup

3 to 4 dried corn husks, soaked in
 cool water until softened
2 tablespoons fermented shrimp
 paste or 3 tablespoons red miso
2 cups vegetable oil
1/2 cup chopped garlic
1 cup thinly sliced shallots (10 to 12)
12 to 15 dried New Mexico (or
 California) chiles or 1 1/2 cups
 dried de árbol, Japonés, or
 chiltepín chiles, softened in hot
 water, seeded, and dried
1 cup dried shrimp, soaked in warm
 water until softened and dried,
 or 1 cup minced grilled chicken
Sea salt
1/3 cup palm sugar or packed light
 brown sugar
1/3 cup fish sauce (*namm pla*)
1/4 cup thick tamarind juice (see
 page 128)

Dry-roasting, or *pow*, was the traditional way of preparing the chiles for this sauce. Today, the chiles are deep-fried in oil, or *todd*, instead, but the name remains the same. This sauce is used to season dishes such as hot-sour soup (page 165), peanut sauce (page 152) for grilled meat, and salad dressing (pages 260 and 266).

For a very spicy flavoring, use the de árbol or *chiltepín* chiles. *Chiltepíns* do not have to be soaked or dried. Be careful to avoid burning the ingredients when deep-frying, or the result will taste bitter. Adding a pinch of sea salt to the oil during frying lessens the splatters and promotes a crisper texture.

Preheat the oven to 500°F. Stack the corn husks and wrap the fermented shrimp paste in them. Put in a small baking pan and bake for 20 minutes. The corn husks and paste will get slightly char-burnt. Let cool, then discard the burnt husks and set the paste aside. Line two large platters with paper towels and set them near the stove.

Heat the oil in a 12-inch skillet over high heat to 300° to 325°F. (You can also test for readiness by sticking the tip of a wooden spoon into the oil; if bubbles form around the spoon, the oil is ready for frying.) Arrange the ingredients in the order in which they will be deep-fried: garlic, shallots, chiles, dried shrimp (grilled chicken does not have to be deep-fried). Lower the heat to medium-high, add the garlic, and fry until golden, 2 to 3 minutes, stirring constantly to prevent from burning and ensure even browning. When the oil starts to spatter, add a pinch of sea salt to the oil. With a strainer, transfer the garlic to one of the platters lined with paper towels.

Repeat with the shallots, which will take 4 to 5 minutes to cook; add another pinch of sea salt to the oil, and make sure the shallots don't burn. Transfer to the lined platter. Fry the chiles for about 2 minutes and transfer to the second platter, then fry the dried shrimp for about 30 seconds; transfer to the platter. Let the oil cool. Retain 1/4 cup of the oil in the skillet and set it aside; strain the rest and save it for stir-frying if desired.

Fit a food processor with the steel blade, add the dried shrimp or grilled chicken and process until it is pureed. Add the garlic and puree. Each ingredient should be pureed before the next is added: Puree the shallots, then the chiles, and then the char-burnt fermented shrimp paste. Scrape down the sides of the bowl and blend well. Add the palm sugar, fish sauce, and tamarind juice and pulse until blended. The sauce should taste spicy-sweet, salty, and slightly sour, all in balance.

Heat the reserved ¼ cup oil in the skillet over high heat for 1 minute. Add the pureed mixture and cook, stirring, for 1 to 2 minutes, or until the oil absorbs the red color from the chiles. Remove from the heat and let cool, then transfer to a glass container with a tight-fitting lid. The sauce will keep in the refrigerator for several months.

Namm Pla
FISH SAUCE

Before *namm pla,* or fish sauce, became the common seasoning, *pla-rah,* or fermented fish, was used. It is still eaten by country folks, especially in the north and northeastern cities near the border of Laos and Cambodia. Traditional home cooks, such as my friend Vithi's aunt, continue to make their own, as did generations before. They gather fish during the monsoons, when fish are especially plentiful. Pounded with salt and roasted rice grains, the fish are fermented in earthenware jars. People in the Northeast are known to exist on only a bit of fermented fish and rice during the long drought season. For the rest of the country, the clear, amber-colored extract made with salt and fish cured in the sunshine takes the place of *pla-rah.*

Quality fish sauce has an exceptional taste and is slightly salty, with an aroma of the sea. The amber liquid is clear, not murky. The best is made by country folks, with fish caught from the sea and salt from seawater. Small whole fish are salted, layered and packed tightly into earthenware jars, and covered with bundled dried banana leaves. The mixture is pressed and weighted down with several bamboo trays and left in the sun to ripen for a couple of weeks, or until the fish has completely disintegrated. The liquid is drained off into a pot. It is at this stage that each fish sauce maker adds his or her own secret touch to enhance the flavor. Some add palm sugar, others dried garlic husks and pineapple peelings, before boiling the liquid over low heat. The pot is stirred continuously for several hours, until the maker decides the perfect balance of taste has been reached. The liquid is then poured into a bottle and left in the sun to mature until it turns light amber.

As in making fine wine, each stage is carefully monitored and every ingredient carefully selected, including the earthenware jar for fermenting the sauce. The result is unlike anything sold in Asian markets here. Unfortunately, the lesser-quality fish sauce from these markets is too often the first introduction for Westerners, and many find it repugnant or downright disgusting. It is a shame and an insult to this marvelous seasoning, because it is like judging wine by tasting only the kind that costs $1.99 a bottle.

Fish sauce is used for its complex taste and aroma, never as a substitute for salt. However, it is salty, so it should be used sparingly. I encourage experimenting to find your preferred brand of fish sauce. I am partial to fish sauce made in Thailand or China. Tiparod fish sauce from Thailand is the most common brand in markets. It is packaged in both glass and plastic bottles; if possible, buy it in a glass bottle. When purchasing fish sauce, hold the bottle to the light. If the liquid is clear and the color of weak tea, then it may be good. The label should indicate it is made with fish extract and salt. If the label lists sugar, preservatives, and/or MSG, avoid it.

Most fish sauce comes in 24-ounce bottles. It is inexpensive, so take a chance and buy more than one bottle. At home, pour a bit into a small bowl and take a whiff. It should smell slightly fishy but not overpowering. Then taste it. Good fish sauce has a sharp salty taste that quickly dissipates. One bottle goes a long way. Keep it in the refrigerator; when it turns dark, discard it and buy a new bottle.

Kao Neuw Ping Sai Goong Pung Nga

ROASTED STICKY RICE WITH
SHRIMP AND SESAME SEEDS

Makes about 20 pieces

For the wrappers

2 packages frozen or fresh banana
leaves or 40 dried or fresh corn
husks
40 flat toothpicks

For the filling

2 tablespoons vegetable oil
1 tablespoon Big Four Paste
(page 86)
½ pound medium shrimp, peeled,
deveined, and minced (or 1 cup
fresh corn kernels, for a
vegetarian version)
½ teaspoon sea salt
¼ cup palm sugar or packed light
brown sugar
1 cup Fresh Grated Coconut Flakes
(page 71)
3 kaffir lime leaves, slivered, or
grated zest of 1 lime

For the rice

1¼ cups Fresh Unsweetened
Coconut Cream (page 69)
1 teaspoon sea salt
2 cups cooked long-grain Thai
jasmine sticky rice (see page 50),
kept warm in the steamer

Vacation was unheard of in our family. While my classmates went to the seashore during school breaks, we stayed home with tutors. It was not until I was in my early teens that my mother decided she could no longer bear the oppressive summer heat in Bangkok. She missed the ocean, having been born and reared near the sea in China. So, for several summers, she packed pots, pans, stoves, and all sorts of cooking utensils into our old Austin, an English car, leaving my father behind with a servant and a bare kitchen. As we drove to Bung Sand, a seaside resort outside of Bangkok, city buildings were gradually replaced by miles of rice fields, and the roadsides were dotted with wooden shacks selling fruits, vegetables, and snacks.

Occasionally, as we neared our destination, we saw young children with bamboo baskets waving pieces of long thin banana or palm wrappers to catch our attention. They were selling *kao neuw ping*, grilled sticky rice wrapped in banana or palm leaves, popular in central and southern Thailand. We always stopped for the chewy sweet-and-smoky rice and coconut, and we knew the sea was just minutes away.

Years later, a friend and I took the train to a seaside resort called Hua Hin. As the train approached the station, women and children rushed up, selling their snack baskets of *kao neuw ping*. As I ate, memories rushed in and I could smell the sea.

The banana leaf bundles can be made a day or two ahead and stored in Ziploc bags in the refrigerator. Bring out an hour before cooking time. These are great for an informal supper or backyard picnic. When friends arrive and ask, "Can I do something to help?" say, "Yes!" and show them how to wrap the sticky rice filling in the banana leaves. Even children can do this.

To prepare the wrappers with frozen banana leaves, thaw the leaves in the refrigerator overnight or on the counter for 30 to 45 minutes. Lay the thawed bundle on a kitchen counter, preferably near the sink, unwrapping it carefully to avoid tearing. One at a time, cut each leaf with scissors into 10-inch squares. Cut off any hard stems. Fill the sink with soapy water and gently wash the cut banana leaves, then rinse well with cold water and dry thoroughly. Set aside.

If using fresh banana leaves, cut the center hard stem, away from each leaf. Cut each leaf into a 10-inch square. Rinse in cold water and dry thoroughly. Set aside.

If using dried corn husks, soak them in a large mixing bowl of lukewarm water for at least 30 minutes. Rinse in cool water a couple of times, cover with fresh water, and set aside.

If using fresh corn husks, remove any corn tassels and rinse the husks thoroughly in cool water. Pat dry and set aside.

To make the filling, heat a 10-inch skillet over medium high heat for 2 minutes, or until when you hold your hand several inches above it, you feel the heat. Add the oil, then add the Big Four Paste and cook, stirring with a wooden spoon, until aromatic, about 30 seconds. Immediately add the minced shrimp (or corn) and cook, stirring and breaking up any clumps, for 2 to 3 minutes, or until the shrimp just turns pink (or the corn is hot). Add the sea salt and sugar, turn the heat to low, and cook, stirring, for another minute, or until the salt and sugar are completely dissolved. Turn off the heat, leaving the skillet on the stove, and add the coconut flakes, mixing well. Add the kaffir lime strands and stir to combine. Transfer the mixture to a mixing bowl.

For the rice, combine 1 cup of the coconut cream and the sea salt in a 1½-quart saucepan and heat over medium heat for 5 minutes, or until the coconut cream begins to boil. Transfer the sticky rice from the steamer to a large mixing bowl, pour the hot coconut cream over it, and mix well with a spoon. Cover and let sit for about 10 minutes.

Arrange the warm sticky rice, the filling, the remaining ¼ cup coconut cream (in a small bowl), a cup of cold water, and the toothpicks on a large work surface near the stove. If using banana leaves, turn a burner to low. For a gas stove, one at a time, carefully hold each leaf over the flame for 1 to 2 seconds, turn over and repeat. If using an electric stove, put the banana leaf directly on the coil. As you work, stack the banana leaves one on top of the other, with the grain going in the same direction and the dull side up.

Place a set of two banana leaves on the work surface, so the grain runs parallel to you. Spread 2 tablespoons of the sticky rice in the center, flattening it with the back of a spoon; dip the spoon in the cold water as needed to prevent sticking. Put ¼ teaspoon of the coconut cream on top of the sticky rice, then spread 1 tablespoon of the shrimp (or corn) filling over the center of the rice.

Join the edge of banana leaf closest to you with the opposite side. Fold the leaves together lengthwise and fold the edge over itself until the package is snug. Secure each end with a toothpick and set aside.

If using dried corn husks, remove the soaked husks from the water and pat them dry. Stack pairs of the dried or fresh corn husks on the work surface, with the grain of the husk running parallel to you, and fill and fold them to seal as above, securing each end with a toothpick.

Light a grill fire. When it is medium-hot, with no shooting flames, place the bundles on the grill and cook, turning frequently, for 7 to 10 minutes, or until the filling is heated through. If the leaves or husks start to burn, spray them with water. Serve hot or at room temperature. (Be sure to provide a bowl for the discarded leaves and toothpicks.)

Kao Tung Na Tung

CRISPY RICE CRACKERS WITH COCONUT, SHRIMP, AND PORK DIPPING SAUCE

Makes 6 to 8 servings

For the dipping sauce

¼ pound boneless lean pork, such as tenderloin or loin, thinly sliced

½ pound shrimp, peeled, deveined, and thinly sliced

1½ cups Fresh Unsweetened Coconut Cream (page 69)

1 tablespoon Big Four Paste (page 86)

2 shallots, minced

1 tablespoon fish sauce (*namm pla*)

1 teaspoon sea salt

¼ cup palm sugar or packed light brown sugar

½ cup unsalted peanuts, dry-roasted (see page 13) and coarsely ground

3 to 4 fresh red bird chiles or 2 to 3 red serrano chiles, slivered

12 to 15 cilantro leaves

Fifteen to twenty 1- to 1½-inch round Rice Crackers (page 61) or rice cracker sheets

I have fond memories from my childhood in Bangkok of the parade of street vendors who wound their way up and down the lanes of shop houses selling snacks, noodles, roasted pigs and ducks, and countless varieties of delectable dishes. In particular, I remember one middle-aged woman, her face weathered by the sun. She was a farmer's wife trying to make extra money by selling *kao tung na tung*, crispy rice crackers with coconut, shrimp, and pork dipping sauce, and *miang lao*, Lao Savory Bite (page 145). These snacks were exotic and yet as Thai as the woman herself. We children squatted close to her basket, watching as she ladled the sauce from a large terra-cotta pot into our bowls, accompanied by a handful of thin golden rice crackers. The rich creamy sauce was packed with delicious surprises and the crunchy rice crackers popped and sizzled in my mouth. Like me, you will enjoy this dish.

Some Asian markets sell two-inch square dried rice crackers wrapped tightly in plastic wrap. They are saltier than the recipe here but can be used as a substitute.

Fit the food processor with the steel blade and grind the pork and shrimp to a paste. It will form a ball. Remove from the bowl and set aside.

In a small saucepan, heat the coconut cream over high heat just until bubbles appear around the edges, then immediately lower the heat to medium-low so you don't curdle the cream. Add the Big Four Paste and the minced pork and shrimp, and stir and cook until the pork loses its pink color and the shrimp turn pink. Add the shallots, fish sauce, sea salt, palm sugar, and ground peanuts and cook for another 5 minutes, stirring occasionally. Transfer the sauce to a serving bowl and let cool completely before serving.

Garnish the sauce with the slivers of red chiles and cilantro leaves, and let each guest spoon the sauce over the crispy rice crackers in his or her bowl.

Kanum Pung Na Goong
SHRIMP TOAST

This Thai snack was created in the early 1900s, when white bread was considered quite chic and was very expensive. Bread was introduced into Thailand by the French in the 1600s and is called *kanum pung*. *Kanum* means snack, and *pung* is the Thai pronunciation of the French word *pain,* or bread. The recipe uses crispy fried white bread to replace the traditional deep-fried crispy rice crackers.

You can prepare all the ingredients ahead for last-minute assembly. An alternative is to prepare the shrimp toasts several hours before deep-frying. Store them in a plastic container with a tight-fitting lid or on a platter tightly covered with plastic wrap. Since the bread is dried, it will not get soggy.

7 square slices white sandwich bread, crusts trimmed off, bread cut into quarters
1/2 pound medium shrimp, peeled and deveined
1 tablespoon Big Four Paste (page 86)
1 tablespoon palm sugar or packed light brown sugar
1/2 cup Fresh Grated Coconut Flakes (page 71)
4 kaffir lime leaves, minced, or grated zest of 1 lime
1 large egg white, beaten until frothy
4 cups vegetable oil

Place the bread squares on a cookie sheet to dry in the sun for several hours or in a 150°F oven for 30 minutes.

Fit a food processor with the steel blade. Put the shrimp, Big Four Paste, and palm sugar in the bowl and process the mixture to a paste. Transfer to a mixing bowl. Add the grated coconut flakes and kaffir lime leaves and mix well, then fold the shrimp mixture into the beaten egg white.

Put the mixture in a small Ziploc bag, seal the bag, and cut across one corner to make a small opening for your makeshift pastry bag. Squeeze about 3/4 tablespoon of the shrimp mixture onto the bread squares; spread evenly with a metal or rubber spatula to cover the bread. Place on a platter, cover with plastic wrap, and refrigerate until ready to deep-fry.

Line a cookie sheet with paper towels and set it near the stove. In a deep 12-inch skillet, heat the oil over high heat to between 350° and 375°F. (You can also test for readiness by dipping the tip of a wooden spoon into the oil; if tiny bubbles appear around it, the oil is ready.) Put the shrimp toast, 6 to 7 pieces at a time, with the shrimp topping down, into the oil. When the shrimp topping turns pink, flip the toast over and fry until the bread is golden brown, about a minute or less. If the oil is too hot and the bread starts to burn, reduce the heat. Transfer the toasts to the lined cookie sheet to drain, then arrange on a serving platter and serve immediately.

Pra-Tubb Rom
FIRE CRACKERS

Makes 3 dozen fire crackers, or 6 to 8 servings

For the dipping sauce

¾ cup sugar

¼ cup rice vinegar or cider vinegar

¼ cup water

Sea salt to taste

6 to 7 fresh bird chiles or 3 to 4
  serrano chiles, minced

1 tablespoon unsalted peanuts,
  dry-roasted (see page 13) and
  ground

½ pound boneless, skinless chicken
  breast, diced

1 tablespoon Big Four Paste
  (page 86)

1 tablespoon fish sauce (*namm pla*)

3 ounces crabmeat, picked through
  for shells and cartilage

1 scallion, minced

One 12-ounce package wonton
  wrappers

1 large egg, slightly beaten

4 cups vegetable oil

Sea salt

Until recently, every Thai celebration included firecrackers. They are illegal in cities now, but in the provinces, where country folks remain wary of unwanted spirits, the tradition persists. These edible "fire crackers" are perfectly legal, even though they pack a big burst of flavor.

The wontons can be assembled in advance and frozen. Place them on a tray or cookie sheet and freeze until frozen hard, then carefully transfer to a Ziploc bag and return to the freezer, where they will keep for a couple of weeks. Do not thaw before frying; frozen wontons will take a minute or two longer to cook.

In a small saucepan, combine the sugar, vinegar, and water with a couple pinches of sea salt and cook over high heat, stirring, until the sugar is dissolved. Lower the heat to medium-low and simmer for another 5 minutes. Remove the pan from the heat. Transfer the liquid to a sauce bowl to cool completely, then stir in the minced chiles. Sprinkle with the peanuts just before serving.

Fit a food processor with the steel blade, add the chicken breast, Big Four Paste, and fish sauce, and process to a paste; the mixture will form a ball. Transfer to a mixing bowl, stir in the crabmeat and scallion, cover, and refrigerate until ready to use.

To assemble, lay the wonton wrappers, a few at a time, on the work surface and put about 1 tablespoon of filling in the center of each wonton skin. Brush the edges with the beaten egg, fold over into a triangle, and pinch the edges to seal. Gently flatten the filling inside. Place on a cookie sheet.

Line a cookie sheet with paper towels and place it near the stove. In a 12-inch skillet or flat-bottomed wok, heat the oil over high heat to between 350° and 375°F. (You can also test for readiness by dipping the tip of a wooden spoon into the oil; if bubbles form around it, the oil is ready for frying.) Sprinkle a couple of pinches of sea salt into the hot oil to reduce splattering (add a bit more during deep-frying to keep the oil from splattering). Drop 5 to 6 wontons at a time into the hot oil and deep-fry until golden brown, 1 to 2 minutes per side. If the oil is too hot and the skins brown too quickly, lower the heat. Remove with a slotted spoon, transferring to the lined cookie sheet. Serve on a platter, with the dipping sauce.

Phu-Ja
CRAB CAKES

The original Thai crab cake is a stuffed and deep-fried whole crab. Years ago, I visited Salvador, Bahia, a city in Brazil, and was astounded to find exactly the same dish there. The Portuguese, who were the first Europeans to enter Thailand, in 1511, were settling in Brazil during the same period. As they navigated the globe, they introduced and exchanged new culinary ideas from many different nations.

If you use frozen crabmeat, thaw it completely and squeeze out as much liquid as you can. The original recipe used slaked lime liquid as a natural leavening agent. Slaked lime is made from burnt limestone, slaked, or crumbled, by the addition of pounded turmeric root, which causes the lime to disintegrate into a fine vermillion paste. Slaked lime, diluted with water, is used in Thai cooking as baking powder is used by Western cooks. I have substituted baking powder.

In a medium bowl, combine the crabmeat, baking powder, and Big Four Paste, mixing well with your hands. Add the scallion, lime zest, coconut flakes, and ¼ cup of the bread crumbs and mix well. In a small bowl, beat 2 of the eggs and the egg white together. Add to the crab mixture and mix thoroughly.

Beat the remaining 2 eggs lightly in a 9-inch pie plate. Put the remaining 2 cups bread crumbs in another pie plate. Scoop up a tablespoonful of the crabmeat mixture, pressing and rolling it into a ball, coat the ball lightly with the egg, and then roll it in the bread crumbs. Lightly flatten the ball with your hand and set aside on a platter. Repeat with the rest of the mixture. Let the cakes sit for at least 10 to 15 minutes before deep-frying. You can cover and refrigerate them for 3 to 4 hours; take them out of the refrigerator 10 to 15 minutes before cooking.

Line a tray with paper towels and set it near the stove. Heat the oil in a 12-inch skillet over high heat to 350°F. Put 5 to 6 crab cakes at a time into the hot oil and fry until golden, 2 to 3 minutes per side. If the crab cakes brown too quickly, lower the heat. With a slotted spoon, transfer to the tray lined with paper towels.

Line a serving platter with the lettuce leaves and place the crab cakes on top. Garnish with the cilantro sprigs, pickled ginger, and lime slices.

1 pound crabmeat, picked over for
   shells and cartilage
½ teaspoon baking powder
1 tablespoon Big Four Paste
   (page 86)
1 whole scallion, minced
1 tablespoon grated lime zest
¼ cup Fresh Grated Coconut Flakes
   (page 71)
2¼ cups Japanese bread crumbs
   (panko; see Cook's Note,
   page 105)
4 large eggs
1 large egg white
3 cups vegetable oil

For the garnishes

6 to 7 romaine lettuce leaves
12 sprigs cilantro
2 ounces sweet pickled ginger
   (see page 140)
1 lime, cut into wedges

Munn Phun Sip

STUFFED POTATOES (THAI CROQUETTES)

Makes 12 croquettes, or 6 servings

12 small red-skinned potatoes
    (about 2 inches in diameter)
½ pound medium shrimp, peeled
    and deveined
½ pound boneless, skinless chicken
    breast, cut into ½-inch pieces
1 tablespoon Big Four Paste
    (page 86)
1 teaspoon fish sauce (*namm pla*)
1 large egg white, slightly beaten
1 tablespoon all-purpose flour
1 tablespoon water
1 large egg
2 cups Japanese bread crumbs
    (panko; see Cook's Note)
2 cups vegetable oil
6 to 7 red leaf lettuce leaves
6 to 7 sprigs cilantro

Thai people call the potato *munn farang,* "foreign tuber," because it was brought to Thailand from the Americas by Europeans in the 1500s. Until recently, it was rarely used. Nonetheless, there are many Thai recipes using the potato in an attempt to imitate Western dishes. This dish was created for King Chulalongkhorn after he visited France in 1897. It is marvelous as a side dish or finger food. You will need small potatoes. Use a sharp vegetable peeler or melon baller to hollow out the potatoes. These can be assembled a day ahead and refrigerated, then fried just before you are ready to serve them.

Fill a large mixing bowl with cold water. Peel the potatoes. Slice about ¼ inch off each top and save for the caps; put the caps in the cold water to prevent them from browning. Trim just enough from the bottom of each potato so it will sit flat. Use a small sharp melon ball cutter to carefully scoop out the inside of each potato, leaving the walls a scant ¹⁄₁₆ inch thick. Add the potatoes to the cold water as you work.

Fit a food processor with the steel blade. Pulse the shrimp, chicken, Big Four Paste, and fish sauce to a paste; it will form a ball. Transfer the mixture to a medium mixing bowl and stir in the beaten egg white, blending thoroughly.

Remove the potatoes and caps from the water and dry thoroughly with paper towels. Put the filling into a small Ziploc bag and cut off a small triangle from one corner. With your makeshift pastry bag, squeeze the filling into each potato shell so that it is three-quarters full.

Fill a pasta pot that has a steamer basket insert halfway with water and bring it to a boil. Meanwhile, line the steamer basket insert with dampened cheesecloth. Put the stuffed potatoes in the steamer basket insert, along with the caps. Cover and steam for 15 minutes, or until the potatoes are cooked but firm. Remove the steamer basket insert from the pot and let the potatoes and caps cool completely.

In a small cup, mix the flour and water to form a thick paste. Smear a bit of the flour mixture on top of each filled potato and top it with a cap, pressing gently to seal. Beat the egg in a pie plate. Put the bread crumbs in another large plate. Roll each stuffed potato gently in the egg, then the bread crumbs, coating completely. Set aside on a plate.

At this point, you can cover the potatoes and refrigerate them until ready to deep-fry. They will keep for 4 to 5 hours. Take them out of the refrigerator half an hour before cooking.

Line a plate with paper towels and set it near the stove. Heat the vegetable oil in a 12-inch skillet or flat-bottomed wok over high heat to between 350° and 375°F. (You can also test the oil for readiness by sticking the tip of a wooden spoon into the oil; if bubbles form around it, the oil is hot enough.) Working in batches, gently slide the stuffed potatoes into the oil and fry them until golden brown, turning them occasionally with tongs to ensure even browning. If the oil is too hot and the potatoes cook too quickly, lower the heat; watch closely, taking care not to let them burn. Transfer to the plate lined with paper towels to drain.

Line a serving platter with the lettuce leaves and garnish with the cilantro sprigs. Arrange the stuffed potatoes on top and serve hot, with a bowl of Classic Cucumber Salad (page 240).

Cook's Note

Panko, Japanese-style bread crumbs, are light and less greasy when deep-fried than ordinary bread crumbs. Panko is available in most Asian markets.

Classical Keang
SOUPS AND STEWS

The secret behind *keang*—soup or stew—is patience. The broth is simmered slowly in a covered pot, allowing the ingredients to cook gently and the flavors to infuse. I've been told by old-timers that the secret of good broth is to "never let the water boil like the ocean wave, but more like the ripple in the river." Often a pot of soup or stew is put on the stove in the morning and left to cook all day, with an occasional checking. By dinner, the broth is richly flavored and the meat is meltingly tender.

Neur Poo Chong—Ginseng
BEEF, LOTUS SEED, AND GREEN PAPAYA STEW

Makes 6 to 8 servings

1 cup dried lotus seeds (or canned hominy), rinsed well in cool water

1½ cups boiling water (if using lotus seeds)

1 green Mexican papaya, chayote squash, or rutabaga

1½ pounds boneless beef sirloin, well trimmed if desired and cut into 1-inch cubes

6 cups bottled or filtered water

2 tablespoons sugar

1 tablespoon fish sauce (*namm pla*)

2 tablespoons soy sauce

3 tablespoons Big Four Paste (page 86)

(continued)

Neur, or beef, *poo chong*, or dragon, *ginseng*—the name of this stew emphasizes a powerful healthy brew. Like many ancient recipes, it is made with broth seasoned with Big Four Paste. The green papaya and its seeds are used as natural tenderizers; the fruit's ability to absorb the rich flavor from the broth is an added plus. The Thais would leave the fat and gristle on the meat, but trim it if you prefer. Dried lotus seeds, an ingredient used mostly in Chinese cooking but adopted by the Thais, are available in most Asian markets, located in the dried food sections (see page 139). They add a surprising texture to the dish. Thais believe that lotus seeds have a rejuvenating effect on the body.

This stew tastes better if allowed to sit for several hours, or overnight in the refrigerator. Do not add the green papaya until shortly before serving. Prepare the crispy fresh cucumber relish during the last stage of cooking, once you've added the green papaya slices.

If you are using lotus seeds, put them in a small bowl, cover with the boiling water, and set aside until the water is cool and the seeds have puffed and softened, about 15 minutes. Drain off the water. Separate and remove the green germ from the center of each seed and discard. Set the seeds aside, or store in a Ziploc bag in the refrigerator until ready to use. They will keep for 2 to 3 days.

Peel the green papaya, chayote, or rutabaga with a vegetable peeler or small paring knife. If using the papaya, cut lengthwise in half and scoop out the seeds with a spoon. Bundle the seeds in a square of cheesecloth, tying it securely, and set aside. Slice each papaya half lengthwise into quarters, then thinly slice each slice on the diagonal into ⅛-inch pieces. You will need 1½ cups for the soup; wrap and refrigerate until ready to use. Leftover green papaya can be finely sliced for Spicy Green Papaya Salad (page 160).

Or, if using the chayote or rutabaga, thinly slice on the diagonal into ⅛-inch pieces to make 1½ cups. Remove seeds from the chayote. Wrap and refrigerate until ready to use.

Put the meat and enough tap water to cover it in a 4-quart saucepan, bring to a boil over high heat, and cook for 5 minutes. Remove the pan from the stove. Drain and rinse the meat, rinse the pan thoroughly, and return the meat to the pan. Add the bottled water and bring to a boil. With a fine-mesh skimmer, remove the scum. Lower the heat to medium and cook, continuing to skim, for 10 minutes. When the broth is clear, add the cheesecloth pouch of papaya seeds, the sugar, fish sauce, soy sauce, and Big Four Paste, with the lotus seeds, if using. Cover, reduce the heat if necessary, and let simmer for 1 hour, or until the meat is very tender and separates easily with a fork. If you have left the fat and gristle on, the meat may take longer to cook.

Remove the cheesecloth pouch of papaya seeds, if using, and discard. Add the green papaya, chayote, or rutabaga slices and simmer. Cook over medium heat for 15 minutes, if using the papaya, or until it turns translucent. The chayote and rutabaga will take another 10 minutes or so to cook.

Once you've added the papaya to the stew, make the cucumber relish by combining all the ingredients in a medium mixing bowl. Toss and let sit until serving time, then transfer to a small serving bowl.

Transfer the stew to a serving bowl. Serve hot, with cooked long-grain rice, preferably Thai jasmine or Indian or California basmati (see pages 37 and 38).

For the cucumber relish

1 cucumber, peeled, cut lengthwise
    in half, seeded, and thinly sliced
    on the diagonal
3 to 4 fresh red bird chiles or
    2 to 3 serrano chiles, minced
1 whole scallion, finely chopped
20 sprigs cilantro, coarsely chopped
2 tablespoons sugar
Juice of 1 lime (about
    2 tablespoons)

Keang Sum Krasudd
THREE KINGS SOUP

Makes 6 servings

One 8.8-ounce package pickled mustard greens (also called sour pickled mustard greens; see page 142), drained, rinsed, and patted dry

6 cups chicken broth (see page 168)

1 tablespoon Big Four Paste (page 86)

1 to 2 tablespoons soy sauce (optional)

¼ pound pork, thinly sliced across the grain

1 boneless, skinless chicken breast (approximately ½ pound), thinly sliced across the grain

2 ounces bean threads (glass noodles), softened in cool water and chopped into 2- to 3-inch lengths

3 scallions, cut into 1-inch pieces

½ pound medium shrimp, peeled and deveined

20 sprigs cilantro, coarsely chopped

The original version of Three Kings Soup called for three kinds of meat wrapped in small bundles of pickled mustard greens. In the past, pork and chicken were fattier and could withstand long periods of cooking without getting tough. Our meats today are leaner and more tender, so I have adapted the recipe while retaining its essence.

Adding a cup of softened bean threads (glass noodles) at the end is my own touch. Bean threads soaked in cold water will retain their shape and clump only slightly if stir-fried. Added to a soup, they will keep their shape as they expand. If bean threads are soaked in hot water, however, they will stick together when stir-fried and are almost certain to disappear in soup, especially if you use poor-quality bean threads, always a hit-or-miss experience.

To prepare the soup ahead, make the broth, but don't add the meat until the last minute. Let it sit for several hours or store overnight in the refrigerator to allow the flavors to blossom. Bring it back to a boil before adding pork, chicken, and shrimp. This is a marvelous soup to serve on a cool wintry day.

Roll the mustard greens, several at a time, into a cigar-shaped bundle and slice across into thin strands. Set aside.

In a 4-quart saucepan, bring the chicken broth to a boil over high heat. Add the pickled mustard greens, cover, and boil slowly over medium-low heat for 45 minutes.

Stir in the Big Four Paste. Taste for saltiness, and add soy sauce depending on your preference. Cover and boil slowly for another 30 minutes.

Increase the heat to medium, add the pork and chicken strips, cover and cook for 7 minutes, or until the meat is just cooked through. Add the bean threads and scallions and cook for another 5 minutes. Add the shrimp; as soon as they turn pink, remove from the heat. Ladle into a soup tureen, garnish with the coarsely chopped cilantro, and serve with cooked long-grain rice, preferably Thai jasmine or Indian or California basmati (see pages 37 and 38).

Keang Bah-Shaw
BEEF AND PUMPKIN STEW

Makes 6 servings

When I discuss *keang bah-shaw* with older Thai friends, their faces light up with pleasant memories, followed by a deep sigh as they lament, "We don't cook like that anymore." This is one of the oldest stew recipes, and it is reserved for special occasions. In the past, Thai people seldom ate beef, as cows, by helping to till and farm the land, were considered sacred friends of the farmers; only injured animals were slaughtered, and the meat was usually very tough. In this recipe, the beef is not only flavored as it slowly cooks in coconut milk, but tenderized.

The stew tastes best if it sits overnight in the refrigerator. Wait to add the squash and cilantro leaves until just before you are ready to serve.

In a large mixing bowl, combine the beef and Big Four Paste. Cover and marinate for a couple of hours in the refrigerator. Remove an hour before cooking to allow to come to room temperature.

In a 12-inch saucepan, heat the coconut milk over high heat until it begins to boil. Lower the heat to medium, add the beef, cover, and let simmer for an hour, or until the beef is tender.

Taste the soup and season with fish sauce and chiles, depending on your taste preference. Cover and let simmer for another 10 minutes. Increase the heat to medium, add the squash, cover, and let simmer for 15 to 20 minutes, or until the squash is tender but still firm.

Ladle the stew into a soup tureen. Garnish with the cilantro leaves and serve with cooked long-grain rice, preferably Thai jasmine or Indian or California basmati (see pages 37 and 38).

1 pound beef top sirloin or chuck roast, cut into 2-inch chunks (about 2 cups)

2 tablespoons Big Four Paste (page 86)

5 cups Fresh Unsweetened Coconut Milk (page 69)

2 to 3 tablespoons fish sauce (*namm pla*)

4 to 5 fresh bird chiles or 2 to 3 serrano chiles, lightly crushed

3 cups cubed kabocha squash or banana squash (1-inch pieces)

20 sprigs cilantro, coarsely chopped

Munn Gew Goong

THE ODD COUPLE: SHRIMP WONTON AND
PORK WITH JÍCAMA MEATBALL SOUP

Makes 6 servings

For the broth

2 pounds beef soup bones
6 cups bottled or filtered water
One ½-inch piece fresh ginger,
    thinly sliced
3 slices *kra-chay* (lesser galangal;
    see page 132), or an additional
    5 slices fresh ginger
3 scallions, coarsely chopped
1 teaspoon sea salt
1 tablespoon pickled Tien Jing
    salted cabbage (see page 143) or
    salt-packed capers, rinsed and
    drained
1 tablespoon sugar

For the wontons

½ pound medium shrimp, peeled
    and deveined
1 tablespoon Big Four Paste
    (page 86)
22 fresh wonton wrappers

For the meatballs (makes about 1 dozen)

½ pound ground pork or ground
    turkey
½ teaspoon sea salt
10 sprigs cilantro, minced
¼ cup minced jícama

20 sprigs cilantro, coarsely chopped

Thai cooking is a lot about surprising textures and flavors. This particular dish, with the soft and chewy texture of the wontons and the subtly pungent flavor of the ginger and the Big Four Paste, is a good example. The combination of ingredients may seem odd, but once you taste it, you will understand why it is easy to fall in love with Thai food.

You may want to do this recipe in stages. If making the stock ahead, let it cool completely before straining the liquid into a plastic or glass container (discard the bones). Seal tightly and refrigerate. It will keep for about a week. Or freeze the broth in a Ziploc bag, leaving room for the liquid to expand when it freezes. It will keep very well for about a month.

Put the soup bones in a large stockpot and cover them with tap water. Bring to a boil over high heat and boil, uncovered, for about 10 minutes. Pour the stock through a fine-mesh sieve. Discard the stock. Clean the pot well and return the bones to the pot. Fill the pot with the bottled water and bring it to a boil, skimming the foam from the surface until the broth is clear. Reduce the heat to a simmer, add the ginger, *kra-chay*, scallions, and sea salt, cover, and let simmer for at least 1 hour. Strain the broth into another large stockpot and discard the bones and solids.

Meanwhile, to prepare the wontons, fit a food processor with the steel blade and grind the shrimp and Big Four Paste to a paste. Transfer to a mixing bowl. Arrange the filling, the opened package of wonton wrappers, a bowl of cold water, and a cookie sheet next to your work area.

Place a wrapper in the palm of your hand, with one corner toward your middle finger. Put ½ to 1 teaspoon of filling just below that point, fold the wrapper over once, toward your wrist, to cover the filling, and then fold once more to form a triangle. Dab a drop of water on the left corner of the triangle. Fold the left corner over the right corner and press to seal. Place on the cookie sheet. Continue until you have 22 wontons.

For the meatballs, fit the food processor with the steel blade, and add the ground pork, sea salt, and cilantro, and pulse until the meat comes together in a ball, about 30 seconds. Transfer to a mixing bowl, add the jícama, and mix well.

To finish the soup, with wet hands, scoop up a teaspoon of the meatball mixture at a time, roll into a ball, and drop into the simmering broth. Let the broth come to a slow boil, then add the pickled cabbage and sugar. When the meatballs are cooked through, about 7 minutes, drop in half of the wontons, let the broth come back to a boil, and add the second batch. Cook for another 5 to 6 minutes, or until the wontons are translucent. Turn off the heat and ladle the soup into a soup tureen. Garnish with the chopped cilantro.

Cook's Notes

Wontons freeze well and are a great addition to soups; or deep-fry them for a quick and exotic appetizer. You may want to make more wontons than the amount suggested for this particular recipe. If so, double the filling recipe. Put the cookie sheet of wontons in the freezer. When they are completely frozen, transfer them to a Ziploc bag and return to the freezer; they will keep for a month. When ready to cook, just drop the still-frozen wontons into boiling water or deep-fry in hot oil.

You can prepare the filling ahead and store in a Ziploc bag in the refrigerator overnight.

Leftover wonton wrappers will keep for a week if well wrapped and refrigerated. You can also slice them into ribbons and add to soups. A sweet alternative is to deep-fry the wrappers in oil and dust with salt, sugar, and cinnamon for a snack.

Leftover jícama can be sliced into matchsticks and added to salads. Thais and Mexicans sprinkle large chunks of jícama with salt, sugar, and red chile powder. It makes a wonderful snack.

Keang Gai Faa

HEAVENLY CHICKEN STEW

Makes 6 servings

10 fresh bird chiles or 8 serrano
    chiles, minced
2 tablespoons Big Four Paste
    (page 86)
4 cloves garlic, minced
¼ cup vegetable oil
One 3-pound chicken, cut with a
    cleaver into bite-sized chunks,
    rinsed, and patted dry
1 cup cold water
2 tablespoons fish sauce (*namm pla*)
5 slices *kra-chay* (lesser galangal;
    see page 132) or one 1-inch piece
    fresh ginger, lightly pounded
3 New Mexico (California) chiles, cut
    into ⅛-inch-wide diagonal slices
¼ cup fresh chile leaves, left whole,
    or 10 arugula leaves, sliced into
    strands

Traditionally, *keang gai faa* required an old hen, seasoned with chile leaves, to be cooked a very long time. I use a regular three-pound fryer, which is more tender, has more meat, and does not take as long to cook. I treasure this old-fashioned dish for its touch of elegance and its slightly bitter-pungent taste, which has been lost in modern Thai cooking. This particular taste is achieved by using young tender chile leaves for cooking or as garnishes for salty-acidic-peppery recipes. I learned to use chile leaves from older traditional Thai cooks who add chile leaves by the handful to stews, spicy curries, and salads. Unless you grow your own chile plants, arugula leaves are a fair substitute.

The amount of chiles depends on your preference. Three to four chiles gives a mild flavor, while 10 chiles will make the stew medium-spicy. The dish holds well and can be made in advance. If you plan to reheat it, wait to add the New Mexico chiles and chile leaves (or arugula strands) until the stew is heated through.

Using a mortar and pestle, pound the chiles, Big Four Paste, and garlic together into a paste. Transfer to a small bowl and set aside.

Heat a 12-inch skillet over high heat for 2 minutes, or until when you put your hand about 2 inches above the skillet, you can feel the heat. Add the oil and heat for 1 minute. Add the chile paste and cook, stirring quickly, until the paste exudes an aroma, about 30 seconds; avoid burning the paste. Add the chicken pieces and brown for about 5 minutes, turning the pieces to brown them evenly. Add the water, fish sauce, and *kra-chay*. When the water begins to boil, lower the heat and cook until the liquid is reduced by half, about 20 minutes.

Add the chiles, stirring to mix, and cook until the liquid is reduced to the consistency of a thick sauce, 7 to 8 minutes. Top with the chile leaves, stir to mix, and transfer to a serving platter. Serve with cooked long-grain rice, preferably Thai jasmine or Indian or California basmati (see pages 37 and 38).

Kreang Kang
SIDE DISHES

Kreang kang, or side dishes, are included in a traditional Thai meal to complement a soup or stew and chile water. When planning a meal, Thai cooks will select meat, poultry, or seafood to be cooked by itself or with seasonal vegetables for a side dish.

Pakk Boog Fai Daeng
RED-HOT STIR-FRIED SWAMP SPINACH

Makes 6 servings

During World War II, when Bangkok was being bombed, my parents moved from their home on Siphraya Road to the countryside. There were times when the bombing was so severe that they could not ride the riverboat to the market in the city, so my mother picked wild greens and *pakk boog*, or swamp spinach, along the riverbanks, which she cooked in endless ways. Years later, my father credited *pakk boog* for saving them from starvation.

Heat a 12-inch skillet over high heat for 2 minutes, or until when you put your hands 1 to 2 inches above the skillet, you can feel the heat. Add the oil and heat for 1 minute, then add the unpeeled crushed garlic and cook, stirring quickly, for 30 seconds before adding the minced garlic. Cook for another 30 seconds, or until all the garlic is golden and the peels are crispy, taking care not to burn the garlic. Add the Big Four Paste, red miso, and chiles, and mix and stir for another minute, or until fragrant. Add the spinach, and stir and toss for another 2 to 3 minutes, or until the leaves are limp but still crunchy. Transfer to a serving platter and serve hot.

¼ cup vegetable oil
7 cloves garlic, 3 minced,
  4 unpeeled, lightly crushed
1 tablespoon Big Four Paste
  (page 86)
1 teaspoon red miso
6 fresh bird chiles or 4 serrano
  chiles, 3 (or 2) minced,
  3 (or 2) lightly crushed
1 bunch (about 2 pounds) swamp
  spinach (see page 18) or
  1½ bunches (about 1½ pounds)
  spinach, with stems and leaves,
  rinsed, and thoroughly dried
  (about 6 cups)

Seur Rong Hai
CRYING TIGER

Makes 6 servings

2 teaspoons dried green
  peppercorns
1 tablespoon Big Four Paste
  (page 86)
10 cloves garlic, 5 minced,
  5 unpeeled, lightly crushed
3 to 20 fresh bird chiles or
  2 to 15 serrano chiles, minced
1 pound boneless, skinless large
  chicken breasts, rinsed and
  patted dry
¼ cup vegetable oil
1 teaspoon fish sauce (*namm pla*)
1 tablespoon sugar
Water as needed
2 tablespoons crispy pork rinds,
  crushed to the consistency of
  coarse cornmeal
20 sprigs cilantro, coarsely chopped

This dish is a true Bangkok creation because of its intense flavors. The chiles must be hot enough to make one howl like a tiger but, at the same time, balanced with a blend of sweet-salty flavors to lessen the fire. Fresh peppercorns give a lingering sensation of warmth.

The original recipe uses fresh Thai green peppercorns. They can be purchased preserved in brine in many Asian markets but may have lost most of their flavor. I prefer dried green peppercorns, available in larger supermarkets. When roasted, they are hotter and produce a lingering heat. If you want slightly weepy tiger (mild), use 2 to 3 fresh bird or serrano chiles; for crying tiger (medium), use 5 to 6 chiles; and for the real howling tiger (very spicy), 15 to 20 chiles or more! The crispy pork rinds used for garnish can be found in the chips section of most supermarkets.

In a small skillet, dry-roast the green peppercorns over medium heat until fragrant, about 2 minutes. Set aside to cool.

Put the Big Four Paste and the minced garlic in a mortar and pound until blended into a paste. Add the unpeeled garlic cloves and pound until the garlic and peels are blended into the paste. Do not worry if the membrane is separated from the cloves. (You may want to remove the peel; I encourage you to try it the authentic Thai way. It may seem unusual, but the reward is the wonderful texture and added taste of delicious crispy garlic peel.) Add the chiles and continue pounding. Add the green peppercorns and, instead of pounding, crush them by pressing them against the side of the mortar in a circular motion. Transfer the paste to a small bowl and set aside. The paste will keep well in a jar with a tight-fitting lid in the refrigerator for a couple of weeks.

Trim any fat from the chicken breast. Cut the breast in half. Working with one half-breast at a time, slice horizontally almost but not quite in half. Open the meat up into a butterfly shape. Put your hand firmly on top of the meat and press down on it to flatten it. Using a very sharp knife, held at a 75-degree angle to the work surface, slice thinly against the grain into 2 to 3 long pieces. Try to keep the pieces the same size and thickness. Set aside on a plate.

Arrange the ingredients near the stove in the order they will go into the skillet: oil, chile paste, chicken, fish sauce, sugar, and a small cup of water.

Heat a 12-inch skillet over high heat for 2 minutes, or until when you put your hand an inch or so above it, you can feel the heat. Add the oil, then add the chile paste, stirring it quickly, until it turns slightly brown and fragrant, 2 to 3 minutes. Add the chicken, lower the heat to medium, and sprinkle a bit of water into the pan to prevent the paste from burning. Try to keep the chicken pieces flat as you sauté them to ensure even cooking. When the chicken is browned, push it to one side of the skillet and add the fish sauce and sugar to the center of the skillet. Stir and blend until the mixture bubbles, then push the chicken pieces into it while you continue to stir until the chicken is coated. If needed, sprinkle a bit more water over it to prevent sticking. Transfer the chicken to a serving platter, garnish with the crushed pork rind and cilantro, and serve hot.

Padd Neur Gai Sai Sen

OMELET STUFFED WITH STIR-FRIED CHICKEN AND BEAN THREADS

Makes 2 servings

For the filling

¼ cup vegetable oil

1 tablespoon Big Four Paste (page 86)

½ pound boneless, skinless chicken breast, sliced lengthwise into paper-thin strips

½ pound medium shrimp, peeled, deveined, and cut into small pieces

2 ounces chicken liver, thinly sliced lengthwise

2 fresh bird chiles or 1 serrano chile, minced (with seeds—fewer seeds for moderately spicy, more for hotter)

1 teaspoon sugar

1 tablespoon fish sauce (*namm pla*)

2 whole scallions, thinly sliced on the diagonal

2 ounces bean threads (glass noodles), softened in cold water and cut into 2- to 3-inch lengths

For the omelet

4 large eggs

Sea salt

2 tablespoons vegetable oil

For the garnishes

2 whole scallions, trimmed

10 to 12 thin slices cucumber

10 to 12 sprigs cilantro

King Chulalongkhorn was the first Thai monarch to travel abroad. While visiting Europe in 1897, His Majesty wrote to the Queen frequently, sharing his experiences, including detailed accounts of foreign foods and fascinating new ways of cooking. In one letter, he described an omelet that had been served to him on the ship. After his return, the Royal Kitchen tried to duplicate the dish, but with a Thai touch. Duck eggs were used instead of chicken, and chicken liver was used in the filling. You may omit it, but I encourage you to try it. The combination of textures and flavors is unlike any Western omelet filling.

Arrange the filling ingredients, in the order they are listed, near the stove. Heat a 12-inch skillet over high heat. Put your hand about 2 inches above the skillet. When you can feel the heat, the skillet is ready for frying. Add the oil and heat it for a minute. Add the Big Four Paste and cook, stirring, until fragrant, about 1 minute. Add the chicken and cook, stirring, until the meat turns white, about 2 minutes. Add the shrimp and cook, stirring, until it turns slightly pink, about 1 minute. Add the liver and cook, stirring, until the shrimp are bright pink and the liver has browned, about 1 minute. Add the chiles, sugar, and fish sauce, mixing well, and reduce the heat to low. Add the scallions and mix well, then add the bean threads and mix well (they will clump slightly). Transfer the filling to a bowl, cover, and keep warm.

Put 2 of the eggs in a small bowl, put the remaining 2 in another small bowl, and beat well. Add a pinch of salt to each bowl and mix well. Clean and dry the skillet, then heat it until very hot. Add 1 tablespoon of the oil and when the oil begins to smoke, add one bowl of the beaten eggs, swirling quickly to make a paper-thin film in the skillet. Lower the heat and shake the pan to loosen the omelet; use a spatula to loosen the edges. When the eggs start to set and the bottom of the omelet is slightly browned, 1 to 2 minutes, immediately slide it onto a big plate, brown side down. Spoon half of the filling into the center. Fold the sides over the filling to make a square. Gently slide the spatula under the folded omelet, put your hand over the top to secure the folds, and invert onto a serving plate. Repeat to make the other omelet. Garnish with the scallions, cucumber slices, and cilantro sprigs and serve hot.

Padd Goong Gup Nor Mai

STIR-FRIED SHRIMP WITH BAMBOO SHOOTS

Makes 6 servings

In Hua-Hin, a seaside resort an hour from Bangkok, there is a family-owned restaurant that specializes in fresh seafood prepared with seasonal vegetables and herbs. One year during a weeklong stay in Hua-Hin I ate dinner there every night and never had the same dish twice. This dish was among my favorites. It's nearly impossible to get fresh bamboo shoots in America, but canned bamboo shoots work fairly well. A good substitute for bamboo shoots is fresh broccoli stems.

In a medium mixing bowl, combine the shrimp with Big Four Paste and toss to coat. Cover and refrigerate for at least 20 minutes or up to 3 hours.

Trim any brown spots from the outer layers of the bamboo shoots. Slice into ⅛-inch-thick circles, then slice into matchsticks. Set aside in a small bowl.

Arrange the ingredients near the stove in the order they will be added to the pan: oil, garlic, shrimp, bamboo shoots, fish sauce, scallions, cilantro, and water.

Heat a 12-inch skillet over high heat for 1 to 2 minutes, then add the oil and heat to 300° to 325°F. (You can also test for readiness by dipping the tip of a wooden spoon into the oil; if there are tiny bubbles around it, it is ready for frying.) Add the garlic and cook, stirring, until lightly browned, 10 to 15 seconds. Increase the heat to high, add the shrimp, and cook, stirring quickly to ensure even cooking, until pink, about 2 minutes. If the shrimp seem to be cooking too quickly, add just a touch of water. Add the bamboo shoots and cook, tossing and stirring, about 2 minutes, adding more water if needed to prevent sticking. Add the fish sauce and scallions. When the scallions are limp, turn off the heat, add the cilantro, and mix well. Immediately transfer the stir-fry to a serving platter and serve.

1 pound medium shrimp, peeled and deveined
1 tablespoon Big Four Paste (page 86)
One 20-ounce can whole bamboo shoots, drained, salted, and rinsed thoroughly
¼ cup vegetable oil
3 cloves garlic, peeled and lightly crushed
1 tablespoon fish sauce (*namm pla*)
2 scallions, sliced into 2-inch pieces
15 sprigs cilantro, coarsely chopped
⅓ cup cold water, if needed

Pla Duk Padd Pedd Ka-Min
SOUTHERN THAI–STYLE CATFISH FILLETS

Makes 6 servings

2 tablespoons Big Four Paste
(page 86)

1 lemon or 2 limes, juiced and
sliced

1½ pounds (about 3 large pieces)
catfish fillets

One 1-inch chunk fresh turmeric,
peeled and very thinly sliced, or
1 teaspoon turmeric powder

1 stalk lemongrass, green parts and
hard outer layers removed,
minced

6 to 7 fresh red bird chiles or
4 to 5 serrano chiles, seeded (or
leave seeds in for a very spicy
result) and minced

¼ cup vegetable oil

2 tablespoons palm sugar or light
brown sugar

¼ cup thick tamarind juice (see
page 128)

1 tablespoon fish sauce (*namm pla*)

4 kaffir lime leaves, slightly torn, or
grated zest of 1 lime

½ cup dry white wine, such as
Chardonnay, or white vermouth

Recently I received a telephone call from a man in Washington, D.C., who had just returned from a vacation in Thailand and could not get one particular dish he'd eaten in southern Thailand out of his mind. He described the dish in vivid detail, from the color to the distinct layers of flavor. After listening, I knew exactly what he had eaten in that restaurant in southern Thailand. Here is the dish that won the heart of a young man from Washington, D.C. I love it too.

The seasoning paste can be made ahead and refrigerated in a jar with a tight-fitting lid for a couple of weeks.

On a large platter, mix 1 tablespoon of the Big Four Paste with the lemon juice. Add the catfish fillets, turning them in the mixture to coat thoroughly. Lay the lemon slices on top of the fish, cover, and set aside. Or, if you are working ahead, cover and refrigerate until ready to cook.

Using a mortar and pestle, pound the lemongrass to a paste. (The lemongrass is pounded first without any liquid, but when the Big Four Paste is added, the liquid will help the lemongrass disintegrate even more.) Add the remaining 1 tablespoon Big Four Paste and pound until blended into a smooth paste. Scrape down the sides of the mortar as needed, mixing well. Add the chiles and pound to a paste, scraping and mixing. Add the turmeric and continue to pound until the mixture turns into a paste. Transfer to a small bowl and set aside.

Drain the marinade liquid from the catfish into a small bowl and add the lemon slices. Line up the ingredients near the stove in the order they are to be added: oil, fish, chile paste, marinade liquid and lemon slices, palm sugar, tamarind juice, fish sauce, kaffir lime leaves, and white wine. Set a 12-inch skillet over high heat for 2 minutes, or until when you place your hand 1 to 2 inches above it, you feel the heat. Add the oil and heat for another minute. Put the catfish gently into the hot oil and cook on each side for 2 to 3 minutes, until the outside turns white and the fish is just partially cooked. Lower the heat if the oil is too hot.

Transfer the catfish to a platter. Add the chile paste to the hot oil and cook, stirring quickly, for a minute, or less, until fragrant. Add the reserved marinade and lemon slices, the sugar, tamarind juice, and fish sauce and stir. Add the kaffir lime leaves and wine. When the liquid comes to a boil, taste to make sure the flavors are well balanced: salty-spicy-sweet-sour. Push the lemon slices aside, return the fish fillets to the skillet, and turn to coat them with the sauce. Cover the pan and cook for another 3 to 4 minutes, until the sauce is thickened. Reduce the heat to low, uncover the pan, and cook for 5 minutes, until the fish is cooked. Turn off the heat, discard the lemon slices, and transfer the fish and the sauce to a serving platter.

The Thai Philosophy of Food

Fresh fish . . . bright eyes shiny gills

Succulent shrimp . . . plump verdant tail

Tender greens . . . crisp splendid spray

Thick rind . . . find barren fruits

Why lament . . . savor curry with bitter rind

**Translated from *Mae Khloa Hoa Paa*
(*Head Cook from the Forest*),
between 1868 and 1900**

The Thai philosophy of food can be summed up in two words: *arroy*, which means "delicious," and *sanuk*, meaning "fun." In Thailand, delicious, fun cooking is accomplished through seasonings, flavors, aromas, and textures.

While writing this cookbook, I invited friends who love Thai food to sample the results from my recipe testing. Their reactions were always the same: love at first bite. On and on, they would rave until their plates were empty. The joy my friends expressed in eating traditional Thai food is what Thai home cooking is all about. It's what I love about my country's exquisite cuisine, and why I savor each gastronomic moment when I visit.

Awaiting my annual homecoming, my friends and family seek out restaurants and homes of friends to share with me. Their selections are always wonderful, but one outing to Chojjitr, a Thai restaurant in Bangkok, was unforgettable. Chojjitr exemplifies the very best of traditional Thai home cooking. The food was truly delicious and fun, and much more. There was *kurn jaa tong pai doey kan,* a blending and balancing. The dishes were superbly seasoned, with each flavored to balance the other, but with elements of contrast and surprise evident throughout the entire meal.

Chojjitr is an exceptional restaurant. Its history portrays the kinship between a great healer and home cook. Knowing how to use and mix herbs and spices is vital to both. The owner's grandfather was a famous herbalist and great cook. Friends and acquaintances who came to him for healing often begged to stay for dinner. One thing led to another, and the herbalist's dispensary became a restaurant eponymously named. The name Chojjitr means "fortune" (*choj*) and "heart and mind" (*jitr*). For over a hundred years, one generation after another, the family has been trained as both herbalists and superb cooks.

My first meal at Chojjitr was on a hot and muggy night after several hours of being stuck in horrendous traffic. To make matters worse, I was suffering from jet lag. Our dishes were carefully chosen by my friend and the owner, reflecting the traditional Thai cook's training to select and prepare dishes with the best seasonal ingredients available. Our host's responsibility as a healer, was to make certain that her foods enhanced our health, and as a cook, that her dishes were also delicious. As we ate, she kept asking me how I was feeling. After the meal, I realized that the drag of jet lag was gone, and I felt rejuvenated and didn't even notice the oppressive heat anymore. I inquired as to how she had worked such a miracle, not only thrilling my taste buds, but healing my body, and that's how I learned the story of her grandfather and the restaurant's background in healing.

My dinner at Chojjitr set me on a quest to discover why and how Thai food came to be what it is today. I wanted to know what made this cuisine so different and special. How, I wondered, had such plain, simple cooking turned into a culinary wonder? From where did the complex and multiple layers of flavors laced with contrasting and surprising textures come?

Many books have been written claiming that Thai food is a combination of Indian and Chinese cooking. I don't believe this, but I do agree the Thais incorporated elements of these cuisines. Long before these two nations influenced the cultural and social fabric of the Thai, however, the Mon, the original inhabitants of the land, ruled a mighty and highly developed civilized nation. They were the first and foremost influence. But it was the definite taste preferences and philosophy of the Thai people themselves that ultimately defined their food.

The process began with the nobility. Impelled to demonstrate their status, and with wealth to enjoy a superior lifestyle, the Thai royalty used food as a means to set them apart from both commoners and foreigners. Unlike contemporary Thailand, until the nineteenth century, the country was predominantly an agricultural society. There was only a handful of important cities where trade and nonagricultural activities occurred. The social structure of the underpopulated country was designed to control labor, not land. Commoners were indentured into the service of a leader, who might be a member of the Royal Court or a noble. When not toiling free for the leader, or off fighting wars, the Thai people lived simply in isolated and self-sustaining communities. Everyone had their own home and land, where rice, vegetables, fruit, and coconut trees were grown. Their diet was occasionally supplemented with meat and fish seasoned with wild herbs and spices foraged from the jungle, but usually they ate very simple food, not only because that was what they had, but also for health reasons, as a guard against the harsh climate and primitive environment. Cultivating the art of dining was not in their interest or grasp until progress came knocking.

Changes first took place in the capital and major cities where the Royal Court, the nobility, and foreign communities were located. During the reign of King Narai in 1656–1688, foreign relations reached its zenith, and that was when the greatest revolution in Thai food took place. The king, a shrewd diplomat, cultivated, encouraged, and sanctioned foreign settlements for political and economic reasons. To counterbalance several aggressive nations that were attempting to monopolize the trade routes by colonizing newly explored countries, he employed many foreigners as his counsels.

Since trade was also important to his war chest, he attempted to control it within the kingdom by appointing Thai-born descendants of foreign ancestors to oversee the trading markets: Chinese, Japanese, Portuguese, Muslims, Indians, Dutch, and Malays. Living in designated communities authorized by the king, with their own governing bodies, they seldom socialized with the commoners. Many of the king's appointees, however, married Thai women.

It was within this small and isolated population that Thai food, as we know it today, germinated, grew, and evolved. It was among these elite groups that new foreign ingredients and cooking tools were first introduced. Skeptical about the foods at first, the commoners then began to try and cultivate them. The era of foreign infusion came to an end when King Narai's chief advisor, a Greek, was found guilty of conspiracy and executed. After the king's death, foreigners were expelled from Siam.

Even though the door was once again closed to foreign influences, descendants of foreigners were assimilated into the society, and with them their foods. The result was a wealth of new styles of cooking, which were carried on, and adapted by, Thai cooks and flourished until Siam was conquered by Burma in 1767. Two years later, when Siam once again emerged as a nation, fragments of the past, especially in cooking, were pieced together and reinstituted as Thai cuisine. The crowning recognition of traditional Thai cuisine came in 1809, when King Rama I celebrated the dedication of the famous Emerald Buddha, brought to Bangkok from the vassal state of Laos, with a sumptuous meal. The menu included chile water, soup, curries, and desserts, including coconut custards and banana chips, and other dishes similar to those the Thai people eat today.

Today, Thai food is one of the best examples of fusion cooking. The result of two hundred years of development, it reflects the influence of centuries of foreigners passing through and settling on the land. Bringing new ideas, methods, and ingredients, they all helped mold and shape Thai food. This continuous adaptation and use of new foods affirms Thai cooks as probably the world's greatest assimilators. The Thais love trying new things, selecting and accepting the best from outsiders and making these their own.

Some food historians believe that in addition to historical influences, the Thais' partiality to intense and sharp flavors is related to the tropical heat. Having grown up in the harsh climate, I can agree, remembering my mother having to coax us to eat. I also remember the attention she paid to the weather when planning the menu or cooking a meal. We ate smaller amounts when the weather was very hot, and more when the air was cool.

Her philosophy of food was similar to that of the proprietor of Chojjitr Restaurant, and of Thai cooks from the ancient time: Food is eaten first for health. Serving dishes that taste good is a pleasurable, yet secondary achievement.

Another reason given for the unique composition of Thai food is the ancient practice of betel-nut chewing. Until this common habit was banned during the reign of King Vajiravudh, Rama VI (1910–1925), every Thai adult indulged in this addictive substance. The pungent and biting taste of the nut, which stained and darkened the teeth and mouth, had a numbing effect, muting the taste buds and curbing the appetite. To make up for the lost sensitivity to taste, food historians have concluded, Thai cooking had to appeal to the other senses. Food had to stimulate both vision and the sense of smell. Thai food can be blue, red, pink, and purple. Snacks and desserts are heavily perfumed with blossoms and scented candles. Fishy, acidic, or pickled smells, as well as burnt aromas, are believed to stimulate the appetite. And the textures in one Thai meal may range from watery, foamy, fluffy, chewy, crispy, and leathery to spongy, slimy, and oily. The surprising jolting, continuous onslaught of textures, perfumes, colors, and flavors is designed to arouse all the senses.

I like to believe that the creative energy that produces the multiple layers of tastes, aromas, and texture come from the joyful spirits of the Thai people. They are Buddhists who believe that life is marked by suffering, impermanence, and constant change. Thus they seek or grasp at every chance to celebrate joy, pleasure, and happiness. Good food and the community spirits of sharing reflect this philosophy.

Arroy in Thai can mean simply delicious, as mentioned earlier, but it can also imply tickling fun, maddening, memorable, and touching one's heart. *Sanuk,* on the other hand, is really the essence of the true Thai philosophy and more difficult to translate. It refers not just to having fun, but to moments of silly, youthful, and spiritual *joie de vivre*. It also means to bring pleasure. When this philosophy is applied to food, the meal is not only delicious, but also distinct and unique for the occasion.

Contrast and Surprise

The fun of cooking Thai food is in part the discovery of a new world of exotic ingredients. Cooking the recipes in this chapter, you'll learn how and why the Thais use certain ingredients. Perhaps you have heard of, eaten, or cooked with some of them before. Some will seem familiar. However, the majority of these dishes are ancient recipes passed down from family members and friends. As you become familiar with the ingredients, you'll want to experiment and incorporate them according to your taste.

Following are the ingredients most commonly used as seasonings, flavorings, and aromatics and to add texture. When used in combination, the results are dishes with harmonious tastes, yet full of contrasting and surprising elements.

One of the reasons Westerners enjoy Thai food is the marvelous and intense flavors. As you get to know these new ingredients, you may use them to add punch, excitement, and surprise to all your cooking. Many are now available in supermarkets. However, you will need to purchase some in an Asian market or from mailorder sources (see page 313). Shopping in Asian markets can be frustrating or intimidating, as items are identified in various Asian languages, but most Asian markets have English-speaking personnel. Ask for the stock person with responsibility in the particular department that has the ingredients you wish to purchase. Be polite, but persistent. Often, when a salesclerk cannot understand what you want, the inclination is just to say, "No, we do not have it." Don't take "No" for an answer; ask to speak to the store manager. Patience and meticulous attention to the purchase of cooking ingredients is part of Thai culture. Shopping in Asian markets may likewise endow you with a new experience in patience, as well as culinary expertise.

Seasonings

Although still based on the traditional basic Big Four Seasonings of salt, garlic, cilantro root, and Thai white peppercorns used in ancient Thai cooking, today's Thai food is more refined and complex. Saltiness is never simply salty, but part of a wide range of saltiness—salty like the sea, or with a fishy aroma, or earthy.

To further enhance flavors, the Thais build layer upon layer of seasonings, beginning with a combination of two basic tastes, salty and peppery, and adding other enticing aromas. Thai cooks seldom use simply salt and pepper, but usually add numerous seasonings to achieve a combination of particular flavors even in the simplest dishes. Old Thai cookbooks sometimes included an instruction at the end of a recipe specifying the dish's predominant taste, followed by secondary and third flavors, as well as cautioning the reader on which specific flavors should never be used. The following are the tastes and flavors most commonly used in Thai cooking, and used in the recipes in the book.

SALTY TASTE

GLURH—SALT: Sea salt and mined salt. For detailed information, see page 84.

SALTY-SEA FLAVOR

PLA-RAH—FERMENTED FISH: Today, this ancient seasoning is identified with the food of northeastern Thailand, where it's made and used more than in other Thai regions. When the rainy season arrives, the rivers and ponds are swarming with fish. To preserve them for future use, cooks make *pla-rah*. Usually small fish are used. They are washed, packed with salt in an earthenware jar, and set in the sun for one to two days, then rinsed and repacked tightly with salt and roasted rice powder, in a sealed earthenware jar. After about a month, the fermented fish is ready for use. It will keep for up to a year in its original earthenware jar, stored in a cool place away from the sun. Small amounts are used as seasonings for soups, stir-fries, and curries and to make briny, salty-tasting sauces.

Fermented fish is sold in glass jars in Asian markets. Read the label before buying; some use artificial preservatives. If possible, buy naturally fermented fish. Store in the refrigerator, keeping the jar tightly sealed, and wrap in plastic wrap to prevent the smell from permeating other foods. Anchovies or sardines packed in salt are a good substitute.

KRAPI—FERMENTED SHRIMP PASTE OR PLANKTON: Each region of Thailand near the ocean is prized for its fermented shrimp paste. Shrimp pastes range in color from slightly pink to dark purple. Some are made with baby shrimp, others with all sizes or with shrimp fragments.

Good fermented shrimp paste is slightly pungent, but not overpowering. It is very salty and a little goes a long way. Shrimp paste is the classic binder for curry paste. Recipes are very specific about which type of shrimp paste is to be used. A popular chile water, *Namm Prikk Krapi* (page 192), made with fermented shrimp paste and very hot chiles, is eaten with seasonal raw vegetables, grilled mackerel, and rice.

Unfortunately, exporters believe that American consumers are naïve about the quality of shrimp paste and will accept any grade. Consequently, the choices of shrimp paste are limited to a few brands from Thailand, Vietnam, and the Philippines, and these are often of inferior quality. Fermented shrimp paste from Thailand is sold in small plastic containers approximately the size of a can of tuna, labeled either white or dark shrimp paste. I always buy the white variety, which is less salty. When you open it, notice how the top is sealed with a layer of paraffin. Pry it loose and save it to reseal the paste; this will keep the shrimp paste from drying out and preserve the aroma. Seal tightly and wrap in plastic before refrigerating. Red miso, or Japanese bean paste, available in Asian and organic markets, as well as some large supermarkets, is a good substitute. Like shrimp paste, red miso or Japanese bean paste will keep refrigerated for months.

NAMM PLA—FISH SAUCE: Ocean fish make the better-quality fish sauces. Tightly packed in sea salt, the fish are sealed in an earthenware jar and allowed to ferment for a couple of weeks. The resulting liquid is drained and boiled with seasonings to enhance the flavor, then bottled and left in the sun to ripen for another 2 to 3 months. The best fish sauce is prized for its light, clear color and slightly briny, fishy taste.

There are many kinds of fish sauce from China, Vietnam, the Philippines, and Thailand. Read the label and buy one without preservatives. Look for a clear light brown liquid. Refrigerate after opening. When the liquid turns dark, discard it. (For more details, see page 96.)

SALTY-FERMENTED TASTE

TOW CHEW—FERMENTED BEAN PASTE, OR SAUCE: To make bean paste, soybeans are mixed with salt, rice powder, and, sometimes, sugar and fermented. Fermented bean sauce is made from whole beans; some turn yellow while others turn brown. Both come packaged in a jar. Bean paste, which is sometimes also labeled bean sauce, is made from pureed beans. The pastes may be packaged in jars or cans and are less salty, with a fermented scent and pasty flavor. Fermented beans, with the liquid extracted, pressed into thin round sheets, and dried, are often used in place of fermented shrimp or fish in vegetarian cooking. The flavor is very intense. Although Thai cooking uses Chinese-style bean paste, red miso or Japanese bean paste can be used as a substitute for fermented bean paste. Store fermented bean paste or sauce in the refrigerator after opening. It will keep for months.

NAMM SEE EWE—SOY SAUCE: There are two kinds of soy sauce. The clear or light-colored variety is called *namm see ewe sai. Namm see ewe dum*, the dark sauce, is a thicker sauce. Not all soy sauces are the same either in quality or taste. Taste before using. Soy sauce from Japan tastes and smells like soybeans, while soy sauces from China are saltier and have a less musty, yeasty aroma. Thai soy sauces vary in taste. Since they are fairly inexpensive, experiment to find your own favorite. After opening it, I keep soy sauce in the refrigerator.

SALTY-SWEET FLAVOR

NAMM SEE EWE WANN—SWEET SOY SAUCE: Sweet soy sauce is available as a thin liquid, which is less sweet, or a thicker liquid, processed with molasses. This sauce is used in combination with salty soy sauce for noodle or stir-fried dishes. Keep at room temperature in your pantry.

SOUR FLAVOR

NAMM SOM SAI CHU—DISTILLED RICE VINEGAR: Made from fermented rice grains, this clear liquid has a sharp, clean taste. Rice vinegar from Thailand is less intense than that from China or Japan. You can use distilled white vinegar or cider vinegar as a substitute. Store in the pantry at room temperature.

SOUR-BITTER TASTE

SOM MEN—BITTER ORANGE: This is actually an immature tangerine. The rind is aromatic, bitter, and acidic; the juice is sour and bitter. Old Thai recipes often used it in combination with calamondin, *som saa* (see below), instead of lime. Old-timers claim that in order to allow the best fruit on tangerine trees to mature, smaller immature fruits would be picked and thrown into streams alongside the orchards; villagers downstream hauled the decaying fruits from the water and used them for cooking—hence the name *som men*, which means "smelly orange." You can substitute unripe oranges or kumquat. Refrigerated in the vegetable bin, bitter orange will keep for a couple of weeks.

NAMM MAH-KRUD—KAFFIR LIME JUICE: Intensely acidic, bitter, and sour, this juice is used in curries, hot-sour soups, salads, and sauces. It's believed to relieve congestion, cleanse the lungs, and settle the stomach. The juice can also be used as a rinse to darken hair and make it shiny. The juice of unripe grapefruits or limes is a fair substitute. Kaffir lime juice can be stored in a container with a tight-fitting lid in the freezer for several months.

SOUR-FRUITY TASTE

SOM SAA—CALAMONDIN OR KALAMANSI: These miniature oranges have a thick green rind. In Thailand, orange rinds never turn orange because of the humidity. Traditionally, calamondin rind was used for its citrus, acidic, and bitter taste. The delicate sweet-sour juice is used in combination with bitter orange, tamarind juice, and/or lime juice in salad dressings. Oddly enough, calamondin is rapidly disappearing from Thai cooking but is now available in Asian and farmers' markets in California. The peel of the Western variety is orange and tends to be less bitter, and the juice is sweeter. Taste before using. Substitute unripe orange or blood orange for calamondin. Store it the same way as any orange.

NAMM SOM MAPLOW—COCONUT VINEGAR: This opaque white liquid, made from coconut juice, is sour with a slightly sweet flavor and fruity aroma. It is used for salad dressings or as seasoning for seafood. Refrigerate after opening.

MADAN—GARCINIA: This fruit resembles an oval green plum. Crisp and very sour, it is eaten raw. Thinly sliced strands are added to salads, stir-fried noodle dishes, or fried rice. Pounded with chiles and shrimp paste, it is used for chile water and added to curries or hot-and-sour soup. Fermented, the fruit is made into a snack or added to clear soups. *Madan* is available during the summer months in Asian markets. Use unripe green plums or nectarines for a substitute.

MAH-NOW—LIME: Limes from Thailand are small and more similar to Key limes and Mexican limes than to supermarket limes. The skin is thin, shiny, and acidic, with a slightly bitter and sour taste. When using the juice in a recipe, taste it first and add accordingly. Fresh limes should feel firm but not hard; when squeezed, they should yield a bit to pressure. Keep in the refrigerator. Thai cooks suggest immersing limes in a bowl of lukewarm water before juicing, which makes it possible to extract more of the juice.

MAH-ENG OR *MA-WAENG KHRUEA*—SOLANACEAE: This fruit is from the same family as tomatoes and chiles. Slightly smaller than a Bing cherry, it turns yellow when ripe and is covered with fine fuzzy hair. The peeled and sliced fruit is added to fermented shrimp paste and chiles to make chile water. It is used to season pungent sour-salty soups or added to salad dressing. Sometimes used as a diuretic, *mah-eng* is occasionally available during the summer months in Asian markets. Tamarillo is a good substitute.

SWEET FLAVOR

NAMM TANN SAI—SUGAR: Thai sugar, made from sugarcane, is coarser and slightly darker than other types of cane sugar. It is usually used in combination with palm sugar. Keep it in a glass jar with a tight-fitting lid in your pantry.

SWEET-FLORAL FLAVOR

NAMM TANN PIPP—PALM SUGAR: Palm sugar is made from the sap of the sugar palm tree, boiled until it turns into a thick brown syrup. Fresh palm sugar is displayed in Thai markets in large mounds. The sticky mass is scraped up with a wooden paddle and smeared onto fresh banana leaves. For wholesale use, palm sugar is sold in large tin containers—thus it's called *namm tann pipp*, tin can sugar! In Asian markets here, palm sugar is sold in small round crystallized blocks or in clear plastic jars. It's very sweet, with a fruity, floral aroma; it is used to flavor, color, and perfume various dishes. Maple syrup and light and dark brown sugar are acceptable substitutes. Store palm sugar in a Ziploc bag in your pantry.

SWEET-SOUR-FRUITY FLAVOR

MAH-KHAM—TAMARIND: Both the tender pods and the leaves of this leguminous tree are used in cooking. The unripe pods are made into chile water. Young tender leaves are eaten raw, added to soups, curries, or salads. The pods ripen during the cool season, and prized crops may be given names such as "golden pods." They measure about 6 to 7 inches and curl into a curve as they mature.

Ripe tamarind is eaten raw. The hard shell is cracked open like an eggshell, revealing a dark yellow or reddish-brown sticky flesh that tastes like sweet-tart preserves. Inside each pod is a shiny dark pitted seed. For cooking, purchase the compressed brown blocks of tamarind wrapped in cellophane, available in Asian markets. Do not buy prepared tamarind juice in jars. It is not really tamarind, and it tastes terrible.

To make tamarind juice, break off a chunk of tamarind, pour hot water over it, and let it sit for 15 to 20 minutes, until softened. When the water has cooled, massage the tamarind to release the pulp. Let it sit for another 15 minutes, for the juice to thicken. Place the softened tamarind pulp and the juice in a glass jar and refrigerate until needed; it will keep for a couple weeks. As you use the juice, add more water to replace what you've removed. The first time you use the juice, it will have a stronger flavor than later and be thick, like applesauce. After 3 to 4 replenishments, the juice will be as thin as buttermilk. At this point, it's time to discard the juice and pulp and start a new batch. Tamarind blocks should be wrapped in plastic wrap and refrigerated; they will keep for about a year. I have substituted a combination of cherry juice and tangy pureed dried apricots for tamarind juice.

Flavorings, Aromatics, and Textures

Most Thai dishes are laced with flamboyant flavorings, with several sharp and intense tastes blended or in contrast with one another. Even a dish that is intended to taste bland is served with sauces for the individual diners to add according to preference. Flavorings with complex aromas ranging from woody, musty, smoky, and acid to floral scents are only part of a vast repertoire. Herbs, spices, flowers, and pickled or salted vegetables, meat, and fish are among hundreds of ingredients used for flavoring.

Aroma is another important element in Thai cooking, used not only to enhance the appetite, but also because the Thais believe that aromatic herbs are medicinal. *Homm yenn* is a Thai phrase used to describe a cooling and calming aroma. It is prized and believed to strengthen the heart, nurture a pregnancy, quench the thirst, clear the lungs, and improve general well-being.

Herbal aromas are used to enhance the taste of meat and seafood and increase one's appetite while masking their gamey smells. Earthy, smoky, and fishy smells are described as *mum,* a difficult translation, but perhaps closest to meaning something that is good and buttery.

Mum also applies to texture, an equally important element. Often textures play the surprising role in a meal. An expert cook uses textures for *sanuk,* or fun. And it's this touch that often lingers in the memory after a meal is eaten.

The following ingredients are used in Thai cooking for flavor, aroma, and texture. Often a single ingredient provides two or all three of these elements.

DRIED SPICES

Spice quality varies greatly. Don't be fooled by fancy, expensive bottles. Some of the best spices are simply wrapped in clear cellophane. Inspect the spice for color, appearance, and, if possible, aroma. Most dried spices used in Thai cooking are available in supermarkets as well as organic and Asian markets. Buy small quantities; spices lose their essence if stored too long. Always buy whole spices instead of powder for maximum quality and shelf life. Dried spices have a fairly long shelf life until opened; then they should be tightly resealed and refrigerated. Roasted and pounded spices should be stored in glass jars with tight-fitting lids.

LOK KRA-WANN—CARDAMOM: Both seeds and leaves are used for flavor and aroma. The small oval hard-shelled pod, which is usually bleached white, contains tiny black seeds. Cardamom is very aromatic, slightly bitter, peppery, and sweet. The fragrance is a bit like lemon. Cardamom is used as a breath freshener and also believed to be good for the digestive system.

PRIKK HAENG—DRIED CHILES: Dried chiles are used for color and their piquant qualities. They are believed to enhance one's appetite, clear the lungs, and increase energy and blood circulation. The following dried chiles are used in the recipes in this book; they are described in detail on pages 89–90.

> *Prikk haeng*—Anaheim or New Mexico (also called California)
> *Prikk chee faa haeng*—de árbol
> *Prikk chee faa haeng*—Japonés
> *Prikk kee nuu* or *prikk nuu kun heang*— *chilipiquín* or *chiltepín*

OP-CHEUY—CINNAMON: Thais prefer cinnamon from China, a sweet, slightly spicy, anise-flavored bark, which is also known as cassia. The brown-reddish bark is thicker than Ceylon cinnamon, comes in loose curls, and has a more intense flavor. One- to 2-inch pieces are broken off and used as is or ground into powder. Generally used for aroma, cinnamon is also believed to cure nausea and colds.

KAN-PHUU—CLOVE: For the best results, use whole cloves instead of powder. The pungent flavor and strong aroma of this sweet-smelling, dark-brown spice are believed to soothe nausea.

LUK PHAK CHEE—CORIANDER SEEDS: The small round, slightly fibrous pods contain tiny seeds that often fall out during harvesting and packaging. Coriander's intensely aromatic, slightly piquant flavor is released when the seeds are roasted and pounded. Its perfume is prized in Thai cooking and believed to act as a mild sedative, reduce flatulence, and aid digestion.

YI-RA—CUMIN OR CARAWAY SEEDS: There seem to be two schools of thought as to what *yi-ra* is. Cumin seeds are tiny, plump, and oblong-shaped with ridges. Young immature green seeds turn light brown. Used primarily for its aroma, cumin is believed to be good for the digestive system and as a breath freshener. Caraway seeds look like cumin but are thinner and darker. Caraway has a very sharp peppery taste and will infuse a dish with its flavor. It is believed to heighten the appetite and enrich the flavor of meat and game.

KREUNG TEDD—CURRY SPICES: *Kreung tedd* is the name given to a blend of spices used in dishes originating in India, Java, and the Middle East. It consists of powdered turmeric, coriander seeds, ginger, cloves, cinnamon, mustard seeds, cardamom, cumin, pepper, and salt. Curry spices are used as flavoring, for their aroma, and as a signal to indicate a dish's foreign origins.

DOK JUN TEDD—MACE: The outer shell covering of the nutmeg is called "closed blossom" by Thais. The brownish yellow petals, or blades, are removed one by one, roasted, and pounded. Mace is used to produce a sweet aroma in Thai dishes influenced by Indian and Indonesian cooking.

JUN TEDD—NUTMEG: This oval-shaped seed has a dark hard outer shell. Use a nutmeg grater to make a fine powder. Nutmeg is favored by the Thais for its intense aroma; it is believed to heighten the effects of alcohol.

POI-KAK—STAR ANISE: These brown pods are in the form of an eight-pointed cluster, with a tiny seed in each segment. Star anise has a sweet, licorice-like flavor resembling that of anise, but it is actually a member of the magnolia family. It is used whole in Thai cooking. The sweet aroma is believed to enhance the appetite.

PRIKK THAI—WHITE PEPPERCORN: Thai white pepper is described in detail on page 85. It is believed that the heat from the peppercorn helps move air through the lungs, thus increasing circulation, while raising the body's core temperature and causing sweat to act as a coolant. It also enhances the appetite.

FRESH HERBS AND SPICES

When buying fresh herbs, look for colors that are vibrant and shiny. The leaves should not be wilted and the stems should be moist. Fresh green herbs will keep well if rinsed and dried thoroughly, wrapped in paper towels, and stored in the refrigerator in Ziploc bags. When you use an herb for the first time, smell it, taste it, and get to know it. Experiment and use it in another recipe, or try a different recipe that calls for it.

PRIKK SODD—CHILES: Fresh chiles are used to flavor and add color to a dish. They are used raw, roasted, slightly pickled, or pounded into a paste and are believed to enhance the appetite and aid blood circulation. In the past, chile leaves were also used to flavor curries and added to seasoning pastes for color. (For more details on fresh chiles, see pages 88–89). The fresh chiles grown in Thailand are nearly impossible to find in American markets. The so-called Thai chiles sold in Asian markets are closest to the Thai chiles called *prikk chee faa*, the Tabasco chile. The following chiles available in America most closely resemble what Thai cooks use.

> *Prikk chee faa*—Anaheim or New Mexico (also called California), ancho, cayenne, Tabasco, de árbol, jalapeño, and serrano
> *Prikk kee nuu*—catarina and *chilipiquín*, or *chiltepín*
> *Prikk yurg*—Hungarian wax

GUEY CHAI—CHINESE CHIVES: A member of the garlic family, these have 12- to 14-inch-long thin, flat, dark green blades. Some have small oblong white flowers. The leaves are chewy, crunchy, and peppery, with a strong musty, garlic-onion flavor. Available in Asian markets, Chinese chives are eaten raw or cooked slightly and used for their aroma and texture. Scallion greens can be used as a substitute. Like garlic,

Chinese chives are believed to be good for colds and coughs.

TUD PHAKK CHEE—CILANTRO, COMMONLY SOLD AS FRESH CORIANDER, ALSO SOMETIMES KNOWN AS CHINESE PARSLEY: Although the whole plant is used, the Thais particularly like the root. Cilantro is one of the basic ingredients in the Big Four Paste (page 86), and its pungent taste and musty aroma make it a basic seasoning in most Thai dishes. The stems and leaves are used as garnishes for color, taste, and scent. Select cilantro with bright green stems and leaves. The leaves should be firm and crisp, and when the stems are gently squeezed, they should exude a strong scent.

Before using, the roots must be cleaned with a brush, then removed from the stems. If cilantro with the roots intact is unavailable, the stems can be used in combination with roasted coriander seeds as a substitute. Cilantro sprigs are left whole for garnishes or to be eaten raw; they are also coarsely chopped or finely minced for garnishes or as an ingredient for fillings. Cilantro roots, stems, and leaves should be thoroughly dried before refrigerating.

KHA—GALANGAL, GALANGA, OR GALANGALE: This rhizome grows underground and resembles a root with its thick, knobby, rounded clusters. The whitish outer layer is shiny and has a pale pink wash with uneven circular dark lines. Used especially for its flavor and aroma, galangal has a hard outer peel; the inner white flesh is crisp and exudes a peppery, ginger, floral scent when sliced. It tastes like ginger with a gentle afterglow. Galangal is believed to be good for the lungs, menstrual problems, and stomach complaints.

Asian markets sell fresh, frozen, dried, and

powdered galangal. Fresh galangal is sometimes sold chopped, which discolors the inner section. The flavor of older galangal will be more intense. The best substitute for fresh galangal is the frozen, even though, when thawed, it turns mushy and has a mild flavor. Use a bit more frozen than is called for in the recipe. Dried galangal must be soaked in warm water to soften it. Squeeze out excess water before using. I do not recommend dried or powdered galangal. If you can't find the fresh or frozen varieties, it is best to substitute fresh ginger.

GA-TIEM—GARLIC: Garlic is one of ingredients in the Big Four Paste (page 86). The most commonly used variety has the familiar clustered bulb, or head, with several cloves enclosed in a papery membrane. The most prized garlic in Thailand is a bulb with only a small single clove. For more details on garlic, see page 84.

KING—GINGER: A gnarled and knobby fibrous stem, mistakenly called a root when it is really a rhizome, ginger grows and spreads near the surface of the soil. Both young and mature ginger are used for flavoring and aroma. Young ginger has a thin light yellow skin. Growing in clusters of two to three stems with pink shoots, young ginger is mild with a gentle, floral aroma. Mature ginger is brown and has skin that looks like brown paper. It has a pungent, peppery taste and is fibrous and more difficult to pound. Dried-out or old ginger can be used for soup stock.

Young ginger is available in the spring in Asian markets, and mature ginger is available all year round in both Asian markets and supermarkets. It should be firm to the touch and not shriveled or moldy. Store ginger in the refrigerator, loosely wrapped in paper towels. Thai cooks keep theirs in a jar filled with sand. Ginger is believed to be good for the lungs, to cure colds and fever, and to settle the stomach and relieve nausea.

KRA-CHAY—LESSER GALANGAL OR CHINESE KEY: Young *kra-chay* is light brown, with stems that resemble a cluster of long fingers. As it matures, it turns woody and very dark, and tastes like mild ginger with a slight floral scent.

Used primarily to flavor seafood dishes, *kra-chay* is sold in Asian supermarkets preserved in brine or frozen. To use, wash well with cool water to remove the brine, and peel. Preserved *kra-chay* should be refrigerated. Keep frozen *kra-chay* in the freezer and thaw just what you need. Both will keep for months. The pungent taste is believed to soothe stomach ailments. Substitute tender young ginger for lesser galangal.

PRIKK THAI SODD—GREEN PEPPERCORNS: These fresh, underripe green berries come in clusters. They are dried and processed into either white or black peppercorns.

Green peppercorns are available in Asian markets packed in glass jars in brine which causes the green color to dull. They are also available in cans (imported from France) in gourmet markets. Rinse before using and store the rest in the refrigerator. However, freeze-dried peppercorns, packaged in small bottles, are a better substitute for the fresh than the pickled variety. These are available in larger supermarkets. Roast them before using to enhance the aroma. Green peppercorns are intensely spicy and aromatic, prized by the Thais for their crunchy texture, fiery flavor, and vibrant color.

BAI MAH-KRUD—KAFFIR LIME LEAF; *PEW MAH-KRUD*—KAFFIR LIME RIND: The double leaf of the kaffir lime has a strong citrus and musty aroma. Thais particularly like it to enhance the flavor of fish and shellfish. Most Asian markets package kaffir lime leaves in plastic wrappers, making it difficult to check quality. Shiny dark green leaves are a good indication of freshness but no guarantee of aroma. Break the seal and slightly crush one of the leaves between your fingers: The aroma should be intense. Dried kaffir lime leaves are not a good substitute for fresh ones. Use the zest or leaves of Mexican limes or fresh firm ordinary limes instead. Added to a container of raw rice, fresh kaffir lime leaves will keep insects away. The leaves can be frozen, but the flavor will be altered and the aroma will disappear. When using frozen leaves, add some fresh lime zest to compensate for the loss of fragrance.

Kaffir lime zest is quite bitter. It is used raw in curry pastes, chile water, or salads and is added to curries, stir-fries, and soups. When a recipe calls for kaffir lime zest or rind, Mexican lime can be substituted.

TA-KAI—LEMONGRASS: Lemongrass has a scallion-like, slightly bulbous base with razor-thin green blades for leaves; the stalks grow in clumps. Recently popular, lemongrass can be purchased in specialty, organic, and Asian markets. The inner core is used in chile pastes, while the leaves are used to flavor soups or to make tea. Its lemon-ginger flavor adds a wonderful aroma to a dish. When you buy lemongrass, the bulb should be thick and feel firm and heavy; the stalks should be tightly bound with green leaves. If you press your fingernail into the bulb, you should smell the characteristic lemony scent. If fresh plump lemongrass is unavailable and what is available appears dry and may be possibly tough, buy twice the amount called for in the recipe. The outer woody leaves should be removed. The white and light purple inner core at the root end can be crushed, pounded, or minced to release its pungent, aromatic oil. For these older dried stalks, slightly crush the end of each bulb and soak them in cool water for a couple of hours before using. Peel off the outer dried leaves until you reach the innermost moist core. To further soften, crush the bulbs with the side of a chopping knife on a cutting board before slicing and mincing.

Keep lemongrass in a glass of water on your counter, changing the water every few days. If it's not used right away, it will begin to sprout roots. Even with roots, it can still be used—or planted for more lemongrass. Believed to cure stomachaches, lemongrass is made into tea (the juice is also used as a mosquito repellent). There is no substitute for this unique herb.

BAI SARANAY—SPEARMINT: The round leaves of this herb have a fruity, refreshing, spicy flavor. The leaves are used as garnishes or added to stir-fries at the last minute for their flavor, aroma, and color. They are finely chopped and mixed with salads. Look for fresh green leaves on firm stems; avoid any that are wilted or brown. To keep mint, trim the stems and put the mint in a glass of water on the counter, or cover loosely with a plastic bag and refrigerate. Its strong aroma is believed to cure stomachaches, act as a cooling agent, and be good for digestion.

BUA BOK—PENNYWORT: The heart-shaped leaves of this plant resemble violet leaves. The slightly bitter leaves are eaten raw in spicy meat salads or with fried noodles. Pennywort is also used for its medicinal qualities. The juice is extracted and drunk during the hot monsoon season as a cooling agent. Pennywort is available in organic and Asian markets. Watercress can be substituted.

PAKK CHEE FARANG—SAWTOOTH HERB: This herb's elongated leaves are dark green with serrated edges, 5 to 6 inches long and 1 inch wide. Sawtooth's musty, earthy flavor and slightly chewy texture complement meat dishes. Like pennywort, it is valued for its medicinal qualities and is believed to refresh and enhance the appetite. It's available in Asian markets; a good substitute is arugula or watercress.

HOM DAENG—SHALLOT: Looking like miniature onions with clusters of two or three cloves, shallots are covered with a thin, reddish brown, papery membrane. The flesh is light purple, tasting like a mild onion, slightly sweet, peppery, and a little bitter. In Thailand, shallots are much smaller, with a stronger flavor, than the ones sold in Asian markets and supermarkets here. Together with garlic, shallots are used in most Thai dishes for flavor, aroma, and texture. Shallot's liquid pulp breaks down easily during pounding, making it a great blending agent for chile pastes.

When you purchase shallots, the bulb should be firm to the touch and the papery skin shiny, not moldy. Keep shallots in a basket together with garlic at room temperature. They are believed to be good for curing a cold or fever and for soothing mouth sores. Red onion can be substituted for shallots.

TON-HOM—SCALLION, SPRING ONION, OR GREEN ONION: The whole stalk of a scallion, both the white bulb and the green leaves, is used by Thais in cooking or, raw, as a garnish. Its sweet flavor, with a slight peppery taste, adds the final touch to many dishes. The vibrant green adds an enticing look. The best scallions are sold with short roots attached. Wash and dry them thoroughly before using; to store, wrap in paper towels and keep in a plastic bag in the refrigerator.

HORAPA—THAI BASIL OR SWEET BASIL: The long pear-shaped, anise-scented leaves are green with a purple hue and purple stems. They are close to European sweet basil. Used for their slight pungent and musty flavor, aroma, and color, the leaves are added whole to curries and stir-fries. Coarsely chopped, they are mixed with salads. Thai basil is believed to be good for intestinal ailments. The juice from pounded leaves is used to stop itching from insect bites. Thai basil is available in organic and Asian markets. Substitute either Italian basil or, for a different flavor, use mint.

GA-PAO—HOLY BASIL OR SWEET BASIL: This variety of basil came originally from India, where the plant is considered sacred. It has a weaker scent than Thai basil and is used predominantly with shellfish and as garnish for salads. It is available in Asian supermarkets. Substitute either Italian basil or mint.

MANG-RUK—SWEET BASIL OR LEMON BASIL: Yet another variety of basil, with a slightly spicy flavor and pleasant floral aroma, *mang-ruk* is used as garnish. The tiny, pinpoint-size seeds are also cooked and eaten as a snack or added to a jasmine-scented sweet-syrupy drink. The seeds must be soaked first in cool water until they expand to ten times their original size. They'll look like frog's eggs with a slippery texture and a surprising crunch in the center. Both the herb and seeds are available in Asian markets. Substitute Italian basil or mint for the leaves.

KA-MIN—TURMERIC: Fresh turmeric, which may be orange or white, is a rhizome in the ginger family; not surprisingly, it looks like miniature ginger. Orange turmeric has dark brown–orange skin; when peeled, the brilliant orange flesh will stain everything. This is also true of the powdered version. Orange turmeric is used for its color, aroma, sweet, crunchy texture, and peppery taste.

Fresh orange turmeric is readily available in Asian and organic markets. It should feel firm. Even if the outer skin has turned quite dark, as long as it is not shriveled or dried, the flesh is still good. Remove any mold, peel, and use the rest. White turmeric or zedoary is extremely rare in America. Larger than the orange, it's often eaten raw with pungent chile water, for its crispy texture, sweet aroma, and taste. Wrap fresh turmeric loosely with paper towels and refrigerate.

Powdered turmeric is used mostly for its intense yellow orange color, as it has little flavor and no aroma. With powdered turmeric, use half of the amount of fresh turmeric called for in a recipe. When fresh turmeric isn't available, instead of using straight powdered turmeric as a substitute, there is another option that closely resembles the taste, flavor, and color of the fresh: Combine 1 tablespoon grated carrot, ½ teaspoon grated fresh ginger, and ½ teaspoon turmeric powder as a substitute for 1 tablespoon minced fresh turmeric.

Turmeric is believed to cure ulcers, to be good for the digestive system, and to cure skin problems.

Fresh turmeric stains easily, but I find that a combination of soap, lemon juice, and salt helps remove stains from your hands. Chopping blocks and dish towels should be washed with bleach and soap.

AROMATIC FLOWERS AND LEAVES

Thais love desserts and snacks heavily perfumed with fresh blossoms or leaves. In the tropical climate when the air is humid and hot, they believe that these floral scents are *hom yenn*—"cool scent"—refreshing and calming for both body and spirit. Make sure that any flowers or leaves you use are pesticide free.

DOK MALI—JASMINE: These fresh blossoms are added to coconut cream or sugar water, allowed to steep overnight and used as an ingredient for desserts. Jasmine-scented candles are burned to perfume ready-made confections by trapping the smoke under a glass dome or jar. Jasmine extract is available in Asian markets. It is artificial with a bitter taste. I recommend that you use fresh blossoms instead or simply substitute orange blossom or orange flower water, which is available in liquor stores.

DOK GULAB—ROSE: Traditional Thai recipes use wild rose petals from the Mon rose in salads or as garnish. These sweet-scented petals taste slightly peppery and sour, with a velvety texture. They are used to give an air of lightness to a meat or seafood salad. Substitute nasturtium blossoms.

BAI TOEY—PANDANUS LEAF OR SCREW PINE: *Bai toey* is the Thai people's vanilla. The dark green, long, broad leaves exude a heavy and musty scent when cooked. They are used to wrap desserts, boiled in syrup for dessert, and cooked with sweet sticky rice. The juice is used as a flavoring and for coloring. The juice and frozen leaves are available in Asian markets. It is preferable to use thawed frozen leaves instead of the extract. Stored in plastic in the freezer, the leaves will keep for several months. Substitute aromatic extracts such as orange or rose water and/or almond extract for pandanus leaf.

BAI TONG—BANANA LEAF: Banana leaves are the most versatile, utilitarian, and environmentally friendly wrappers. They are used by street vendors in Thailand to wrap both raw and cooked food. Folded into pouches to hold food for steaming, the leaves keep the contents moist and release a pleasing aroma. Thais also transform the leaf into artistic shapes and forms to hold flowers and incense.

Frozen banana leaves are available in Asian markets. Thaw completely before using. Carefully unwrap the leaves and cut off the hard stems. Soak in cool soapy water and wash each leaf carefully so as not to tear them. Rinse once more with cool water. Dry, fold, and wrap in paper towels. Store in a plastic bag, refrigerated, for up a week. Fresh or dried corn husks can be used as a substitute in most recipes.

DRY-ROASTED, DRIED, PICKLED, PRESERVED, AND SALTED INGREDIENTS

For hundreds of years, the Thai people have been preserving foods by drying, roasting, or pickling to save surplus harvests for future lean times. Herbs and spices are dried in the sun. Vegetables and fruits are dried, salted, pickled in brine, or cured with vinegar. Sometimes fruits are pureed with sugar to preserve them. Fish, shrimp and other shellfish, duck eggs, and meat are cured with salt. Thais love the flavor, aroma, and texture of these ingredients and are connoisseurs about using them for cooking.

Dry-Roasted Ingredients

Chiles, garlic, ginger, and shallots are the ingredients most commonly dry-roasted directly on the fire or in a skillet, or thinly sliced and fried in oil until crispy. The result is an appealing smoky-burnt flavor and aroma and a crispy, crunchy texture. These are used as garnishes or combined with other ingredients and pounded into a paste for seasoning.

Both cooked and raw rice grains are dry-roasted in a skillet. Dry-roasted cooked rice grains are pounded for desserts, while dry-roasted raw rice is ground to be added to salads. And raw peanuts are shelled, dry-roasted, and pounded, used not only for many main dishes, but also for desserts and snacks.

King Pow

DRY-ROASTING GINGER

Dry-roasting ginger is best done on an outdoor charcoal or propane grill. However, it can be roasted directly over the open flame of a gas stove burner or wrapped in aluminum foil and roasted in a toaster or regular oven with satisfactory results.

To dry-roast ginger over a grill or the flame of a gas stove burner, pierce a 2- to 3-inch chunk of fresh ginger with a long-handled grilling fork. Hold the ginger directly over the flame and grill, turning until the skin is char-burnt. Cool completely, then peel off the burnt skin and use the inner section.

To dry-roast the ginger in a toaster oven, put a chunk of ginger on a piece of aluminum foil. Sprinkle with a few drops of vegetable oil, wrap securely, and put in the toaster oven. Turn the heat to 400°F and bake for 20 minutes, or until the ginger softens. Remove and cool completely before peeling off the outer skin.

Ga-Tiem Pow, Hom Pow

DRY-ROASTING GARLIC OR SHALLOTS

Follow the same process as for dry-roasting ginger above. Use a whole garlic head or several shallot bulbs, first slicing off the top. If a recipe calls for both ingredients, wrap together and bake at 400°F in a toaster or regular oven for 30 minutes. The inner softened flesh of the roasted garlic or shallots can be easily squeezed out from the burnt skins.

Hom Chew
CRISPY SHALLOTS

Makes about ¾ cup

10 to 15 shallots, sliced into
paper-thin rings (1 cup)
2 cups vegetable oil
Sea salt, if needed

Be sure to deep-fry the shallots slowly to ensure even browning; very hot oil will burn some and leave others uncooked. Adding sea salt keeps the oil from splattering and makes the shallots crisper. These will keep for a month.

Separate the shallots into individual strands and rings. In a 10-inch skillet, heat the vegetable oil over medium heat for 2 minutes, or until it is very hot but not smoking. Add the shallots and cook, stirring constantly with a wooden spoon, until the shallots slowly brown to golden, 15 to 20 minutes. If the oil begins to dance and splatter, lower the heat and sprinkle in a few pinches of sea salt. Remove from the heat. Put a strainer over a large metal mixing bowl and drain the shallots in the strainer. Transfer the shallots to a cookie sheet lined with paper towels. When completely cool, transfer to a glass jar with a tight-fitting lid and store at room temperature for up to a month. Strain the oil through a coffee filter and save it to use for stir-fried dishes or to make Crispy Garlic (below).

Ga-Tiem Chew
CRISPY GARLIC

Makes about ¾ cup

30 garlic cloves, peeled
(1 cup)
2 cups vegetable oil
Sea salt, as needed

As with crispy shallot, slow-cooking and patience are the key to golden crispy garlic. Thai often deep-fry the papery skins together with the garlic cloves.

Fit a food processor with the steel blade, add the garlic cloves, and pulse 20 to 30 times, or until the garlic is coarsely chopped.

Fry the garlic, using the same technique as for making crispy shallots (above). Be sure to stir constantly, and let the garlic brown slowly until golden, 10 to 15 minutes. Be patient; this takes longer than you think it should. Drain as for crispy shallots, cool, and store the garlic in a jar with a tight-fitting lid at room temperature for up to a month.

Dried Ingredients

NEUR HEANG—DRIED BEEF: To make dried beef, thinly sliced beef is first cured with a mixture of dried herbs, spices, and seasonings and sun-dried. The leathery strips are then deep-fried and served as an accompaniment to spicy chile water and curries. A favorite food among northern and northeastern Thais, beef strips are eaten simply with sticky rice, bitter greens, and spicy chile water. Hot and chewy American jerky is a fair substitute, or you can make your own (see page 208). Dried beef, as well as fish, is also grilled or steamed. Minced and pounded, it is added to soups or combined with other ingredients for chile paste.

PLA HEANG—DRIED FISH: Both fresh and saltwater fish are salted and dried. Often the whole fish is dried, but some are gutted and boned first. Grilled and pounded, dried fish is added to chile paste and chile water. Minced, it's used as a binder for chile paste to make traditional Thai jungle soup, Yellow Curry (page 226), and Sour-Orange Curry (page 233).

Another popular preparation is to deep-fry dried fish in oil until very crispy and serve it as a side dish with chile water and curry. Unfortunately, the dried fish exported to America is of very poor quality. I prefer dried fish from Japan, both the whole tiny fish as well as bonito (fish shavings) as a substitute. These are available in organic and Asian markets and some large markets. After opening, rewrap the fish securely in plastic (otherwise, the refrigerator will smell like salted fish) and refrigerate. It will keep for several months.

MED BUA—DRIED LOTUS SEEDS: These small white puffed seeds with black pointed ends look somewhat like hominy after they are soaked and softened. Each seed has a young green shoot in the center, which should be removed. The soft-ened seeds are added to soup for their slightly sweet, floury flavor and crunchy texture, and for the ability to absorb other flavors. Dried lotus seeds packaged in cellophane are sold in Asian supermarkets and keep well in a Ziploc bag in the pantry. Canned hominy, drained and rinsed several times, can be substituted.

HED HOM—DRIED SHIITAKE MUSHROOMS: There are many grades of dried shiitake mushrooms. The Japanese shiitakes are clean and beautifully packaged, with each mushroom carefully arranged, but they are expensive. Chinese shiitakes, on the other hand, are jumbled together regardless of size or shape. They take more time to clean than the Japanese shiitakes, but are worth the effort because their meaty flesh absorbs flavors and tastes better. Both are available in supermarkets and organic and Asian markets. Dried mushrooms will keep well wrapped in plastic in your pantry.

To reconstitute dried shiitakes, pour boiling water over them and let cool to room temperature. When the mushrooms are soft and silky, wash and massage them in several changes of water. Slice off the hard stems, and save to flavor a broth or discard. Rub the caps with salt in a colander and let stand for 10 to 15 minutes. Rinse off the salt and squeeze dry. They can be left whole, quartered, or sliced into long thin strands. Store in a sealed plastic bag in the refrigerator until ready to use; they will keep for a few days.

HED HUNU HEANG—DRIED WOOD EAR, TREE EAR, OR CLOUD EAR MUSHROOMS: These shriveled dried black flakes look like dried leaves. When soaked in boiling water, they revive, puff up, and stretch into glossy black, rubbery caps. Each mushroom has a hard woody knot where it was attached to the tree trunk. After soaking, pinch it off. Wash the mushrooms in several changes of cold water. Place in a colander, sprinkle with salt, and let sit for at least 10 minutes, then rinse in cold water and pat dry. The mushrooms can be cooked whole or finely sliced for soup or stir-fry. They have a musty aroma and crunchy chewy texture, and absorb other flavors well. The Chinese have long believed, and Western scientists have confirmed, that these strange funghi thin the blood and help circulation. These dried mushrooms are available in some supermarkets and organic markets and in any Asian market. To store dried wood ear mushrooms, wrap in plastic; they will keep for many months in the pantry.

GOONG HEANG—DRIED SHRIMP: Tiny shrimp, from both fresh and salt water, are salted and dried. They are eaten as is or used for cooking. Dried shrimp are also deep-fried for garnishes. When soaked in warm water to soften, they can be pounded and used as a binder for curry paste, chile paste, and chile water. Asian markets carry different sizes packaged in cellophane. Some supermarkets carry them in the Mexican food section. Inspect carefully and select those with a pink-orange color. The smallest ones are good for *Miang Khum*, Savory Bite (page 146), while the larger ones are good for making curry or chile pastes. Avoid dried shrimp ground into powder. Seal leftover dried shrimp in the original bag with a rubber band and freeze. They will keep for a long time.

TUA RISUNG—PEANUTS: Using peanuts, like chiles, with dishes is deemed to be most distinctly Thai. It is true that Thai people love peanuts, but not as much as the Malaysians or their Muslim neighbors. Dried and sold in or out of the shell in Asian markets, peanuts are seldom salted. Freshly harvested peanuts are sometimes boiled in salt water and sold as a snack. Supermarkets here carry unsalted Spanish peanuts with their skins.

In cooking, peanuts can add a surprising crunchy element. Dry-roasted and pounded coarsely, they make a garnish with a crispy, crunchy, and rich, nutty texture. Dry-roasted and ground peanuts should be stored in a glass jar with a tight-fitting lid in the pantry. They will keep for 2 to 3 weeks. Unsalted whole peanuts should be wrapped in plastic bags and refrigerated.

Pickled Ingredients

NOR MAI DORNG—PICKLED BAMBOO SHOOTS: Young tender shoots sliced paper-thin and pickled in brine have a salty-sour taste with a crunchy and chewy texture. They are used in hot-and-sour soup. Rinse the amount needed several times in cold water and refrigerate the rest. They will keep for a month.

Bamboo shoots preserved with salt, oil, and fresh chiles make a wonderful side dish or condiment. I love them best with a bowl of steaming-hot rice. They are sold in jars in Asian markets. Refrigerate after opening.

GA-TIEM DORNG—PICKLED GARLIC: Whole heads of garlic are used pickled, and both the cloves and pickling juice are used in cooking. Eaten whole, thinly sliced, or minced, the cloves taste sweet, sour, salty, pungent, and crunchy at the same time and are desirable for both the pickled flavor and aroma. The juice is added to soups or salad dressings. Refrigerated, pickled garlic will keep for months.

KING DORNG—PICKLED GINGER: Paper-thin slices of young, tender ginger are first soaked and cured with sea salt and lime juice, which changes their off-white color to a beautiful pink.

Then the ginger is pickled in a mixture of sugar and vinegar. Traditional Thai cooks carve the delicate slices into flowers, birds, and stars prior to pickling. Aside from its artistic presentation, pickled ginger's sweet and crunchy taste makes a wonderful contrast to spicy Thai dishes, and pickled ginger is often served as a condiment or an accompaniment. Pickled ginger is also used by the Japanese for sushi.

Pickled ginger is found in most Asian markets, and in larger supermarkets in the ethnic foods section along with other Asian ingredients. Generally, there are two kinds of pickled ginger. One is light pink and the other bright red. Buy the light pink variety.

If you prefer to make your own, homemade pickled ginger is easy and tastes better. Here is how.

King Dorng
YOUNG GINGER IN VINEGAR

Makes 1 cup

In a small saucepan, combine ¼ cup of the sea salt and the water. Heat over high heat, stirring, until the sea salt is dissolved. Remove from the heat to cool.

In a medium mixing bowl, combine the sliced ginger with the salted water; let sit for 1 hour or until the ginger slices are softened. Drain in a strainer, rinse in several changes of water, and pat dry.

Leaving the sliced ginger in the strainer, add the lime juice, tossing to combine. Let sit for 30 minutes. The ginger will turn pink. Squeeze to extract the excess liquid and transfer the sliced ginger to a clean 16-ounce glass jar.

In a small saucepan, combine the remaining 1 teaspoon sea salt, the sugar, and vinegar; heat over medium-high heat until the salt and sugar are dissolved. Cool completely, then pour the mixture over the sliced ginger. Cover and seal with the lid. Refrigerate for 1 to 2 weeks before serving. It will keep for several months.

¼ cup plus 1 teaspoon sea salt
1 cup water
½ pound fresh young ginger, peeled and thinly sliced to yield 2 cups
Juice of 2 limes
1 cup sugar
1 cup rice vinegar or cider vinegar

PAKK GADD DORNG—SOUR PICKLED MUSTARD GREENS: Salted and covered with brine, young mustard greens turn khaki-colored and are salty-sour with a crunchy, slightly chewy texture. If you like kosher pickles, you will love these greens. They add surprising contrast to many dishes and turn a simple soup into a richly flavored, irresistible treat. Most of the time, you will find them, sliced lengthwise in half, packaged in clear plastic wrap. The packages hold 1 cup. Sometimes Asian markets have them in large plastic or wooden bins.

Wash pickled mustard greens several times with cool water before cooking or eating raw. Store in a sealed plastic bag and refrigerate; they will keep for several months. But pickled mustard greens are easy to make. Here is how.

Pakk Gadd Dorng
PICKLED MUSTARD GREENS

Makes 2 quarts

3 pounds Chinese mustard cabbage
1½ cups coarse sea salt or kosher salt
4 cups bottled water

The fresh mustard greens used for pickling are called Chinese mustard cabbage, broad-leaf mustard cabbage, or *gai choy*. The thick, broad, curved stems cluster in a semiclosed head, somewhat like romaine lettuce. Both the stems and leaves are bright green. The greens are available in Asian markets, especially in the spring and summer.

Clean the mustard greens and pat dry. Spread them on a wooden tray and leave in the sun to dry for a day, or until they are wilted. Slice each mustard green lengthwise in half and set aside.

Combine ¼ cup of the salt with the bottled water in a medium saucepan and boil over medium heat for about 30 minutes, or until the salt is completely dissolved. Cool completely.

Layer the mustard greens in a 2-quart glass jar with the remaining 1¼ cups salt, filling the jar. Pack the greens down into the jar and cover with the cool salt water. Close the lid tightly and leave the jar at room temperature for a week. The mustard greens will change color from green to khaki. After a week, store the pickled mustard greens in the refrigerator. They will keep for at least a month.

Preserved Ingredients

KAI YEW MAH (HORSE'S URINE EGG!)—THOU-SAND-YEAR-OLD EGGS: These preserved eggs are really about a month old, not nearly as old as the name implies. After a paste of lime, baking soda, rice husks, and salt forms a coat on the egg, it's left to ferment or ripen. The egg white turns a beautiful translucent black, which tastes like salted gelatin, while the yolk takes on gray, brown, and black hues and a creamy, soft, rich texture. The eggs, to be eaten with hot mustard or stir-fried with garlic, chiles, and fresh basil, come individually wrapped in plastic in Styrofoam egg cartons, sold in Asian markets. Store the eggs in the refrigerator. They will keep for several months.

Salted Ingredients

TUNG CHAI—SALTED CABBAGE: Sometimes called Tien Jing salted cabbage, after the city where it originated, salted cabbage may also be labeled preserved cabbage. Packaged in squat brown plastic or ceramic containers, salted cabbage looks like thin, brown, wet cornflakes and smells musty and fermented. A little bit of salted cabbage adds taste and texture to soups, noodles, or scrambled eggs. Rinse the amount you need several times in cold water. Store the rest in the covered container in the refrigerator, and it will keep for years. Use salted capers as a substitute.

KAI KEM—SALTED EGGS: For these, large raw duck eggs are immersed in salted water in large wooden or ceramic bins for 10 to 14 days. Sold individually from a large bin or packaged in Styrofoam egg cartons, they are available in Asian supermarkets. Boiled like regular hard-cooked eggs and cut in half with the shell on, they reveal firm whites and yolks. They are very salty, with a grainy texture, and are used to accompany curries and rice dishes. A bowl of soft-cooked rice gruel and a salted duck egg is a great breakfast on a cold, gray day. Keep both raw and cooked salted eggs in the refrigerator. The raw eggs will keep for weeks, while the cooked ones will keep for several days.

PLA KEM—SALTED FISH: Thai people adore the strong fish smells of the sea. Fish of all sizes and varieties, both fresh and saltwater, are salted and dried. Markets throughout Thailand have entire sections devoted to selling only dried and salted fish. They look like exhibits in a natural history museum, with every imaginable kind and size of fish, salted and dried, neatly arranged and piled high in rows of baskets. Each species promises a unique flavor and texture. Most are very salty, chewy, and crunchy. Some are soft and taste very much like anchovies. Larger fish are salted and sliced across the midsection. Their firm and meaty flesh can be shredded into bite-sized pieces and added to stir-fries.

Unlike thin anchovy fillets, most salted fish from Thailand stay intact when cooked. Some are pounded before being added to soup. Sometimes salted fish is sold preserved in oil in jars. It is steamed with fresh chiles, garlic, and cilantro leaves and eaten with rice. For those who love anchovies, salted fish fillets from Taiwan, Hong Kong, and China can be bought in Asian markets. Once salted fish is opened, seal tightly in a plastic bag before refrigerating; otherwise, the refrigerator will smell like salted fish.

HOA CHAI POH—SALTED RADISH OR DAIKON: Packaged in clear cellophane along with a dozen or so whole radishes, these look like long, flat, rubbery dark beige tubes. Sometimes they are sliced into long thin strands. While they may appear uninteresting and strange, the crunchy, stringy texture of the radish added to soups and noodle dishes creates a nice surprise. Use directly from the package or rinsed with water. Salted radish is very salty, and a tiny bit goes a long way. Wrapped in plastic in the refrigerator, it will keep for years. Italian salted capers make a fair substitute.

GIEM BOUY—SALTED PLUMS: These dried, shriveled, grayish brown fruits, no bigger than an olive, are covered with fine salt. Sold beautifully packaged in small clear plastic containers or wrapped in cellophane, salted plums can be found in the candy section of Asian markets. Regular supermarkets sometimes sell them in the section where Mexican dried herbs and spices are sold.

As a child, I loved to suck on a salted plum until the meat around the hard seed disintegrated—along with the inside of my mouth! Nowadays, I use them to flavor and add an unexpected element to steamed fish. Salted plums will keep for months in the pantry.

Now the fun begins. Armed with all the varieties of flavors and seasonings, you are ready to test and taste. The following recipes incorporate the multiple layerings and combinations of Thai seasonings. You will enjoy both cooking and eating your creations.

Aharn Wung
SNACKS AND APPETIZERS

Snacking is an obsession shared by all Thais. They snack between meals from the time they awake until bedtime. In Thailand, it is effortless to buy one's favorite snack. One only steps onto the street to find at least one or two kinds for sale on the sidewalk. Especially in shopping areas, pedestrians must weave around the vendors who jam the sidewalk with their stands, portable kitchens, tables, and chairs.

On the other hand, appetizers, or *gab glam*, are served to accompany liquor. These social

hours were once strictly for men and continue to be so in small provincial towns. Makeshift portable bars selling homemade liquor are set up under shade trees or wooden lean-tos. A few stools surround a small table where you will find tiny plates of lime slices, bitter seeds, roasted salted peanuts mixed with fresh hot chiles, and other simple easy-to-make dishes to be eaten with 100-proof liquor. Rarely do you find a woman at one of these stands except during the holidays.

Miang Lao
LAO SAVORY BITE

The word *lao* suggests that this recipe is of Laotian origin, when in fact it is not. *Miang lao* is a canapé version of the recipe on page 146. The balls of filling, wrapped in greens and sitting on top of the crispy rice crackers, look something like the chewing tobacco favored by northern Thais, Laotians, and Burmese.

Once I took a chance and served *miang lao* at a formal catered event. The guests had never seen or tasted anything like it before. At first, only a few people were intrigued enough to try it. However, as word spread, it became the hit of the party! The *miang* balls can be prepared a day in advance. The rice crackers will keep in Ziploc bags for at least a week. Leftover mustard greens (including the stems) can be used for other recipes such as Three Kings Soup (page 108)

In a small bowl, combine the dried shrimp and boiling water. Set aside until the water cools. Drain the softened shrimp and pat dry with paper towels. Pound the shrimp in a mortar to the consistency of coarse cornmeal. Transfer to a large mixing bowl and combine with the ground pork. Set aside.

In a small saucepan, combine the palm sugar, fish sauce, and tamarind juice and cook over medium heat until the sugar dissolves and the mixture thickens. Remove from the heat and set aside to cool.

Add the cooled tamarind mixture to the dried shrimp-and-pork mixture. Mix well, then add the peanuts, ginger, crispy shallots and garlic, and the pork rind; mix well. Set aside.

Carefully remove the pickled mustard greens from the package. Rinse in cold water and gently squeeze out the excess water. One at a time, separate each leaf from the cluster, spreading the individual leaves on paper towels to dry.

Slice the hard stems off the leaves, taking care not to tear the leaves. Carefully cut each leaf into a 3-inch square. Put 1 teaspoon of filling in the center of each square. Fold the leaf over the filling and shape it into a tight tiny ball by gently squeezing it in the palm of your hand.

Place the rice crackers on a serving tray. Top each rice cracker with a filled mustard leaf ball. Together they pack a sensational punch.

2 tablespoons small dried shrimp
1 cup boiling water
¼ pound cooked ground pork (1 cup)
2 tablespoons palm sugar or light brown sugar
1 tablespoon fish sauce (*namm pla*)
2 tablespoons thick tamarind juice (see page 128)
2 tablespoons unsalted peanuts, dry-roasted (see page 13) and finely ground
One 1-inch chunk fresh ginger, peeled and minced
¼ cup Crispy Shallots (page 138)
¼ cup Crispy Garlic (page 138)
2 tablespoons crispy pork rind, ground (see page 114; optional)
½ cup vegetable oil
One 8.8-ounce package (1 cup) pickled mustard greens (also called pickled sour mustard greens—select a package with more dark green leaves than stems; see page 142)
50 Rice Crackers (page 61)

Miang Khum
SAVORY BITE

For the sauce
(makes about 2 cups)

1 tablespoon small dried shrimp

1 cup boiling water

One 1-inch chunk fresh ginger

½ teaspoon vegetable oil

1 teaspoon fermented shrimp paste
or 1 tablespoon red miso

One 12-inch square fresh banana
leaf (see page 135), 3 fresh corn
husks, or 3 dried corn husks,
soaked in warm water until
softened

1 stalk lemongrass, green parts and
hard outer layers removed,
minced

5 shallots, minced

2 tablespoons fish sauce (*namm pla*)

½ cup palm sugar or packed light
brown sugar

½ cup Roasted Fresh Grated
Coconut Flakes (page 71)

(continued)

This snack from Central Thailand is said to be the dish that most perfectly balances nutritious and harmonious elements. It was originally a Mon dish, and the concept is based on the ritual of betel-nut chewing, an ancient and addictive practice with social and religious significance. A bitter, astringent, and spicy-tasting leaf would be wrapped around a slice of betel nut smeared with slaked lime and chewed (similar to chewing tobacco). Sometimes aromatic roasted coconut flakes were added to give extra flavor as well as lessen the sting.

Miang means "fermented tea leaf" and *khum* means "one bite." As a snack, *miang* is prepared in several hundred variations. *Miang khum* uses a leaf similar to a betel leaf, called *chaa pluu*, which is glossy green and has a chewy, crunchy texture and musty-bitter, slightly spicy taste. An intensely sweet aromatic sauce is ladled on top of the tiny condiment cubes on the leaf, creating a fabulous, explosive, and unanticipated culinary experience.

This is a dish the guests assemble themselves, and it is a great icebreaker for a dinner party (although it is not hallucinogenic like the original versions!). The sauce keeps for several weeks stored in the refrigerator in a jar with a tight-fitting lid. Reheat in the microwave or in a saucepan; if it is too thick, dilute with water.

For the sauce, in a small mixing bowl, combine the dried shrimp with the boiling water. Let sit until the water cools. Drain and pat dry with paper towels. Pound the softened shrimp in a mortar until it is the consistency of coarse cornmeal. Transfer to a small bowl and set aside.

Preheat the oven to 400°F. Rub the ginger with the vegetable oil and wrap in aluminum foil. Wrap the shrimp paste or miso in the banana leaf, folding it over several times (or stack the corn husks and wrap in them). Roast the ginger and the banana leaf bundle for 20 minutes. Cool completely.

CRACKING THE COCONUT

146

Peel and mince the ginger. Pound the ginger in the mortar until pureed. Add the lemongrass and pound to a paste. Scrape down the sides of the mortar with a spoon, add the shallots, and pound and blend. Add the softened dried shrimp and pound and blend well. Add the cooled roasted shrimp paste and pound and blend well.

Transfer the mixture to a small saucepan. Add the fish sauce and palm sugar. Set over high heat and cook, stirring constantly with a wooden spoon, until the sugar is dissolved and the sauce is slightly thickened, 1 to 2 minutes. The sauce should be the consistency of honey. Add the roasted coconut flakes, stirring to combine. Transfer to a small bowl to cool.

To serve *miang khum*, put each condiment in a separate sauce bowl. Place the bowl of sauce and the bowl of chiles, together with serving spoons, in the center of a large platter. Arrange the mustard greens around them. Place one or two pieces of dried shrimp, roasted peanuts, shallots, ginger, and lime in the center of each leaf. Add a pinch of coconut matchsticks over them.

Have each guest carefully pick up a leaf and fold it into a pouch, top with fresh chiles or leave them out, depending on preference, and spoon a dollop of the sauce over it, then fold the leaf over the ingredients into a bundle and enjoy.

Cook's Note

If using cabbage, cut thirty-six 3-inch circles from the leaves, using a sharp biscuit cutter or a paring knife and a template.

For the condiments

¼ cup small dried shrimp
½ cup unsalted peanuts, dry-roasted (see page 13)
2 shallots, cut into ¼-inch dice
One 2-inch chunk fresh young ginger, peeled and cut into ¼-inch dice, or regular ginger, peeled, rubbed with a couple of pinches of sea salt, allowed to sit, then rinsed and dried well
1 lime, unpeeled, cut into ¼-inch dice, and seeds removed
¾ cup Roasted Fresh Coconut Matchsticks (page 71)
4 to 5 fresh bird chiles or 2 to 3 serrano chiles, cut into tiny chunks (with seeds, for a spicy dish)

For the wrappers

36 fresh mustard green, stems trimmed, or 15 to 20 cabbage leaves (see Cook's Note)

Todd Munn

DEEP-FRIED FISH PATTIES

Makes about 24 patties, or 6 to 8 servings

**For the dipping sauce
(makes about ¾ cup)**

8 to 9 fresh bird chiles or 3 to 4
    serrano chiles

2 teaspoons sea salt

3¼ cups water

6 cloves garlic, minced

2 tablespoons sugar

2 tablespoons rice vinegar or cider
    vinegar

2 tablespoons thick tamarind juice
    (see page 128) or 7 dried apricots,
    soaked in warm water until
    softened and pureed

½ teaspoon cornstarch

¼ cup seeded and thinly sliced
    cucumber

6 sprigs cilantro, coarsely chopped

1 teaspoon coarsely ground
    unsalted peanuts, dry-roasted
    (see page 13)

(continued)

Every great Thai cook has a recipe for these patties, which are juicy and tender inside, crispy and crunchy on the outside. Kaffir lime is the predominant flavor. Traditionally the fish was filleted and scraped with a metal spoon, and pork fat added. Handfuls of the mixture were then slapped against the side of a ceramic or metal bowl until the flesh broke down to the point where a small amount would float in a bowl of ice-cold water.

The dipping sauce can be made ahead; stored in a jar with a tight-fitting lid in the refrigerator, it will keep for several days. The seasoning paste can also be made ahead and refrigerated for several weeks.

To make the dipping sauce, holding each chile by the stem, slice it lengthwise. In a small bowl, combine 1 teaspoon of the sea salt and 3 cups of the water. Add the sliced chiles and soak for 15 minutes. Fan the chiles in the water to remove the seeds, then rinse and pat dry with paper towels. Holding each chile together, slice crosswise very thin.

Put the remaining 1 teaspoon sea salt and the garlic in a mortar. Pound until the garlic turns to a paste. Add the chiles and pound just enough to bruise them. Transfer to a small bowl and set aside.

In a small saucepan, combine the sugar, vinegar, tamarind juice, the remaining ¼ cup water, and the cornstarch; mix well. Bring to a boil over high heat and continue to boil, stirring, until the sugar dissolves and the sauce thickens, 1 to 2 minutes. Remove from the heat and let cool.

For the seasoning paste, put the sea salt and garlic in the mortar and pound until the garlic turns into a paste. Add the chiles and pound until incorporated. Add the cilantro roots and stems, pounding until incorporated into the paste. One by one, add the lemongrass, galangal, and shallot, pounding each thoroughly into the paste before adding the next ingredient. Set aside.

For the fish patties, fit the food processor with the steel blade. Process the catfish for 30 seconds to 1 minute, until it turns into a paste and forms a ball. Transfer to a medium mixing bowl and stir in the seasoning paste. Set aside.

In a saucepan, bring 3 cups water to a boil over high heat and add a couple of pinches of sea salt. Add the beans and boil for 2 to 3 seconds, or just until the color brightens. Drain and rinse well with cold water. Pat dry. Gather the beans into a tight bundle and slice crosswise very thin. Add to the fish mixture along with the kaffir lime leaves. Fold in the beaten egg whites.

Line a platter with paper towels and set it near the stove. Have a bowl of cold water nearby to wet your hands; this will prevent the fish mixture from sticking to your hands as you shape the patties. Shape the mixture into flattened disks the size of silver dollars, placing them on a tray or platter lined with plastic wrap.

In a 12-inch skillet, heat the oil over high heat to between 350° and 375°F. (You can also test for readiness by dipping the tip of a wooden spoon into the oil; if bubbles form around it, the oil is ready.) Put 8 to 9 patties at a time into the hot oil and deep-fry until golden brown, turning as needed. Transfer to the paper towel–lined platter to drain. Just before serving, transfer the dipping sauce to a small bowl. Garnish with the cucumber, cilantro, and crushed peanuts. Serve the patties piping hot on a platter, with the dipping sauce.

For the seasoning paste (makes ⅓ cup)

1 teaspoon sea salt

6 cloves garlic, minced

2 dried New Mexico (or California) chiles, soaked in warm water until softened, seeded, and minced

15 sprigs cilantro with roots and stems, minced

1 stalk lemongrass, green parts and hard outer layers removed, minced

One ½-inch piece galangal or 1-inch piece fresh ginger, peeled and minced

1 shallot, minced

For the fish patties

1 pound catfish fillets, to yield about 2 cups, sliced

Sea salt

6 wing beans or green beans

5 kaffir lime leaves, sliced into thin strands, or grated zest of 1 lime

2 large egg whites, beaten until foamy

3 cups vegetable oil

Ngon Rood

"FENDER BENDER" FRIED STUFFED SNOW PEAS OR SQUASH BLOSSOMS

Makes 6 servings

¼ pound boneless lean pork, sliced
  into ½-inch strips
¼ pound medium shrimp, peeled,
  deveined, and sliced lengthwise
  into ½-inch strips
1 tablespoon Big Four Paste
  (page 86)
1 tablespoon fish sauce (*namm pla*)
1 teaspoon sugar
2 tablespoons unsalted peanuts,
  dry-roasted (see page 13) and
  coarsely ground
24 snow peas or zucchini blossoms
12 to 14 chives (for zucchini
  blossoms only)

For the batter

2 cups all-purpose flour
1 teaspoon baking powder
½ teaspoon sea salt
½ teaspoon freshly ground Thai
  white pepper
1⅓ cups bottled or filtered water

4 cups vegetable oil

Ngon means "fender," and *rood* means "car." In the late 1800s, when horse carriages were gaining popularity among well to-do Thais and the early automobiles were reserved for only the royal family and very wealthy Europeans, the creator of this dish named it for the curved fender of the carriage. Originally, the recipe used *dok khae,* the white or red flower of a plant in the bean family. When stuffed, coated, and deep-fried, the flower does resemble a carriage fender. Here, I have substituted snow peas or zucchini blossoms.

The batter, which is my mother's recipe, comes out light and crispy, and the stuffed peas or blossoms can even be reheated without getting soggy. Warm them on a wire rack set on top of a baking sheet for 7 to 10 minutes at 350°F, or until crispy.

There are several options for preparing this recipe ahead. One is to make the filling and refrigerate it overnight. Another is to stuff the snow peas or blossoms several hours before cooking and refrigerate. One hour before deep-frying, bring them out of the refrigerator. *Ngon rood* are served with Thai Tabasco, Siracha hot sauce, which can be purchased in Asian markets.

Fit a food processor with the steel blade and process the pork and shrimp until coarsely ground. Add the Big Four Paste, fish sauce, and sugar and process for 30 seconds to 1 minute, or until the mixture turns into a paste and forms a ball. Transfer to a mixing bowl, add the peanuts, and mix well. Set aside, or cover and refrigerate until ready to use.

If using snow peas, carefully remove the thin thread running down the side of each snow pea and split it open. Remove any peas inside the pods. Set aside. If you are using zucchini blossoms, bring a large saucepan of water to a boil. Drop the chives into the boiling water for 1 to 2 seconds; remove and rinse in cold water. Pat dry and set aside.

Fill a small Ziploc bag with the filling and cut a tip off one corner of the bag to create a makeshift pastry bag. Gather the filling toward the cut corner and squeeze about ½ to 1 teaspoon of filling into each snow pea or zucchini blossom. If you are using zucchini blossoms, tie the tops with the parboiled chives. Set aside, or refrigerate until ready to deep-fry.

For the batter, in a medium mixing bowl, combine the flour, baking powder, sea salt, and white pepper. Add the water and mix with a whisk or fork just until smooth, taking care not to overmix. Let the batter stand for 10 to 15 minutes.

Place a platter lined with paper towels near the stove. Heat the oil in a 12-inch skillet or flat-bottomed wok over high heat to between 350° and 375°F. (You can also test for readiness by dipping the tip of a wooden spoon in the oil; if tiny bubbles gather around it, the oil is ready for frying.) Dip the pods or blossoms in the batter, coating thoroughly and letting the excess drop off, and carefully drop them into the oil; deep-fry 5 to 6 at a time, turning as needed, until deep golden, about 3 minutes. Remove with a slotted spoon and drain on the platter lined with paper towels. Serve immediately with Thai Tabasco, or Siracha hot sauce.

Saté Kup Namm Jimm Tua Ri-Sung
SATÉ WITH PEANUT SAUCE

Makes 6 to 8 servings

**For the peanut sauce
(makes about 1 cup)**

2 tablespoons vegetable oil

1 shallot, minced

½ cup smooth peanut butter

3 tablespoons palm sugar or light
brown sugar

2 tablespoons fish sauce (*namm pla*)

½ teaspoon cayenne

1 cup Fresh Unsweetened Coconut
Cream (page 69)

1½ teaspoons Roasted Chiles in Oil
(page 94), or more to taste

¼ cup thick tamarind juice (see
page 128)

(continued)

Saté with peanut sauce came originally from Indonesia. One of the best recipes is from the island of Java. It is different from the saté served in Thai restaurants. Saté, sometimes spelled *satay,* is now considered and recognized as a Thai dish. The peanut sauce served as a dipping sauce with the grilled meat and rice crackers is very popular with Americans—so much so that bottled peanut sauce can be bought today at gourmet food stores and most markets. However, the commercial version is as different from the original recipe and taste as bottled mayonnaise is from homemade.

In this recipe, which is like the ancient one, the meat is aromatic, tender, and slightly crispy. The secret is in the marinade and the way the meat is laced on the skewer. Traditional Thai recipes instruct one to thread the meat in and out tightly into a bundle on the skewer, or until the skewer bends with the weight of the meat. The recipe calls for pork, beef, and chicken, which follows the traditional way of eating saté, but you can make it with just one kind of meat by tripling the amount of that ingredient. Homemade peanut sauce is easy to make once you have the key ingredients, Roasted Chiles in Oil and tamarind juice. I encourage you to try it; there is simply no comparison in taste. When making the sauce, begin by adding the amount of Roasted Chiles in Oil called for, and taste for spiciness. Keep adding small amounts until it suits your taste.

In a 9-inch skillet, heat the vegetable oil over high heat for 1 minute. Add the shallot and stir-fry until limp but not burned, about 1 minute or less. Lower the heat to medium, add the peanut butter, palm sugar, fish sauce, cayenne, and coconut cream, and stir until the peanut butter is dissolved. Cook, stirring, until the sauce begins to bubble and thicken, then add the roasted chiles and stir. Remove from the heat and stir in the tamarind juice. Taste for a balance of creamy, salty, sweet, sour, and spicy flavors; some cooks like to top the sauce with more oil from the roasted chiles before serving. Transfer to a bowl to cool completely, or store in a jar in the refrigerator until ready to serve. Bring to room temperature before serving.

For the saté, in a medium mixing bowl, combine the ground coriander seeds, cumin, peppercorns, lemongrass, turmeric, and sea salt. Add the coconut cream and mix well. Divide the marinade using three mixing bowls and put the beef, pork, and chicken in separate bowls. Mix to coat thoroughly. Cover and let sit for up to 1 hour at room temperature, or, if making ahead of time, cover and refrigerate; it will keep overnight. Remove from the refrigerator an hour before grilling, to come to room temperature. Thread the meat onto the soaked bamboo skewers, place on a platter, and cover with plastic wrap. Place 1 or 2 bread squares each on skewers and set them on a platter.

When ready to cook, start a grill fire.

Dip each meat skewer into the can of pineapple juice, then spray the meat generously with vegetable oil spray. Lay the skewers close to one another, to keep the meat moist, on the hot grill and cook, turning frequently, for 2 to 3 minutes, until well-done. Grill the bread squares for 5 to 10 seconds, turning to toast until crispy on both sides. Serve the saté and toasted bread piping hot with the peanut sauce and Classic Cucumber Salad (page 240).

Cook's Notes

Both the marinade and peanut sauce can be made ahead and stored in jars with tight-fitting lids in the refrigerator. They will keep for several days. When I make the saté for large catered parties, as soon as the meat is cooked, I brush the skewers generously with pineapple juice and wrap 5 to 6 skewers in aluminum foil. This way, I can hold them in a 150°F oven for an hour, and the meat stays juicy and tender.

For the saté

1 tablespoon coriander seeds, dry-roasted (see page 13) and ground

1 tablespoon cumin seeds, dry-roasted (see page 13) and ground

1 teaspoon Thai white peppercorns, dry-roasted (see page 13) and ground

1 stalk lemongrass, green parts and hard outer layers removed, minced

1 teaspoon turmeric powder

1 teaspoon sea salt

1 cup Fresh Unsweetened Coconut Cream (page 69)

½ pound *each* boneless beef sirloin, pork tenderloin, and boneless, skinless chicken breast, sliced into 1- by 6-inch paper-thin slices

40 bamboo skewers, soaked in water

15 to 20 cubes (1-inch square) French or Italian bread (without crusts)

One 6-ounce can pineapple juice

Vegetable oil spray

Mah Haw

GALLOPING HORSE

Makes 24 pieces, or 6 servings

For the filling
(makes about 1 cup)

2 tablespoons vegetable oil
6 cloves garlic, minced
½ pound ground pork or turkey
¼ cup palm sugar or packed light
   brown sugar
2 tablespoons fish sauce (*namm pla*)
2 tablespoons unsalted peanuts,
   dry-roasted (see page 13) and
   coarsely ground

For the galloping horse

3 to 4 tangelos; ½ pineapple,
   peeled and eyes removed (see
   page 28); 12 fresh figs; or
   3 to 4 Japanese persimmons
24 cilantro leaves
3 to 4 fresh red serrano chiles, sliced
   into 24 thin slivers

Thais have a custom of naming dishes for a legend or famous event, with a metaphor, or for the appearance of a dish. *Mah haw*, galloping horse, was created during the era of King Rama VII (1910–1925). Educated in England, the King had a passion for the theater, and he modeled his court after the sophisticated, decadent European style. He was also an avid horseman. This dish was named in recognition of his horse-riding hobby.

Sections of tangerine or pineapple chunks make "the horse," or base, which is topped with savory meat to symbolize the rider. Here I prefer to use tangelos, which have fewer seeds and are easily peeled and separated into sections. Pineapple, fresh figs, and Japanese persimmon are also wonderful substitutes.

The filling can be made and shaped ahead. Let cool completely and refrigerate in an airtight container for up to a day.

For the filling, in a 9-inch skillet, heat the vegetable oil over high heat for 1 to 2 minutes. Add the minced garlic and cook, stirring, until golden, about 15 seconds; do not burn. Add the ground pork and cook, stirring, until completely cooked through, 2 to 3 minutes. Pour off any accumulated oil and liquid and transfer the mixture to a mixing bowl.

Add the palm sugar and fish sauce to the skillet and cook, stirring, over medium heat until the sugar is dissolved and the mixture looks syrupy, about 3 minutes. Return the meat mixture to the skillet and mix well. Taste for balance: It should taste equally sweet and salty. Add more fish sauce or sugar if needed. When the meat is glazed with the syrup, stir in the peanuts, blending well. Remove the skillet from the heat to cool.

When the filling is cool, shape into balls about ¾ inch in diameter.

If using tangelos, peel the fruit and pry apart the sections, removing the white membrane. You will need 24 sections. Carefully remove any seeds, so as not to bruise the fruit. Make a slit lengthwise down the center of the back of each section, as though you were deveining a shrimp, taking care not to cut all the way through, creating a pouch for the filling. Insert a ball of filling in the slit and garnish with a cilantro leaf and red chile sliver. Place on a serving platter.

If using pineapple, cut the pineapple lengthwise in half and slice across into thin slices. Put a small ball of filling on top of each pineapple slice and garnish with a cilantro leaf and red chile sliver.

If using figs, simply slice each fig lengthwise in half. Gently press an indentation into the center of the fruit, insert a ball of filling, and garnish with a cilantro leaf and red chile sliver.

If using persimmons, peel the fruit and slice thinly crosswise. Put a ball of filling on top of each slice and garnish with a cilantro leaf and red chile sliver.

Yumm

SALADS

Thai salads combine meat, seafood, cooked and raw vegetables, and fruits, seasoned and matched with an intensely flavored dressing. Served with other complementary dishes and cooked rice, Thai salads comprise an ideal or traditional meal. The art of making Thai salads is both complex and easy and I have devoted an entire chapter to the subject (pages 235–271). The recipes included in this section were selected specifically to demonstrate one of the main elements in Thai cooking: contrast and surprise. Each salad is not only delicious, or *arroy*, but also fun, or *sanuk*.

Yumm Goon Cheang

GRILLED CHINESE SAUSAGE SALAD

Makes 6 servings

**For the dressing
(makes about ½ cup)**

½ teaspoon sea salt

3 tablespoons sugar

1 tablespoon fish sauce (*namm pla*)

1 clove garlic, minced

1 tablespoon Roasted Dried Chile Powder (page 91) or cayenne, or more to taste

Juice of 1 lime (about 3 tablespoons)

2 tablespoons fresh orange juice

(continued)

As teenagers, my cousin Susie and I were sent all the way from Bangkok to a boarding school in Kentucky. Talk about culture shock! We could not get used to American food and longed for our mothers' cooking. Cousin Susie had a really bad craving for the traditional dry sweet and salty Chinese sausages. She wrote to her parents begging them to send some. I loved them too, but didn't have the nerve to ask my parents to mail them all the way from Thailand. When they arrived in the mail, we thought we had gone to heaven!

You can find these sausages, made with chicken, pork liver, and pork, in the deli section of Asian markets. The sausages look like hot-dog-sized salami and are packaged similarly to hot dogs, with about a dozen sausages wrapped in vacuum-tight plastic. Once opened, they should be stored in a plastic bag in the refrigerator. They will keep for about a month.

The amount of Roasted Dried Chile Powder in the dressing depends on your preference. For a mild dressing, add 1 tablespoon; for a medium-spicy one, add 2 tablespoons; for a spicy dressing, add 3 to 4 tablespoons. Stored in a jar with a tight-fitting lid in the refrigerator, the dressing will keep for a couple of days. The fruit juice may lose its flavor; taste and adjust if necessary before using.

For the dressing, in a small saucepan, combine the sea salt, sugar, and fish sauce and cook over medium heat, stirring, until the salt and sugar are completely dissolved, about 2 minutes. Set aside to cool to room temperature.

Add the garlic, roasted chile powder, lime juice, and orange juice to the fish sauce mixture, stir, and taste for balance. The sauce should be spicy, sweet, sour, and salty, in that order of strength (i.e., spicy should be the strongest taste). Add more chile powder for a spicier salad. Set the dressing aside.

For the salad, in a medium saucepan, bring 2 cups water to a boil. Plunge the sausages in for 30 seconds, or until the color lightens; drain and dry completely with paper towels.

Preheat the broiler and position the broiler rack 5 inches from the flame. On a baking sheet, fold some aluminum foil into a shallow tray big enough to hold the sausages, crimping the edges to catch any fat and juices the sausages will release. Place the baking sheet under the broiler and brown the sausages, checking and rotating them every 2 to 3 minutes to ensure even browning and prevent burning (a moderate amount of blackening is fine). Transfer the sausages to a plate lined with paper towels to drain and cool.

Slice the sausages into 1/8-inch diagonal slices and put them in a large mixing bowl. Add the cucumbers, onion, jícama, and lettuce and toss. Add the cherry tomatoes and toss again. Pour the dressing over the salad and mix gently. Transfer to a serving platter and garnish with the peanuts, cilantro, and mint.

For the salad

6 Chinese sausages or sweet
  Portuguese sausages
  (about 5 ounces)
2 pickling cucumbers, peeled, sliced
  lengthwise in half, seeded, and
  thinly sliced on the diagonal
1/2 medium sweet onion, thinly
  sliced
1 cup jícama sliced into 2-inch-long
  thin matchsticks
5 romaine lettuce leaves, torn into
  bite-size pieces
10 cherry tomatoes, halved
  lengthwise
1/4 cup unsalted peanuts,
  dry-roasted (see page 13)
  and coarsely ground
20 sprigs cilantro, coarsely chopped
20 fresh mint leaves, coarsely
  chopped

Yumm Hoy Kew Jean
WATER CHESTNUT SALAD

For the dressing
(makes about 1/2 cup)

1/4 teaspoon sea salt

1 tablespoon palm sugar or light brown sugar

1 tablespoon granulated sugar

2 tablespoons fish sauce (*namm pla*)

1/4 cup thick tamarind juice (see page 128)

For the salad

1/4 pound cooked crabmeat, picked over for shells and cartilage

1/4 pound cooked shrimp, halved lengthwise

6 ounces cooked chicken, turkey, or pork, sliced into long thin strips

1 tablespoon fresh lime juice

2 tablespoons unsalted peanuts, dry-roasted (see page 13) and coarsely ground

3 tablespoons Crispy Shallots (page 138)

3 tablespoons Crispy Garlic (page 138)

12 to 15 fresh water chestnuts, peeled and sliced into 1/8-inch-thick disks (or 1/2 small jícama, peeled and thinly sliced) cut into shapes with metal cookie or canapé cutters or sliced into matchsticks (about 1 cup)

4 to 5 fresh bird chiles or 2 to 3 serrano chiles, finely minced

20 cilantro leaves, finely minced

The women of the Thai Royal Court are famous for carving vegetables and fruits. Dishes such as this salad, in which water chestnuts are peeled, thinly sliced, and exquisitely carved into miniature flowers, fruits, and animals, are a signature of the Royal Court. It is a gorgeous dish. Be creative and use bite-sized metal cookie or canapé cutters in shapes such as stars, animals, fruits, and flowers to stamp out shapes from thin slices of water chestnut or jícama. Or simply slice them into thin matchsticks.

The amount of fresh chiles depends on your personal preference. For a milder salad, use 3 to 4 bird chiles or 2 serrano chiles, removing the seeds; 4 to 5 bird chiles or 3 serrano chiles, with or without seeds, will produce a well-balanced spicy-sweet flavor. The dressing must be sharp to complement the sweet taste of the water chestnuts or jícama. Store the dressing in a jar with a tight-fitting lid in the refrigerator; it will keep for a week.

For the dressing, in a small saucepan, combine the sea salt, palm sugar, sugar, and fish sauce and cook over medium heat, stirring, until the sugar is dissolved, about 2 minutes. Add the tamarind juice and cook until thickened, another 1 to 2 minutes. Remove from the heat and cover to keep warm.

For the salad, in a large mixing bowl, combine the crabmeat, shrimp, and chicken. Pour on the warm dressing; add the lime juice and mix well. Let sit until cool, about 10 minutes.

Mix the peanuts, crispy shallots, and crispy garlic into the salad. Add most of the water chestnuts (or jícama), reserving 7 to 8 pieces for garnish. Transfer the salad to a serving platter. Garnish with the reserved water chestnuts (or jícama), the chiles, and cilantro. Mix well before serving.

Yumm Pew Som Saa
ORANGE ZEST SALAD

Bitter-citrus flavors are quite popular in Thailand. I remember that we never threw away orange or pomelo (see page 237) peels. Instead, they were threaded on twine to dry in the sun and saved for cooking or medicinal brews. This recipe calls for green calamondin, a very small round orange the size of a kumquat. Only the elderly Thai cooks know what this fruit is like, since it has completely disappeared from Thai cooking. I have adapted the recipe, using a combination of kumquats and Valencia, blood, and/or navel oranges.

For a mild dressing, use 1 tablespoon of the Roasted Dried Chile Powder; 2 tablespoons will make the flavors quite intense. Stored in a jar with a tight-fitting lid, the dressing will keep in the refrigerator for a week.

For the dressing, in a small saucepan, combine the palm sugar and fish sauce and cook over medium heat, stirring, until the sugar is dissolved, about 2 minutes. Add the tamarind juice, lower the heat, and simmer slowly until thickened, about 2 minutes more. Stir in the roasted chile powder and set aside.

For the salad, put the sliced kumquats in a medium mixing bowl. Using a small paring knife, slice the peel from the oranges as if you were peeling an apple, working over the saucepan of dressing to catch the juices. Cut between the membranes to separate the orange sections from the pith, adding the wedges to the kumquat slices. Mix gently.

In a large mixing bowl, combine the cooked shrimp and chicken. Pour on the dressing, mix well, and let sit for 10 minutes.

Just before serving, add the crispy shallots, crispy garlic, and peanuts to the salad and mix gently. Add the kumquats and oranges; mix again. Transfer to a serving platter, garnish with the mint strands, and serve immediately.

For the dressing
(makes 1/2 cup)

- 1/4 cup palm sugar or packed light brown sugar
- 3 tablespoons fish sauce (*namm pla*)
- 1/4 cup thick tamarind juice (see page 128)
- 1 to 2 tablespoons Roasted Dried Chile Powder (page 91) or cayenne

For the salad

- 6 kumquats, unpeeled, sliced crosswise into paper-thin circles, seeded, and any juices reserved
- 2 to 3 Valencia, blood, or navel oranges, or a combination
- 1/2 pound cooked shrimp, halved lengthwise
- 1/2 pound cooked chicken, turkey, or pork, sliced into thin 2-inch-long strands
- 1/2 cup Crispy Shallots (page 138)
- 1/4 cup Crispy Garlic (page 138)
- 3 tablespoons unsalted peanuts, dry-roasted (see page 13) and coarsely ground
- 30 fresh mint leaves, sliced into thin strands

Som Tumm Ma-Rah Gor

SPICY GREEN PAPAYA SALAD

Makes 1 serving

2 tablespoons fish sauce (*namm pla*)

1 tablespoon palm sugar or light
brown sugar

1 clove garlic, minced

5 to 6 fresh bird chiles or
3 to 4 serrano chiles

3 ounces green Mexican papaya,
peeled, seeded, and shredded, or
2 medium tart Granny Smith
apples, peeled, seeded,
shredded, and soaked in water
with fresh lemon or lime juice, to
yield 1½ cups

1 green bean, sliced into thin slivers
on the diagonal (optional)

3 cherry tomatoes, quartered

½ tart green plum, sliced into thin
ribbons, or 4 to 5 thin
matchsticks fresh pineapple

1 tablespoon fermented fish
(see page 125) or 1 salt-packed
anchovy fillet, washed and
patted dry

1½ tablespoons fresh lime juice

9 to 10 unsalted peanuts, dry-
roasted (see page 13) and slightly
pounded

**For the garnishes and
accompaniments**

4 to 5 green beans, parboiled for
1 minute in salted water

One 1-inch cabbage wedge

8 to 10 arugula leaves

Patpong Road, Bangkok's red-light district, is one of the best places in Thailand to get spicy green papaya salad. This is because many of the women working in the bars and brothels are from Northeast Thailand, where the dish is a regional classic. In Bangkok, stands belonging to food vendors are set up like salad bars, with an array of seasonings from which customers may choose. The original northeastern Thai name for this salad is *tumm som,* literally "pounded spicy." It calls for seasonal vegetables pounded with seasonings including lime and tamarind juice, fermented fish, fresh or dried chiles, garlic cloves for the aroma, and baby eggplant for musty-bitter flavor and texture. Green papaya is the latest addition.

The fruit was first introduced to the Thais in the seventeenth century, when it was brought over from the Americas through the Philippines. Today, every Thai city has its own recipe. This is a salad made to accommodate an individual's preference. The recipe is written for a single serving of the classic formula, which should be used as a guide for your own version. Taste and alter the seasonings to your liking. The salad should taste spicy, salty, sour, and sweet—in that order. To make the salad for more than one, increase the amount of each ingredient per number of guests. Experiment with other vegetables and fruits with slightly sweet flavors and crunchy textures, such as green beans, cucumber, cabbage, or pineapple instead of green papaya.

The green papaya to use for this recipe is the Mexican papaya, which is three to four times larger than the Hawaiian papaya commonly available in supermarkets. One medium Mexican papaya is enough for 6 to 8 servings. Green Mexican papayas are available in Asian markets.

Like the green papaya salad vendors, you can have everything prepared for last-minute assembly. Then simply pound the ingredients together and serve. Papaya shredded by hand is best (see page 28), because the texture is perfect for pounding. If you have a food processor, you can use the shredder disk and force chunks through the food tube. A box grater isn't a good alternative, as it tends to bruise the papaya flesh, turning it soggy. If substituting apples for the green papaya, be sure to soak them in lime- or lemon-infused water to prevent browning.

In a small saucepan, combine the fish sauce and palm sugar and cook over high heat until the sugar dissolves, about 30 seconds. Transfer to a small bowl to cool.

Using a mortar and pestle, pound the garlic and chiles together; the chiles should be bruised but still whole. Add the shredded green papaya and mix with a spoon, pounding slightly. Add the green bean, if desired, and mix with the spoon, again pounding lightly. Add the cherry tomatoes and plum and mix and gently pound until slightly bruised. Add the fish sauce mixture, fermented fish (or anchovy), and lime juice and pound gently to incorporate into the mixture (if using anchovy, first push the salad to one side of the mortar and, in the center of the mortar, crush the anchovy into a paste). Taste for balance: the paste should be spicy, sour, salty, and sweet, in that order. Add the peanuts and pound lightly. Mix well with the spoon.

Transfer to a plate and garnish with the green beans, cabbage, and arugula.

Cook's Notes

Green Papaya Salad is traditionally served with long-grain Thai jasmine sticky rice (see page 50) or Rice Cooked with Coconut Cream (page 39) and Grilled Chicken (page 162). If serving with sticky rice, soak the rice overnight; steam it at the same time you are making the salad. The rice will be ready by the time you are finished with the last-minute cooking of the salad. If your choice is the rice with coconut cream, you can cook it an hour ahead of serving and keep it warm.

Gai Yang
GRILLED CHICKEN

For the marinade

2 tablespoons Big Four Paste
    (page 86)
One 1-inch chunk fresh ginger,
    minced
8 cloves garlic, minced
1 teaspoon cumin seeds,
    dry-roasted (see page 13)
    and ground
1 teaspoon caraway seeds, dry-
    roasted (see page 13) and ground
One 2-inch chunk fresh turmeric,
    peeled and minced, or
    1 teaspoon turmeric powder
3 tablespoons vegetable oil

One 3-pound chicken, fat trimmed,
    halved lengthwise, rinsed
    thoroughly, and patted dry
Vegetable oil spray

This chicken tastes best if marinated overnight or for at least 3 to 4 hours. Cooking time is about 1 hour. After grilling, you can keep the chicken warm and moist for up to 30 minutes by wrapping it in aluminum foil, and placing it in a 150°F oven. You can also grill it ahead, cool it completely, and refrigerate. Reheat in a 500°F oven, uncovered, for 5 minutes, then lower the heat to 300°F and cook for another 10 minutes, or until hot.

For the marinade, in a medium mixing bowl, combine the Big Four Paste, ginger, garlic, cumin, caraway, and turmeric. Whisk in the oil until well blended.

Place a chicken half, skin side down, on a chopping board. Pound with a mallet or heavy frying pan to crack the bones and flatten slightly. Flip it over and repeat the process. Repeat with the other half.

Transfer the marinade to a large Ziploc bag, add the chicken halves, seal the bag, and toss the chicken pieces until coated with the marinade. Let sit at room temperature for at least 30 minutes or up to 1 hour. Or refrigerate and marinate for at least 3 hours, or overnight; remove the chicken from the refrigerator at least an hour before cooking to allow it to reach room temperature.

Prepare the grill. (Set a gas grill to medium-high.) When the coals are white-hot, spray the chicken generously with vegetable oil spray and put it skin side down on the hot grill. Sear for 1 to 2 minutes, or until the skin is golden. Flip it over and spray the top with vegetable oil spray. After 1 to 2 minutes, cover the coals with ashes or remove the chicken from the grill and lightly spray the coals with water to cool them. Return the chicken to the grill to continue cooking. (If you are using a gas grill, lower the heat to medium.) Cover the grill and grill-roast the chicken for about 1 hour, checking frequently and turning occasionally to prevent burning. When the chicken is completely cooked, the juices will run clear if you prick the thigh joint and an instant-read thermometer inserted in the thigh will read 160°F. Transfer to a platter, tent with foil to keep hot, and let rest for 10 minutes until ready to serve. Chop into bite-sized pieces and serve.

Keang
SOUPS AND STEWS

A traditional Thai dinner, which is the most elaborate of all Thai meals, usually includes two kinds of *keang*, in addition to other side dishes. One is a spicy stew or curry and the other is a soup with a clear broth that is not spicy. Today, except for special occasions, modern Thai families only serve one or the other with rice, condiments, and/or accompaniments.

Keang Koa Goong
SPICY AROMATIC STEW WITH SHRIMP AND APRICOTS

Makes 6 servings

This ancient recipe uses *kratorn*, a tropical fruit with a sour-acidic flavor. I substitute firm, sour, underripe fresh apricots. This is a trick I learned from my Thai friend Vithi. Years ago, while attending UCLA, he rented a house with a large apricot tree and found that the green unripened apricots were the perfect Western alternative for flavoring this spicy *keang*.

The chile paste for this particular *keang koa* is one of many variations (see page 166) created by Than Phu Ying (Her Ladyship) Prann (see page 310), the famous author of the first Thai cookbook, *Mae Khloa Hoa Paa*. She is also referred to as the title of her book, which is translated as "Head Cook from the Forest." Many of her poems, which I've translated, are found at the beginning of the chapters of this book. Because of her Persian ancestry, she was partial to aromatic spices such as caraway and coriander seeds. She also disregarded the basic rule for making authentic *keang koa* chile paste by eliminating the major ingredient, kaffir lime. The end result is an elegant soup with exquisitely balanced flavors and vibrant color.

For the chile paste, combine the sea salt and garlic in a mortar and pound into a paste. One by one, add the chiles, coriander seeds, caraway seeds, lemongrass, galangal, and shallots in sequence, adding each new ingredient only after the previous one is pureed and incorpo-

**For the chile paste
(makes about 3/4 cup)**

1 teaspoon sea salt

6 cloves garlic, minced

3 to 4 dried New Mexico
   (or California) chiles, softened in
   warm water and minced

1 teaspoon coriander seeds, dry-
   roasted (see page 13) and ground

1/2 teaspoon caraway seeds, dry-
   roasted (see page 13) and ground

1 stalk lemongrass, green parts and
   hard outer layers removed, minced

One 1/2-inch chunk galangal or
   1-inch chunk fresh ginger, peeled
   and minced

2 shallots, minced

1 teaspoon fermented shrimp paste
   or 1 tablespoon red miso

(continued)

For the stew

2 cups Fresh Unsweetened Coconut
   Milk (page 69)

6 to 7 fresh red bird chiles or
   3 to 4 serrano chiles, lightly
   pounded (optional)

½ cup Fresh Unsweetened Coconut
   Cream (page 69)

¼ teaspoon sea salt

¼ cup fish sauce (*namm pla*)

¼ cup sugar

5 tablespoons thick tamarind juice
   (see page 128)

6 to 7 slightly unripe, firm apricots,
   quartered and pitted (3 cups)

1 pound medium shrimp, peeled
   and deveined

rated into the paste. Throughout the process, use a tablespoon to push the paste back into the center of the mortar as necessary. Transfer to a bowl and set aside.

For the stew, in a 3-quart saucepan, heat the coconut milk over high heat for 2 to 3 minutes, or until it boils. The cream will rise to the top; skim it off into a 12-inch skillet. Lower the heat and leave the coconut milk at a simmer. For a spicy soup, add the optional chiles to the coconut milk.

Add ¼ cup of the fresh coconut cream and the chile paste to the skillet and mix until blended. Put the skillet over high heat and cook, stirring constantly, until the cream takes on the sheen of the red chile and the sauce thickens, about 5 minutes. Be careful not to burn the paste. Remove from the heat.

Increase the heat under the saucepan of coconut milk and bring to a gentle boil. Stir in the chile paste mixture and mix well. Add the sea salt, fish sauce, sugar, and tamarind juice. Taste the soup for a balance of spicy, sweet, salty, and sour flavors. Lower the heat to a gentle boil and add the apricot slices. Cook for another 5 to 7 minutes, or until the apricots are softened. Add the shrimp and cook, stirring to separate the shrimp. As soon as the shrimp turn firm and pink, 1 to 2 minutes, transfer the soup to a serving bowl. Dollop with the reserved ¼ cup coconut cream and serve.

Keang Tomm Yumm Goong
HOT-SOUR SHRIMP SOUP

Makes 6 servings

This fiery soup originated in the central and southern regions of Thailand, where shrimp freshly caught from the ocean is used. There are many ways to make it, but all cooks agree that a well-seasoned broth and fresh seafood are crucial. In Bangkok, the soup is sweetened with sugar and has a reddish hue from the Roasted Chiles in Oil. Bangkokians are partial to sweet tastes, and the appearance of a dish is as important as the taste. Using 5 or 6 fresh chiles will result in a milder soup, while 20 will make the soup super-fiery.

Have a square of cheesecloth ready. In a 3-quart saucepan, heat the oil over high heat for 1 to 2 minutes, or until it begins to smoke. Add the shrimp shells and dried chiles and cook, stirring, until the shells turn pink and the chile pods turn black, 30 seconds to 1 minute. Remove the saucepan from the heat and, with a slotted spoon, transfer the shells and chile pods to the square of cheesecloth. Tie it securely with twine and return the bundle to the saucepan.

Carefully pour the chicken broth into the hot pan and bring to a boil over high heat. Add the galangal, lemongrass, cilantro roots or stems, kaffir lime leaves, and fresh chiles. Lower the heat to medium-low, cover, and let the spices infuse the chicken broth for 15 to 20 minutes.

Add the sea salt and fish sauce, and taste to see if you need more spice or salt. Add the mushrooms, raise the heat to high, and boil for 10 minutes.

Remove the cheesecloth bag, lemongrass, and kaffir lime leaves. Add the roasted chiles, taste for spiciness, and add more if needed. Add the shrimp and cook for 1 to 2 minutes, or just until the shrimp turn pink. Remove from the heat and add the lime juice. Taste: You should have an equal balance of spicy, salty, and sour. Transfer the soup to a serving bowl. Garnish with the cilantro leaves and serve hot.

1½ tablespoons vegetable oil

10 shrimp shells (reserved from shrimp, below), rinsed and patted dry

6 dried de árbol chiles, softened in warm water and dried thoroughly on paper towels

4 cups chicken or vegetable broth

One ½-inch chunk galangal or 1-inch chunk fresh ginger, thinly sliced and lightly crushed

3 stalks lemongrass, green parts and hard outer layers removed, sliced lengthwise in half, and bruised lightly

3 cilantro roots or 10 stems, thoroughly rinsed

6 kaffir lime leaves, torn, or zest of 1 lime, removed with a peeler in strips and julienned

5 to 6 fresh bird chiles or serrano chiles, lightly crushed, or more to taste

½ teaspoon sea salt, or more to taste

2 tablespoons fish sauce (*namm pla*)

One 15-ounce can straw mushrooms, rinsed, halved, and patted dry, or 1 cup fresh oyster mushrooms, cleaned and sliced

1 tablespoon Roasted Chiles in Oil (page 94), or more to taste

1½ pounds medium shrimp, peeled, deveined, rinsed, and patted dry

3 tablespoons fresh lime juice

¼ cup coarsely chopped cilantro leaves

Keang Gai Kub Ma-Kheau Tedd

CHICKEN SOUP WITH STUFFED TOMATOES

Makes 6 servings

For the chile paste
(makes ½ cup)

9 almonds, softened in boiling
   water, peeled, and finely
   chopped
1 teaspoon sea salt
6 cloves garlic, minced
6 fresh cilantro roots or stems,
   minced
10 dried de árbol or Japonés chiles,
   softened in warm water and
   minced
1 tablespoon coriander seeds,
   dry-roasted (see page 13) and
   ground
1 teaspoon caraway seeds, dry-
   roasted (see page 13) and ground
Grated zest of 1 kaffir lime or
   regular lime
One 2-inch chunk fresh turmeric,
   peeled and minced, or
   1 teaspoon turmeric powder
2 shallots, minced

(continued)

The original recipe recorded by Than Phu Ying (Her Ladyship) Prann (see page 163) uses pureed chicken liver, heart, and gizzard combined with corn kernels as a filling for cherry tomatoes. In the past, food was never wasted and a good cook invented ingenious ways of using left-over ingredients, in this case resulting in a delicious soup. I have adapted the filling recipe, using shrimp and corn kernels instead.

For the chile paste, using a mortar and pestle, pound the almonds and ½ teaspoon of the sea salt to a puree. Transfer to a small bowl. Add the remaining ½ teaspoon sea salt and the garlic to the mortar and pound until pureed. Add the cilantro roots or stems and pound, then add the chile and pound. Use a tablespoon to scrape the ingredients down into the center of the mortar as needed. Add the coriander seeds and car-away seeds and pound. Add the kaffir lime rind and turmeric and pound to a puree. Add the minced shallots. Add the reserved almond puree, pound and mix together, and set aside.

With a small paring knife, core each tomato. Use the end of a vegetable peeler to scoop out the seeds.

Fit a food processor with the steel blade and grind the shrimp to a paste. Transfer to a mixing bowl, add the corn kernels and ¼ teaspoon of the sea salt, and mix well. Transfer the mixture to a small Ziploc bag. Cut a small triangle from one corner, big enough for the corn kernels to pass through, and, using this makeshift pastry bag, squeeze the filling mixture into the tomatoes, filling each about two-thirds full. Set aside.

In a 4-quart saucepan, heat the vegetable oil over high heat for 1 to 2 minutes, or until hot. Add the garlic and cook, stirring to prevent burn-ing, until golden, about 15 seconds. Add the chile paste and cook, stir-ring constantly, until fragrant, about 3 minutes—do not let the paste stick to the pan; add a bit of the broth if needed. Add the chicken and cook, stirring, until it is coated with the paste and the outside is firmed and cooked, 1 to 2 minutes. Add the chicken broth. When the broth begins to boil, season with the remaining 1 teaspoon sea salt, the sugar, fish sauce, and Kaffir lime leaves; taste for a balance of salty and spicy. Lower the heat to medium and let the soup boil gently for 15 to 20 minutes, or until the chicken is cooked through.

Just before serving, add the stuffed cherry tomatoes to the boiling soup. When the shrimp filling turns pink and the skin of the tomatoes begins to curl away, about 2 minutes, remove from the heat. Transfer to a serving bowl and serve immediately.

Cook's Notes

Both the chile paste and the chicken broth (page 168) can be made ahead and refrigerated. The stuffed cherry tomatoes can be refrigerated overnight. Serve the soup with cooked long-grain jasmine rice (see pages 37 and 38) and Classic Cucumber Salad (page 240) for a perfect meal.

For the soup

16 cherry tomatoes
¼ pound medium shrimp, peeled,
    deveined, and minced
½ cup sweet corn kernels
1¼ teaspoons sea salt
3 tablespoons vegetable oil
5 cloves garlic, lightly crushed
5 cups chicken broth
1 pound boneless, skinless chicken
    breasts, cut into bite-sized pieces
1 tablespoon sugar
2 tablespoons fish sauce (*namm pla*)
4 kaffir lime leaves, torn, or grated
    zest of 1 lime

Keang Jeurn Woon Senn

CLEAR SOUP WITH BEAN THREADS

Makes 6 servings

For the chicken stock

One 3-pound chicken, rinsed and
   thoroughly dried
6 cups bottled or filtered water
A very thin slice fresh ginger
4 cloves garlic, unpeeled, smashed
1 rib celery, chopped
1 medium yellow or white onion,
   quartered
1 teaspoon sea salt

For the soup

¼ pound ground pork
1 tablespoon soy sauce
10 Thai white peppercorns, dry-
   roasted (see page 13), 7 finely
   ground, 3 slightly crushed
½ teaspoon sesame oil
2 tablespoons fish sauce (*namm pla*)
1 teaspoon sugar
1 teaspoon salted Tien Jing cabbage
   (see page 143)
1 cup slivered fresh shiitake
   mushroom caps (or use dried
   shiitakes, softened in boiling
   water)
1 cup shredded cooked chicken
   (reserved from the stock)
2 ounces bean threads (glass
   noodles), softened in cool water
   and cut into approximately
   3-inch lengths
3 whole scallions, cut into
   ½-inch lengths
¼ pound small shrimp, peeled and
   deveined
10 sprigs cilantro, coarsely chopped
2 tablespoons Crispy Garlic
   (page 138)

As with all other broths, this one can be made ahead and refrigerated or frozen. Making a good broth requires practice. If you allow this soup to boil gently, the pork patties will remain whole, the chicken and shrimp will be moist, not tough, and the bean threads will expand without falling apart. The secret seasonings for Thai soups are salted Tien Jing cabbage and crispy garlic. As an alternative to pork patties, use either sliced, shredded, or ground beef or turkey for the patties. Squid, clams, and mussels are great in the soup too. Soft tofu is another wonderful addition.

For the stock, in a 6-quart stockpot, combine the chicken, water, ginger, garlic, celery, onion, and salt and bring to a boil over high heat. Cover, lower the heat to medium-low, and boil gently for 1 hour.

Strain the broth and set aside. Remove the chicken from the bones, discarding the skin. Shred enough of the chicken into bite-sized pieces to make 1 cup and reserve for the soup; reserve the rest for another use. Wash the stockpot, return the broth to the pot, cover, and bring to a gentle boil over medium heat.

Meanwhile, for the soup, in a small bowl, mix the ground pork with the soy sauce, finely ground peppercorns, and the sesame oil. Set aside.

Season the broth with the slightly crushed peppercorns, the fish sauce, sugar, and salted cabbage. Pinch off teaspoonfuls of the pork mixture, pat with your fingers into small patties, and drop into the broth. Let the broth come to a boil and add the shiitake mushrooms and the reserved chicken, gently stirring to separate the chicken pieces. Cover and let the soup simmer over low heat for no longer than 30 minutes. Fifteen minutes before serving, add the bean threads and scallions.

Just before serving, add the shrimp. When they turn pink, remove the pot from the heat and ladle the soup into a large soup bowl. Garnish with the chopped cilantro and crispy garlic. Serve hot.

Kreang Kang
SIDE DISHES

Side dishes are often determined by what's fresh and available in the market and what strikes a cook's fancy. If it is a very special find, the entire menu will be designed to complement it. The following recipes represent a range of Thai cooking from the traditional to the contemporary. Several are rare old recipes, not even known to modern Thai cooks, while others are popular not only with today's Thais, but among foreigners who love Thai food as well.

Padd Moo, Goong, Sapparod
STIR-FRIED PORK, SHRIMP, AND PINEAPPLE
Makes 6 servings

My cousin Susie exports canned pineapples from Thailand. Every day she chases after pineapples, trying to get her orders filled before the big corporations buy them up, and while they're still growing in the fields. She is a tough customer to please when it comes to pineapple, and she doesn't approve of American canned pineapple at all. However, she does approve of this recipe—as long as fresh pineapple is used. Substitute ripe but tart peaches, peeled and sliced into bite-sized chunks, for fresh pineapple if necessary.

In a 12-inch skillet, heat the oil over high heat for 1 to 2 minutes, or until it is very hot and just barely smoking. Add the garlic cloves and cook, stirring and tossing, until golden, about 15 seconds. Add the pork and cook, stirring, until cooked through, about 2 minutes. Add the pineapple chunks and cook, stirring, until darkened and soft, 1 to 2 minutes. Season with the sea salt, sugar, and fish sauce and mix well. Add the shrimp and cook, stirring, until pink, about 1 minute. Add the chiles and mix well. Transfer to a serving plate and sprinkle with the ground peppercorns and chopped cilantro. Serve hot.

2 tablespoons vegetable oil

6 cloves garlic, lightly pounded

6 ounces lean boneless pork, sliced across the grain into thin 3-inch strips

2 cups bite-sized chunks fresh pineapple (see page 28)

1 teaspoon sea salt

2 tablespoons sugar

3 tablespoons fish sauce (*namm pla*)

6 ounces medium shrimp, peeled and deveined

4 to 6 fresh red bird chiles or 2 to 3 serrano chiles, sliced into thin slivers

1 teaspoon Thai white peppercorns, dry-roasted (see page 13) and ground

10 sprigs cilantro, coarsely chopped

Haw Mok Pla

STEAMED FISH CUSTARD IN BANANA POUCHES

Makes 6 servings

⅓ cup Keang Koa Chile Paste
  (page 210)
2 cups Fresh Unsweetened Coconut
  Cream and Milk (combined to
  make consistency of whole milk;
  page 69)
½ teaspoon sea salt
2 tablespoons fish sauce (*namm pla*)
1 tablespoon sugar
6 large eggs, separated
1½ pounds red snapper fillets, cut
  crosswise into ¼-inch-wide slices
  (3 cups)
One 1-pound package frozen
  banana leaves, thawed (or 8
  custard cups or 6 medium
  artichokes, parboiled 20 minutes,
  inner leaves and chokes
  removed)
4 to 5 Napa cabbage leaves, rinsed
  and thoroughly dried
⅓ cup Fresh Unsweetened Coconut
  Cream (page 69)
6 to 8 cilantro leaves
6 to 8 fresh Thai basil leaves or mint
  leaves
3 fresh red bird chiles or 2 serrano
  chiles, seeded and slivered
6 kaffir lime leaves, finely sliced, or
  zest of 1 lime, removed with a
  peeler in strips and julienned

One wintry day while I was visiting Thailand, my friend Vithi took me for a picnic on top of a mountain. He wanted me to see the azaleas and rhododendrons blooming. We stopped at a market and bought our food there, including *haw mok*. When we reached the mountaintop, the air was crisp and clear, and the wind chilly and brisk. Several government drug agents wearing heavy jackets laden down with machine guns were patrolling the area. They looked very forlorn, so my intrepid friend invited them to join us. We all huddled close together among the glorious blooms on top of the world and savored the warm and spicy *haw mok*.

Banana leaf pouches are best for steaming *haw mok*. They add a special fragrance to the dish. The pouches can be made ahead and will keep for a day; stack them together and store in a Ziploc bag in the refrigerator. Heat-proof custard cups can be substituted for the banana pouches. Using these requires an extra 10 minutes for the custards to cook. Another alternative is parboiled whole artichokes: Remove the inner leaves and the chokes, fill with the fish mixture, and steam for 45 to 50 minutes.

Gentle heat for steaming guarantees a soft custard. Do not rush, and try not to lift the lid to peek. *Haw mok* can be served hot, at room temperature, or cold, with cooked long-grain rice (see pages 37 and 38). It is best not to reheat *haw mok,* because the custard will lose its delicate texture and become gelatinous.

Put the chile paste in a large mixing bowl and slowly whisk in the coconut cream and milk. Add the sea salt, fish sauce, and sugar and mix well. In a small bowl, beat the egg yolks until smooth. Add the egg yolks to the coconut cream mixture, then add the snapper and mix well. Set aside.

Wash and dry the banana leaves. Using scissors, carefully cut the leaves into 12- to 14-inch manageable oblong pieces, then trim into 8-inch rounds. Turn a gas or electric burner to medium and wave the banana rounds over the flame or slide over the heating element, turning once, to soften. To make the square banana leaf pouches, stack two banana rounds, with the dull sides facing each other; make sure the veins of the banana leaves run parallel. Make a 1-inch-wide tuck or pleat, about 1½ inches deep, at any point on the circumference and secure with a toothpick. Repeat the same process at exactly the opposite point and secure with a toothpick. Make a tuck that is perfectly centered between the first two tucks and secure with a toothpick, then make one more tuck directly opposite this one. You will have a square container. Snip off any toothpick portions that extend beyond the pouch with scissors. Repeat with the remaining banana leaves. You should have 6 to 7 pouches.

Tear the soft leaves from the hard stems of the Napa leaves, discarding the stems. Line the banana pouches (or custard cups or artichokes) with the leaves. Beat the egg whites until frothy and fold gently into the fish mixture. Spoon the fish mixture into the pouches (or custard cups or artichokes) leaving a ½-inch space at the top. Garnish each one with a teaspoon or more of thick coconut cream, a cilantro leaf, a basil leaf, and a few red chile slivers and kaffir lime leaf strands.

Fill a pasta pot that has a steamer basket insert half-full of water and bring it to a rapid boil. Put as many filled banana pouches (or custard cups or artichokes) as you can successfully fit in the steamer basket insert, set the insert in the pasta pot, and lower the heat to medium. Cover and steam for 25 minutes, or until the custard is firm (a bamboo skewer inserted in the center should come out clean). Repeat steaming until all the custards are cooked.

Mus-Yao Than
STUFFED TROUT

Makes 6 servings

For the filling
(makes ⅓ cup)

1 teaspoon coriander seeds
¼ teaspoon caraway seeds
1 teaspoon Thai white peppercorns
½ teaspoon cardamom seeds
4 whole cloves
½ teaspoon freshly grated nutmeg
½ teaspoon ground cinnamon
1 teaspoon sea salt
6 cloves garlic, minced
8 cilantro stems with roots, minced
One ½-inch chunk galangal or
   1-inch chunk fresh ginger,
   peeled and minced
1 stalk lemongrass, green parts and
   hard outer layers removed,
   minced
Grated zest of ½ kaffir lime or
   regular lime
3 shallots, minced

(continued)

Mus-yao is an ancient Thai word meaning "fish," and *than* means "fragrant-sweet." This dish reveals its Near Eastern influence because of the nutmeg, cardamom, and cloves. At first, this recipe sounded odd to me, but I found it a wonderful and surprising treat, full of contrast—distinctly Thai—and definitely befitting this chapter.

The filling can be prepared in stages or all at once and stored in the refrigerator for a day. Be aware that the spices will intensify the longer the filling sits. The fish can be steamed and breaded several hours in advance. Wrap it securely with plastic wrap and refrigerate. An hour before serving, remove the fish from the refrigerator to come to room temperature. Deep-fry just before serving.

I like using Japanese bread crumbs (panko) because they are very light and not greasy when deep-fried. However, you can dust the fish with flour or use unseasoned regular bread crumbs.

In a 9-inch skillet, dry-roast the coriander seeds, caraway seeds, and Thai peppercorns together over high heat for 1 minute, or until fragrant. Transfer the roasted spices to a plate to cool. Roast the cardamom seeds in the skillet for 30 seconds, or until fragrant. Transfer them to the plate with the other roasted spices and repeat the process with the cloves. Cool completely, then grind the spices in an electric coffee or spice grinder. Combine them with the grated nutmeg and cinnamon and set aside.

Using a mortar and pestle, pound the sea salt and garlic together to a paste. One at a time, add the cilantro stems, galangal, lemongrass, kaffir lime zest, shallots, and spice mixture in sequence, adding each new ingredient only after the previous one is pureed and incorporated into the paste. Transfer to a small bowl and set aside.

In a 10-inch skillet, heat the 5 tablespoons oil over high heat for 1 to 2 minutes, or until hot. Add the paste and cook, stirring, until fragrant, another 1 to 2 minutes. Add the fish sauce and sugar, mix well, and remove the skillet from the heat. Add the peanuts and kaffir lime leaf strands and mix well. Cool completely and set aside.

In a small mixing bowl, lightly beat the egg white. Mix in the flour. Stuff each fish cavity with half the filling, pressing down gently on the filling. Spoon the egg white and flour mixture along the openings, then press gently to seal the openings.

Wrap each fish securely in 5 or 6 softened corn husks and place on a heat-proof round platter. Fill a wok halfway with water and set a round wire rack (a cake cooling rack will do) inside. Turn the heat to high. When the water begins to boil, put the plate with the fish on top of the wire rack, cover the wok, and steam until the fish is cooked through, about 15 minutes. Remove the platter from the wok and set aside to cool.

Lightly beat the eggs in a shallow bowl and put the Japanese bread crumbs in another shallow bowl. Carefully remove the fish from the corn husks and pat dry with paper towels. Dip the fish into the egg coating, then dredge in the bread crumbs, coating completely. Let the breaded fish sit for 15 to 20 minutes at room temperature

Line a platter with several paper towels and place near the stove. In a 12-inch skillet or flat-bottomed wok, heat the remaining 3 cups vegetable oil over high heat to 350°F. (You can also test for readiness by dipping the end of a wooden spoon into the oil; if tiny bubbles form around the spatula, the oil is ready.) Carefully slide one of the breaded fish into the oil and fry until golden brown on the first side, 2 to 3 minutes. Turn to fry and brown the other side. Transfer to the platter lined with paper towels to drain, and deep-fry the second fish. Serve immediately on a platter, garnished with the lime wedges.

For the trout

- 5 tablespoons plus 3 cups vegetable oil
- 1 tablespoon fish sauce (*namm pla*)
- 1 tablespoon sugar
- ¼ cup unsalted peanuts, dry-roasted (see page 13) and coarsely ground
- 3 kaffir lime leaves, thinly sliced into strands, or grated zest of 1 lime
- 1 large egg white
- 1 tablespoon all-purpose flour
- 2 boned whole trout (about ¾ pound each), rinsed and patted dry
- 10 to 12 dried corn husks, soaked in warm water until softened
- 2 large eggs
- 2 cups Japanese bread crumbs (panko; see Cook's Note, page 105)
- 1 to 2 limes, sliced into wedges

Padd Pla Mueg Namm Prikk Pow

STIR-FRIED SQUID WITH ROASTED CHILES IN OIL

Makes 6 servings

1 pound fresh squid
1 teaspoon sea salt
2 tablespoons vegetable oil
10 cloves garlic, minced
1 to 2 tablespoons Roasted Chiles in
    Oil (page 94)
2 tablespoons soy sauce
4 to 6 fresh red bird chiles or
    3 to 4 serrano chiles, seeded
    and sliced into thin slivers
1 cup fresh Thai basil leaves, Italian
    basil leaves, or mint leaves

Many seafood restaurants in southern Thailand display their catch of the day on ice at the entrance to the establishment so their customers can select their own seafood and specify how they want it cooked. Whenever I see squid, I choose to have it stir-fried with Roasted Chiles in Oil and a handful of fresh Thai basil leaves. Besides squid, this same technique can be used for shrimp, clams, or mussels.

For tender, crunchy, delicious fried squid, it's important to make sure the squid is very cold and thoroughly dry, and that the skillet is very hot.

Clean the squid, following the instructions on page 17. In a colander in the sink, massage the squid with the sea salt. Let it sit for 5 to 10 minutes. Rinse with several changes of cool water and dry thoroughly with paper towels. Separate the tentacles and set aside on a plate. Slice the squid bodies crosswise into 1-inch rings and lay them next to the tentacles on the plate.

In a 12-inch skillet, heat the oil over high heat for 1 to 2 minutes, or until it begins to smoke. Add the garlic and cook, stirring to prevent burning, until it turns golden, about 15 seconds. Add the roasted chiles, lower the heat to medium, and cook, stirring, until the mixture is dissolved, about 10 seconds. Turn the heat back up to high and add the soy sauce. The mixture will bubble immediately. Add the fresh chiles and squid tentacles and cook, stirring, until the tentacles begin to curl, about 1 minute. Add the rest of the squid and cook, stirring, until white and firm, 1 to 2 minutes. Turn off the heat and stir in the basil leaves. Transfer to a serving platter and serve hot.

Padd Kee Mau Neur

DRUNKEN STIR-FRIED BEEF

Makes 6 servings

Padd kee mau is a legendary Thai dish. The chile paste is so hot and spicy that it will either cure a hangover or make you drink so much alcohol that you will end up getting drunk and need more to cure your hangover. If it is not hot, it is not *kee mau*!

Padd kee mau is delicious with beef, chicken, pork, lamb, tofu, seafood, or noodles.

For the chile paste, using a mortar and pestle, pound the sea salt and garlic into a paste. One by one, add the chiles, lemongrass, lime zest, galangal, and shallots in sequence, adding each new ingredient only after the previous one is pureed and incorporated into the paste. Set aside or refrigerate.

Heat a 12-inch skillet over high heat until you feel the heat when you hold your hand 3 to 4 inches above it. Add the vegetable oil. When the oil begins to smoke, after 10 to 15 seconds, add the chile paste and cook, stirring, until aromatic, 20 to 30 seconds. If it is browning unevenly, add a teaspoon or two of the sherry to the pan. When the oil turns red from the chile paste, add the beef slices and cook, stirring and mixing, until the meat is cooked through, about 2 minutes. If the skillet is too dry, add 1 to 2 tablespoons or more sherry as you stir-fry.

Add the green beans, mixing well, then add the fish sauce. Once again, if the mixture is dry, add a tablespoon or two of sherry, and continue to stir-fry until the green beans are softened but still crispy, 1 to 2 minutes. Turn off the heat and stir in the mint leaves. Transfer to a serving platter and serve hot.

Cook's Note

Use 2 to 3 fresh bird chiles for a milder paste, 5 to 6 bird chiles for medium-spicy, and 10 or more for the real drunken chile paste. You can substitute serrano chiles but in smaller proportions.

**For the chile paste
(makes about ⅓ cup)**

½ teaspoon sea salt

3 cloves garlic, minced

1 dried New Mexico (or California) chile, softened in hot water, split lengthwise, stem and seeds removed, dried thoroughly, and sliced very thin

10 to 12 fresh bird chiles or 7 to 8 serrano chiles, minced (see Cook's Note)

1 stalk lemongrass, green parts and hard outer layers removed, minced

Grated zest of 1 kaffir lime or regular lime

One ¼-inch slice galangal or ½-inch slice fresh ginger, peeled and minced

2 shallots, minced

For the stir-fried beef

3 tablespoons vegetable oil

2 tablespoons dry sherry or white wine, plus more if needed

1 pound boneless lean beef (flank steak or top sirloin), thinly sliced across the grain into long bite-sized pieces

2 cups green beans, parboiled in salted water for 1 minute and thinly julienned on the diagonal

2 tablespoons fish sauce (*namm pla*)

10 sprigs fresh mint, leaves only (½ cup leaves)

Pla Ping Kab Yumm Mah-Muen

GRILLED TUNA WITH GREEN MANGO SALAD

Makes 4 to 6 servings

1 pound fresh tuna steak
2 tablespoons Big Four Paste
   (page 86)
One ½-inch piece fresh ginger,
   peeled and minced
1 tablespoon soy sauce
1 lemon, halved, juiced, and sliced
3 to 4 dried Japonés chiles
½ to 1 teaspoon olive oil

For the green mango salad

Juice of 1 lemon
Sea salt, as needed (for mango)
1 large green mango, peeled and
   grated, or 2 medium-tart Granny
   Smith apples, unpeeled,
   quartered, seeded, and sliced
   into matchsticks
3 tablespoons palm sugar or light
   brown sugar
1 tablespoon fish sauce (*namm pla*)
1 teaspoon Roasted Dried Chile
   Powder (page 91)
3 shallots, thinly sliced
Vegetable oil spray

Generally, Thais prefer grilling a whole fish with the head and bones intact, and they are especially fond of smaller fish grilled until very crispy. Every last remnant of fish is eaten with great relish. Recently, however, Western and Japanese ways of cooking large fish steaks such as tuna and salmon have been adapted by Thai cooks. This is one of their adaptations.

Place the tuna steak on a platter. In a small bowl, mix together the Big Four Paste, ginger, soy sauce, and lemon juice. Pour the marinade over the fish, turn to coat, and top with the lemon slices. Cover with plastic wrap and refrigerate for 1 hour.

Preheat the oven to 375°F. Put the chiles on a piece of aluminum foil and drizzle with the olive oil. Fold the foil to make a packet and roast in the oven for about 15 minutes. The chiles should turn black. Set them aside to cool.

If you are using the mango, in a bowl, mix together 3 cups water, the lemon juice, and a couple of pinches of sea salt. Add the mango and leave in the water until ready to mix the salad. If using Granny Smith apples, mix 3 cups water with the lemon juice, add the sliced apples, and leave in the water until ready to mix the salad.

In a small saucepan, combine the palm sugar and fish sauce and cook over medium heat for 1 minute, or until the sugar dissolves. Transfer to a bowl to cool completely, then stir in the chile powder.

Remove the mango or apple from the water and squeeze out the excess liquid. Pat dry with paper towels, and put in a large mixing bowl. Add the shallots and toss gently. Just before serving, add the chile dressing and mix well.

Preheat a grill until it is very hot. Spray the fish generously with vegetable oil spray, put on the hot grill, and baste it with the marinade. Cook for 1 to 2 minutes, spray the fish again with vegetable oil spray, and turn it over. Lower the heat to medium-high, or move the fish to a cooler part of the grill, and grill for another 7 to 10 minutes, or until the fish is cooked through.

Place the grilled tuna on a large serving platter, with the mango salad on the side. Garnish with the crispy toasted chiles and serve.

Kho Op Maw Din

RICE IN AN EARTHENWARE POT

Makes 6 servings

Both small and large clay earthenware pots can be purchased in Asian markets. The clay gives a musty-earthy aroma to the rice. If you don't have a clay pot, an enameled cast-iron casserole is a good substitute.

Prepare the ingredients ahead, but leave the assembly to the last minutes before baking. You can substitute 4 cups of softened bean threads (see page 304) for the cooked rice. Shrimp, crabmeat, or clams also make tasty additions. For a spicy casserole, drizzle a tablespoon of Roasted Chiles in Oil (page 94) on top of the meat and vegetables before baking. Serve with Fresh Chiles with Fish Sauce (page 93).

In a small bowl, combine both soy sauces, the white wine, ginger, and sesame oil. Put the chicken pieces in a bowl. Pour the mixture over the chicken, cover with plastic wrap, and let sit at room temperature for at least 15 to 20 minutes or up to 1 hour.

Preheat the broiler. Broil the sausage for 1 to 2 minutes, or until the top turns crispy, turn the sausage, and broil for another 1 to 2 minutes. If using Portuguese sausage, lower the heat to 350°F and cook for another 2 minutes. Transfer the sausage to a plate lined with paper towels to cool. Slice into scant ⅛-inch-thick diagonal pieces and set aside.

In a small bowl, mix the cornstarch and water; set aside. In a 12-inch skillet, heat the vegetable oil over high heat for 1 to 2 minutes, or until the oil just begins to smoke. Add the garlic and cook, stirring, until golden, about 15 seconds. Add the chicken with the marinade and cook, stirring, until cooked through, 1 to 2 minutes. If using the oyster sauce, add it now. Add the mushrooms and snow peas and cook, stirring, until the peas turn bright green, about 1 minute. Add the chicken broth. When the broth begins to boil, whisk the cornstarch and water well and add it to the stir-fry. Cook, stirring, until the sauce is the consistency of light gravy, 1 to 2 minutes. Remove from the heat.

Meanwhile, preheat the oven to 375°F. Spray the inside of an earthenware or enameled cast-iron pot with vegetable spray. Place the cooked rice in the pot. Ladle the chicken and vegetable mixture on top. Spoon the sauce evenly over the top. Garnish with the sausage. Bake 5 to 7 minutes, until the rice is heated through. Garnish with the chopped cilantro.

1 tablespoon soy sauce
1 tablespoon dark sweet soy sauce,
    or 1 tablespoon regular soy sauce
    plus 1 teaspoon molasses
1 tablespoon dry white wine or
    white vermouth
One ¼-inch chunk fresh ginger,
    peeled and minced
1 teaspoon sesame oil
6 ounces boneless, skinless chicken
    breast, sliced across the grain
    into bite-sized pieces
1 Chinese sausage or sweet
    Portuguese sausage
1 teaspoon cornstarch
2 tablespoons water
2 tablespoons vegetable oil
2 cloves garlic, unpeeled, lightly
    pounded
1 tablespoon oyster sauce (optional)
1 cup fresh shiitake mushrooms,
    thinly sliced lengthwise, or one
    15-ounce can straw mushrooms,
    drained, salted, rinsed, patted
    dry, and cut in half
1 cup tender snow peas or snap
    peas
1½ cups chicken broth
Vegetable oil spray
2 cups cooked long-grain rice,
    preferably Thai jasmine or Indian
    or California basmati (see pages
    37 and 38)
6 sprigs cilantro, coarsely chopped

Chile Water
THE CROWN JEWEL

Namm prikk tray ornately arranged
Crowned with jewel and flowery morsels
Carved from greens so simple and plain
Utterly enchanting to the Divine
Who disregards His kingly manner
To feast in rapture and ecstasy

**Translated from a poem by Jeangjai Teddvisa,
"Recipes for Salads and Chile Water from
Thailand," published by the
Thai Women's Association, 1966**

Namm prikk, or chile water, is the crown jewel of Thai food. A uniquely Thai invention, in name and appearance it bears resemblance to a relish, salsa, condiment, or seasoning sauce. But it's not like any of these: *Namm prikk* is an entity unto itself. One precious spoonful of this intensely flavored sauce, extreme in taste, is very potent. When served with other dishes, it is not used as a seasoning, but is instead eaten with its own assortment of complementary accompaniments. Each is strictly prescribed and made specifically to match the flavor, aroma, and texture of the particular *namm prikk* recipe.

Whether at the table of commoner or king, traditionally *namm prikk* took center stage. Ordinary folks considered a meal of chile water, bitter greens, and rice to be satisfying and wholesome. In the worst and in the best of times, to have a bit of *namm prikk* with rice was a blessing. According to Royal Court protocol, a formal menu for the king consisted of nine dishes. *Namm prikk,* the ninth dish, would be placed in the center of the table—the pivotal point of presentation—as the crown jewel of the meal. Nearby would be set a tray of accompaniments including carved vegetables, fruit, tender blossoms, grilled meat, poultry, and/or seafood. All were prepared by formal rules created by the royal cooks.

An ancient food, *namm prikk* was eaten by Thais as early as the Sukothai Kingdom (A.D. 1288). Records of that time mention a paste that was the main staple, made with a roasted and fermented bean paste, wild onion, and Thai peppercorns and diluted with lime juice. The same paste was also used as a seasoning in other dishes, particularly *keang*, or soup and stew. The Thai principle of combining intensely salty, spicy, sweet, and sour tastes, enhanced by a musty and fermented aroma, is the foundation of the dish.

Down through the centuries, *namm prikk* has inspired hundreds of recipes, evolving into one of Thailand's most complex and extraordinary culinary creations. Today, it represents a composite of flavors, aromas, and textures that satisfy all the desires of the Thai palate. Garlic and shallots eventually replaced the wild onion for their more aromatic fragrances and pungent tastes. Chiles are used in combination with the Thai peppercorns for spiciness. Different fruits, particularly those with sharp, sour tastes and intense perfumes are added, in combination with the lime juice, for distinct flavors, aroma, and textures. In place of fermented beans, fermented and roasted or grilled meat, poultry, seafood, and insects are added, multiplying the layers of complex flavors and textures.

Thai people cannot do without *namm prikk*. Like their ancestors, when they travel, a jar goes along. It soothes the spirit and soul and serves as a reminder of home in foreign and unfamiliar places. Among connoisseurs of Thai food, *namm prikk*, because of its exacting seasonings, is the true test of sophisticated palates. It's also a dish that separates the ordinary cook from a great one. In the past, although Royal Court ladies might never have to cook for their families, each strove to excel in the art of making *namm prikk*. For the accompaniments, the ladies of the court would transform ordinary fruits and vegetables into flowers, animals, or astrological constellations.

In its celebration as a dish, and as a presentation fit for the gods and kings, *namm prikk*, with its accompaniments, truly represents the creative expression of Thai culinary skill. It also mirrors the Thai belief that food is prepared and eaten as an expression of love, for good health, *sanuk*, or "fun," and *arroy*, for its deliciousness.

An authentic Thai meal is not complete without *namm prikk*. Yet foreigners, because of its extreme flavors and aromas, are seldom served the dish. It is believed that only when someone has fully embraced the Thai culture is he or she able to appreciate this unique culinary creation. Young generations of Thais brought up in traditional households are appreciative of *namm prikk*, but few know its evolution, or the cultural and social customs it represents. Fewer still know how to make it. Most modern Thai families satisfy their cravings by buying ready-made *namm prikk* in markets. However, some traditional Thai families continue to make their own. I was fortunate to be introduced to one such family.

One wet monsoon day, a friend, *Khun* (Mr.) Sutorn, took me to a home located on a Buddhist temple ground in Nonthaburi, a city near Bangkok. My friend's intention was for both the husband and the wife to teach me how to cook. After driving along one muddy lane after another, penetrating deep into endless, iridescent-green tunnels of banana groves, we finally arrived at an old wooden house perched dangerously over a swollen river.

The house is also a convenience store, resembling a 7-Eleven market in America. But at this store, the neighbors paddled tiny wooden boats to the dock to shop. The husband, *Lung* (Uncle) Nol, as he was called, was not at home. But his wife, *Paa* (Aunt) Shoup, welcomed us as we joined a group of lively friends and family members. During the next two hours, as the selling and buying and social activities intensified, the children, caught up in the frenzied spirits, began to dive off the porch into the muddy river, squeaking with delight. None of these activities seemed to disturb Paa Shoup as she, a neighbor, and I squatted on the wooden floor among bags of groceries to prepare the evening meal.

Paa Shoup had first taken me to her vegetable garden to pick fresh yard-long beans; *pakk boog*, swamp spinach; and *mah-eng*, a tiny hairy yellow fruit resembling a green cherry tomato. We washed, sliced, diced, and pounded as we talked among ourselves about food, cooking, and children. By the time Lung Nol came home, all the ingredients were prepared and ready for him.

He's the cook in the family. As he took over the kitchen, Paa Shoup quietly finished the pounding for the last dish, *namm prikk krapi*, chile water with fermented shrimp paste.

As we gathered on the wooden porch over the river for our meal, a straw mat for sitting was placed next to several large ceramic jars filled with blooming water lilies and goldfish. The sun had almost set, leaving the river shimmering in the twilight. The women lit candles on the wooden floor near us. The house was suddenly quiet. The only noise was the occasional sound of water lapping against the wooden planks. The cool breeze was a welcome refreshment after the afternoon of cooking. The women brought out bowls and plates containing dinner and placed them on the mat. Set in the center of all the other dishes, just as in ancient times, was Paa Shoup's *namm prikk krapi*. It was accompanied with a plate of grilled *pla too*, or mackerel; crunchy baby eggplants; an omelet made with water mimosa, or swamp spinach; and parboiled yard-long beans bound in bite-sized bundles. Khun Sutorn whispered softly to me that although Lung Nol is known as the cook of his family, it's Paa Shoup who is a really great cook.

Anatomy of Namm Prikk

Among the hundreds of *namm prikk* recipes, I have selected a handful that I hope will be a good beginning for your love affair with this amazing dish. The ingredients for these recipes are readily available. Follow the few basic rules, but be creative and inventive. Have *sanuk* (fun).

The guidelines for *namm prikk* include starting with the freshest and finest of seasonal ingredients; selecting a dominant ingredient; and matching the rest to complement it. Then,

remember to add an element of surprise. It may be an ingredient with a contrasting texture, for example, crunchy or crispy as opposed to smooth. A good chile sauce should taste salty, followed by a spicy sting and sharp sour taste. It's meant to be strong, so use it sparingly.

Namm prikk has a variation called *lon*. Seasoned with coconut cream, it's a rich, creamy, sweet sauce. Lime juice balances the sweetness. In contrast to *namm prikk, lon*'s predominant taste is sweet-and-sour, with a secondary taste of saltiness and spiciness. In addition, the consistency of *lon* is different, as it's watery. Minced and cooked pork, chicken, shrimp, or fish is added as the binder and for texture.

Common Flavoring Ingredients for Namm Prikk and Lon

SALTINESS: fish sauce, sea salt, soy sauce, anchovy

SOUR AND FRUITY: green apple, bitter orange, calamondin, lime juice, unripe mango, raw plum, unripe tamarind pod, tamarind juice, tomatillo, unripe tomato, pineapple, kiwi

SPICY: fresh bird, jalapeño, serrano, or Anaheim chile with stem, in red, yellow, or green; dried *chiltepín*, Japonés, or de árbol chile; fresh Thai white peppercorns

SWEET: palm sugar, white sugar, brown sugar

BINDER: fermented fish, fermented shrimp paste, red miso or Japanese fermented bean paste, roasted eggplant, roasted mushrooms, unripe tomato with a lot of seeds

AROMATIC: chile leaf, coconut cream, cilantro root, cilantro stems and leaves, garlic, shallot, fresh turmeric

CONTRAST AND SURPRISE: deep-fried dried fish, grilled dried fish, grilled fresh fish, dried shrimp, fish roe, salted egg, salted fish, grilled pork, dried beef, grilled chicken

Pounding Namm Prikk

Refresh your memory by following the directions on pounding and pureeing, or *tumm*, using a mortar and pestle (see page 12).

In a mortar, start by pounding the sea salt and garlic to a paste. Add the whole chiles and pound to bruise, with a few heavily crushed for a spicy chile water. Add the binder, blending and mixing the ingredients well. For additional fruity flavors and textures, add the ingredients called for in the individual recipe and pound to crush lightly. Season with fish sauce, tamarind, and/or lime juice. Taste and season to your preference. *Namm prikk* and *lon* taste best the same day they are made. Prepare the ingredients ahead for last-minute pounding and assembling.

Serving Namm Prikk

Arrange fresh and parboiled vegetables, grilled fish, meat, sausage, and pickles on a large platter. Place a small bowl of *namm prikk* in the center. Serve with hot long-grain Thai jasmine rice or jasmine sticky rice (see pages 37 or 50). Dip raw and parboiled vegetables directly into the *namm prikk*. Spoon a small amount, approximately ¼ teaspoon, of it onto grilled fish, meat, or sausages. Remember, *namm prikk* is extreme in taste; a tiny amount goes a long way. Try all of the accompaniments with *namm prikk* to discover the wonderful arrays of flavors and textures. *Namm prikk*, the accompaniments, long-grain rice, and a soup make a wonderful meal.

Soft Sweet Sticky
Rice Bundles

(page 58)

Southern Thai–Style
Catfish Fillets

(page 118)

Sticky Rice from
Nong Kao

(page 75)

Water Chestnut Salad

(page 158)

Steamed Fish Custard
in Banana Pouches

(page 170)

Chile Water
from Lanna

(page 190)

Sweet Green Curry
with Meatballs

(page 222)

Heavenly
Shrimp Salad
(page 267)

Cool Noodles with
Baby Shrimp
(page 281)

Crispy Noodles

(page 306)

Krueng Kang

Accompaniments are chosen by a set of rules invented by the past *namm prikk* recipe creators. There are four major categories that serve as guides to choosing the appropriate pairings. I have eliminated ingredients that are not available in America, substituting many that closely resemble the original.

NAMM PRIKK   Seasoned with Sour Fruits such as Lime, Sour Orange, or Tomatillo

> *Fresh Vegetables:* Cherry tomatoes, carrot, cucumber, green beans, tender young ginger, arugula, watercress
>
> *Parboiled Vegetables or Vegetables Boiled in Fresh Unsweetened Coconut Cream:* Swamp spinach, Japanese eggplant, green beans, baby zucchini, zucchini blossoms, broccoli rabe (rapini)
>
> *Vegetables Dipped in Batter and Deep-Fried:* Cilantro, Japanese eggplant, zucchini blossoms, pumpkin, sweet potato, banana squash, kabocha squash
>
> *Meat, Poultry, Seafood, or Egg:* Deep-fried mackerel or other fish with high oil content, such as sardines or salmon; grilled shrimp; cooked pork laced with sweet caramelized sauce; open-faced spinach omelet

NAMM PRIKK   Made with Oranges, Fresh Vegetables, Sour and Unripened Fruits, Dried Shrimp, Dry-Roasted Fermented Shrimp Paste, or Dry-Roasted Shallots

> *Fresh Vegetables:* Cucumber, tomato, watercress, arugula
>
> *Vegetables Stir-Fried in Oil or Parboiled Vegetables:* Swamp spinach, radicchio, green beans, peas

> *Pickled Vegetables:* Pickled ginger, pickled onion
>
> *Meat, Poultry, Seafood, or Egg:* Grilled catfish, deep-fried trout, salted eggs.

NAMM PRIKK   Made with Tamarind Juice, Dry-Roasted Garlic, or Dry-Roasted Fresh Chiles

> *Fresh Vegetables:* Cucumber, tomato, watercress, arugula, Napa cabbage
>
> *Meat, Poultry, Seafood, or Egg:* Salted beef jerky, cooked pork laced with sweet caramelized sauce, pork stir-fried with Big Four Paste (page 86), chicken or pork sausages

LON

> *Fresh Vegetables:* Cucumber, tomato, Belgian endive, white cabbage, green beans, Napa cabbage
>
> *Vegetables Dipped in Batter and Deep-Fried:* Chile leaves, cilantro, zucchini blossoms
>
> *Meat, Poultry, Seafood Dipped in Batter and Deep-Fried or Egg:* Tempura catfish, salmon, or trout, grilled shrimp

Preparing the Accompaniments

VEGETABLES

Unless otherwise noted, each vegetable makes enough for 6 to 8 servings. Fresh vegetables should be served cold or at room temperature. Most cooked vegetables should be served at room temperature, except for deep-fried vegetables, which taste best piping hot. Both fresh and cooked vegetables can be prepared ahead. Store them separately in Ziploc bags in the refrigerator.

Fresh Vegetables

ARUGULA: 2 to 3 ounces; use only young tender leaves, with stems.

CUCUMBER: 1 cucumber, peeled, halved lengthwise, seeded, and each half quartered lengthwise.

CARROT: 1 medium carrot, peeled and thinly sliced across; use sharp mini-canapé cutters to cut into flowers, diamonds, and other decorative shapes.

CABBAGE: 1 small head cabbage, tender inner parts only, sliced into long thin wedges.

NAPA CABBAGE: 1 small head Napa cabbage, tender inner heart only, sliced into long wedges.

BELGIAN ENDIVE: 1 endive, sliced lengthwise into eighths.

GINGER: Use only young tender ginger, peeled and sliced paper-thin on the diagonal; allow 2 to 3 slices per serving.

SNAP PEAS: Allow 2 to 3 whole peas per serving.

BANANA SQUASH, KABOCHA SQUASH, PUMPKIN, OR SWEET POTATO: 2 to 3 ounces for each serving; peel and very thinly slice (⅛ inch). In a medium mixing bowl, combine 1 teaspoon baking soda with 3 cups water and soak the sliced squash, pumpkin, or sweet potato in the mixture for 15 minutes. Rinse several times with cool water; pat dry.

SWAMP SPINACH: 4 ounces tender leaves and stems (or substitute regular spinach).

ZUCCHINI: Use only baby zucchini and leave whole; allow 2 to 3 pieces per serving.

ZUCCHINI BLOSSOMS: 1 to 2 blossoms per serving.

Bundled Vegetables

Cooked swamp spinach and broccoli rabe (rapini) can be shaped into bite-sized bundles. Parboil or stir-fry them, and let cool, then wrap the leaves around the stems, shaping them into small bundles.

Parboil yard-long beans, slice each one into approximately 9-inch lengths, and tie each piece into a loop.

Pickled Vegetables

Both pickled ginger and pickled onion can be purchased in some supermarkets and in Asian markets. Pickled ginger, which is also used for Japanese sushi, can be found packaged in plastic containers in the refrigerated deli section as well as in glass jars on shelves with ethnic food, while pickled onions in glass jars are on the shelves among the other pickles and relishes. See page 140 for a recipe for making your own pickled ginger.

Cooking Techniques for the Accompaniments

PARBOILED VEGETABLES

Fill a 4-quart saucepan about two-thirds full with water and bring to a boil over high heat. Add a couple of pinches of sea salt. Add one type of vegetable at a time and boil just until its color brightens. Remove and rinse in cool water. Pat dry and set aside until ready to serve.

BOILED VEGETABLES IN FRESH UNSWEETENED COCONUT CREAM

In a 4-quart saucepan, bring 2 cups Fresh Unsweetened Coconut Cream (page 69) to a boil.

Add one kind of vegetable at a time and cook for 1 minute. Remove the vegetable with a strainer and set aside. Boil the remaining coconut milk for 7 to 10 minutes over medium heat, or until it thickens. Transfer to a small bowl and let cool. Drizzle the coconut cream on top of the cooked vegetables and serve.

VEGETABLES DIPPED IN BATTER AND DEEP-FRIED

Prepare eggplant, banana squash, kabocha squash, pumpkin, or sweet potato according to the directions above. In a 12-inch skillet or flat-bottomed wok, heat 3 cups vegetable oil over high heat to 350°F. (You can also test for readiness by dipping the tip of a wooden spoon into the oil; if tiny bubbles begin to form around the spoon, the oil is ready.) Coat the vegetables with the batter (see page 150) and deep-fry 6 to 7 pieces at a time until golden. Drain on a plate lined with paper towels, then transfer to a serving platter and serve hot.

STIR-FRIED VEGETABLES

In a 12-inch skillet, heat 1 to 2 tablespoons vegetable oil over high heat for 1 to 2 minutes, or until the oil begins to smoke. Add one kind of vegetable at a time and cook, stirring, until softened but still crisp, 1 to 2 minutes. Transfer to a serving platter.

MEAT, POULTRY, SEAFOOD, AND EGG ACCOMPANIMENTS

Beef, Pork, and Chicken

These can be grilled, caramelized, or stir-fried; ½ pound will serve 6 people.

To grill: Marinate the meat or poultry in the marinade (page 87) for at least 30 minutes. Preheat a gas grill on high for 10 minutes or prepare a charcoal grill. Spray the meat or chicken generously with vegetable oil spray and place on the gas grill. Turn the heat on the gas grill to medium-high and grill, basting the meat with the marinating liquid and turning as necessary until cooked through. If using a charcoal grill, transfer the meat to a platter, then spray the hot coals with water to cool them. Return the meat to the grill and continue to cook. Let cool before slicing into thin strips.

To caramelize with sweet sauce: Rub beef, pork, or chicken strips with 1 teaspoon Big Four Paste (page 86) and marinate for 15 to 20 minutes. In a 12-inch skillet, heat 2 tablespoons vegetable oil over high heat for 1 to 2 minutes, or until the oil begins to smoke. Add the marinated meat to the hot oil and cook, stirring and tossing, until cooked through, 1 to 2 minutes. Add ¼ cup granulated sugar and ¼ cup fish sauce and toss to coat the strips with the mixture. Cook, stirring and tossing, until the liquid evaporates, another 3 to 4 minutes. Transfer the meat to a plate to cool.

To stir-fry: In a 12-inch skillet, heat 1 tablespoon vegetable oil over high heat for 1 minute. Add 1 teaspoon Big Four Paste (page 86), stirring constantly to prevent burning. Add strips of beef, pork, or chicken and cook, stirring to mix, until cooked through, 2 to 3 minutes. Transfer to a plate to cool.

Sausage

Use mild or sweet sausages, such as Chinese sausage, chicken and apple, turkey, or sweet Italian sausage. Two to three links of sausage, grilled and sliced, will serve 6 people.

To grill: Preheat a gas grill on high heat for 10 minutes. Generously spray the sausages with vegetable oil and place on the grill. Lower the heat to medium and grill for 7 to 10 minutes, or until cooked through. Set aside to cool, then slice into diagonal bite-sized pieces. If using a charcoal grill, see the instructions for beef, pork, and chicken above.

Fish

Ocean fish with a high oil content, especially whole mackerel, whole sardines, or salmon fillets, are preferred for grilling or deep-frying. Generally, 2 medium (¾ pound each) mackerel, 6 small sardines, or ½ to ¾ pound salmon fillet is sufficient for 6 people. Smoked boneless trout is an alternative to grilled fish.

To grill: Preheat a gas grill on high heat for 10 minutes. Rinse and dry the fish thoroughly, then rub with a bit of sea salt and 2 tablespoons olive oil. If using whole fish, insert a sprig of fresh rosemary in the cavity of each. Spray the fish generously with vegetable oil spray and grill over medium-high heat for 10 minutes, or just until cooked through.

To deep-fry: Dry the fish thoroughly with paper towels. In a 12-inch skillet or flat-bottomed wok, heat 3 cups vegetable oil over high heat to 350°F. Add a pinch of sea salt to prevent the oil from splattering, slide in the fish, and deep-fry until crispy and golden brown. Transfer to paper towels to drain.

Another way to deep-fry fish is to coat it with a homemade batter (see page 150) or purchase prepackaged tempura (available in supermarkets and Asian markets); follow the instructions on the package.

Shrimp

A dozen medium or large shrimp, peeled and boiled or grilled, will serve 6 people.

To boil: In a 4-quart saucepan, bring 3 cups water to a boil over high heat. Add a pinch of sea salt, then add the shrimp. Within 10 to 12 seconds, the shrimp will turn pink. Drain, rinse with cool water, and pat dry.

To grill: Preheat a gas grill on high for 10 minutes. Spray the shrimp generously with vegetable oil spray and grill over medium-high heat for 1 to 2 minutes, until pink. Transfer to a plate and cool.

Egg

Salted eggs are sold in Asian markets. One to 2 eggs will serve 6. Uncooked salted eggs will keep in the refrigerator for a month.

To boil salted eggs: Put the eggs in a small saucepan along with water to cover and bring to a boil over high heat; boil for 2 minutes. Turn off the heat and let the eggs sit until the water is completely cool. Do not remove the shells. Place each egg on the chopping board and, holding it firmly, with a sharp knife, slice lengthwise in half. Slice across each half lengthwise to make 4 pieces in all.

An open-faced spinach omelet is wonderful as an accompaniment, served cold. The recipe follows.

Pakk Kom Shoup Kai Todd
OPEN-FACED SPINACH OMELET

Makes 6 servings

In a 12-inch skillet, heat 2 tablespoons of the vegetable oil over high heat for 1 to 2 minutes, until the oil begins to smoke. Add the garlic cloves and cook for 1 minute. Add the spinach and cook until wilted but still crispy, about 2 minutes. Transfer to a platter to cool, then squeeze out the excess liquid and chop the cooked spinach into bite-sized pieces. Set aside. Discard the garlic cloves.

In the same skillet, heat the remaining 2 tablespoons vegetable oil over high heat. In the meantime, in a medium mixing bowl, lightly beat the eggs. Add the sea salt and ground white peppercorns and beat until foamy. Put the cooked spinach into the skillet and spread it around. Pour the beaten eggs over the spinach and swirl the skillet around to spread the eggs evenly and coat the spinach. When the edges of the omelet begin to pull away from the skillet and the eggs start to set, flip the omelet over and cook for 1 to 2 minutes. Slide the omelet onto a platter. When it's cool to the touch, slice into 10 to 12 wedges.

¼ cup vegetable oil
2 cloves garlic, peeled and slightly pounded
1 pound spinach, stems and leaves rinsed and thoroughly dried (4 cups)
3 large eggs
Sea salt to taste
¼ teaspoon ground Thai white peppercorns

Namm Prikk Pakk Chee

CHILE WATER WITH CILANTRO

Makes 1 cup

¼ cup dried shrimp

1 tablespoon fermented shrimp paste or 1½ tablespoons red miso

3 dried corn husks, softened in warm water and dried, or aluminum foil

½ teaspoon sea salt

6 cloves garlic, minced

7 to 8 fresh bird chiles or 4 to 5 serrano chiles, lightly pounded

1 tablespoon palm sugar or light brown sugar

¼ pound cilantro sprigs, finely chopped (1 cup)

Juice of 1 small lime

This is one of the oldest *namm prikk* recipes. It is both marvelous and different. If you love the aroma and taste of cilantro, you will love this *namm prikk*.

Soak the dried shrimp in lukewarm water for 15 minutes, or until softened. Rinse, pat dry with paper towels, and transfer to a food processor fitted with the steel blade. Puree, then transfer to a small bowl and set aside.

Preheat the oven to 400°F. Wrap the shrimp paste in the softened corn husks and place in the preheated oven for 20 minutes. Let cool.

In a mortar, pound the sea salt and garlic to a paste. Add the chiles and pound to crush some chiles completely while leaving a few whole and slightly bruised. Add the palm sugar and pound to blend. Add the cilantro and pound lightly to mix and blend. Add the fermented shrimp paste and dried shrimp; mix well before adding the lime juice. Taste for balance: spicy, salty, and sour. Transfer to a serving bowl and serve.

Accompaniments

Raw cucumber, arugula; parboiled swamp spinach, green cabbage; deep-fried fish; and cooked long-grain rice, preferably Thai jasmine or Indian or California basmati (see pages 37 and 38)

Namm Prikk Goong Nang
CHILE WATER WITH FRESH SHRIMP

Makes 1 cup

This recipe is from Surad-Thani, a city in the southern part of the country, near the Gulf of Thailand. It is an exquisite sauce, combining roasted ingredients with spicy chiles and tangy-fruity kiwi and kumquat or sour tangerine.

Preheat the oven or grill to 350°F for 10 minutes. Place the shrimp on a baking sheet and spray generously with vegetable oil spray. Bake or grill the shrimp for 5 to 7 minutes, or until the shrimp turn pink. Set aside to cool. Mince the shrimp and set aside in a bowl.

Raise the oven temperature to 400°F. Wrap and fold the shrimp paste in the softened corn husks (or in aluminum foil) and roast for 20 minutes. Remove from the oven to cool.

Using a mortar and pestle, pound the garlic and fermented shrimp paste into a paste. Add the chiles and pound to crush some completely while leaving a few whole and slightly bruised. Add the shrimp, fish sauce, and palm sugar, mixing and blending well. Add the kiwi and pound slightly to bruise, then add the kumquats, pounding to bruise and mix well. Add the kaffir lime leaves, mixing and blending well. Taste for balance of salty, spicy, sour, and fruity. Transfer to a serving bowl.

Accompaniments

Raw cucumber, tomato, watercress, arugula; parboiled spinach and/or broccoli rabe (rapini) in fresh unsweetened coconut cream (see page 184); and cooked long-grain rice, preferably Thai jasmine or Indian or California basmati (see pages 37 and 38)

¼ pound medium shrimp, peeled and deveined

1 tablespoon fermented shrimp paste or 1½ tablespoons red miso

3 dried corn husks, softened in warm water and dried (optional)

6 cloves garlic, minced

8 to 10 fresh bird chiles or 7 to 8 serrano chiles

1 tablespoon fish sauce (namm pla)

1 tablespoon palm sugar or light brown sugar

1 small kiwi, peeled and slivered

4 kumquats, unpeeled, thinly sliced and seeded, or 1 small sour tangerine, peeled, seeded, and thinly sliced, with any juice reserved

3 kaffir lime leaves or grated zest of ½ lime

Namm Prikk Ong

CHILE WATER FROM LANNA

Makes 1 cup

6 cloves garlic, minced

2 shallots, minced

1 dried New Mexico (or California) chile, softened in warm water, seeded, dried, and minced

8 dried de árbol or Japonés chiles, soaked in warm water until softened, seeded, dried, and minced

1 tablespoon fermented shrimp paste or 1½ tablespoons red miso

¼ pound ground pork

1 medium tomato, chopped

2 tablespoons vegetable oil

1 to 2 tablespoons water

Lanna was the name of the ancient kingdom of northern Thailand when it was a separate nation. It was conquered by Burma in 1662 and did not become a part of Thailand until 1792. This *namm prikk* recipe is one of several favorites of Thais from other parts of the country. It reminds me of a spaghetti meat sauce.

Using a mortar and pestle, pound the garlic and shallots together into a paste. Add the chiles and pound until mixed and pureed. Add the fermented shrimp paste, mixing and blending well. Transfer the mixture to a small mixing bowl, add the ground pork and tomato, and mix well. Set aside.

Heat a 10-inch skillet over high heat for 1 minute, then add the oil. When the oil begins to smoke, add the chile mixture and cook, stirring, for 1 minute. Add 1 tablespoon of the water and cook, stirring and adding up to 1 more tablespoon of water if needed, until the pork is cooked through and the liquid has evaporated, 4 to 5 more minutes. Transfer to a serving bowl to cool before serving.

Accompaniments

Raw cucumber, green cabbage, Napa cabbage; grilled sausages; and cooked long-grain Thai jasmine sticky rice (see page 50)

Namm Prikk Numm

CHILE WATER WITH ANAHEIM CHILES

Makes 1 cup

The word *numm* is a name of a chile similar to hot Hungarian chiles. It also means young and tender, and is often used to refer to a young boy who has just reached puberty. It's another example of the Thai people's sense of *sanuk* (fun), using the same word to mean both a chile and a young boy. I've substituted Anaheim chiles, which are available in supermarkets.

Preheat the oven or grill to 500°F for 10 minutes. Broil or grill the chiles, turning frequently, until the skin is charred and burnt, 5 to 7 minutes. Put in a plastic bag, seal tightly, and let cool.

Gently massage the chiles inside the bag to loosen the burnt skin. Remove the chiles and rinse with water; leave the seeds intact. Pat the chiles dry, coarsely chop, and put them in a medium mixing bowl. Set aside.

Thread the cherry tomatoes onto the bamboo skewers and grill, or broil until the skins are slightly burnt. Remove from the skewers and set aside to cool. Coarsely chop and add to the bowl of chiles.

Lower the oven to 400°F. Slice off the top of the head of the garlic and rub it with 1 teaspoon of the vegetable oil. Do the same with the shallots. Wrap the garlic and shallots separately in the banana leaves (or in aluminum foil) and put both pouches in the oven to roast for 30 minutes. Remove to cool.

Squeeze the pulp from the garlic cloves and shallots onto a chopping board. Mince them together, then add to the bowl of chiles and tomatoes.

In a small mixing bowl, combine the red miso, sea salt, sugar, and lime juice and mix well. Pour over the chile mixture, mix well, and taste for a balance of salty, spicy, sour, and sweet. Transfer to a serving bowl and garnish the top with the chopped fennel leaves.

Accompaniments

Raw cucumber, green cabbage, Napa cabbage; deep-fried eggplant, pumpkin, banana squash, sweet potato, kabocha squash; and cooked long-grain Thai jasmine sticky rice (see page 50)

10 fresh Anaheim chiles
8 cherry tomatoes
1 to 2 bamboo skewers, soaked in water
1 head garlic
3 shallots
2 teaspoons vegetable oil
3 to 4 fresh banana leaves (see page 135; optional)
1½ tablespoons red miso
1 teaspoon sea salt
1 teaspoon sugar
Juice of 1 lime
1 sprig fresh fennel leaves, finely chopped

Namm Prikk Krapi

CHILE WATER WITH FERMENTED SHRIMP PASTE

Makes 1 cup

1 tablespoon dried shrimp

1 tablespoon fermented shrimp paste or 1½ tablespoons red miso

3 to 4 dried corn husks, softened in warm water and dried (optional)

3 tablespoons minced garlic

15 to 18 fresh bird chiles, with stems and seeds for a spicy sauce, half stemmed and seeded for a mild sauce

3 tomatillos, husked, rinsed, and thinly sliced

2 teaspoons palm sugar or brown sugar

Juice of 1 to 2 limes (3 to 6 tablespoons)

8 to 9 baby eggplants or 12 fresh peas

The countless variations of this sauce are a favorite subject for discussion among *namm prikk* aficionados. The fermented shrimp paste and dried shrimp have to be of the best quality, preferably made from baby ocean shrimp and with a light pink color. Fermented shrimp paste made from matured shrimp is more pungent, smells fishy, and is darker, with a purplish pink hue. A lesser amount of this kind of paste should be used, or it may be grilled before using. At least a dozen or more fiery-hot chiles, sour fruit with a slightly musty and bitter taste, and lime juice are added as contrasts to the pungency of the shrimp paste. Gently pounded tiny eggplants are added for the extra texture and another surprising contrast.

If you cannot find good fermented shrimp paste at an Asian market, red miso and Japanese bean paste make good substitutes. Organic markets carry freshly made miso, which has a nice compact texture that is similar to that of Thai fermented shrimp paste. The amount of chiles and lime juice depends on your preference: 6 to 7 chiles for mild, 8 to 12 for medium, and 12 to 16 chiles, or more, for a real Thai taste. If you like the flavor of chiles but not the spiciness, seed the chiles and use more. For a sour taste, start with 2 to 3 tablespoons of lime juice, then adjust for a balance of salty-spicy-sour that you like. The sauce will keep for a couple of days, although it tastes best the day it is made. Store in a jar with a tight-fitting lid in the refrigerator.

Soak the dried shrimp in lukewarm water for 15 minutes, or until softened. Rinse, pat dry with paper towels, and transfer to a food processor fitted with the steel blade. Puree, then transfer to a small bowl and set aside.

Preheat the oven to 400°F. Wrap the fermented shrimp paste in the softened corn husks (or in aluminum foil). Roast for 30 minutes. Remove from the oven to cool, and set aside.

Using a mortar and pestle, pound the garlic into a paste. Add the pureed shrimp and pound into a paste. Add the bird chiles and pound to crush some completely while leaving a few whole and slightly bruised. Add the fermented shrimp paste, mixing with a spoon. Add the tomatillos, pounding to bruise them. Add the palm sugar and 2 to 3 tablespoons lime juice; taste before adding more to taste. Mix with a spoon, then add the whole baby eggplants, pounding slightly to bruise. The sauce should be thick like a cake batter, with an intense salty-spicy-sour taste. Transfer to a serving bowl.

Accompaniments

Grilled mackerel or sardines; raw cucumber; parboiled green beans; Open-Faced Spinach Omelet (page 187); deep-fried eggplant; and cooked long-grain rice, preferably Thai jasmine or Indian or California basmati (see pages 37 and 38)

Namm Prikk Dum

BLACKENED CHILE WATER

Makes 1½ cups

40 dried Japonés chiles, soaked in
warm water until softened, half
seeded and half not, and dried,
or 80 dried *chiltepín* chiles,
softened, left whole
Sea salt
2 heads garlic
1 teaspoon vegetable oil
One 1-inch chunk galangal, or
1½-inch chunk fresh ginger,
peeled and minced
2 tablespoons fish sauce (*namm pla*)
¼ cup thick tamarind juice (see
page 128)

At a chile festival held at the San Diego Museum of Natural History, I
made this *namm prikk,* using tiny, fiery piquant bird, or *chiltepín,*
chiles, and served it with long-grain Thai jasmine sticky rice, steamed
swamp spinach bundles, and grilled chicken. It was the hottest, most
flavorful chile dish served. Those who like extremely spicy food like
the Thais should substitute *chiltepín* chiles for the Japonés chiles. Do
not soften or seed them, just dry-roast them as they are. It is best to
dry-roast them outdoors because of the fumes. If you are roasting
indoors, turn on your oven exhaust fan as well as several fans around
the work area and open the windows. Store the sauce in a jar with a
tight-fitting lid in the refrigerator; it will keep for 1 to 2 weeks.

Put the dried chiles in a 12-inch skillet over medium-high heat, add a
couple of pinches of sea salt, and dry-roast, tossing and stirring frequently to prevent burning and ensure even cooking, until the chiles
are blackened, 4 to 5 minutes. Transfer to a bowl to cool completely.

Preheat the oven to 400°F. Cut the tops off the garlic heads to reveal the
cloves. Put the heads of garlic on a piece of aluminum foil, drizzle with
the vegetable oil, and wrap in the foil. Roast for 30 minutes. Cool completely, then squeeze the softened garlic cloves into a bowl.

Fit a food processor with the steel blade, add the dry-roasted chiles, garlic, and galangal, and puree until the ingredients turn to a paste, about
1 minute. While the machine is running, add the fish sauce and
tamarind juice; puree. Transfer to a glass jar or a serving bowl.

Accompaniments

Grilled sausages, grilled pork strips; raw cucumber and broccoli florets; parboiled green beans and parboiled baby zucchini with blossoms; and cooked long-grain rice, preferably Thai jasmine or
Indian or California basmati (see pages 37 and 38)

Cook's Note

A teaspoon or more of this sauce will give a spicy punch to your
favorite salsa or guacamole recipe.

Namm Prikk Mah-Kheua Pow
GRILLED EGGPLANT CHILE SAUCE

2 medium Japanese eggplants
5 to 7 jalapeño chiles
1 teaspoon sea salt
1 head garlic, roasted (see page 137)
    and peeled
5 shallots, roasted (see page 137)
    and minced
2 tablespoons fish sauce (*namm pla*)
2 tablespoons thick tamarind juice
    (see page 128)
Fresh lime juice

I learned how to make this *namm prikk* from my friend Vithi's cook. Only in her teens, she was already skillful at making *namm prikk*. I make this instead of caponata, the Italian eggplant dish, to spread on bruschetta Calabrese. My companion, Italo, a Calabrese, always asks as he devours it, "What did you do to the eggplant? Man, is this good!" This sauce tastes best when freshly made, although it will keep overnight in the refrigerator. The taste may alter during storage; taste for a balance of spicy-salty-sour flavors.

Heat a gas grill to high for 10 minutes, then lower the heat to medium-high (or preheat the broiler). If using charcoal grill, wait until the shooting flames have disappeared and white ash covers the charcoal. Grill (or broil) the eggplants and jalapeño chiles until the skins are blackened. Put both in a plastic bag, seal securely, and let cool, then peel off the skin. Shred the eggplant into thin strands and set aside. Remove the chile seeds, or not, depending on your preference for spiciness. Set aside.

Using a mortar and pestle, pound the sea salt and garlic to a paste. One at a time, add the shallots, eggplants, and chiles and pound until the mixture is a coarse mush. Stir in the fish sauce and tamarind, mixing well. Add lime juice to taste. You should taste a balance of salty-spicy-sour. Transfer to a serving bowl.

Accompaniments

Grilled tuna, beef, pork, or chicken; steamed or parboiled broccoli rabe (rapini); raw green cabbage; and cooked long-grain Thai jasmine sticky rice (see page 50)

Jell Bonn

SPICY CHILE WATER

Makes about 1½ cups

30 dried de árbol or Japonés chiles,
   half soaked overnight in cool
   water, half not
2 dried New Mexico (or California)
   chiles, soaked overnight in cool
   water
1 lime or lemon
One 2-inch chunk galangal or
   2½-inch chunk fresh ginger
Vegetable oil for rubbing, plus
   2 cups
1 cup red lentils or regular lentils
Sea salt
½ cup loosely packed fresh Thai
   basil leaves
¾ cup Crispy Garlic (page 138)
½ cup Crispy Shallots (page 138)
¼ cup thick tamarind juice (see
   page 128)
2 tablespoons soy sauce
1 tablespoon sugar

Jell means sauce, and *bonn* means spicy in northeastern Thai dialect. In markets all over Thailand, little old women sit on straw mats, selling homemade *jell bonn* in small plastic containers. Each one tastes different and each is fabulous. *Jell bonn* made without tamarind juice is like a thick paste. In the past, farmers and foragers took the thick *jell bonn* with them on long trips away from home. Diluted with lime or tamarind juice, it's ready as a *namm prikk* to be eaten with greens and rice. *Jell bonn* is simply marvelous on hot jasmine rice or with sticky rice. It can be stored in a jar with a tight-fitting lid in the refrigerator for 2 to 3 weeks.

Drain the soaked chiles and cover again with cool water. Slice the lime in half, squeeze the lime juice into the water, and add the slices. Slit each chile open lengthwise, put it back into the water, and fan it back and forth to remove the seeds. Dry the seeded chiles with paper towels. Put on a cookie sheet in a 150°F oven to dry for 1 to 2 hours. Remove and set aside.

Increase the oven temperature to 400°F. Put the galangal on a piece of aluminum foil, rub it with a little vegetable oil, and wrap in the foil. Roast for 30 minutes. Cool, then peel, mince, and set aside.

Meanwhile, soak the lentils in cool water for 20 minutes, or until softened. Rinse and dry completely on paper towels. Set aside.

Line a large platter with paper towels and set it near the stove. In a 10-inch skillet, heat the 2 cups vegetable oil over high heat to 300° to 350°F. Add a pinch of sea salt to prevent the oil from splattering, then add the basil leaves. Fry until crispy, 20 to 30 seconds. With a strainer, transfer the leaves to drain on the paper towel–lined platter. Fry the softened lentils until golden, 15 to 20 seconds, then transfer them with the strainer to the paper towels. Fry the seeded chiles in the oil, adding a couple pinches of sea salt, to prevent the chile fumes from rising, until they turn black, 15 to 20 seconds. With the strainer, transfer to the paper towels. Repeat with the remaining 15 dried chiles. Set aside to cool.

Fit a food processor with the steel blade and puree the crispy fried lentils. Add the garlic, shallots, all of the chiles, and the roasted galangal and puree to a coarse-textured paste. Add the tamarind juice, soy sauce, 1 teaspoon salt, and the sugar. Pulse to blend. Transfer to a bowl and stir in the crispy fried basil leaves. Store in a glass jar with a tight-fitting lid, or transfer to a serving bowl.

Accompaniments

Pickled ginger; stir-fried swamp spinach; fresh green beans, raw cucumber, cherry tomatoes, white cabbage; salted eggs, grilled mackerel or salmon; and cooked long-grain Thai jasmine sticky rice (see page 50)

Namm Prikk Mah-Kheua Tedd
TOMATO CHILE PASTE

Makes 2 cups

2 tablespoons dried shrimp,
  softened in warm water and
  pureed (see page 192)
1 teaspoon fermented shrimp paste
  or 1 tablespoon red miso
6 cloves garlic, minced
10 fresh bird chiles or 5 to 6 red
  serrano chiles
2 tablespoons vegetable oil
1 cup chopped tomatoes
¼ cup finely chopped tomatillos
2 tablespoons fish sauce (namm pla)
2 tablespoons sugar
1½ tablespoons fresh lime juice

A ritual I look forward to each time I return to Thailand is a reunion with my classmates from boarding school. For the occasion, I always cook something Western, while some of my friends either make Wattana's noodles, terrible greasy noodles with soggy vegetables named for the school, or some very spicy curry, and *namm prikk*.

Mexican food is the rage in Bangkok. I hand-carried tortilla chips from America and made this *namm prikk* to go with them instead of the regular salsa. My friends loved the combination. The sauce will keep overnight, and you should make it at least 1 to 2 hours before serving to let the flavors blend and ripen. The lime juice may lose some of its tang as the sauce sits. Right before serving, taste and season for balance.

Using a mortar and pestle, pound the dried shrimp and fermented shrimp paste into a coarse paste. Add the minced garlic and pound to a paste. Add the fresh chiles and pound to crush most of them completely, leaving a few whole and slightly bruised. Transfer to a small bowl and set aside.

In a 10-inch skillet, heat the oil over high heat for 1 minute. Add the paste and cook, stirring, until fragrant, about 1 minute. Add the chopped tomatoes and tomatillos and cook until both are limp, about 1 minute. Season with the fish sauce and sugar and cook, stirring, until the sauce thickens and the sugar is dissolved, about 1 minute more. Transfer to a bowl and cool completely, then add the lime juice.

Accompaniments

Raw cucumber, green cabbage, Napa cabbage, carrots; and corn tortilla chips

Lon Pla Gapong

SAVORY COCONUT CREAM SAUCE
WITH CANNED SALMON

Makes 2½ cups

While many Americans look down on dishes made with canned food, Thai people considered it exotic during the 1950s and 1960s, and it was considered very chic to serve something made with canned goods.

Buy the best-quality canned salmon, with large chunk meat packed in water. Crown Prince and Rubinstein's are brands that are reliable. This easy recipe should be made just before serving. I think you'll find it quite chic.

In a medium saucepan, cook the salmon, coconut cream, and shallots over high heat, stirring frequently to prevent the coconut cream from curdling, for 3 minutes. Lower the heat to medium and add the tamarind juice, palm sugar, fish sauce, both slivered and whole chiles, and kaffir lime leaves. Cook, stirring, for another minute. Taste and adjust the seasoning for a balance of creamy, sweet, spicy, and salty. Remove from the heat, transfer to a serving bowl, and let cool to room temperature. Garnish with the chopped cilantro.

Accompaniments

Raw cucumber slices; parboiled green beans; deep-fried eggplant and banana squash

One 7.5-ounce can large chunk
   salmon packed in water, drained
   and shredded
1 cup Fresh Unsweetened Coconut
   Cream (page 69)
2 large shallots, thinly sliced
6 tablespoons thick tamarind juice
   (see page 128)
2 tablespoons palm sugar or light
   brown sugar
3 tablespoons fish sauce (*namm pla*)
9 fresh serrano chiles, left whole
   and slightly bruised, 4 seeded
   and slivered
3 to 4 kaffir lime leaves, torn, or zest
   of 1 lime, removed with a peeler
   in strips and bruised slightly
5 sprigs cilantro, coarsely chopped

Thai Curry

THE SIGNATURE DISH

Keang masman	sweet heart made
Cumin scent	fanned mad desire
Singular bite	tainted his dream
Ache passionate stir	for maiden's fern

**Translated from a poem by King Rama II,
"King Buddha Loes La,"
between 1768 and 1824**

Khun Yuy (*Khun* is a Thai word for grandmother) is in her late eighties. She owns a restaurant in Pitsnulok in Central Thailand and is respected as one of the city's best curry makers. When I first met her, she was meticulously dressed in a simple sarong and white blouse. Thin as a rail, with graying hair crowned around her wrinkled face, she was still quick with her hands as she sat on a wooden stool, slicing meat as thin as tissue paper.

My cousin Susie is a business associate of Khun Yuy's daughter. For months before my annual visit to Thailand, Susie had begged and had cajoled the daughter into letting me watch her mother cook, something she had never permitted anyone to do. Khun Yuy finally relented. At the crack of dawn, with roosters crowing in the still-darkened streets, Khun Yuy's daughter picked me up at my hotel, dropped me off at her mother's restaurant, and promptly disappeared. I paid my respects to Khun Yuy, who paused in slicing a massive pile of beef long enough to inspect me, then offered me coffee. As I stood awkwardly in the center of the small shop house,

I suddenly detected the distinct and overpowering peppery-sweet perfume of curry in the already hot and humid morning air.

The curry aroma saturated the air in the small shop house and the dark street where the outdoor kitchen was situated. On top of several butane stoves were two large pots, each filled with bubbling, shimmering reddish curry illuminated by neon lights from the roof overhang above. The cook, a middle-aged woman in a flowery sarong, although acutely aware of my presence, never looked up from her immense wok as she stirred and cooked. I was left to myself with a young woman, the cook's assistant. She ran back and forth between the cook and Khun Yuy, stealing glances at me from the corners of her eyes and smiling sheepishly.

I asked if I could help. Khun Yuy seemed surprised by my question but, continuing to work, she ordered the young assistant to give me the cucumbers to slice. I squatted on the cement floor with a big basket of cucumbers, which I quickly peeled, then washed in a sink outside, staying clear of the cook. I sliced the cucumbers paper-thin and piled them into a plastic bowl. Khun Yuy looked up through her bifocal glasses at the sliced cucumber, then ordered the young assistant to give me more vegetables. We prepped and cooked in quiet frenzy. By 8 A.M., the restaurant was ready for business.

The buffet-style steam table in the front of the shop was filled with *keang pet gai,* chicken curry; *keang keow wann pla glay,* sweet green curry with fish patties; *penang neur,* beef curry; *keang leurng,* yellow curry with chunks of catfish; and *padd pet keang koa,* stir-fried spicy curry with green beans. A large plastic bowl brimmed with cucumber salad, my contribution. Another

was stuffed with curry condiments: crispy fried beef jerky, sweet-sour pork strips, sliced salted eggs, and crispy fried dried chiles. Next to these bowls were several makeshift butane stoves with pots of soup and sauces for cold vermicelli. It was a spectacular sight.

Customers packed the small shop house. Many waited outside to order take-out. It wasn't until later in the afternoon, after the luncheon crowd had disappeared, and just about everything had been sold out, that Khun Yuy acknowledged me with a wry smile.

After cleaning up the kitchen, the cook and her young assistant stacked wooden chairs on top of the tables, then crawled underneath the wooden staircase and dragged out a giant stone mortar. It took both of them to lift and set it on the floor in the center of the shop house. It was the biggest mortar I had ever seen. The cook squatted down in front of it and with one hand fed it handfuls of salt, chiles, and garlic while holding an enormous stone pestle and pounding the ingredients together with her other hand. Mounds of lemongrass, galangal, kaffir lime zest, and shallots were piled high on an enameled tray nearby. A large glass jar of fermented shrimp paste sat next to her.

I blurted out a request to the cook to let me try my hand at pounding in this granddaddy of mortars. The cook, who hadn't spoken a word to me since my arrival, looked at me with astonishment. Still not saying a word, she scooted away from the mortar and handed me the pestle.

Squatting down in front of the mortar, I realized how immense the thing was. The rim of the mortar came up almost to my chest. I would have to raise myself above it in order to give me proper leverage. I asked for a stool, which was quickly brought over by the young assistant, looking at me perplexed and anxious. In contrast to my little mortar at home, which I have to brace with one hand to keep it from skipping, this mortar never moved. It was one solid piece of rock. With both hands, I held onto the club-sized pestle and pounded with all my might. Khun Yuy perched on a wooden stool, smoking a cigarette. The cook squatted next to me, and the young assistant stood in the front of the shop house. All watched intently as I pounded away. It took several minutes to get used to the size of the mortar and pestle, but I kept on pounding. I could feel myself sweating from the workout.

When finally the familiar rhythmic song of an even pounding sang out from the mortar, a chorus of laughter burst out from the women. Khun Yuy asked me where I'd learned to cook. I explained my passion for cooking, and how I return to Thailand year after year to learn all I can from people like her.

As I continued to pound, Khun Yuy drew heavily on her cigarette, then began to speak of her childhood and cooking. Her father, she told me, was a farmer and a great curry maker. He was famous especially for his roasted duck curry. According to Khun Yuy, when her father cooked, it was a grand production, taking all day. Preparation started early in the morning, when he would climb the tall coconut tree that grew in front of their home to hack off ripe coconuts. He then whacked each open with a machete and grated the thick creamy white meat inside, which he mixed and massaged with water, making pristine, fragrant coconut cream and milk.

Her mother, meanwhile, picked fresh herbs, spices, and vegetables from their garden. These included chiles, galangal, lemongrass, kaffir lime, and shallots, all of which her father pounded into the curry chile paste. Mother then went to the nearby bamboo grove to chop and gather young shoots. She would later boil and slice them for her father to add to the duck curry. In the meanwhile, Khun Yuy was sent down to the

pond near their home to pick tender shoots of swamp spinach, growing wild on the water's edge. It would be eaten raw as one of the condiments for the curry.

Ducks, slaughtered and roasted by a friendly neighbor and given to her father, were a sure invitation to a great meal. By midafternoon, unexpected visitors would begin to stop by the house, bringing homemade moonshine. Father always invited everyone to stay for dinner. When he began to cook the curry, the smell of the chile paste simmering in the rich coconut cream drifted from the outdoor kitchen onto the porch, where the friends sat waiting with their moonshine. As she spoke, Khun Yuy smiled, saying that she could still taste her father's wonderful curry.

While the cook and the young assistant took over the pounding, Khun Yuy and I talked about *keang pet*, Thai curry. She is proud, she said, to be known as one of the best *keang* makers. It is an honor among Thai cooks, because *keang pet* is considered to be the signature dish of Thai food. It is, by far, the best example of the genius of ancient Thai cooks. They were the ones who experimented with newly introduced foreign ingredients and combined them with their simple seasonings to create a renowned culinary invention.

I told Khun Yuy of my obsession with researching and learning the history of Thai curry. Khun Yuy was curious and asked me to tell her what I had learned thus far. I told her about the word *keang,* that is a Mon word, describing the technique of making stew-like dishes by adding ingredients to a pot of liquid simmered over fire. Because of this, many considered *keang* to have originated with the Mon. We concurred that *keang* is a curious word because it used to describe both the process of using clear liquid and the practice of using coconut cream for cooking. While one results in a soup-like dish, the other is more stew-like. The word is also used for both nonspicy and spicy *soups*, such as curry.

Khun Yuy chimed in, remembering the old-fashioned *keang* her mother made. Both her father and mother used to cook just as I described earlier, with terra-cotta pots over charcoal braziers. There is nothing like the delicious taste of *keang* cooked this way. She thought for a moment before commenting on what I had said about the origins of curry. Maybe, she wondered aloud, *keang* did come from the Mon, for there are still many Mon living in Pitsnulok and their cooking is just like the Thais'.

I shared with her the different views held by food historians, particularly the idea of curry made with coconut cream originating with the Indians and being adapted by the Thais. But, I explained, others think that curry may actually have come from the Ceylonese, who introduced, and converted, the Mon to Buddhism in the seventh century.

Khun Yuy pronounced quite definitely that Thai curry is not like Indian curry. She had eaten Indian curry. Indians use far more dried spices than are used in Thai curry. We both agreed that the Arab traders and Islamic missionaries probably introduced the use of aromatic dried spices for curries to the Thais.

Khun Yuy noted that in her local market, Indians and Arabs are still the major spice traders. I commented that her restaurant menu included not only curries from Central Thailand, such as *keang pet* (with chicken) and *keang koa* (with green beans), but also *penang* (beef curry) and *keang leurng* (with catfish) recipes that orig-

inated in southern Thailand. Khun Yuy concurred, and started to list curries from the North that she sometimes made without coconut cream, a typical regional variation. And her cook, who was born in Northeast Thailand, made several kinds of fiery-hot curries from her region.

But it was the Thai Royal Court, I explained, that perfected the making of Thai curry, along with the ritual of serving curry with an assortment of accompaniments to complement and contrast tastes. At this point in our conversation, Khun Yuy became very excited. She then revealed to me that after her husband's death, a distant relative, who had served for several years in the Royal Court, had come to live with her. It was the relative who not only taught Khun Yuy how to make the curries, but first brought fame to her restaurant. The curry pastes had been her family's secret recipes.

It was late by then, and Khun Yuy had finished a whole pack of cigarettes and downed several pots of tea. When I got ready to leave, she patted me lightly on my back and told me she was glad I had come. She invited me to return anytime to visit and cook with her. She instructed me, as we parted, "When you go back to America, you tell them about our foods. Tell them what you told me. Tell them it took many generations of cooks to perfect our wonderful curries. And don't forget to tell them about my father and his famous roasted duck curry."

The Anatomy of Keang

Keang, **Thai curry,** can be served as a one-dish meal, or *aharn jarn deow,* with rice and a long list of accompaniments including salted, dried, or crispy fried meat, fish, or eggs, or a simple tray of hard-boiled eggs, cucumber relish (see page 107), and Fresh Chiles with Fish Sauce (page 93). For a truly decadent meal, *Mee Krob*, or Crispy Noodles (page 306), laced with sweet-sour caramelized syrup is the absolute best accompaniment for curry. Its crispy and crunchy texture, together with the sweet-and-sour flavors, makes a perfect match for spicy curry. As an entrée, Thai curry commands the star position among other dishes, which are served to complement it.

Making *keang* begins with the *namm prikk keang,* or chile paste, to season the broth. Understanding the nature of fresh and dried herbs and spices and how to use them in their correct combination is essential in making the paste. Equally important is the preparation of the ingredients. Pounding the right proportion of fresh and dried herbs and spices in the correct sequence results in the perfectly blended paste that makes all the difference in delicious curry.

After the chile paste, the next step is to learn to match meat, poultry, and seafood with the freshest of seasonal vegetables. These enhance as well as contrast with the flavors and textures of the curry. The result is a curry that tastes spicy-salty, with a slight sweet flavor, and is very aromatic.

Chile Paste and Curry Ingredients

BAI TEDD SODD, KREUNG TEDD SODD

FRESH HERBS AND SPICES

Following is a list of fresh and dried herbs and spices used in making the chile paste and/or aromatics. Also included are suggestions for main ingredients to use in making Thai curry.

BAI GA-PAO, BAI HORAPA—BASIL: Both Thai basil and holy basil are used as aromatics to perfume the curry and, in some cases, to lessen the meaty or fishy smell. Holy basil is best for gamier meats and strong-flavored fish. Add some while the curry is boiling and another handful just before serving. Use fresh mint as a substitute.

PRIKK SODD—CHILES: Chiles are used for flavor, color, and aroma, both in chile paste and to season the curry. Thai curries are often named after the color of the chiles used in making the chile paste: for example, *keang pet*—spicy red curry; *keang keow wann*—sweet green curry; and *keang leurng*—yellow curry. Traditional chile pastes were milder and made with the seeds removed from the chiles. Today, Thais prefer spicy curry. For a mild curry, use seeded dried New Mexico (or California) chiles. For medium-hot, use dried New Mexico chiles combined with de árbol or Japonés chiles, with or without seeds. For an extremely spicy curry, use dried de árbol or Japonés chiles and fresh bird or serrano chiles in the chile paste and add several slightly bruised fresh chiles to the curry while it is cooking. Green chiles are reserved for green-colored curries. Too many chiles will dominate the taste, overwhelming the salty-rich flavors. Too few, though, and the dish lacks its essence.

KHA—GALANGAL: Too much galangal makes curry bitter; too little, and the curry will lack flavor. When a chile paste recipe calls for galangal and lemongrass together, always use two portions of lemongrass to one portion of galangal. Galangal, lemongrass, and kaffir lime are a threesome used with meat, while galangal only is always used with fish. If galangal is unavailable, use fresh ginger as a substitute. (For more about galangal, see page 131.)

GA-TIEM—GARLIC: Garlic adds the pungency essential to the chile paste. It is also the major element in binding and blending other harder herbs and spices during the pounding process. Two portions of garlic to one portion of shallots is the rule of thumb for most curry pastes.

PEW MAH-KRUD—KAFFIR LIME ZEST; *BAI MAH-KRUD*—KAFFIR LIME LEAVES: Always use equal portions of kaffir lime zest and galangal in a chile paste. Too much kaffir lime zest will make the curry bitter. When using the zest, either grate it or peel it as you would other citrus with a vegetable peeler, removing only the strips of the colored part and leaving the white pith behind. If the recipe calls for additional kaffir lime zest and leaves to perfume the broth, add them to the boiling broth to heighten the release of their aromatic oils. (For more details about kaffir lime, see page 132.)

KRA-CHAY—LESSER GALANGAL: Lesser galangal is always used with seafood, especially fish. When pounding the chile paste, always add lesser galangal last, before adding the binder, to prevent splattering. If adding a chunk of lesser galangal to the broth, slightly crush it to release its perfume. (For more details about *kra-chay*, see page 132.)

KA-MIN—TURMERIC: Popular in southern Thailand for its dramatic color, fresh turmeric is believed to enhance the flavor of beef, pork, and gamier meats. Yellow turmeric is used in chile paste; white turmeric is eaten raw as an accompaniment. Substitute turmeric powder for fresh.

KREUNG TEDD

DRIED HERBS AND SPICES

For the most intense flavor and aroma, always roast whole seeds before pounding; use sparingly.

LUK PHAK CHEE—CORIANDER SEEDS: Use two portions of coriander seeds to one portion of cumin or caraway seeds.

YI-RA—CUMIN OR CARAWAY: *Yi-ra* is always used in the chile paste for meat and poultry curries.

JUN-TEDD—NUTMEG: A pinch of grated nutmeg in the chile paste for beef curry heightens the flavor.

NUER KUB PAKK SAI NAI KEANG

MAIN INGREDIENTS FOR THAI CURRY

Meat, including beef, lamb, and pork: These are the most popular. Thais love the flavors from cooking meat with bones, sinew, tendon, and fat left intact. Chop bone-in meats into 2-inch chunks. Slice boneless meats into long thin strips against the grain to ensure tender and juicy results.

Poultry, including chicken, duck, squab, and other wild game: Again, Thais aren't bothered by bones because of the rich flavors they render to the dish. Roasted duck and chicken are prized in making curry for their rich flavors and marvelous aroma. For game birds, a tablespoon or two of whisky helps to tenderize the meat.

Seafood, including fish, eel, lobster, shrimp, and other shellfish: Seafood seasoned with fresh herbs brings an element of the sea to a curry.

Fruits and Vegetables, including fresh bamboo shoots, pickled bamboo shoots, unripe bananas, green beans, cauliflower, tender young coconut meat, eggplant, mushrooms, onions, hearts of palm, potatoes, sweet potatoes, pumpkin, summer squash, green tomatoes, baby watermelon, green mangoes, star fruit, apples, lychees, grapes, and pineapples: Each provides balance and contrasting texture and flavor to the curry.

Namm Prikk Keang
CURRY CHILE PASTES

Pounding Chile Paste

Review the section on pounding and pureeing (*tumm*; page 12). For easy and speedy pounding, mince all fresh herbs and spices and grind the roasted dried spices. Measure carefully, and arrange all the ingredients in proper sequence. Add each new one only after the preceding ingredient has been pounded into the paste. Start with the sea salt and garlic, and pound into a paste before adding the chiles. This will prevent the paste from splattering. Then, if the recipe calls for it, add roasted dried spice powder, lemongrass, kaffir lime zest, and shallots. The binder, which may be fermented shrimp paste, pureed dried fish, pureed dried shrimp, or red miso, always goes in last.

Making Curry

Keang, or curry, comes in two consistencies: *keang heang*, a dry curry, and *keang namm konn*, a stew-like curry. A dry curry is thickened to a gravy-like consistency, while the other type is more like a watery stew. Both kinds use water, broth, or coconut cream as the liquid.

KEANG HEANG
DRY CURRY

Two portions of thick coconut cream to one portion of chile paste is the rule of thumb for cooking. First cook the chile paste with coconut cream over medium-high heat—this is the most important step in making the curry. The chile paste needs time to blend with and infuse the coconut cream. When the tiny bubbles of coconut oil rise to the surface and the liquid has thickened and turned the color of the paste, it's time to add the main ingredients and seasonings. With meat and poultry, the curry needs additional coconut milk to tenderize, as well as flavor. After the chile paste is cooked, add enough coconut milk to barely cover the meat or poultry and cook uncovered over medium-heat, stirring frequently to ensure even cooking, until the liquid evaporates and the meat or poultry is tender. Curry with fish or shellfish also uses thick coconut cream to enrich and enhance the flavor. Curry with vegetables uses less coconut cream. In fact, coconut milk will usually do.

KEANG NAMM KONN
STEW-LIKE CURRY

The consistency of a stew-like curry is important. Leaving the curry watery will ruin the dish. A well-prepared curry of this type is one in which the sauce clings to and coats the rice.

To make stew-like curry, boil coconut milk

to separate the cream from the whey. Add the meat or poultry to the boiling coconut milk to tenderize it. Mix additional coconut cream with the skimmed-off coconut cream, and add the chile paste to cook in and infuse the cream. When the coconut oil bubbles separate and cover the surface with the dramatic color of the chile paste, transfer the meat or poultry from the coconut milk to the chile paste and cook until it is coated with the mixture, then return it to the simmering coconut milk. Again, as in making dry curry, add the seasoning only when the broth comes to a boil, adding a handful of fresh basil just before serving.

As for *keang heang*, a stew-like curry with meat, poultry, or seafood uses more coconut cream, while a vegetarian curry uses only coconut milk.

Krueng Kang
ACCOMPANIMENTS

Like *namm prikk*, chile water, traditional Thai curry is always served with long-grain Thai jasmine rice, or *kanum jean*, cool noodle nests (pages 280 or 281), and accompaniments. Pairings are carefully considered and specific. They include grilled meat or fish; beef jerky or deep-fried meat; grilled fish or shrimp; cucumber relish; raw, pickled, grilled, and/or deep-fried vegetables; and boiled, fried, or salted egg. The preparation and portions are similar to servings for *namm prikk* (see pages 183–186). Most ingredients can be purchased or made except beef jerky. Thai beef jerky is unlike any sold in American or Asian markets. Thais love this sinewy, chewy, sweet, and salty beef jerky. You'll love it too.

Neur Sawan
BEEF JERKY

Makes 4 to 6 servings

1 teaspoon cumin seeds
2 tablespoons coriander seeds
1 teaspoon Thai white peppercorns
5 tablespoons palm sugar or light brown sugar
1 cup soy sauce
1 pound boneless beef top sirloin, sliced paper-thin

Put the cumin seeds in a 9-inch skillet and dry-roast over medium-high heat, sliding the skillet back and forth to ensure even roasting, until the seeds are fragrant, about 45 seconds. Remove to a plate to cool. Add the coriander seeds and Thai peppercorns to the skillet and dry-roast for about a minute or less, until they exude a pleasing aroma. Transfer to the plate. Cool the seeds, then grind in an electric spice or coffee grinder.

Transfer the ground spices to a large shallow pan and add the palm sugar and soy. Add the beef, stir well to coat thoroughly, cover, and marinate overnight in the refrigerator.

Put the marinated steak on wire cooling racks and dry in the sun for a day, turning occasionally to ensure even drying. Alternatively, dry the steak in a 150°F oven for at least 8 hours, until dry and leathery. Store in the refrigerator. To serve, shred and deep-fry in hot oil until crispy.

Keang
THAI CURRY

Traditional Thai cooks learned the secrets of making a well-balanced curry paste from their families. The knowledge was passed down through hands-on experience and by word of mouth. Because there are so many chile paste variations and so much to remember, clever devices are useful in memorizing the lists of ingredients for each particular curry paste. Some basic rules will help, beginning with the origins of different kinds of curry. For the older and more traditional curry recipes, the basic ingredient for the chile paste is the Big Four Paste (page 86). This was the foundation from which all variations were created. Curries with foreign influences or from southern regions always include *kreung tedd,* or dried spices.

The following chile paste recipes start with the earliest and move to the most recent creations. Each *namm prikk keang,* or chile paste, starts with the Big Four Paste, to which additional ingredients are added. The curry recipes are from the Thai Royal Court, except *keang som,* Sour-Orange Curry. It is an ancient dish and best represents the curry of the common people. I love its light and delicate flavors combined with tender seasonal vegetables.

All the curry recipes include a list of accompaniments to be served along with rice. Each is a fabulous meal, representing the true culinary wonder of Thai food and most worthy of the time and effort it takes to prepare them.

Keang Koa

Keang koa is a dry curry generously seasoned with kaffir lime leaves. There are several variations on the basic chile paste used for *keang koa.* One is made with dried shrimp or grilled fish, for a seafood *keang koa.* Another includes ground roasted peanuts for *keang kao* with meat and vegetables. One in particular could easily be mistaken for the chile paste used for *keang masmun* because of its Arabic seasonings: ground roasted dried mace, nutmeg, cloves, and cardamom. To experiment with this recipe, 1 tablespoon of the combined spice powder is sufficient.

The multiple versions of the ingredients for the actual dish are as varied as the chile pastes for *keang koa.* The most common has a crunchy texture—the result of adding peanuts. Other interesting variations are made by using pickled vegetables, such as salted mustard greens, paired with tamarind juice for an extra sour-fruity flavor.

Keang koa is less colorful than most curries. When cooking the chile paste, the coconut oil does not need to be allowed to separate from the cream before the other ingredients are added.

The amount of chiles for the paste depends on your preference. For a milder paste, use 3 to 4 New Mexico (or California) dried chiles. For a medium-spicy paste, use 2 New Mexico dried and seeded chiles and 6 to 7 de árbol or Japonés chiles with seeds. For a really spicy paste, use 7 to 12 de árbol or Japonés chiles with seeds and 6 to 7 fresh bird or serrano chiles with seeds. Basic chile pastes are foundations that allow you to add or subtract the amount of dried and fresh chiles. *Keang koa* chile paste can be stored in a jar with a tight-fitting lid in the refrigerator for at least 1 month.

Keang Koa Chile Paste

1 teaspoon sea salt

6 cloves garlic, minced

1 tablespoon minced cilantro roots and stems

2 dried New Mexico (or California) chiles, softened in warm water and seeded

9 dried de árbol or Japonés chiles, softened in warm water, half seeded, half not

½ teaspoon Thai white peppercorns, dry-roasted (see page 13) and ground

½ teaspoon caraway seeds, dry-roasted (see page 13) and ground

1 teaspoon minced galangal or 1 tablespoon minced fresh ginger

1 stalk lemongrass, green parts and hard outer layers removed, minced

1½ teaspoons grated kaffir lime zest or 1 tablespoon grated regular lime zest

2 shallots, minced

1 teaspoon fermented shrimp paste

Using a mortar and pestle, pound the sea salt and garlic to a paste. One at a time, add the cilantro roots and stems, chiles, peppercorns, caraway seeds, galangal, lemongrass, lime zest, and shallots in sequence, adding each new ingredient only after the previous one is pureed and incorporated into the paste. Finish by adding the fermented shrimp paste, mixing and blending well.

Variations

Keang koa paste is also used for *haw mok* (page 170). For a vegetarian chile paste, add 2 tablespoons roasted ground peanuts and 1 tablespoon of red miso instead of the shrimp paste.

For a great stir-fry, use 1 to 2 tablespoons of *keang koa* paste; 2 tablespoons vegetable oil; ½ pound each of meat, chicken, or seafood sliced; and 2 cups firm crispy vegetables, such as cauliflower, bamboo shoots, baby corn, or zucchini

Keang Koa Fuk Kup Gai

CURRY WITH KABOCHA SQUASH AND CHICKEN

Makes 6 servings

Thai people love the sweet taste and soft texture of cooked squash and use it more often than Americans. The best-tasting squashes for curry are kabocha and banana squash. A vegetable peeler does a quick and easy job of peeling the thick rind of kabocha squash. To make this dish ahead, cook the chicken without the squash; cool completely before storing in the refrigerator. When ready to serve, heat with another 1/2 cup of coconut milk before adding the squash, and follow the remaining recipe instructions.

Sprinkle the chicken pieces with a couple pinches of sea salt and let sit for at least 30 minutes and no more than 1 hour. Rinse in several changes of cool water and pat dry with paper towels.

In a 12-inch skillet, combine 1 cup of the coconut cream and the chile paste and cook over high heat, stirring to prevent burning, 1 to 2 minutes. Slowly stir in another 1 cup coconut cream and cook, stirring, until the coconut cream thickens, 3 to 5 minutes. Add the chicken pieces and cook, stirring to coat, until the chicken is partially cooked, about 3 minutes. Add the coconut milk, palm sugar, and fish sauce. Taste, and add a teaspoon of sea salt if needed. Lower the heat to medium-high and cook, uncovered, until the chicken is cooked through and the liquid is reduced by half, 20 to 25 minutes.

Add the squash, mix well, and cook, uncovered, until the liquid has evaporated and the squash is tender, about 10 minutes. Add the tamarind juice, mix well, and bring to a boil. Lower the heat to medium and cook for another 3 to 5 minutes. Transfer to a serving bowl and garnish with the kaffir lime strands, the remaining 2 tablespoons coconut cream, and the chile slivers.

Accompaniments

1/4 pound smoked mussels; 2 tomatoes, sliced and topped with Thai basil leaves; 3 to 4 sliced pickled sweet cucumbers; 6 to 7 pieces pickled watermelon rind; and cooked long-grain rice, preferably Thai jasmine or Indian or California basmati (see pages 37 and 38)

2 pounds boneless, skinless chicken breasts, cut into 2-inch pieces
Sea salt
2 cups plus 2 tablespoons Fresh Unsweetened Coconut Cream (page 69)
3/4 cup Keang Koa Chile Paste (page 210)
1 cup Fresh Unsweetened Coconut Milk (page 69)
3 tablespoons palm sugar or light brown sugar
2 tablespoons fish sauce (*namm pla*)
1 small kabocha squash (West Indian pumpkin), cut into bite-sized pieces (2 cups)
3 tablespoons thick tamarind juice (see page 128)

For the garnishes

1/4 cup kaffir lime leaves, sliced into thin strands, or the zest of 1 lime, removed with a peeler in strips and julienned
5 to 6 fresh bird chiles or 3 to 4 serrano chiles, seeded and slivered

Chu-Chi

Chu-chi is a dry curry, like *keang koa*, but it is spicier. Because of its extremely spicy and salty flavors, *chu-chi* is particularly delicious with firm, oily fish, such as tuna, halibut, or salmon. It is also delicious with shrimp, as you will discover in the following recipe. Always top *keang chu-chi* with a generous amount of kaffir lime strands or cilantro leaves. *Chu-chi* tastes best when served fresh right off the skillet to the platter.

Chu-Chi Chile Paste

Makes about ¾ cup

1 teaspoon sea salt
6 cloves garlic, minced
1 tablespoon minced cilantro roots
    and stems
1 dried New Mexico (or California)
    chile, softened in warm water and
    seeded
15 dried de árbol or Japonés chiles,
    softened in warm water
1 tablespoon dried shrimp, softened in
    warm water and pureed (optional)
½ teaspoon Thai white peppercorns,
    dry-roasted (see page 13) and
    ground
½ teaspoon caraway seeds, dry-
    roasted (see page 13) and ground
1 teaspoon minced galangal or
    1 tablespoon minced fresh ginger
1 stalk lemongrass, green parts and
    hard outer layers removed, minced
1 teaspoon grated kaffir lime zest or 1
    tablespoon grated regular lime zest
2 shallots, minced
1 tablespoon Fresh Grated Coconut
    Flakes (page 71)
1 teaspoon fermented shrimp paste or
    1 tablespoon red miso

Using a mortar and pestle, pound the sea salt and garlic into a paste. One at a time, add the cilantro roots and stems, chiles, dried shrimp, if desired, the peppercorns, caraway seeds, galangal, lemongrass, lime zest, and shallots in sequence, adding each new ingredient only after the previous one is pureed and incorporated into the paste. Add the grated coconut and mix well, then add the fermented shrimp paste and mix well. The chile paste can be stored in the refrigerator for at least a month.

Keang Chu-Chi Goong
CHU-CHI SHRIMP

I had the spiciest *chu-chi* with my cousin Susie at Surad Thani, on the way to Koh Samui, a seaside resort in southern Thailand. She watched me eat a whole plate of *keang chu-chi goong* along with other fiery spicy dishes. Needless to say, Cousin Susie now thinks I have an iron stomach.

Massage the shrimp with a few pinches of sea salt and place in a colander in the sink to drain for 10 minutes. Rinse with cool water and dry thoroughly with paper towels.

In a 12-inch skillet, heat the oil over high heat for 2 minutes to 325°F. (You can also test for readiness by dipping the tip of a wooden spoon into the oil; if bubbles form around it, the oil is ready for frying.) Deep-fry the shrimp until golden, 1 to 2 minutes. Remove with a slotted spoon and drain on a tray lined with paper towels. Cover lightly with more paper towels and set aside.

In a 12-inch skillet, mix the 2 cups coconut cream with the chile paste and set over high heat. Cook, stirring to prevent the paste from burning, until the mixture begins to bubble, about 2 minutes. Lower the heat to medium-high and continue to cook, stirring occasionally, until the mixture thickens and the oil separates, releasing tiny bubbles the color of the chile paste, about 7 minutes. Add the fried shrimp, stirring to coat well, increase the heat to high, and season with the fish sauce and palm sugar. Cook, stirring well, for 1 to 2 minutes, then transfer to a serving platter. Garnish with the fresh chile slivers, mint leaf strands, and kaffir lime leaf strands.

Accompaniments

Cucumber relish (see page 107); pickled ginger; and cooked long-grain rice, preferably Thai jasmine or Indian or California basmati (see pages 37 and 38)

1½ pounds large shrimp, shelled and deveined

Sea salt

2 cups vegetable oil

2 cups plus 2 tablespoons Fresh Unsweetened Coconut Cream (page 69)

½ cup Chu-Chi Chile Paste (page 212)

2 tablespoons fish sauce (*namm pla*)

2 tablespoons palm sugar or light brown sugar

For the garnishes

6 to 7 fresh red bird chiles or serrano chiles, half seeded, half not, and slivered

15 fresh mint leaves, sliced into thin strands

10 kaffir lime leaves, sliced into thin strands, or ¼ cup finely chopped cilantro leaves

Panang

This is another dry *keang*, named after the city of Penang, which borders southern Thailand and Malaysia. The chile paste is very similar to *keang koa*, except it uses ground roasted peanuts as the thickener. Cashews can be used as a substitute. Seasoned with palm sugar and rich creamy coconut cream, *panang* is sweeter than *keang koa*. This chile paste is fairly mild. To make it really spicy, double the amount of chiles and leave the seeds intact. The strands of kaffir lime zest are as important to this dish as the roasted peanuts. The paste will keep for at least a month stored in a jar with a tight-fitting lid in the refrigerator.

Panang Chile Paste

Makes ½ cup

1 teaspoon sea salt

6 cloves garlic, minced

1 tablespoon minced cilantro roots and stems

15 dried de árbol or Japonés chiles, softened in warm water, half seeded, half not

1 teaspoon Thai white peppercorns, dry-roasted (see page 13) and ground

1 teaspoon minced galangal or 1 tablespoon minced fresh ginger

2 stalks lemongrass, green parts and hard outer layers removed, minced

1 tablespoon minced kaffir lime zest or 1½ tablespoons minced regular lime zest

1 shallot, minced

1 teaspoon fermented shrimp paste or 1 tablespoon red miso

3 tablespoons unsalted peanuts, dry-roasted (see page 13) and ground

Using a mortar and pestle, pound the sea salt and garlic into a paste. One at a time, add the cilantro roots and stems, chiles, peppercorns, galangal, lemongrass, kaffir lime zest, and shallot in sequence, adding each new ingredient only after the previous one is pureed and incorporated into the paste. Add the fermented shrimp paste, stirring to blend well, then add the peanuts. Transfer to a jar with a tight-fitting lid and refrigerate until ready to use.

Panang Neur
PANANG WITH BEEF

There is an old restaurant in Phitsnulok in Central Thailand that sells a variety of curries, served cafeteria-style. It's been in the business for more than thirty years. The cook makes a wonderful *panang neur* using beef tri-tip, with its tendon and sinew still attached. The curry is cooked slowly for two to three hours until the meat is so tender you can cut it with a fork. Just before transferring it to a serving bowl, the cook adds a handful of finely julienned kaffir lime leaf strands and lightly mixes the curry. The citrus-musty aroma makes her *panang* famous all over Phitsnulok. *Panang neur* keeps well overnight in the refrigerator.

3 cups Fresh Unsweetened Coconut Cream (page 69)
1/2 cup Panang Chile Paste (page 214)
2 pounds beef tri-tip, thinly sliced against the grain into 2-inch-long bite-sized strips
3 tablespoons fish sauce (*namm pla*)
1/4 cup palm sugar or packed light brown sugar
6 to 7 kaffir lime leaves, torn, or grated zest of 1 lime
20 kaffir lime leaves, sliced into strands, or zest of 2 limes, removed with a peeler in strips and julienned
10 to 12 fresh red bird chiles or 4 to 5 serrano chiles, half seeded, half not, and slivered

In a 4-quart saucepan, mix 2 cups of the coconut cream with the chile paste and heat over high heat, stirring, until it begins to boil. Lower the heat to medium-high and cook, stirring occasionally, until thickened, about 10 minutes more. Add the beef, stirring to coat well. Season with the fish sauce and palm sugar and cook, stirring, until the mixture comes back to a boil. Add the torn kaffir lime leaves, and add the remaining 1 cup coconut cream. Lower the heat to a gentle simmer and cook, stirring occasionally to prevent sticking and to ensure even cooking, until the meat is tender and the liquid has evaporated, about 1 hour.

Stir in one third of the kaffir leaf strands and transfer to a platter. Garnish the top with the remaining kaffir lime strands and the chile slivers. Serve hot or warm.

Accompaniments

Cucumber relish (see page 107); 6 ounces spicy kim chee (Korean pickled cabbage); and cooked long-grain rice, preferably Thai jasmine or Indian or California basmati (see pages 37 and 38)

Keang Pet Daeng
SPICY RED CURRY

This is the most versatile paste, used to make both stew-like curries and stir-fries. *Keang pet* means spicy stew and is known in America as red curry. The most famous Thai cook, Than Phu Ying (Her Ladyship) Prann, during the reign of King Chulalongkhorn (1868–1910), emphasized in her cookbook that the paste must be carefully pounded and the ingredients added in proper sequence. Other Thai cooks suggest adding cumin or caraway to the paste to enhance the flavor of beef, pork, or mutton. For fish, add *kra-chay* (lesser galangal) for the aroma.

If you are serving *keang pet* with beef, pork, or lamb, the meat must be cooked in coconut milk to tenderize it before it's added to the cooked paste. Poultry, fish, shrimp, and other shellfish should be rinsed and dried thoroughly before adding them to the paste. Roasted meat or poultry, a real treat in this curry, should be boned. A curry containing roasted meat or poultry should be flavored with sour-fruity ingredients, such as tomatoes, green apples, green grapes, pineapple, or apricots.

A favorite vegetable used in *keang pet* is eggplant. Other vegetables with a soft but firm texture, such as potatoes, sweet potatoes, pumpkins, and green bananas, are also marvelous additions. Crunchy vegetables, such as bamboo shoots, green beans, fresh lima beans, and fava beans, are delicious too. The chile paste will keep stored in a jar with a tight-fitting lid in the refrigerator for at least a month.

Keang Pet Chile Paste

Combine the cumin and caraway seeds, if using, in a 9-inch skillet and dry-roast over medium-high heat, sliding the skillet back and forth to ensure even cooking, until the seeds exude a wonderful aroma, 1 minute or less. Transfer to a plate to cool. Repeat the process with the Thai white peppercorns and coriander seeds. Cool completely before grinding to a powder in an electric spice or coffee grinder. Transfer to a bowl and set aside.

Using a mortar and pestle, pound the sea salt and garlic into a paste. One at a time, add the cilantro roots and stems, dried chiles, fresh chiles, ground spices, nutmeg, galangal, lemongrass, kaffir lime zest, and shallots in sequence, adding each new ingredient only after the previous one is pureed and incorporated into the paste. Add the fermented shrimp paste and stir well. Transfer to a jar with a tight-fitting lid and refrigerate until ready to use.

½ teaspoon cumin seeds (for meat *keang*)

½ teaspoon caraway seeds (for meat *keang*)

½ teaspoon Thai white peppercorns

1 tablespoon coriander seeds

1 teaspoon sea salt

6 to 7 large garlic cloves, minced

1 tablespoon minced cilantro roots and stems

15 dried de árbol or Japonés chiles, softened in warm water, half seeded, half not, and minced

7 to 8 fresh red bird chiles or 4 to 5 serrano chiles, minced (with or without seeds)

¼ teaspoon freshly grated nutmeg (for meat or poultry *keang*)

1 teaspoon minced galangal or 1 tablespoon minced fresh ginger (for seafood *keang*)

1 stalk lemongrass, green parts and hard outer layers removed, minced

Minced zest of 3 to 4 kaffir limes or minced zest of 1 regular lime

2 shallots, minced

1 teaspoon fermented shrimp paste or 1 tablespoon red miso

Keang Pet Moo Yang Kub Klouy Dipp

RED CURRY WITH ROASTED PORK
AND GREEN BANANA

Makes 6 to 8 servings

**For the marinade
(makes ½ cup)**

3 cloves garlic, lightly crushed
1 tablespoon minced fresh ginger
¼ cup pineapple juice
¼ cup soy sauce

For the curry

1 pound pork tenderloin
1 teaspoon baking soda
2 cups water
4 green bananas or plantains,
    peeled and sliced into ¼-inch
    diagonal slices (4 cups)
3 cups Fresh Unsweetened Coconut
    Milk (page 69)
1 cup plus 3 tablespoons Fresh
    Unsweetened Coconut Cream
    (page 69)
½ cup Keang Pet Chile Paste
    (page 217)
1 yellow onion, cut into eighths
2 tablespoons fish sauce (namm pla)
1 teaspoon sea salt
1 tablespoon sugar
3 to 4 kaffir lime leaves, torn and
    bruised, or the zest of 1 lime,
    removed with a peeler in strips
    and lightly bruised
3 to 4 fresh bird chiles or serrano
    chiles, or more, lightly crushed
1 cup fresh Thai basil leaves

Kum Peng Pedd, an ancient city in Central Thailand, is the banana capital of the country. My friend Cat took me there to tour its archaeological ruins. Along the way, we loaded up the trunk of her car with our purchases: long stalks of beautiful ripe bananas, banana chips, banana cooked in syrup, and dried bananas. That evening, we dined at a restaurant near a river that served us this roasted pork and green banana curry. I cannot imagine that there's a banana dish left in Thailand that we didn't try on that trip!

Finding green bananas in supermarkets is never a sure thing, but green plantains are more readily available. Either may be used here; soaking the peeled, sliced fruit in baking soda and water prevents discoloration and removes any sap and slime. This curry will keep well overnight, but wait to add the banana until just before serving. Reheat the curry before adding the banana, and follow the rest of the instructions to finish the recipe.

For the marinade, in a small mixing bowl, combine the garlic, ginger, pineapple juice, and soy sauce. Put the pork in a shallow baking dish and pour the mixture over it. Marinate at room temperature for 1 hour; or, if you wish to marinate it longer, cover and refrigerate for no longer than 3 hours.

Preheat the oven to 350°F. Pour off the marinade and roast the pork for 25 to 30 minutes, or until an instant-read thermometer registers 160°F. Remove from the oven and set aside to cool, then cut into 1-inch cubes.

In a small mixing bowl, combine the baking soda with the water and pour over the green bananas. Let sit for 30 minutes.

Rinse the bananas in several changes of cool water, drain, and dry thoroughly with paper towels. Set aside.

Heat the coconut milk in a 4-quart saucepan over high heat until boiling. Lower the heat to medium. With a spoon, skim off the cream that has risen to the top and transfer to a 10-inch skillet. Leave the coconut milk in the saucepan at a simmer over low heat. Add 1 cup of the fresh coconut cream and the chile paste to the skimmed cream in the skillet, blending well, and bring to a boil over high heat. Lower the heat to medium and cook, stirring occasionally, until the oil rises to the surface with tiny bubbles, 7 to 10 minutes. Stir in the pork and banana slices and bring the mixture to a boil. Add the onion and bring to a boil once more.

Transfer the pork mixture to the saucepan with the simmering coconut milk and increase the heat to medium-high. Stir in the fish sauce, sea salt, and sugar and bring to a boil, stirring occasionally. Add the kaffir lime leaves, crushed chiles, and half of the basil. Return to a boil, then lower the heat to medium and let simmer, uncovered, for 10 to 15 minutes, or until the broth thickens and the bananas are tender but firm. Transfer to a serving bowl. Garnish the top with the remaining 3 tablespoons coconut cream and the remaining basil.

Accompaniments

Fresh Chiles with Fish Sauce (page 93); 12 to 15 tender arugula leaves; 1/2 cucumber, thinly sliced on the diagonal; 6 to 7 cloves pickled garlic, thinly sliced; 2 kosher pickles, thinly sliced on the diagonal; 2 cups Crispy Noodles (page 306); and cooked long-grain rice, preferably Thai jasmine or Indian or California basmati (see pages 37 and 38)

Keang Keow Wann

SWEET GREEN CURRY

The chile paste for this stew-like *keang* uses fresh green chiles instead of dried red chiles to give it the green color. Traditional recipes add the leaves from the chile plant. Some Thai restaurants in America use spinach leaves, while others add food coloring to obtain the green color! I use a combination of the typical fresh bird and serrano chiles for flavor, along with green jalapeño and poblano—sometimes called pasilla—chiles for color. Puree the chiles and squeeze out the liquid before pounding in the pulp; otherwise, it will splatter and could burn your skin or eyes. Wear rubber gloves to extract the juice to prevent burning your skin. Or, if you don't use gloves, sprinkle pinches of sea salt on sliced lime and rub your hands with them, then wash your hands with soap and water.

In the summer when my chile plants can afford to be plucked, I add some leaves to the chile paste, as is done in the traditional way. I add ½ cup fresh kaffir lime leaves while the curry is cooking and garnish the finished *keang* with a handful of fresh chile leaves and Thai basil. The result is a beautiful curry worthy of its name, and the aroma is hard to match.

Versions of *keang keow wann* made with fish balls, shrimp balls, meatballs, or chicken are particularly favored by the Thais. Green baby eggplants and whole fresh green chiles are added together with green beans and fresh tender bamboo shoots. Regular Japanese eggplant, without its purple skin, is a good substitute for green baby eggplants. Tomatillo is another good addition. *Keang keow wann* is exceptional when made with roasted duck cooked with fresh pineapple, grapes, or lychees.

The chile paste will keep in a jar with a tight-fitting lid in the refrigerator for at least a month.

Keang Keow Wann Chile Paste

Makes ¾ cup

Slit the jalapeño and poblano chiles lengthwise. Soak in lukewarm water with 1 teaspoon of the sea salt for 15 minutes. To seed the chiles without burning yourself, remove the seeds while the chiles are in the water. Then discard the liquid along with the seeds and pat the chiles dry with paper towels.

Slice the chiles into chunks and process in the food processor until pureed, about 1 minute. Transfer the chile puree to a 15-inch square of cheesecloth, and wring out the juice into a bowl. Set the liquid aside for cooking the curry. Combine the remaining pulp with the minced bird chiles.

Combine the cumin and caraway seeds in a 9-inch skillet and dry-roast over medium-high heat, sliding the skillet back and forth to ensure even roasting, until the seeds exude a wonderful aroma, 1 minute or less. Transfer to a plate to cool. Repeat the process with the Thai white peppercorns and coriander seeds. Cool completely, then grind in an electric spice or coffee grinder to a powder. Transfer to a bowl and add the grated nutmeg. Set aside.

Using a mortar and pestle, pound the remaining 1 teaspoon sea salt and the garlic into a paste. One at a time, add the cilantro roots and stems, ground spices, chiles, galangal, lemongrass, kaffir lime zest, and shallots in sequence, adding each new ingredient only after the previous one is pureed and incorporated into the paste. Add the fermented shrimp paste and mix well. Transfer to a jar with a tight-fitting lid and refrigerate until ready to use.

3 to 4 fresh green jalapeño chiles
1 fresh poblano chile
2 teaspoons sea salt
15 fresh bird chiles or 6 serrano chiles, half seeded, half not, and minced
½ teaspoon cumin seeds
½ teaspoon caraway seeds
¼ teaspoon Thai white peppercorns
1 tablespoon coriander seeds
¼ teaspoon freshly grated nutmeg
9 cloves garlic, minced
1 tablespoon minced cilantro roots and stems
1 teaspoon minced galangal or 1 tablespoon minced fresh ginger
1 stalk lemongrass, green parts and hard outer layers removed, minced
1 teaspoon grated kaffir lime zest or 2 teaspoons grated regular lime zest
2 shallots, minced
1 teaspoon fermented shrimp paste or 1 tablespoon red miso

Keang Keow Wann Bah Shaw Neur

SWEET GREEN CURRY WITH MEATBALLS

1 pound ground beef

½ teaspoon sea salt

1 ear fresh corn, kernels cut from the cob and minced (1 cup)

3 to 4 tablespoons chile juice (reserved from making the chile paste)

3 cups Fresh Unsweetened Coconut Milk (page 69)

1 cup plus 3 tablespoons Fresh Unsweetened Coconut Cream (page 69)

¾ cup Keang Keow Wann Chile Paste (page 221)

2 tablespoons fish sauce (*namm pla*)

1 tablespoon sugar

5 to 6 kaffir lime leaves, torn, or grated zest of 1 lime

5 to 6 fresh green bird chiles or serrano chiles, halved lengthwise

1¼ pounds banana squash, golden acorn squash, or pumpkin, peeled, seeded, and cubed (2 cups)

1 cup fresh Thai basil leaves

This is an old-fashioned recipe and a favorite of mine. I love the surprising texture of the fresh corn in the meatballs. When I eat this curry, I envision a group of women-in-waiting, in the inner circle of the Royal Court during the time of King Chulalongkhorn. In my fantasy, the women are taking delicate bites and analyzing the particulars of this exquisite dish.

This dish can be made ahead and will keep well overnight, but do not add the banana squash until ready to serve. Bring the curry to a boil before adding the squash, then follow the remaining recipe instructions.

In a large mixing bowl, combine the ground beef, sea salt, corn, and 1 tablespoon of the reserved chile juice. Take a handful of the mixture at a time and hit it against the bowl until the meat becomes sticky and congeals. The process will make the meatballs crispy and crunchy. Set aside.

In a 3-quart saucepan, bring the coconut milk to a boil over high heat. Lower the heat to medium. With a spoon, skim off the cream that has risen to the top and transfer it to a 12-inch skillet. Let the coconut milk continue to simmer over low heat.

Add 1 cup of the fresh coconut cream and the chile paste to the skillet of skimmed cream, blend well, and bring to a boil over high heat. Lower the heat to medium-high and cook, stirring occasionally, until the oil separates and tiny bubbles the color of the chile cover the surface of the cream, about 15 minutes. Transfer the mixture to the saucepan with the simmering coconut milk and increase the heat to medium-high. When the broth begins to boil, season it with the fish sauce, sugar, kaffir lime leaves, and fresh chiles. Add the banana squash and half of the basil and cook until the squash is partially softened, about 5 minutes. Add the remaining reserved chile juice. Shape the meat mixture into balls about 1 inch in diameter and drop them into the broth. Cook until the meatballs are cooked through and the squash is tender, 5 to 10 minutes more.

Transfer to a serving bowl and garnish the top with the remaining 3 tablespoons coconut cream and the remaining basil leaves. Serve hot or warm.

Accompaniments

Fresh Chiles with Fish Sauce (page 93); 2 cups cucumber relish (see page 107); ½-pound smoked salmon, cut into strips, or sliced smoked eel; and cooked long-grain rice, preferably Thai jasmine or Indian or California basmati (see pages 37 and 38), or *kanum jean* (pages 280–292)

Keang Kari
THAI-INDIAN CURRY

Keang kari is an aromatic stew-like Thai-Indian curry that includes roasted garlic and shallots. It's usually prepared with meat, lamb, or chicken, along with yellow or white onions, potatoes, whole shallots, and sweet potatoes or pumpkin. Seafood is seldom used, but occasionally shrimp are included, with cherry tomatoes. Crispy shallots top and garnish this fabulous and rich curry.

Keang Kari Chile Paste

Makes ¾ cup

6 heads garlic

3 shallots

One 1-inch chunk fresh ginger

1 tablespoon olive or vegetable oil

1 tablespoon coriander seeds

½ teaspoon cumin seeds

½ teaspoon caraway seeds

1 teaspoon sea salt

15 dried de árbol or Japonés chiles, softened in warm water, half seeded, half not, and minced

2 tablespoons Madras curry powder (see page 292)

1 stalk lemongrass, green parts and hard outer layers removed, minced

One 2-inch chunk fresh turmeric, peeled and minced (1 tablespoon), or 1 teaspoon turmeric powder

1 teaspoon fermented shrimp paste or 1 tablespoon red miso

Preheat the oven to 400°F. Slice off the tops of the garlic and shallots. Place the garlic, shallots, and ginger on a sheet of aluminum foil, drizzle the oil over them, and wrap in the foil. Roast for 30 minutes. Let cool completely.

Squeeze the soft garlic from the cloves into a bowl and set aside. Peel the ginger, mince, and set aside in a separate bowl. Squeeze the soft shallots from the skin, mince, and set aside in another bowl.

Put the coriander seeds in a 9-inch skillet and dry-roast over medium-high heat, sliding the skillet back and forth to ensure even roasting, until the seeds exude a wonderful aroma, 1 minute or less. Transfer to a plate to cool. Repeat the process with the cumin and caraway seeds. When the seeds are completely cool, grind in an electric spice or coffee grinder. Transfer to a bowl and set aside.

Using a mortar and pestle, pound the sea salt and roasted garlic together into a paste. One by one, add the ginger, shallots, chiles, ground spices, curry powder, lemongrass, and turmeric in sequence, adding each new ingredient only after the previous one is pureed and incorporated into the paste. Add the fermented shrimp paste and mix well. Transfer to a jar with a tight-fitting lid and refrigerate until ready to use.

Keang Kari Gai

THAI-INDIAN CURRY WITH CHICKEN

My father's favorite Thai dish is *keang kari*. Our servant, Somm, used to make the chile paste with only one chile because my father couldn't eat spicy food. For the rest of the family, with hearty stomachs and more heat-resistant palates, she made *prikk namm pla,* chopped chiles and fish sauce. *Keang kari* with chicken and potatoes is the Yu family's favorite curry.

The cooking technique for the chicken included in this recipe may seem excessive. But trust me, you will be well rewarded for your diligence. The end result is marvelous.

In a 4- to 6-quart saucepan, bring the coconut milk to a boil over high heat. Lower the heat to medium-high. With a spoon, skim off the cream that has risen to the top and transfer it to a 12-inch skillet. Add the chicken to the saucepan and lower the heat so it simmers.

Add 1 cup of the fresh coconut cream and the chile paste to the skimmed cream in the skillet and bring to a boil over high heat. Lower the heat to medium-high and cook until the oil separates and tiny bubbles the color of the chile paste cover the surface, about 10 minutes.

Transfer the chicken pieces to the skillet and stir to coat well. Increase the heat to high and cook, stirring, until the skin of the chicken is well coated with the mixture and browned, about 3 minutes. Add the chicken and chile paste mixture to the simmering coconut milk and turn the heat to high. When the sauce comes to a boil, add the sugar, fish sauce, onions, potatoes, bay leaves, and chiles. Lower the heat to medium, cover, and cook for 20 minutes, or until the chicken is cooked through and the potatoes are tender.

Transfer to a serving bowl, top with the remaining 2 tablespoons coconut cream and the crispy shallots, and serve hot.

Accompaniments

Fresh Chiles with Fish Sauce (page 93); cucumber relish (see page 107); ½ pound smoked mussels; 2 pickled garlic cloves, thinly sliced; and cooked long-grain rice, preferably Thai jasmine or Indian or California basmati (see pages 37 and 38)

3 cups Fresh Unsweetened Coconut Milk (page 69)
One 3-pound chicken, cut into bite-sized pieces, rinsed, and thoroughly dried
1 cup plus 2 tablespoons Fresh Unsweetened Coconut Cream (page 69)
¾ cup Keang Kari Chile Paste (page 224)
1 tablespoon sugar
2 tablespoons fish sauce (*namm pla*)
2 medium yellow onions, cut into eighths
1 pound potatoes, peeled and cut into 1-inch cubes
2 to 3 bay leaves
5 to 6 fresh red bird chiles or 3 to 4 serrano chiles, sliced lengthwise in half (with or without seeds)
¼ cup Crispy Shallots (page 138)

Keang Leurng
YELLOW CURRY

Keang leurng is a fiery, spicy soup thickened with pureed dried shrimp or grilled fish instead of the usual coconut cream. Grilled mackerel is often used for added flavor, but grilled tuna or other kinds of meaty fish with a high oil content are good substitutes. *Keang leurng*'s golden-yellow color is a southern Thai signature, because yellow turmeric is used in almost everything made in southern Thailand. Whole dried chiles with seeds are used in the paste, so the end result is a very spicy curry. For a milder curry, you can remove the seeds. This will make the dominant tastes of the curry sour and salty, then spicy, instead of spicy-sour-salty.

Keang leurng is almost always made with seafood and tangy fruit such as pineapple, tomato, or star fruit. The chile paste will keep very well in a jar with a tight-fitting lid in the refrigerator for a couple of weeks.

Keang Leurng Chile Paste

Makes ¾ cup

1 teaspoon sea salt

9 large cloves garlic, minced

15 to 20 dried de árbol or Japonés chiles, softened in warm water and minced (with or without seeds)

1 tablespoon minced fresh turmeric or 1 teaspoon turmeric powder

2 shallots, minced

1 tablespoon fermented shrimp paste or 1½ tablespoons red miso

2 ounces mackerel or tuna, grilled, boned, and pureed in a food processor (¼ cup)

Using a mortar and pestle, pound the sea salt and garlic into a paste. One at a time, add the chiles, turmeric, and shallots in sequence, adding each new ingredient only after the previous one is pureed and incorporated into the paste. Mix in the fermented shrimp paste until smooth. Add the fish and mix well. Store in a jar with a tight-fitting lid in the refrigerator until ready to use.

Keang Leurng Subparod
YELLOW CURRY WITH FISH AND PINEAPPLE

Makes 6 servings

When I lived in Ventura, California, during the 1970s, a weekly ritual of mine was a drive to Chinatown in Los Angeles to buy groceries and eat at Jitrada, a Thai restaurant on Hollywood Boulevard. It was a tiny place known for the best Thai food in the city and was frequented by Thais living in Los Angeles. The owner, who was from southern Thailand, made the tastiest and spiciest *keang leurng* I've ever had in this country. It always reminded me of home.

Stand the pineapple on end and quarter it lengthwise. Leaving the core in, cut each wedge crosswise into 1/2-inch slices. Set aside.

Put the fish steaks in a colander in the sink, massage the fish with the sea salt, and let sit for 10 minutes. Rinse in several changes of cold water, pat dry with paper towels, and slice into 2-inch chunks.

In a 3-quart saucepan, combine the chile paste with the bottled water and bring to a boil over high heat. Lower the heat to medium, add the chiles, and simmer for about 10 minutes. Add the pineapple, fish sauce, palm sugar, and tamarind. Taste for a balance of spicy-sour and salty. Increase the heat and bring the broth to a boil again, then lower the heat to simmer. Cook for about 10 minutes, or until the pineapple is soft but still firm. Add the fish and stir to mix gently. Simmer for another 10 minutes, or until the fish is cooked through. Transfer to a serving bowl.

Accompaniments

Fresh Chiles with Fish Sauce (page 93); sweet gherkins; Beef Jerky (page 208); and cooked long-grain rice, preferably Thai jasmine or Indian or California basmati (see pages 37 and 38)

One 1 1/2-pound pineapple, peeled and eyes removed (see page 28)

2 pounds tuna steaks or halibut steaks

1 tablespoon sea salt

3/4 cup Keang Leurng Chile Paste (page 226)

3 cups bottled or filtered water

10 to 12 fresh red bird chiles or 5 to 6 serrano chiles, halved lengthwise (with or without seeds)

3 tablespoons fish sauce (*namm pla*)

3 tablespoons palm sugar or light brown sugar

1/2 cup thick tamarind juice (see page 128)

Keang Masmun

MASMUN CURRY

Keang masmun is the most renowned Thai dish, and one of the best loved, among Westerners. It is probably because of its aromatic perfume, which is reminiscent of Indian-style curry. Ironically, it was the Thais who invented this curry, using dried herbs and spices acquired from Arab traders. It is the heartiest of all Thai stew-like curries, prized for its exuberant dry-roasted flavors. The chile paste is elaborate and includes more ingredients than the previous curry recipes. Take the time, though—it is worth it. The chile paste will keep for a month or more if properly stored in the refrigerator.

Keang masmun is a rich and decadent dish. Boiled peanuts and roasted whole shallots are sometimes added for texture and flavor. Palm sugar as well as tamarind juice (see page 128) or calamondin juice (see page 127), or both, may be included to produce a balance of sweet, tangy, fruity flavors. A famous *keang masmun* combines potatoes and sweet potatoes with beef or chicken and, sometimes, pairs pineapple with beef or deep-fried chicken. As I researched *masmun* recipes, I discovered each author and cook has his or her own version and provides a convincing argument as to why it should be prepared that particular way. One thing all Thai cooks agree upon, however, is that the meat must be thoroughly dried and cooked in coconut milk to tenderize before adding it to the chile paste. I have taken bits and pieces from all my best sources for my own version, which, I must say, is fabulous.

Keang Masmun Chile Paste

Makes 1 cup

Preheat the oven to 400°F. Slice off the tops of the garlic and the shallots. Place the garlic, shallots, and galangal on a large piece of aluminum foil. Drizzle the oil over them and wrap in the foil. Wrap the lemongrass in another piece of aluminum foil. Put both pouches in the oven and bake the lemongrass for 20 minutes and the garlic, galangal, and shallots for 30 minutes. Remove and set aside to cool completely.

Squeeze the cooked garlic from the cloves. Peel the galangal and mince. Squeeze the cooked shallots from the skin and mince. Set the garlic, galangal, and shallots aside in separate bowls. Mince the roasted lemongrass and set aside.

Combine the cumin and caraway seeds in a 9-inch skillet and dry-roast over medium-high heat, sliding the skillet back and forth to ensure even roasting, until the seeds exude a wonderful aroma, about 1 minute. Transfer to a plate to cool, then repeat the process with the coriander seeds, cardamom seeds, and cloves. Grind in an electric spice or coffee grinder. Transfer to a bowl, add the nutmeg, cinnamon, and mace, and set aside.

Using a mortar and pestle, pound the sea salt and garlic into a paste. One at a time, add the cilantro roots and stems, chiles, coriander seeds, ground spices, cardamom, cloves, galangal, lemongrass, kaffir lime zest, and shallots in sequence, adding each new ingredient only after the previous one is pureed and incorporated into the paste. Add the fermented shrimp paste and mix and blend well. Store in a jar with a tight-fitting lid in the refrigerator until ready to use.

3 heads garlic
2 shallots
One 1-inch chunk galangal or ginger
1 tablespoon olive oil or vegetable oil
6 stalks lemongrass, green parts and hard outer layers removed
1 tablespoon coriander seeds
½ teaspoon cumin seeds
½ teaspoon caraway seeds
1 teaspoon cardamom seeds
6 whole cloves
½ teaspoon freshly grated nutmeg
1 teaspoon ground cinnamon
½ teaspoon ground mace
1 teaspoon sea salt
10 to 12 sprigs fresh cilantro with stems and roots, minced
2 dried New Mexico (or California) chiles, softened in warm water, seeded, and minced
15 dried de árbol or Japonés chiles, softened in warm water, half seeded, half not, and minced
Minced zest of 1 kaffir lime or regular lime
2 teaspoons fermented shrimp paste or 1 tablespoon red miso

Keang Masmun Neur
MASMUN CURRY WITH BEEF

Makes 6 servings

¼ cup unsalted raw peanuts

3 cups Fresh Unsweetened Coconut Milk (page 69)

2 pounds good-quality boneless beef top sirloin, sliced against the grain into thin 2-inch strips

2 cups Fresh Unsweetened Coconut Cream (page 69)

1 cup Keang Masmun Chile Paste (page 229)

2 tablespoons fish sauce (*namm pla*)

2 tablespoons palm sugar or light brown sugar

3 tablespoons thick tamarind juice (see page 128)

3 bay leaves

¼ teaspoon ground mace

4 whole cloves, dry-roasted (see page 13)

1 cup 1-inch cubes yellow or white onion

7 shallots, roasted and peeled (see page 137)

5 unpeeled kumquats or 1 peeled sour tangerine, sliced paper-thin and seeded

Juntujuk, a weekend market in Bangkok, is immense—larger than several football fields. You can buy anything; that is, if you take the time to walk for miles and search. The ready-made food section is housed in a gigantic enclosed area. On hot and humid days, the aroma from hundreds of prepared foods can drive you crazy with hunger. There are several stalls that sell curry, boldly displayed in *uncovered* large aluminum pots. There's every color of curry and every kind of curry: dry or liquid, and with meat, poultry, seafood, or meatballs. *Keang masmun,* with its glorious dark red sauce and whole peanuts and shallots floating on top, is the most dramatic of the lot.

Fill a small saucepan with water, add the peanuts, and boil gently over medium heat for 1 hour. Drain the peanuts, rinse with several changes of cool water, and transfer to a bowl. Add water to cover and rub the peanuts together with your hands to loosen the skins. Pour off the water and skins; set aside.

In a 3-quart saucepan, bring the coconut milk to a boil over medium heat and boil for 2 minutes. When the cream rises to the top, skim it off into a 12-inch skillet. Add the beef to the boiling coconut milk and return to a boil. Lower the heat to a simmer and cook for about 10 minutes, or until the meat is partially cooked. Skim off the scum and discard. Leave the beef to simmer while you cook the chile paste.

Add the fresh coconut cream and chile paste to the skillet with the skimmed coconut cream and mix well. Heat over high heat for 2 minutes, or until the mixture begins to boil. Lower the heat to medium-high and cook until the oil separates and bubbles the color of the chile paste cover the surface, 15 to 20 minutes.

With a slotted spoon, transfer the beef from the saucepan to the skillet. Stir well. Increase the heat to high and cook for 2 minutes, then transfer both the beef and chile paste mixture into the simmering coconut milk. Turn the heat to high. When the mixture comes to a boil, add the fish sauce, palm sugar, tamarind juice, boiled peanuts, bay leaves, mace, cloves, onion, and roasted shallots. Return the broth to a boil once more, then lower the heat to medium. Cook for about 10 minutes, or until the beef is tender and the onion is cooked, stirring occasionally to prevent sticking. Add the kumquats and mix well. Transfer to a serving bowl and serve hot.

Accompaniments

Fresh Chiles with Fish Sauce (page 93); Big Salad (page 254); pickled garlic; pickled ginger; salted egg; and cooked long-grain rice, preferably Thai jasmine or Indian or California basmati (see pages 37 and 38)

Keang Som
SOUR-ORANGE CURRY

Every region in Thailand has a version of *keang som*. It is an ancient and simple curry soup cooked with seasonal vegetables. The dominant taste of the broth is salty-sour, followed by spicy and slightly sweet. Young tender vegetable shoots and greens are among the favorite vegetables for *keang som*. Firm-fleshed vegetables, such as summer squash, baby watermelon, mushrooms, and/or green papaya, are allowed to simmer in the broth for a longer period, to soften as well as to absorb the flavors from the seasonings. Leafy vegetables, on the other hand, are added just before serving. Some, such as peas or green beans, should be parboiled in salted water and rinsed in cold water before being added to the broth. This retains their natural green color, adding dramatic contrast to the orange curry. Taste the broth to ensure a balance of flavors before you add the main ingredients.

The binder for the chile paste can be grilled fish or fermented shrimp paste. For a vegetarian version, use red miso. Using fish results in a thicker broth with the aroma of the sea. The latter is lighter, cleaner, and refreshing. The paste will keep well in a jar with a tight-fitting lid in the refrigerator for at least a month.

Keang Som Chile Paste

Makes ½ cup

1 teaspoon sea salt

9 cloves garlic, minced

15 dried de árbol or Japonés chiles, softened in warm water, half seeded, half not

2 shallots, minced

1 tablespoon minced *kra-chay* (lesser galangal; see page 132) or fresh ginger

1 tablespoon minced galangal or fresh ginger

1 tablespoon fermented shrimp paste or 1½ teaspoons red miso

2 ounces mackerel or tuna, grilled or broiled, skin and bones removed, and shredded (¾ cup)

Using a mortar and pestle, pound the sea salt and garlic into a paste. One at a time, add the chiles, shallots, *kra-chay*, and galangal in sequence, adding each new ingredient only after the previous one is pureed and incorporated into the paste. Add the fermented shrimp paste and mix well, then add the grilled fish. Store in a jar with a tight-fitting lid in the refrigerator until ready to use.

Keang Som Pak Orn

SOUR-ORANGE CURRY WITH TENDER VEGETABLES

Makes 4 servings

When I decide to make *keang som,* I shop at my favorite farmers' market for the freshest and most tender seasonal vegetables. The secret of *keang som* is gentle and slow cooking. This allows the spicy flavors to develop and infuse the broth. I use my old earthenware pot from Thailand to cook it slowly in a brazier (charcoal burner) in my outdoor kitchen. You can substitute a *cazuela,* a Mexican earthenware pot, or an enameled cast-iron casserole. Remember to put a heat diffuser between the flame and the earthenware pot to prevent the pot from cracking. If using a regular metal pot, be patient and let the broth simmer as gently as possible. *Keang som* broth can be made ahead and refrigerated. Minutes before serving, warm it gently and add the vegetables.

Parboil the French beans in boiling salted water for just 3 to 4 seconds. Immediately drain and rinse with cold water. Repeat with the peas. Set aside.

In a 4-quart saucepan, *cazuela,* or enamel casserole, dissolve the chile paste in the bottled water and cook over medium heat, stirring, for 5 minutes. Season the broth with the sugar, fish sauce, if desired, and the tamarind juice and boil for 1 to 2 minutes. Taste for a balance of salty-sour-spicy-sweet flavors. Lower the heat, add the mushrooms, and simmer for 5 minutes, or until tender. Add the zucchini and simmer for another 2 minutes, or until cooked but still firm. Increase the heat to medium, add the Napa cabbage, spinach, and dandelion leaves, and bring to a boil. Reduce the heat to a simmer and cook for another 5 minutes, or until the vegetables are crisp yet tender. Add the green beans and sweet peas, transfer to a serving bowl, and serve hot.

Accompaniments

Smoked trout, smoked salmon, and deep-fried shrimp, or, for a vegetarian curry, deep-fried sweet potato and Japanese eggplant (page 195); and cooked long-grain rice, preferably Thai jasmine or Indian or California basmati (see pages 37 and 38)

3 ounces French beans, snapped in half

3 ounces sugar snap sweet peas

¾ cup Keang Som Chile Paste (page 232)

4 cups bottled or filtered water

1 tablespoon sugar

1 tablespoon fish sauce (*namm pla;* optional)

½ cup tamarind juice (see page 128)

3 ounces fresh oyster mushrooms, cleaned, or shiitake mushrooms, cleaned and quartered

2 cups whole baby zucchini with blossoms or 4 ounces larger zucchini, sliced crosswise on a diagonal (1 cup)

6 to 7 tender Napa cabbage leaves and tender hearts, sliced into bite-sized pieces

2 ounces baby spinach with stems and leaves

1 ounce dandelion leaves or arugula leaves

The Secret of Thai Salads

Pla Too, through perilous sea you made your journey
I thank you
Pla Too, your noble sacrifice for my sustenance
I thank you
Pla Too, your delectable flesh is my existence
I thank you
[*Pla too*, mackerel, has been the favorite fish of
Thai people for centuries.]

Translated from *Mae Khloa Hoa Paa*
(Head Cook from the Forest),
between 1868 and 1900

Yumm, or Thai salad, is believed to have originated in Burma. The word describes the process of using your hands to mix vegetables, fruits, blossoms, and roots together with a dressing. Sometimes small amounts of meat are added. Historically, *yumm* was tossed with a simple dressing of sour-sweet-salty-spicy flavors made with lime juice, sugar, salt, and chiles. *Yumm* is a dish that exemplifies the Thai cook's sense of *sanuk,* or fun, and creativity, making it *arroy,* or delicious. Thai salads are created as *kreung kang,* or side dishes. A salad is chosen to complement other dishes on the menu. Thus, variations may include meat, poultry, or seafood, mixed with vegetables or fruits and seasoned with fresh herbs and spices. *Yumm* is one of the easiest dishes to make. My first cooking lesson as a young child at a Thai boarding school was making a Thai salad.

Wattana Wittaya Academy, where I was enrolled when I was five years old, was founded during the time of King Chulalongkhorn in 1874. Originally the school was called Wang Lung, or the "back palace" school. Located in the inner sanctum of the royal palace, it resembled a small city run entirely by women who served the King, the Queen, the royal consorts, and their children. Young girls from privileged families were accepted into this inner court to serve and to learn the art and etiquette of becoming a refined, cultured Thai woman. By the time Wang Lung expanded and moved onto land donated by the Queen, it had become a boarding school for girls of noble families. The foreign missionaries who taught at the school tried valiantly to turn their young charges into educated and independent women. Unfortunately, the parents only wanted their daughters to become sophisticated and marriageable.

Among my aristocratic classmates, I was one of a handful of children whose parents were ethnic Chinese. Under a strict regimen and along with regular subjects, we were still taught as if we were going to become royal courtesans. Traditional lessons included sewing, tatting, embroidering, crocheting, and knitting, all of which we managed to fail dismally. Our desperate teacher decided to teach us how to cook, beginning with how to carve fruits and vegetables. This, too, ended abruptly, with the class gleefully devouring our mistakes. Her next attempt was a class on how to make *yumm*, or Thai salad.

We washed, cleaned, sliced, and pounded. We cleaned a fish, pulling off its head and shredding the meat. We pounded the ingredients for the dressing, and sliced and carved cucumbers into flowers. We used the "rabbit," an instrument we had only seen used by adults at home, to grate the coconut into mounds of snowy flakes. By far, the best part of the day was dinner that night when we ate our *yumm*, instead of the usual inedible fare, as the rest of the children watched with envy.

Periodically I make this same grilled fish salad, and sometimes in rather faraway places without a kitchen and with sparse choices of ingredients. It is quite remarkable that a simple salad has become one of the most popular and creative dishes. Every region in Thailand has its own exceptional version. But it was the Royal Court and the nobility who took this simple concept and made it a showcase for cooks to display their talent and imagination. This occurred during the reign of King Chulalongkhorn (1868–1910), when Thai cuisine reached its peak and the Royal Court became a creative and inventive culinary center. This was because His Majesty adored cooking and eating. The King also loved to travel all over the country to visit his people. He was curious and appreciative of regional ingredients as well as of their simple cooking. When he traveled, a large group of members of the Royal Court always accompanied him. Adding their own touches, members of the court began to re-create the King's favorite dishes when they returned to the royal palace. Being creative people, they began to alter, change, and invent their own versions of traditional dishes. *Yumm* was among the dishes that took the court by storm. An example is *laab,* an extremely spicy salad from northeastern Thailand, traditionally made with raw or partially cooked beef, which the court made with roasted chicken or duck.

The popularity of Thai salads was infectious, and for a while, it was as if every Thai household went on a binge in creating *yumm.* Each cook believed hers or his was the best. Certain methods or ingredients became guarded secrets and were never shared. When friends asked for the recipes, it was expected that an ingredient or two would be left out purposely. The Thai salad became a subject of much discussion among cooks and food connoisseurs. As a result, Thai salad has become a dish with complex theory and history behind it, including prescribed combinations of provocative, contrasting ingredients, textures, and tastes.

Luckily, in 1966, in a spirit of cooperation, an association of Thai women decided to write a series of cookbooks. The result was the preservation of ancient Thai home recipes that other-wise might have been lost. From famous families of great cooks, the women came together to share their family recipes and methods of cooking. One of the books was on Thai salads, and it is one of the best Thai cookbooks on the subject. The book explains the complicated theory of Thai salad, and how to mix and match ingredients and dressings.

The Anatomy of Thai Salads

A Thai salad is like a classical ballet. There is a prima ballerina, and a supporting cast to accentuate the star's performance. Thai salads are often named after their major star ingredient, as with *yumm mah-muen*, mango salad; *yumm pla duk*, grilled catfish salad; or *yumm som ohh*, pomelo salad. Other meats, poultry, seafood, fruits, or vegetables are carefully selected to complement and/or add contrasting flavors and textures. Garnishes add enticing aromas and brilliant colors. The dressing binds all these ingredients together.

Thai salads are made from the freshest and best of each season's bountiful gifts. In the hot, humid summer months, a particular kind of raw mango is added to salads for its sweet, nutty flavor and crisp texture. It is ideal with dried shrimp and sweet palm sugar, creating a surprising, inconceivable, yet delicious combination. The monsoon season brings a profusion of greens and edible blossoms, including banana blossoms. Salads are made with banana blossoms tossed in fresh, rich coconut cream and topped with tender cooked pork strips and roasted crispy coconut flakes. With the arrival of the cool season, when the weather turns balmy and the night chilly, pomelo, a citrus fruit similar to a large grapefruit, yields its jewel-like, succu-lent, tart, sweet, and crispy crop. The fruit is sectioned and used to accompany grilled shrimp garnished with toasted coconut flakes.

Thai cooks are partial to vibrant colors and employ them not only for artistic purposes, but to convey symbolic meanings. Red, for example, the color of rubies, represents richness. Green is the emerald, representing wealth; yellow or orange is gold, representing abundance; white is for purity; and purple is the color of royalty. In Thai cooking, color carries the cook's message. Through a beautiful presentation, the cook honors guests, sets the mood, and extends a visually appealing and appetizing invitation to dine even before the food has touched one's lips. A salad's earthy-brown cooked-meat color serves as the background canvas on which captivating hues of green, red, yellow, orange, and purple are spread. Unlike Westerners, who tend to dislike black food, Thai are partial to it and often contrast black with bright colors.

Finally, here are some ancient words of advice passed down from generations of Thai cooks that I find very helpful when I duplicate old recipes, or when I create my own Thai salad:

Always combine white and palm sugar. White sugar is sweet but lacks the aroma of palm sugar. Palm sugar is so dark that if used alone it will discolor other ingredients. Its strong flavor also will dominate a dish. Pairing white and palm sugar makes a good balance. Light brown sugar, date sugar, or maple sugar can be used as a substitute for palm sugar.

Tamarind juice (see page 128), which is fruity, tart, and slightly sweet, is paired with orange or other citrus juice, but never vinegar and rarely lime juice. Experiment with different fruit juices such as concentrated apple, cherry, pineapple, or pomegranate.

Coconut cream must be paired with a fruity, tart flavor such as tamarind, bitter orange, or kumquat. Ancient Thai cooks rarely used lime, feeling it was too sharp and acidic, and that it tended to dominate other flavors, making it difficult to produce a delicate balance. Often a recipe using coconut cream calls for slivers of tart fruit as a garnish to balance the nutty, sweet flavor of the coconut. Star fruit, tart plums, apricots, grapes, and tart green Granny Smiths are delicious additions.

Use fish sauce as an accent to give the dish a slight hint of the sea. Use good-quality sea salt in combination with high-quality fish sauce.

Salads made with grilled beef, pork, sausage, poultry, fish, and shellfish are often seasoned with kaffir lime leaves and/or lemongrass. In addition, fish is always seasoned with *kra-chay* (lesser galangal; see page 132). A combination of green Mexican and Key limes is a good substitute for kaffir lime. Use young ginger as a substitute for *kra-chay*. If young ginger is not available, use regular ginger: Salt it with a couple of pinches of sea salt, let it sit for 5 to 10 minutes, rinse, and squeeze dry.

There are five basic dressings for Thai salad. Each dressing branches into several variations, although the primary flavors remain the same. Each ingredient is carefully selected to complement the ingredients in the salad. At the same time, wise Thai cooks recognize and honor individual taste preferences. Individual cooks and guests are directed to taste the dressing, then add flavors to suit personal tastes.

These recipes apply the same rule. Use each as a guide and alter it to fit your individual preference. Just as each salad dressing is created and chosen by a Thai cook to complement the primary ingredient or the star of the salad, it must also balance with the supporting cast, or secondary ingredients. Primary consideration is given to the overall tastes and textures and how they complement or contrast with each other. The final touch is the garnishes, which are selected for aroma and color.

Thai salad is easy to make. Preparation can be in stages for last-minute assembly. Most dressings can be stored in a glass jar with a tight-fitting lid and refrigerated for a day or two. Dressings with fresh coconut cream and tamarind juice can be partially made ahead, but these ingredients should be added at the last minute, just before serving. Ingredients for Thai salad will keep well and remain fresh if stored in separate Ziploc bags and refrigerated. Garnishes such as Crispy Garlic (page 138), Crispy Shallots (page 138), Roasted Fresh Grated Coconut Flakes (page 71), and roasted ground peanuts can be made in large quantities and stored in glass jars at room temperature.

Dressing One

SWEET, SALTY, SOUR

Makes 1 cup

In a small saucepan, combine the sea salt, fish sauce, palm sugar, and granulated sugar and cook over low heat, stirring, just until the sea salt and sugar are dissolved. Remove from the heat and transfer to a mixing bowl to cool. When cooled completely, stir in the lime juice.

1/2 teaspoon sea salt
1/4 cup fish sauce (*namm pla*)
2 tablespoons palm sugar or light
    brown sugar
1/4 cup granulated sugar
1/2 cup fresh lime juice

Primary Ingredients

Dressing One is used with crispy vegetables and fruits such as cucumber, cabbage, green mango, and jícama. Sometimes soft, slippery, chewy ingredients such as grilled mushrooms and grilled peppers are used. Less conventional but interesting ingredients include grilled eggplant and grilled okra.

Secondary Ingredients

This dressing, which can be added to the primary ingredients, is used with soft and chewy ingredients such as cooked shrimp and pork, grilled fish, raw baby eggplant, and crispy fried dried shrimp. To counterbalance these soft-textured ingredients, crispy vegetables such as lettuce, Chinese celery, and sweet onion are added.

Aromas and Colors

Fresh, clean herbs and aromatics such as mint and Thai or holy basil are usually combined with musty, peppery aromatic herbs including lemongrass, kaffir lime leaves, and garlic. Ingredients with smoky aromas from deep-frying, such as Crispy Garlic (page 138) and Crispy Shallots (page 138), as well as nutty, earthy aromas from peanuts, are also popular. Bright and cheerful fresh chiles and herbs are added for the grand finale.

Yumm Taeng Kua

CLASSIC CUCUMBER SALAD

Makes 4 servings

1 cucumber, peeled, halved
   lengthwise, seeded, and thinly
   sliced on the diagonal (2 cups)
1 whole scallion, minced
¼ cup Dressing One (page 239)

Cucumber salad is served with grilled meat, poultry, and seafood, as well as with Thai curry, as an accompaniment or relish. Variations can be made to complement a particular entrée.

Put the cucumber and scallion in a small mixing bowl and add the dressing. Mix well and let sit for 10 minutes before serving.

Variations

1. Omit the scallion and add 1 to 2 shallots, thinly sliced, and 12 sprigs cilantro, coarsely chopped.

2. In addition to the ingredients in the basic recipe, add 1 to 2 fresh bird chiles or serrano chiles, seeded, if desired, and minced, and 12 mint leaves, minced.

3. In addition to the ingredients in variations 1 and 2, garnish the basic salad or either of the above variations with 1 to 2 tablespoons dry-roasted (see page 13) and ground unsalted peanuts.

4. In addition to the ingredients in variations 1, 2, and 3, garnish the basic salad or any one of the above variations with 1 table-spoon crispy fried dried shrimp (prepared as described on page 305).

Yumm Appurn

APPLE AND SMOKED SALMON SALAD

Makes 6 servings

King Chulalongkhorn traveled to Europe in 1897 on his yacht, *Maha Chakri*. During the long journey, he kept a diary, which includes many entries recounting his yearning for Thai foods, and took to improvising some of his favorite Thai dishes. This recipe was His Majesty's own creation, using fresh apple and dried shrimp. I have taken the liberty of substituting smoked salmon for the dried shrimp.

In a large mixing bowl, combine the lemon juice, lemon rind, and 3 cups cold water. Quarter the apples, leaving them unpeeled, and remove the core and seeds, putting the apple quarters in the lemon water as you proceed. Slice each quarter very thinly and return the slices to the lemon water.

At serving time, drain the apple slices and rinse with cool water. Pat dry with paper towels and arrange on a platter. Scatter the smoked salmon over the apple slices and top with the sliced shallots. To serve, mix the minced fresh chiles with the dressing and pour over the salad. Toss well and serve.

Variation

Two to 3 tablespoons chopped fresh cilantro stems and leaves and 3 to 4 tablespoons coarsely ground dry-roasted (see page 13) unsalted peanuts are delicious additions.

Juice of 1 lemon (rind reserved)
2 Granny Smith apples
¼ pound smoked salmon, shredded (1 cup)
2 shallots, thinly sliced
4 to 5 fresh bird chiles or 2 to 3 serrano chiles or more, minced
¾ cup Dressing One (page 239)

Yumm Kratorn

APRICOT, SHRIMP, AND PORK SALAD

Makes 6 servings

6 to 8 slightly firm apricots, sliced lengthwise into eighths
1 teaspoon sea salt
½ pound medium shrimp, peeled, deveined, cooked, and slivered (1 cup)
¼ pound boneless pork, cooked and slivered (1 cup)
5 to 6 fresh bird chiles or
   3 to 4 serrano chiles, seeded (if desired) and minced
¾ cup Dressing One (page 239)
3 tablespoons unsalted peanuts, dry-roasted (page 13) and coarsely ground
2 tablespoons Crispy Garlic (page 138)

The original recipe uses *kratorn,* a tropical fruit the size of a big apple. It has a pulpy, soft texture with a very tart and acidic flavor. Almost-ripe apricots are a good substitute. Minced fresh chiles give the dish that extra zing. However, you can adjust the amount of chiles according to your own preference.

Set a colander in the sink, add the apricots, and toss with the sea salt. Let sit for 5 minutes. Rinse with cool water and pat dry with paper towels. Transfer to a large mixing bowl and add the cooked shrimp and pork.

Combine the minced chiles with the dressing and pour the mixture over the salad. Toss gently and transfer to a serving platter. Garnish with the peanuts and crispy garlic.

Variations

Firm peaches or seedless grapes are good alternatives to the apricots. To peel peaches, parboil them in hot water for 20 to 30 seconds and immediately rinse in cool water. Peel off the skin, then slice into long bite-sized wedges. No need to peel the grapes—just cut them in half.

For the dressing, instead of lime juice, heat 3 tablespoons Fresh Unsweetened Coconut Cream (page 69) and 1 teaspoon Roasted Chiles in Oil (page 94) and add to the dressing. Garnish the salad with ground crispy fried pork rinds (see page 114).

Yumm Prikk Yurg

GRILLED ANAHEIM CHILES WITH MINCED PORK AND MINCED SHRIMP

Makes 6 servings

Prikk yurg, the long slender chile that Thai cooks use for this salad, is spicy and aromatic. When char-burnt and seeded, it retains much of its flavor, even as its firm flesh softens. Dark green Anaheim chiles are a good substitute. Taste the chiles to determine spiciness. If an extra kick is needed, add 1 to 2 tablespoons chopped green serrano chiles to the dressing.

Char the Anaheim chiles over high heat, directly on an electric burner, over a gas flame, or on an outdoor grill, turning occasionally until the skin is burnt and blackened. Put the chiles in a plastic bag, seal, and set aside to cool.

Massage the chiles in the bag to loosen the skin, then rinse them under cool water to remove the skin. Slit each chile open lengthwise and remove the seeds. Pat dry with paper towels. Cut each chile into thin long strands and set aside.

In a small saucepan, bring the coconut cream just to a boil over medium heat and cook, stirring constantly, for 3 minutes. Remove from the heat and let cool until lukewarm. Add it to the dressing and set aside.

In a large mixing bowl, combine the roasted and fresh chiles, pork, and shrimp. Toss gently, then add the dressing. Toss to mix and transfer to a serving platter. Garnish with the crispy shallots and garlic.

6 to 7 Anaheim chiles
¼ cup Fresh Unsweetened Coconut Cream (page 69)
1 cup Dressing One (page 239)
2 to 3 fresh bird chiles, minced
¼ pound boneless pork, cooked and sliced into thin slivers (1 cup)
½ pound medium shrimp, peeled, deveined, cooked, and slivered (1 cup)
1 tablespoon Crispy Shallots (page 138)
1 tablespoon Crispy Garlic (page 138)

Variations

For the dressing, increase the amount of coconut cream to ½ cup; mix ¼ cup of it with 1 tablespoon pureed softened dried shrimp and add the mixture to the dressing. Just before serving the salad, pour the remaining coconut cream on top as an additional garnish.

You can also garnish the salad with a sliced hard-boiled egg.

Yumm Tupp Tim

POMEGRANATE SALAD

Makes 6 servings

1 large pomegranate

½ pound boneless pork, cooked and shredded (2 cups)

½ pound boneless, skinless chicken breast, cooked and shredded (2 cups)

1 to 2 tablespoons Roasted Dried Chile Powder (page 91) or cayenne

¾ cup Dressing One (page 239)

¼ cup Crispy Garlic (page 138)

¼ cup Crispy Shallots (page 138)

Tupp tim, or pomegranate, means ruby, symbolizing richness and fertility. The Chinese consider it nectar for the gods and in Thailand, pomegranate trees are grown in the backyard as good luck charms. The fruit, much smaller than what we find here in America, is used as garnish and in salads. This is a spectacular dish and very easy to make.

Remove the seeds from the pomegranate. You should have about 1½ cups of seeds. In a large mixing bowl, combine 1 cup of the pomegranate seeds, the pork, and chicken. Toss lightly.

In a small mixing bowl, mix the chile powder with the dressing. Pour it over the salad; toss lightly. Transfer to a serving platter, garnish with the crispy garlic, crispy shallots, and the remaining pomegranate seeds, and serve.

Dressing Two

S W E E T ,   S A L T Y ,   S O U R ,   S P I C Y

Makes 1 cup

In a small saucepan, combine the sea salt, fish sauce, and sugar and heat over low heat until the sugar is dissolved, about 2 minutes. Transfer the mixture to a small mixing bowl to cool, then stir in the lime juice, garlic, and chiles.

½ teaspoon sea salt
¼ cup fish sauce (*namm pla*)
5 tablespoons sugar
½ cup fresh lime juice
2 cloves garlic, minced
8 fresh bird chiles or 6 serrano chiles, half seeded, half not, and minced

Primary Ingredients

Dressing Two is used with raw, boiled, grilled, or deep-fried seafood, including mussels, squid, octopus, and fish. Sometimes it is used with grilled chicken, eggplant, or mushrooms. *Laab,* the famous northeastern Thai salad made with raw or slightly cooked beef, or roasted chicken or duck, is served with this dressing. One odd recipe from southern Thailand uses a preserved meat similar to baloney, while the city folks in Bangkok use Spam!

Supporting Cast

Possibilities include crispy vegetables with sweet, peppery, and slightly sweet-tangy flavors, such as Napa cabbage, white cabbage, romaine lettuce, escarole, Chinese celery, sweet onion, green mango, plum, and star fruit. Grilled vegetables are balanced with grilled or other cooked seafood, chicken, or pork.

Aromas and Colors

Herbs with refreshing, clean, citrus, and/or musty aromas are used to contrast with the briny aromas of seafood and shellfish in the salad. These include lemongrass, kaffir lime leaves, ginger, *krachay* (lesser galangal; see page 132), mint, cilantro leaves, scallions, and fresh red chiles.

Yumm Goong Mung Gorn
GRILLED LOBSTER SALAD

1 cup white wine
½-inch piece ginger, thinly sliced
3 whole scallions
3 sprigs cilantro
1 teaspoon Thai white peppercorns
Salt
Olive oil
Two 1½-pound live lobsters
2 shallots, thinly sliced
2 stalks lemongrass, green parts and
    hard outer layers removed,
    minced
5 to 6 kaffir lime leaves, slivered, or
    zest of 1 lime, removed with a
    peeler in strips and julienned
6 to 7 fresh bird chiles or 4 to 5
    serrano chiles, minced (optional)
½ cup Dressing Two (page 245)
4 sprigs mint, leaves only, sliced
    into long thin strands, plus
    6 whole sprigs
6 to 7 tender young Napa cabbage
    leaves

During the long hot summer, Thais take their families to the seaside to escape the heat of the city. They camp on the beach or rent inexpensive bungalows along the beaches of Rayong and Hua Hin on the Gulf of Thailand, away from the prestigious hotels that cater to foreign tourists. Food stalls built from huge palm fronds line the seashore, with vendors selling raw mussels, oysters, and shellfish mixed with a very spicy and sour dressing as an appetizer. There are also grilled fish and tiger prawns in an intensely spicy *yumm*. Grilled lobster salad is the ultimate splurge for these vacationing Thai families.

Fill a large stockpot three-quarters full with water and bring it to a boil. Add the white wine, ginger, scallions, cilantro, and Thai white peppercorns and let it boil for 5 minutes. Add the lobsters, cover, and boil 10 minutes. The lobsters should look red and the head can be easily pulled from the socket. Remove the lobsters from the water and let sit until cool. Split the lobsters in half lengthwise, leaving the shells intact. Discard the intestines. Rinse and pat dry. Sprinkle the lobster halves with a pinch of salt and brush generously with olive oil.

To broil: Preheat the broiler for 10 minutes. Place the lobsters sliced side up on a metal sheet pan. Broil 7 to 10 minutes.

To grill using a charcoal grill: Wait for shooting flames to disappear, then place the lobsters cut side down on the grill and cook 5 to 7 minutes, or until brown.

To grill using a gas grill: Preheat the grill to 500°F for 10 minutes and cook the lobsters as for the charcoal grill. Remove and cool completely before extracting the meat from the shells. Slice into bite-sized pieces.

In a large mixing bowl, combine the lobster, shallots, lemongrass, and kaffir lime leaves. Toss gently.

In a small mixing bowl, combine the fresh chiles, if using, with the dressing and pour over the salad. Add the mint strands and mix well. Line a serving platter with the cabbage leaves and put the lobster on top. Garnish with the mint sprigs and serve.

Yumm Pla Too
GRILLED MACKEREL SALAD

Makes 6 servings

At fish markets in Thailand, *pla too,* mackerel, is sold steamed and packaged in small bamboo baskets. At home, it is fried in oil until crispy. Thais eat all parts of the fish, including the head, bones, and tail. It's been a long time since my first attempt to make this salad. As a foreign student living in Kentucky, I was so desperate for home cooking that I made the recipe with canned sardines. These days I am fortunate to have two friends, Flora Mace and Joey Kirkpatrick, whose passion, aside from making glass sculptures and fishing, is smoking their own salmon, which sometimes I use to make this salad. It is heavenly.

Prepare the grill or preheat the oven to 375°F. In a small mixing bowl, combine the garlic, 1½ teaspoons of the sea salt, and the olive oil. Rub the mixture over the fish. Wrap it in an aluminum foil pouch and grill over a medium-hot fire, or roast in the oven, until just cooked through, 15 to 20 minutes. Check for doneness by piercing the fish with a fork; it should flake easily. Cool, then slice the fish into bite-sized chunks.

In a small mixing bowl, toss the ginger with the remaining 1 tablespoon sea salt and let it sit for 5 to 7 minutes. Transfer to a strainer and pour several changes of cool water over it. Squeeze to extract the excess liquid and transfer the ginger to a large mixing bowl. Add the grilled fish, shallots, and pickled garlic and toss gently. Add the dressing and toss gently once more.

Line a serving platter with the cabbage leaves. Put the salad on top of the cabbage leaves and garnish with the coconut flakes, peanuts, chile slivers, and cilantro. Just before serving, pour the dressing over everything and toss gently.

2 cloves garlic, minced

1½ tablespoons sea salt

¼ cup olive oil

1 pound whole mackerel or tuna steaks

One 3-inch piece fresh young ginger, slivered, or a 1-inch piece regular ginger, peeled and slivered

4 shallots, thinly sliced

3 cloves pickled garlic, thinly sliced, or ¼ cup salt-packed capers, rinsed and drained

½ cup Dressing Two (page 245)

6 to 7 Napa cabbage leaves

2 tablespoons Roasted Fresh Grated Coconut Flakes (page 71)

3 tablespoons unsalted peanuts, dry-roasted (see page 13) and coarsely ground

6 to 7 fresh red bird chiles or 3 to 4 red serrano chiles, seeded and slivered

½ cup cilantro leaves

Yumm Dok Gurab

ROSE OR NASTURTIUM SALAD

Makes 6 servings

1 whole boneless, skinless chicken
    breast, cooked and shredded
    (1 cup)
¼ pound boneless pork, cooked
    and sliced into thin strips (1 cup)
½ pound medium shrimp, peeled,
    deveined, cooked, and halved
    lengthwise (1 cup)
½ cup Dressing Two (page 245)
5 tablespoons thick tamarind juice
    (see page 128)
1½ cups (unsprayed) rose or
    nasturtium petals (see headnote)
¼ cup Crispy Garlic (page 138)
¼ cup Crispy Shallots (page 138)
2 tablespoons unsalted peanuts,
    dry-roasted (see page 13) and
    coarsely ground
¼ cup cilantro leaves

Dok gurab mon is a heavily scented wild red rose. It is used to make perfume, scented candles, and potpourri, as well as for cooking. This particular salad was adapted by the Thais from a Persian recipe. Since it is difficult in America to find roses that have not been sprayed with chemicals, I have substituted nasturtium blossoms, which are readily available, sold as edible flowers. During the spring and summer, nasturtium blossoms blanket my front yard, and I pick them myself to make this gorgeous salad.

In a large mixing bowl, combine the chicken, pork, and shrimp. In a small mixing bowl, mix the dressing with the tamarind juice, and pour over the meat mixture. Toss gently.

Just before serving, add the rose or nasturtium petals and toss gently. Transfer to a serving platter and garnish with the crispy garlic, crispy shallots, peanuts, and cilantro. Toss once again, then serve.

Yumm Moo Yor

BALONEY SALAD

During the Vietnam War, Udorn Radchatani was a designated rest and recreation town for American soldiers. As a result, this little northeastern provincial town underwent culture shock, and it has never fully recovered. In the early 1980s, after the war, when the Americans had left, the town housed several refugee camps. While visiting the refugee site, I ate at a restaurant on the riverbank known for its local food. One of the dishes was *yumm moo yor,* a salad made with something that looked like baloney. I thought it was a joke, but it wasn't. The restaurant proprietor explained that local folks had learned to make this type of sausage from the Europeans several centuries ago. The locals insisted that this preserved meat wasn't an import resulting from the war, but was as Thai as they were. It may not have been baloney, but the American soldiers loved it because it reminded them of home.

I have many American friends whom I consider to be "closet baloney lovers." They are ashamed to confess their fondness for this lowly and underrated lunch meat. This salad is really wonderful when made with top-quality baloney. Searing it on a hot grill brings out a marvelous smoky flavor. For those who really have a thing against baloney, try this dish with grilled sausage.

In a large skillet or on a griddle, cook the baloney until browned on both sides. Cool and slice into bite-sized wedges.

In a large mixing bowl, combine the baloney, Chinese celery, onion, tomato, and pickled garlic and mix well. Pour the dressing over the salad and toss.

Line a serving platter with the lettuce and place the salad mixture on top of the lettuce. Arrange the cucumber slices around the salad and top it with the jalapeño.

Variation

Substitute 1 can Spam or 1 pound sausage, grilled, for the baloney.

½ pound sliced baloney

3 stalks Chinese celery, sliced into 1-inch pieces, or 1 rib regular celery, thinly sliced on the diagonal

½ cup thinly sliced sweet onion

1 tomato, sliced into bite-sized wedges

2 cloves pickled garlic, peeled, or 8 pickled pearl onions, thinly sliced

½ cup Dressing Two (page 245)

6 to 7 red-leaf lettuce leaves or butter lettuce leaves

1 cucumber, peeled, halved lengthwise, seeded, and thinly sliced on the diagonal

1 fresh red jalapeño chile, slivered

Laab Ped Yang
LAAB WITH ROAST DUCK

1 pound roast duck meat, with skin, finely chopped (1½ cups)

1 tablespoon minced *kra-chay* (lesser galangal; see page 132) or fresh ginger

Juice of 2 limes, or to taste

¼ cup Dressing Two (page 245)

1 tablespoon Roasted Rice Powder (page 49)

1 to 2 tablespoons Roasted Dried Chile Powder (page 91)

3 shallots, minced

2 scallions, minced

½ cup minced sawtooth herb (see page 133), arugula, or watercress

2 kaffir lime leaves, sliced into thin strands, or zest of 1 lime, removed with a peeler and julienned

¼ cup minced cilantro leaves

10 sprigs mint, leaves only, slightly torn

For the accompaniments

6 to 7 tender young Napa cabbage leaves

7 to 8 cherry tomatoes

6 yard-long beans or 12 French green beans, sliced into 3-inch lengths

6 to 7 arugula leaves

7 to 8 sprigs cilantro

There is a hole-in-the-wall restaurant in the central province of Pitch-sanulok owned by a woman from northeastern Thailand. She and her sister cook the food while their young niece takes the orders, serves the customers, washes the dishes, and collects the money. The place is total chaos. The customers, however, are tolerant and patient, knowing that when (and if) they do get the food they ordered, it will be wonderful. Everything is served on tiny tin plates, and it is so spicy you don't need more than a couple of the miniature plates of food. I usually eat the *laab* with roast duck that they serve with hot sticky rice. It is absolutely fabulous.

Even though you may prefer less-spicy *laab,* I suggest you make it as the Thais do, really strongly flavored. Eat small portions accompanied by fresh vegetables and sticky rice. This salad has to be intense, or it's not authentic. Serve it as a snack with cold beer or Thai whiskey on ice.

Most Asian supermarkets have a deli section that sells roast duck and roast pork. Save the bones to make a rich broth for noodle soup. If you can't find "ready-made" roast duck, make your own by roasting a 4½- to 5½-pound duck, rubbed all over with 2 tablespoons Big Four Paste (page 86). Place it in a preheated 450°F oven, lower the oven temperature to 375°F, and roast for 15 minutes per pound, or until the drumsticks can be moved easily. (The duck should be slightly under-cooked.) Cool completely before removing and shredding the meat.

In a large mixing bowl, combine the roast duck with the *kra-chay* and half the lime juice. Pour the dressing over it and mix well. Taste for sourness: It should be very sharp. Add some or all of the remaining lime juice if needed, and set aside for 10 minutes.

Just before serving, add the roasted rice powder and chile powder to the duck and mix gently. Add the shallots, scallions, sawtooth herb, and kaffir lime and toss gently but thoroughly. Add the cilantro and mint leaves and toss again. Taste for a balance of spicy-sour-salty, and adjust as necessary. Transfer to a serving platter and garnish with the accompaniments.

Variations

Substitute roast chicken or fish for the roast duck.

Classic *laab* uses finely chopped medium-rare grilled top sirloin, with minced galangal instead of *kra-chay*. Squeeze a generous amount of lime juice onto the meat after mixing it with the minced galangal, let it sit for 10 minutes, and then add the dressing. Proceed with the remaining instructions for *laab*.

Yumm Kanum Jean

NOODLE SALAD WITH LIMA BEANS, GREEN BEANS, AND PINEAPPLE

Makes 6 servings

2 tablespoons dried shrimp, softened in warm water and pureed (see page 192)

1 teaspoon fermented shrimp paste or 1 tablespoon red miso

1 tablespoon sugar

Juice of 1 lime

2 shallots, minced

6 to 7 fresh bird chiles or 3 to 4 serrano chiles, slightly pounded (optional)

½ cup Dressing Two (page 245)

1 bundle Japanese somen noodles (see page 278)

½ cucumber, peeled, halved lengthwise, seeded, and thinly sliced on the diagonal

1 cup baby lima beans, parboiled in salted water for 1 minute, rinsed with cool water, and drained

¼ cup blanched almonds, coarsely chopped

6 green beans, parboiled in salted water for 20 seconds, rinsed with cool water, and sliced into thin circles

½ cup fresh pineapple matchsticks

Kanum jean is a Mon-style vermicelli noodle (see page 274). This southern Thai salad combines the soft silken texture of the noodles with the crunchy, pasty seed called *sato*. Its shape and musty aroma remind me of lima beans, which is what I have substituted here. *Lok neing*, another seed grown in southern Thailand, is also traditionally used in this recipe. It tastes a bit like blanched almonds, so I use them as a substitute.

In a medium mixing bowl, blend the pureed dried shrimp and fermented shrimp paste into a paste. Add the sugar, lime juice, shallots, chiles, and dressing, mix well, and set aside.

In a 4-quart saucepan, bring 4 cups of water to a boil. Add the noodles, stirring to separate them. Lower the heat to medium-high, to prevent the water from boiling over, and cook the noodles for 2 to 3 minutes. Drain the noodles and rinse with several changes of cold water. Return the noodles to the saucepan and fill with cool water. Lift a fingerful of noodles from the water, twist and loop the strands around your finger, and squeeze gently to extract the water. Place the noodle nest on a serving platter and repeat the process with the rest of the noodles.

Scatter the cucumber, lima beans, almonds, green beans, and pineapple on top of the noodle nests. Just before serving, pour the dressing over the salad and mix well.

Dressing Three

SWEET, SOUR, SALTY, SPICY, ACIDIC, MUSTY

Makes 1 cup

In a small saucepan, combine the sea salt, fish sauce, palm sugar, granulated sugar, and vinegar and cook, stirring, over medium heat until the sugar dissolves. Cool completely, then add the lime juice, cilantro roots, chiles, and garlic. Mix well.

1 teaspoon sea salt

¼ cup fish sauce (*namm pla*)

3 tablespoons palm sugar or light brown sugar

¼ cup granulated sugar

2 tablespoons white vinegar or cider vinegar

½ cup fresh lime juice

1 tablespoon minced cilantro roots or stems

6 to 7 fresh bird chiles or 3 to 4 serrano chiles, minced

1 clove garlic, minced

Primary Ingredients

This is the most versatile dressing and is used with innumerable combinations. Often a salad made with this dressing begins with the dynamic duo—pork and shrimp. Chicken, hard-boiled eggs, and pork or beef liver are added for a truly sumptuous salad.

Secondary Ingredients

Parboiled vegetables with crunchy, tender, or slippery textures—spinach, bean sprouts, wood ear mushrooms, and green beans—are used. Slightly crispy and crunchy vegetables, such as bamboo shoots, arugula, lettuce, cucumber, and tomato, are matched with very crispy vegetables, such as Chinese celery and sweet onions. Slippery, soft bean thread noodles as well as baked and deep-fried tofu are sometimes added for an extravagant effect.

Aromas and Colors

Smoky, musty, and earthy aromatic ingredients top salad made with this dressing. They are Crispy Garlic (page 138), Crispy Shallots (page 138), dried chiles, dried shrimp, and pork skin, as well as roasted peanuts, watermelon seeds, and, of course, fresh red chile slivers.

Yumm Yai

BIG SALAD

Makes 6 to 8 servings

12 dried wood ear mushrooms
Sea salt
2 ounces cooked pork skin strands
1 teaspoon fresh lime juice
¼ pound lean boneless pork, cooked and slivered (1 cup)
¼ pound pork or beef liver, cooked or grilled and slivered (½ cup)
¼ pound medium shrimp, peeled, deveined, cooked, and slivered (1 cup)
1 skinless, boneless chicken breast, cooked and slivered (1 cup)
¼ pound cleaned squid, grilled and slivered (¼ cup)
¼ cup pork fat, slivered (optional)
¼ cup slivered cooked pork stomach (optional)
¼ cup slivered cooked pork heart (optional)
2 ounces baked tofu, slivered
¼ pound very firm tofu, sliced into thin strips
2 ounces bean threads (glass noodles), softened in hot water and sliced into bite-sized pieces
½ cucumber, peeled, halved lengthwise, seeded, and sliced paper-thin on the diagonal
2 ounces fresh bean sprouts, parboiled 10 seconds in salted water
2 Napa cabbage leaves, finely sliced
10 dried shrimp, softened in warm water and coarsely chopped (see page 192)

(continued)

This classic Thai salad reminds me of a 1960s version of America's chef's salad, loaded with so many kinds of meats and cheeses on a plate you could hardly mix in the dressing. *Yumm yai* is called "big salad" because it has twenty ingredients, not including garnishes. The contrasting textures and flavors will not only surprise, but even startle and confuse your palate! This is an authentic recipe, although you may adjust the ingredients to your preference (some people aren't wild about eating innards). Many deli sections in Asian supermarkets sell cooked pork stomach and heart. You can find cooked pork skin packaged in clear cellophane wrap in the refrigerated section of Asian supermarkets; they look like translucent noodles. Pork innards can also be purchased in Asian supermarkets. They must be massaged with sea salt, then boiled in water with several slices of fresh ginger. Baked tofu is available in most health food stores, as well as in Asian markets. It is also called savory baked tofu or baked bean curd. Unlike regular tofu, which is pure white, baked tofu has been seasoned with spices and soy sauce, giving it a light brown color. The water has also been extracted from the curd, making it firm and compact.

In a medium mixing bowl, soak the wood ear mushrooms in warm water until softened. Drain the mushrooms and remove and discard the hard stems. Massage the mushrooms with sea salt, let sit for 5 minutes, and rinse in several changes of cool water.

In a 4-quart saucepan, bring 3 cups water to a boil. Add the mushrooms and boil for 6 to 7 minutes, until tender. Drain, then rinse in several changes of cool water. Pat dry, slice into thin long slivers, and set aside.

Massage the pork skin with the lime juice and 1 teaspoon sea salt and let sit for 15 minutes. Rinse with cool water, pat dry, and set aside.

In a large mixing bowl, mix all the ingredients except the dressing, hard-boiled eggs, mint leaves, cilantro, and chile slivers. Transfer to a large serving platter. Just before serving, toss with the dressing and let the salad sit for 5 minutes to let the flavors marry. Garnish with the hard-boiled eggs, mint leaves, cilantro, and chile slivers.

Variation

For a smaller version, called *yumm noi*, or "little salad," reduce the number of ingredients to 6 items: the cooked pork and shrimp, hard-boiled eggs, cucumber, sweet onion, and chopped cilantro sprigs, tossed with ½ cup of the dressing.

1 head pickled garlic, cloves
   separated and peeled, or 4
   pickled onions, thinly sliced
1 cup Dressing Three (page 253)
2 hard-boiled eggs, shelled and
   quartered
15 fresh mint leaves, slightly torn
15 sprigs cilantro, coarsely chopped
2 fresh red jalapeño or serrano
   chiles, seeded and slivered

Yumm Kamoy
A THIEF'S SALAD

Makes 6 servings

½ pound boneless pork, cooked and sliced into long thin strips (2 cups)

½ pound medium shrimp, peeled, deveined, cooked, and sliced lengthwise in half (1 cup)

1 boneless, skinless chicken breast, cooked and shredded (1 cup)

2 hard-boiled eggs, shelled and quartered

1 cucumber, peeled, halved lengthwise, seeded, and thinly sliced on the diagonal

1 whole scallion, sliced into 1-inch pieces

7 to 8 tender young romaine lettuce leaves, torn into bite-sized pieces

½ cup thinly sliced sweet onion

2 to 3 sprigs cilantro, torn into small sprigs

1 cup Dressing Three (page 253)

10 fresh mint leaves, slightly torn

1 to 2 fresh red bird or serrano chiles, seeded and slivered

Growing up in Bangkok, I never heard of a thief stealing food. That was a problem more prevalent in the countryside. The name of the salad is a metaphor for whatever a thief could steal to make a meal. City thieves, however, stole jewels and money. I do remember one incident. When everyone was asleep, we were awakened by someone yelling *"kamoy"* (thief), followed by the sound of running footsteps scurrying on a wooden floor. Soon an Indian night watchman pounded at the neighbors' door, trying to get them to open it, hoping to catch the thief. The thief was never caught. In fact, no one ever believed that there was actually a thief. The rumor was that it was our neighbor's husband, a heavy gambler, who tried to unfasten her gold necklace while she was asleep.

In a large mixing bowl, combine all the ingredients except the dressing, mint leaves, and chiles. Add the dressing and toss gently. Transfer to a serving platter, and garnish with the mint leaves and chile slivers.

Variation

Yumm yurn, the Vietnamese version of this salad, omits the lettuce and instead includes: 1 cup thinly sliced Napa cabbage, ⅓ cup thinly sliced fresh water chestnuts or jícama, and 1 tablespoon toasted watermelon seeds or almond slivers.

Yumm Nuoen Jo-Cho

JO-CHO BEARD SALAD WITH
BEAN THREADS AND SHRIMP

Makes 6 servings

Jo-Cho is a name for the elderly Chinese who in the past grew long beards. The description reminds me of an old Chinese scholar who lived in a lane near my childhood home. I thought he was a ghost, dressed as he was in traditional Chinese costume with a long white beard and braided hair meticulously combed. My mother said he had a gift from the spirits and could tell fortunes. Before I left for America, she secretly asked him to read fortunes for my brother, sister, and me. Years later, when I married, she sent my fortune to me. Upon reading it, I found accurate details of my life.

In a medium mixing bowl, soak the bean threads in cool water for 15 minutes, or until pliable. Drain.

Fill a 4-quart saucepan three-quarters full with water and bring it to a boil. Add the softened bean threads and cook for 1 to 2 minutes. Drain and rinse the bean threads with several changes of cold water. Gently squeeze the water from the bean threads. Slice the bean threads into 3-inch lengths. Transfer to a large mixing bowl.

Just before serving, add the remaining ingredients except for the dressing, cilantro, chiles, and crispy shrimp to the bean threads. Add the dressing and toss gently until coated. Transfer the salad to a serving platter and garnish with the cilantro leaves, chiles, and dried shrimp, if using.

Variation

Instead of the shrimp, add 2 tablespoons dry-roasted (see page 13) and ground unsalted peanuts and 1 teaspoon minced lemongrass.

¼ pound bean threads (also known as glass noodles; see page 168)

6 to 7 young romaine lettuce leaves, torn into bite-size pieces

1 tomato, sliced into bite-sized wedges

3 ribs Chinese celery, sliced into 1-inch lengths, or 1 rib celery, thinly sliced

½ medium sweet onion, thinly sliced

½ pound medium shrimp, peeled, deveined, cooked, and halved lengthwise (1 cup)

¼ pound boneless pork, cooked and slivered (1 cup)

1 head pickled garlic, cloves separated and peeled, or 3 pickled onions, thinly sliced

¾ cup Dressing Three (page 253)

15 sprigs fresh cilantro, coarsely chopped

3 to 4 fresh bird chiles or 2 to 3 serrano chiles, seeded and slivered

1 tablespoon dried shrimp, deep-fried until crisp (see page 305; optional)

Yumm Gai Yang

GRILLED CHICKEN SALAD

Makes 6 servings

2 Anaheim chiles

3 boneless, skinless chicken breasts, grilled and shredded into bite-sized pieces

¾ cup Dressing Three (page 253)

3 shallots, thinly sliced

½ green mango, peeled and grated, or ½ green Granny Smith apple, unpeeled, thinly sliced and soaked in fresh lemon juice and water

3 kaffir lime leaves or zest of 1 lime, removed with a peeler in strips and julienned

⅓ cup unsalted peanuts, dry-roasted (see page 13) and coarsely ground

15 fresh mint leaves, slightly torn

When I was contemplating opening my restaurant, Saffron, I spent a lot of time consulting with my friend George, who had several restaurants in San Diego, named after his wife, Piret. He tried to talk me out of going into the restaurant business. When he finally realized that I was determined, he helped me through every step. Since the restaurant I planned to open would primarily sell Thai grilled chicken, George advised me to find as many ways as possible to use leftover chicken. At Saffron, we have since created and sold more than a dozen kinds of grilled chicken salads. This is one of them, and quite coincidentally, inspired by a northeastern Thai recipe using leftover grilled chicken.

Grill the chiles over a hot grill flame, electric burner, or gas flame until the skin is completely charred. Put them in a plastic bag, seal tightly, and set aside to cool. Rub the chiles against the sides of the bag until the burnt skins drop off. Remove the chiles; rinse to remove any remaining skin and the seeds. Pat dry with paper towels, slice into bite-sized pieces, and set aside.

In a large mixing bowl, mix the grilled chicken with half of the dressing and set aside for 5 to 7 minutes. Add the rest of the ingredients except the peanuts and mint leaves, then toss lightly with the remaining dressing. Mix in the peanuts and transfer to a serving platter. Garnish with the mint leaves and serve.

Yumm Nuer
BEEF SALAD

This is one of the most popular salads served in Thai restaurants in America. Ironically, it's not very highly regarded in Thailand. Many Thai people abstain from eating it because of the tough quality of most beef, as well as the fact that cows are considered sacred. Old Thai recipe books suggest several ways to tenderize the meat. The traditional recipe is quite similar to making *laab* (page 250), for which raw meat is used to make the salad and served with vegetables as accompaniments. This recipe is a newer version with the vegetables mixed in. It is quite delicious and easy to make.

In a large Ziploc bag, combine the meat with pineapple juice, seal, and refrigerate for at least 1 hour and no longer than 3 hours.

Preheat a gas or charcoal grill on high heat. Remove the meat from the pineapple juice and spray it generously with vegetable oil spray. Cook over the hot grill fire for 2 minutes. Spray the meat again with vegetable oil, flip it over and baste with the pineapple juice. Cook for another 2 to 3 minutes, flipping occasionally, until the meat is medium-rare. Remove from the grill to a platter and set aside until lukewarm.

Slice the meat across the grain into thin bite-sized pieces and transfer to a large mixing bowl. Add the juice of 1 lime, toss gently, and taste for a sour taste before adding more lime juice if necessary; the taste should be very sharp. Let sit for 10 minutes.

Just before serving, add the lemongrass and kaffir lime strands to the meat and mix well. Add the rice powder and chile powder; mix again. Pour the dressing over the meat and toss lightly, then add the onion, cucumber, and lettuce. Toss the mixture gently, add the cherry tomatoes, toss gently again, and transfer to a serving platter. Garnish with the mint leaves and cilantro.

Cook's Notes

If the tri-tip is thicker than 1 inch, slice it across in half. The cooked meat should be lukewarm when mixed with lime juice.

If you cook the meat ahead, wrap it in aluminum foil and reheat it in a 150°F oven for 20 minutes before the final preparation.

---

1 pound beef tri-tip (see Cook's Notes) or flank steak

6 ounces frozen pineapple juice concentrate

Vegetable oil spray

Juice of 1 to 2 limes

2 stalks lemongrass, green parts and tough outer layers removed, minced

3 kaffir lime leaves or zest of 2 limes, removed with a peeler in strips and julienned

1 tablespoon Roasted Rice Powder (page 49)

1 tablespoon Roasted Dried Chile Powder (page 91)

1 cup Dressing Three (page 253), made without the vinegar

1 medium sweet onion, thinly sliced

1 cucumber, peeled, halved lengthwise, seeded, and thinly sliced on the diagonal

8 young romaine or iceberg lettuce leaves, torn into bite-sized pieces

1 cup cherry tomatoes, sliced in half

10 mint sprigs, leaves only, slightly torn

15 sprigs cilantro, coarsely chopped

Dressing Four

SWEET, SALTY, SOUR, SPICY, MUSTY, CHAR-BURNT, CREAMY

Makes 1 cup

½ teaspoon sea salt

¼ cup fish sauce (*namm pla*)

3 tablespoons palm sugar or light brown sugar

3 tablespoons granulated sugar

1 to 2 tablespoons Roasted Chiles in Oil (page 94)

3 tablespoons fresh lime juice or very tart orange juice

¼ cup thick tamarind juice (see page 128)

¼ cup Fresh Unsweetened Coconut Cream (page 69)

In a small saucepan, combine the sea salt, fish sauce, palm sugar, and granulated sugar and heat over medium heat until the sugar is dissolved. Transfer the mixture to a mixing bowl to cool completely, then stir in the remaining ingredients. Refrigerate in a jar with a tight lid until ready to use.

Primary Ingredients

Dressing Four is best with crispy vegetables that have earthy and musty tastes, such as mushrooms, fennel, and jícama. Another good group includes delicate ingredients, such as banana blossoms, young pea shoots, and zucchini blossoms. Raw tart fruit, such as green mango, star fruit, green apple, grapes, and pineapple, are a third group of ingredients.

Secondary Ingredients

Soft, chewy meat, such as grilled chicken, squid, and pork, are among the ingredients that complement the star ingredients, used alone or in various combinations.

Aromas and Colors

Smoky, earthy, aromatic ingredients are used to top these salads. They include Crispy Garlic (page 138), Crispy Shallots (page 138), and Roasted Fresh Grated Coconut Flakes (page 71). Mint, basil, and cilantro leaves, which add a refreshing, clean taste, are combined with red and yellow chile slivers as garnish.

Yumm Nuer Kap Nor Mai
BEEF WITH BAMBOO SHOOTS SALAD

Makes 6 servings

After the Vietnam War, thousands of Southeast Asian refugees emigrated to America. Many settled in San Diego, California, and moved into houses that had once been used as military housing. These bungalows have big front and back yards, which, with the new residents, quickly blossomed into family vegetable and herb gardens. King, the Laotian cook at my restaurant, and her family live in one of these houses, where they grow edible plants and trees, including bamboo. In the springtime, King cuts off the tender bamboo shoots and brings them to me as a gift. The fresh shoots remind me of home, and I make this salad with them. If the fresh shoots are not available, canned are fine.

In a 4-quart saucepan, heat the coconut cream and milk over medium-high heat for 2 minutes, until boiling. Stir in the beef slices, lower the heat to medium, and cook until all the liquid has evaporated, about 30 minutes. Transfer the meat to a large mixing bowl to cool.

If using fresh bamboo shoots, fill a 2-quart saucepan with water and bring to a boil. Add 1 teaspoon sea salt and the bamboo shoots and boil for 2 to 3 minutes; drain. Rinse the bamboo shoots several times in cool water, drain again, pat dry with paper towels, and transfer to a bowl. If using canned bamboo shoots, drain, place the shoots in a strainer, sprinkle with a few pinches of sea salt, and massage lightly. Let sit for 5 minutes, then rinse with cool water and pat dry. Set aside.

Just before serving, add the lemongrass to the beef and toss slightly. Add the dressing and mix well, then add the bamboo shoots and mix again. Transfer the salad to a serving platter. Garnish with the kaffir lime leaf strands and serve.

2 cups Fresh Unsweetened Coconut Cream and Milk (combined to the consistency of whole milk; page 69)

½ pound flank steak, thinly sliced across the grain into 2-inch strips

Sea salt

One 8-ounce canned sliced bamboo shoots or 1 cup sliced fresh bamboo shoots (see page 20)

1 stalk lemongrass, green parts and outer hard layers removed, minced

¾ cup Dressing Four (page 260)

5 kaffir lime leaves or zest of 1 lime, removed with a peeler in strips and julienned

Yumm Plameug Soud
FRESH SQUID SALAD

Makes 6 servings

1 teaspoon sea salt

1 pound squid, cleaned and
    tentacles removed (see page 17)

4 Napa cabbage leaves, thinly sliced

1/2 cucumber, peeled, halved
    lengthwise, seeded, and thinly
    sliced on the diagonal

3 to 4 ribs Chinese celery, sliced into
    1-inch lengths, or 1 rib regular
    celery, thinly sliced

3 to 4 tender romaine lettuce leaves
    or iceberg lettuce leaves, torn
    into bite-sized pieces

1/2 medium sweet onion, thinly
    sliced

1/2 cup green or red seedless grapes,
    halved

1/4 pineapple, peeled, eyes and core
    removed (see page 28), and finely
    chopped (1/2 cup)

2 whole scallions, finely chopped

1/4 cup sesame seeds, dry-roasted
    (see page 13)

6 to 7 fresh red bird chiles or
    3 to 4 serrano chiles, seeded and
    slivered

1/2 cup Dressing Four (page 260)

Near my childhood home on Siphraya Road in Bangkok, there's a Buddhist temple named Wat Keo Faa, which means "Heavenly Glass Jewel Temple." When wealthy people died, they were taken there for cremation, preceded by several days of lying in state. The family of the deceased would provide entertainment on the temple grounds, including traveling theater troupes and silent movies to entertain the deceased and invited guests. Neighbors were also welcome. Food vendors set up stalls selling snacks, desserts, and drinks during showtime. It was at just such a funeral on the temple grounds that my brother, sister, and I watched our first Charlie Chaplin movie, sitting on the grass and eating grilled squid on sticks, among other delectable snacks.

In a 6-quart saucepan, bring 4 cups water to a boil. Add 1/2 teaspoon of the sea salt and the squid, including the tentacles. When the water comes to a boil and the squid turns white, about 2 minutes, drain the squid and rinse several times with cool water. Drain again, squeeze out the excess water, and pat dry with paper towels. Cut the pouches of squid crosswise into bite-sized pieces; leave the tentacles whole, or slice lengthwise in half. Place in a large mixing bowl.

In a strainer in the sink, massage the Napa cabbage with the remaining 1/2 teaspoon salt and let sit for 10 minutes.

Rinse the cabbage in several changes of cold water, squeeze dry, and spread it on a serving platter. Scatter the remaining vegetables and the fruits on top of the cabbage, top with the squid, and garnish with the scallions, sesame seeds, and chiles. Just before serving, add the dressing and toss lightly.

Variation

Substitute escarole for the lettuce, apple slices for the grapes, and cashews for the sesame seeds.

Yumm Hua Plee

BANANA BLOSSOMS WITH CHICKEN SALAD

Makes 6 servings

In Lampoon, a city in northern Thailand where my sister Marian once lived, banana trees grow wild along the roadside. They were considered worthless by the villagers because they were so abundant. Anyone could pick the ripened bananas or cut the leaves for making pouches or wrapping food. I would wait anxiously for the fruits to ripen and when they did, I ate my fill like a happy monkey. Whenever I spotted the burgundy-colored blossoms hanging forlornly on the trees, I asked my sister's gardener to chop off several with a machete for the cook to make *yumm hua plee*.

Squeeze the excess water from the banana blossoms and transfer to a medium mixing bowl. Mix with the coconut cream and let sit for 10 minutes. Transfer to a serving platter.

In another medium mixing bowl, combine the chicken with the dressing. Place on top of the banana blossoms. Garnish with the coconut flakes, peanuts, crispy shallots, and crispy garlic. Toss just before serving.

2 heads banana blossoms (see page 23), finely sliced and soaked in lemon- or lime-infused water, or 1 large head Belgian endive, finely sliced (2 cups)

3 tablespoons fresh Unsweetened Coconut Cream (page 69)

3 boneless, skinless chicken breasts, cooked and shredded (2½ to 3 cups)

½ cup Dressing Four (page 260)

2 tablespoons Roasted Fresh Grated Coconut Flakes (page 71)

2 tablespoons unsalted peanuts, dry-roasted (see page 13) and coarsely ground

3 tablespoons Crispy Shallots (page 138)

2 tablespoons Crispy Garlic (page 138)

Yumm Tua Plu
WING BEAN SALAD

Makes 6 servings

2 tablespoons unsalted peanuts, dry-roasted (see page 13) and ground

¾ cup Dressing Four (page 260)

¼ cup Fresh Unsweetened Coconut Cream (page 69)

1 pound wing beans or asparagus, trimmed, parboiled in salted water until bright green, rinsed with cool water, and thinly sliced (3 cups)

½ pound medium shrimp, shelled, deveined, cooked, and sliced lengthwise in half

¼ pound boneless pork, cooked and sliced into long thin pieces

2 tablespoons Roasted Fresh Grated Coconut Flakes (page 71)

12 dried shrimp, softened and pureed (see page 192)

6 to 7 fresh bird chiles or 3 to 4 serrano chiles, minced

For several years, I returned to Thailand during the months of December and January. This is the cool season, when the weather is most pleasant, and it is also the season for *tua plu,* wing beans. It seemed that every restaurant in the whole country had *yumm tua plu* on its menu. One of the best I found was at Hong Teow Restaurant, near the Rai-Kram Hotel in Chiang Mai in northern Thailand. The cook used the very young and tender wing beans, which she parboiled so that they retained their emerald green color. She garnished the salad with tiny dried shrimp, which were crispy and crunchy.

In a small mixing bowl, combine the ground peanuts with the dressing; mix well and set aside. In a small saucepan, bring the coconut cream to a boil over medium-high heat. Set aside to cool.

In a large mixing bowl, combine the wing beans, shrimp, and pork and toss lightly. Add the dressing mixture and mix well. Transfer to a serving platter. Spoon the coconut cream over the salad and garnish with the roasted coconut flakes, dried shrimp puree, and minced chiles. Toss once more before serving.

Yumm Phra Ram Dern Dong
BEEF AND SWAMP SPINACH SALAD

Makes 6 servings

Phra Ram is the God-Hero in the Thai version of a Hindu epic, *The Ramayana*. This dish is named for an episode where Phra Ram spends years in the forest searching for his wife, See Da, who was abducted by the Monkey King, Todsagun. Unlike other Thai salads, this is served hot. It is best to have all the ingredients prepared and lined up in order for last-minute stir-fry and assembly.

Heat a 12-inch skillet over high heat for 1 to 2 minutes, or until when you put your hand 3 to 4 inches above the skillet, you can feel the heat. Add 3 tablespoons of the oil and heat for 1 minute. Add the garlic and cook, stirring, until just browned, about 20 seconds. Add the beef and cook, stirring, until the beef is well-done, about 2 minutes. If the beef sticks to the skillet, add a tablespoon of water to the pan. Transfer to a serving platter.

Add the remaining 2 tablespoons oil to the skillet and return it to high heat. Add the spinach and cook, tossing and stirring, until wilted, 1 to 2 minutes. Transfer the spinach to the platter, next to the beef.

In a small mixing bowl, combine the dressing with the ground peanuts. Pour the dressing over the beef and spinach, garnish with the cilantro and roasted peppercorn powder, and toss well before serving.

5 tablespoons vegetable oil
3 to 4 cloves garlic, lightly crushed
1 pound boneless top sirloin, thinly sliced across the grain
4 cups swamp spinach leaves or a bunch of spinach with stems and leaves, rinsed and thoroughly dried
3/4 cup Dressing Four (page 260)
3 tablespoons unsalted peanuts, dry-roasted (see page 13) and ground
15 sprigs cilantro, minced
1 teaspoon roasted Thai white peppercorn powder (see page 85)

Dressing Five

SWEET, SALTY, SOUR, SPICY, MUSTY, CHAR-BURNT, CREAMY, BRINY

Makes 1½ cups

2 tablespoons fish sauce (*namm pla*)
3 tablespoons palm sugar or light brown sugar
1 cup Fresh Unsweetened Coconut Cream (page 69)
2 tablespoons Roasted Chiles in Oil (page 94)
2 ounces dried smoked tuna or salmon, minced (¼ cup; see Cook's Notes on page 47)
6 tablespoons thick tamarind juice (see page 128)

In a small saucepan, combine the fish sauce and palm sugar and heat over medium heat until the sugar is dissolved, about 1 minute. Remove the pan from the heat and stir in the coconut cream. Add the roasted chiles in oil, smoked fish, and tamarind juice. Store in a glass jar with a tight-fitting lid in the refrigerator for 1 to 2 days.

Primary Ingredients

Dressing Five is used with citrus fruits such as pomelo or orange. Among the other favorites are mixed fruits, including ripe sweet papaya, pineapple, pears, peaches, and apricots.

Secondary Ingredients

Grilled chicken and fish, as well as shellfish, or both, play nicely against the sweet-soft fruits. Crispy and crunchy vegetables, such as Chinese celery and lettuce, add contrast.

Aromas and Colors

Salads made with this dressing are topped with Crispy Garlic (page 138), Crispy Shallots (page 138), Crispy Dried Chiles (page 90), Roasted Fresh Grated Coconut Flakes (page 71), dry-roasted (see page 13) ground peanuts, and fresh red chile slivers. Fresh mint, cilantro leaves, and kaffir lime strands are also added.

Yumm Goong Sawan
HEAVENLY SHRIMP SALAD

Makes 6 servings

I discovered this recipe in an old Thai cookbook and tested it at a catering party. The guests went wild. Several asked me to put it on my restaurant menu. Now, when papaya is ripe and sugary sweet, this heavenly salad is one of the restaurant's most popular summer dishes. Instead of shrimp, I use grilled chicken.

Spread the papaya cubes out on a serving platter. In a large mixing bowl, combine the shrimp, kaffir lime leaf strands, and lemongrass. Toss lightly and put the mixture on top of the papaya cubes. Pour the dressing over the shrimp and papaya, garnish with the cilantro, mint, and peanuts, and toss gently just before serving.

Variations

Instead of papaya, substitute fresh peaches, pears, mangoes, or nectarines.

Instead of shrimp, substitute grilled chicken, turkey, imitation or real crabmeat, or lobster.

3 cups cubed (1-inch cubes) ripe papaya

1½ pounds medium shrimp, peeled, deveined, and cooked

7 kaffir lime leaves or zest of 1 orange, removed with a peeler in strips and julienned

1 stalk lemongrass, green parts and tough outer layers removed, minced

¾ cup Dressing Five (page 266)

15 sprigs cilantro, leaves only, minced

15 sprigs mint, leaves only, sliced into thin strands

2 tablespoons unsalted peanuts, dry-roasted (see page 13) and coarsely ground

Yumm Som Ohh

POMELO AND SHRIMP SALAD

Makes 6 servings

1 pomelo or 1 grapefruit plus
   2 tangelos
1½ pounds medium shrimp,
   peeled, deveined, cooked, and
   halved lengthwise
¾ cup Dressing Five (page 266)
¼ cup Roasted Fresh Grated
   Coconut Flakes (page 71)
2 tablespoons Crispy Shallots
   (page 138)
2 tablespoons unsalted peanuts,
   dry-roasted (see page 13) and
   coarsely chopped
6 to 7 fresh bird chiles or
   3 to 4 serrano chiles, slivered
5 kaffir lime leaves or zest of
   1 orange, removed with a peeler
   in strips and julienned

From the beginning of November through February, markets all over Thailand sell ripened pomelos, a citrus fruit resembling an oversized grapefruit. They are displayed by the hundreds in stacks only a juggler or acrobat could have designed. Pomelo is my father's favorite fruit. He would always buy at least a half dozen of these golden balls and line them up neatly on the floor along the wall inside our house. In the morning, my father would pick up a pomelo, balance it in his hand, and sniff the top of the fruit where the stem had been. Once he'd determined the fruit was ripened to his satisfaction, he gave it to our servant. She immediately skillfully peeled and sectioned the fruit and lined up the perfect wedges on a plate for my father, who ate them with great relish.

Traditionally, Thai cooks shredded the pomelo into individual crystalline-pink strands and bejeweled them with plump pink shrimp. Besides tasting exquisite, this salad is a beautiful piece of art.

To prepare the pomelo, begin by slicing about ½ inch off the top of the fruit, where the stem was removed. Score the rind into quarters. Starting from the top, peel away the thick rind until you reach the membrane. Separate the fruit in half and then again into quarters. Tear the fruit into sections. Slice across the very top of each section and peel the fruit off the membrane. Separate the section into individual strands. The juice sacs of the pulp are firm and can be separated without bruising them. Spread them on a serving platter.

Or, for grapefruit and tangelos, peel the fruit and separate into sections. Slice across the very top of each section and carefully peel the fruit off the membrane. Break the sections into bite-size chunks and spread them on a serving platter.

In a medium mixing bowl, combine the shrimp with half of the dressing. Put the mixture on top of the fruit. Garnish with the coconut flakes, crispy shallots, peanuts, chile slivers, and kaffir lime strands. Just before serving, pour the rest of the dressing over the salad and toss gently.

Cook's Note

Select a pomelo that feels heavy for its size. Press a fingernail into the stem end and smell: It should be fragrant.

Variations

Substitute other shellfish, such as cooked mussels or crabmeat, for the shrimp. Squid or shredded grilled chicken is also delicious.

Yumm Pla Yang
GRILLED FISH SALAD

Makes 6 servings

½ pound salmon fillet, grilled and flaked

1 stalk lemongrass, green parts and hard outer layers removed, minced

One ½-inch piece fresh ginger, peeled and sliced into thin strands

3 shallots, thinly sliced

¾ cup Dressing Five (page 266)

12 arugula leaves or 24 watercress leaves

½ green mango, peeled and grated, or 1 tart Granny Smith apple, unpeeled, thinly sliced, soaked in fresh lemon juice and water, and patted dry

10 fresh water chestnuts, peeled and sliced into matchsticks, or ½ cup jícama matchsticks

5 kaffir lime leaves, sliced into thin strands, or 3 kumquats, thinly sliced and seeded

3 to 4 fresh bird chiles or 2 to 3 serrano chiles, slivered

The original recipe uses fish coated with a light batter and deep-fried until *grob,* or crispy. Thai love deep-fried food, the greasier, the better. Another variation is to grill small whole fish until crispy. Over the past several years, fresh Atlantic salmon has been introduced into Thailand and has quickly become a favorite fish in Bangkok. In this variation, I have made the dish lighter and less greasy by grilling the fish fillet.

In a medium mixing bowl, combine the grilled fish, lemongrass, ginger, and shallots, stir in the dressing, and toss gently.

Line a serving platter with the arugula leaves and scatter the mango and water chestnuts over them. Spread the grilled fish mixture over the top, garnish with the kaffir lime strands and chile slivers, and serve.

Cook's Note

For fun, try making paper-thin cutouts from slices of water chestnuts or jícama, using miniature cookie or canapé cutters.

Yumm Pun Rah Mai

FRUIT SALAD

Unlike Western-style fruit salads, which favor sweet and well-ripened fruits, this salad pairs slightly tart fruits with crispy and crunchy ones. Other contrasting ingredients include bean threads, several kinds of cooked meat, and a garnish of several spoonfuls of thick coconut cream.

In a medium mixing bowl, soak the bean threads in cool water for 15 minutes, or until pliable. Drain.

Fill a 4-quart saucepan three-quarters full with water and bring it to a boil. Add the softened bean threads and cook for 1 to 2 minutes. Drain and rinse the bean threads with several changes of cold water. Gently squeeze the water from the bean threads. Slice the bean threads into 3-inch lengths. Transfer to a large mixing bowl.

In a small saucepan, bring the coconut cream to a slow boil over medium heat and cook for 2 minutes. Transfer to a small bowl to cool.

In a large mixing bowl, combine the bean threads, pork, shrimp, lemongrass, cilantro, scallion, and Chinese celery. Transfer to a serving platter.

In another mixing bowl, combine the fruits. Put the fruits on top of the meat and vegetable mixture. Pour the dressing over everything, and drizzle with the coconut cream. Just before serving, toss gently.

2 ounces bean threads (also known as glass noodles; see page 304)

¼ cup Fresh Unsweetened Coconut Cream (page 69)

½ pound boneless pork, cooked and sliced into long thin pieces (1 cup)

¼ pound medium shrimp, peeled, deveined, cooked, and halved lengthwise

1 stalk lemongrass, green parts and hard outer layers removed, minced

7 sprigs cilantro, leaves only, coarsely chopped

1 whole scallion, finely chopped

4 ribs Chinese celery or 1 rib regular celery, finely chopped

¼ pound fresh pineapple, peeled, cored, eyes removed (see page 28), and slivered (½ cup)

¼ pound seedless green or red grapes, halved (½ cup)

A few sections of pomelo, julienned into fine strands, or 1 navel orange, peeled and sectioned (½ cup)

1 peach, peeled and sliced into bite-sized wedges (½ cup)

½ star fruit, thinly sliced, or 1 pear, cored and thinly sliced (½ cup)

1 cup Dressing Five (page 266)

Noodles

A THAI BLESSING

Poetic songs resonate through stately abode

A husband's ode for wife's gastronomic feast

Singing lines faceted with praises

Sweet melody chimes with rhythms

None surpass wife's legendary fame

Written by Chao Phraya (Lord) Phasagonvong for his wife, Than Phu Ying (Her Ladyship) Prann, between 1868 and 1900

I was nine years old when my mother's close friend, who happened to be our neighbor, became my younger sister's godmother. She was a widow living in a large teak house with her three daughters. At the time, she was financially secure as a sales representative for an American company. Shortly after this new arrangement between our families, my sister's godmother began to experience one unfortunate incident after another. After a string of bad luck, she decided to alter her fate and sought protection against evil spirits. She consulted the head abbot from our neighboring Buddhist temple, who made astrological calculations for an auspicious date to perform a protective ceremony. Precisely at nine o'clock in the morning, ten monks from the temple and the head abbot were picked up in a rented Mercedes and brought to the godmother's house.

A week before the ceremony date, the godmother's tranquil household had taken on the atmosphere of a war zone. The cook watched helplessly as the godmother's female relatives—grandmothers, aunts, and their servants—invaded her domain armed with their pots and pans, mortars and pestles, even their knives. Sounds of pestles hitting against the stone mortars drowned out the cook's favorite soap operas, which she regularly listened to on the transistor radio. The aromas of garlic, chiles, and ginger, mingled with the scent of jasmine blossoms and musty pandanus leaves, saturated the air. It is hard to imagine the frenzy and chaos that existed up until the morning when the monks stepped out of the Mercedes to find the house and kitchen orderly, spotless, and serene.

The monks were escorted past rows of kneeling friends and family members into a starkly empty living room, from which all furniture had magically disappeared, replaced by an elaborate altar with a golden Buddha that sparkled radiantly next to eleven yellow cushions placed neatly against the wall. The monks marched in single file toward the cushions and sat down. Everyone else gathered in front of them and sat on the polished wood floor. The godmother's elderly brother lit the candles on the altar, and the monks began to chant loudly in a monotonous, strange, mysterious language I did not understand. After a short while, the chanting stopped and the head abbot, who sat closest to the altar, got up to pick up a ball of white twine from the tray in front of the Buddha statue. He wrapped the twine several times around the statue before unrolling it as he walked toward the seated monks and stringing the thin white twine across their folded hands. Then he put the remaining ball of twine neatly on a tray near the last monk before returning to his cushion to pick up the twine in front of him. Once again,

they began to chant. I squirmed on the sticky floor, watching the grown-ups doze in the dark, stuffy room. Only the godmother was attentive and alert, with her hands folded in prayer.

Finally, the chanting stopped as abruptly as it had begun, jolting the sleepers from their naps. All the monks got up and walked outside, except for the head abbot, who took the ball of twine and tossed it through one of the windows to the waiting monks. He then joined them and began to wrap the entire house and fence with the twine. By and by, they returned to the living room with the remaining twine, which the head abbot placed on the tray in front of the altar. He then picked up a silver bowl filled with scented water and walked outside to where the godmother and her guests had gathered at the front entrance to the house. He began to anoint the crowd with the water, beginning with the godmother, for whom he uttered a blessing. Immediately she was transformed from a brooding, anxious woman to a jovial and peaceful woman. With her wish granted, she once again felt safe and confident. As she escorted the monks back to their cushions, the women relatives rushed to the kitchen. It was precisely eleven o'clock and time to serve the monks lunch.

The women emerged from the kitchen with twelve heavy silver trays, holding identical plates and bowls brimming with food. They crawled and scooted carefully along the floor, watching their heads, so as not to be higher than the seated monks. They pushed the trays in front of them, trying not to spill the food. An individual tray was presented to each monk, and the twelfth tray was placed in front of the Buddha statue on the altar. Once again, the monks chanted. The marvelous aromas made my stomach growl loudly. I checked out the trays and observed a plate brimming with *kanum jean*— bundles of long thin white rice noodles resembling the blessed twine now wrapped around the outside of the godmother's house. Shiny black crispy-fried chiles, wedges of young tender banana blossoms, green tamarind shoots, and the golden yolks of salted duck eggs garnished the pristine white strands. A bowl of glistening *namm prikk*—chile curry sauce—was nestled next to them. After a short prayer, the monks started eating lunch while chatting happily with the godmother. She beamed with pride when they complimented her on the delicious food. They consumed several helpings while we sat and watched.

When the monks finally finished, every plate was empty except for the twelfth tray, which remained untouched. Then the guests began to feast. The godmother took another tray of food to the spirit house, a miniature wooden house on top of a tall cement pillar beside her house. The front patio of the spirit house, which served as an offering platform, was adorned with fresh flower leis and a porcelain incense holder. The godmother sat the silver tray on the offering platform, lighting candles and incense as she softly offered a prayer. Inside the house were tiny porcelain men and women dolls representing the good spirits, seated in a circle as if they were conversing. They were the permanent residents invited to live in the spirit house to look after the godmother and her family. Later, after the guests left, the godmother and her three daughters contentedly ate the cold, stale noodles from the offering trays. They weren't concerned with the taste. To them, it was a sacred meal, blessed by the head abbot and symbolically shared by the Buddha statue and good spirits who lived in the spirit house.

Like my sister's godmother, Thai families traditionally serve *kanum jean*, or cool rice vermicelli, for special occasions and as ceremonial offerings to the Buddhist monks. The white strands of noodles symbolize sacredness, purity, and protection against evil spirits. The noodles are served cool or at room temperature, with a sauce and a selection of accompaniments. The bland yet slightly fermented taste of the noodles, combined with their delicate, slippery, smooth texture, makes them a perfect medium for absorbing the savory sauces. The word *Jean,* in Thai, commonly means China. Among most Thai people, *kanum jean* is thought to have originated in China.

Yet a second popular theory among Thai food historians is that *kanum jean* did not come from China but, rather, originated in India and was brought to Thailand by Brahmin Indians, who practiced a Hindu ritual of using the sacred white cotton thread to bless the soul. Still others believe *kanum jean* is neither Chinese nor Indian but originated with the Mon, the indigenous people of Southeast Asia. Proponents of this theory explain that *kanum* is a Mon word meaning "cooked and ready to be served." The Mon-Khmer, a subculture of the Mon, use the word *kanum* to describe a snack, a dessert, or a specially prepared dish for special occasions. *Jean,* on the other hand, is a Mon-Burmese word meaning "long strands." The pronunciation of the word *jean* is similar to the word the Thais and Burmese use for "Chinese," thus the confusion. The historians further emphasize the Mon ritual of serving *kanum jean* as an offering to spirits or during special celebrations. In addition, the traditional Mon method of making *kanum jean* is similar to the way the ancient Thais made it and very different from the way the Chinese made their noodles. This traditional way is both difficult and laborious.

During one of my annual visits to Thailand,

I made it my mission to find someone who still made *kanum jean*. Although there are stalls in markets all over the country that sell the dish freshly made, most market vendors buy the noodles ready-made from a factory. When I questioned them, everyone concurred that the process of making them is too time-consuming. Many had no idea how they are made. My search led me to befriend an elderly woman from Pitsanulok in Central Thailand who had owned a *kanum jean* and curry stand for decades. She and her husband made their own *kanum jean* every day. According to her, in the past, families only made *kanum jean* for special occasions, and the project would involve everyone in the household and their neighbors. As she described the method, I understood why it took so long and so many people to make.

First, both long-grain rice and glutinous rice grains are soaked overnight until softened. Then, the rice grains are kneaded and pounded in a large stone mortar big enough to hold a small child. A long wooden pestle that requires two people to lift it is used to pound the rice grains into a smooth glutinous rice paste, which is then mixed with water and left to ferment for two to three days. After being soaked in several changes of water, the dough is kneaded again, making it even more glutinous, and then put inside a strainer bag.

The bag is like a pastry bag, fashioned from a wide round piece of thin cotton cloth sewn around a brass disk resembling a strainer with pinholes. The cloth is gathered tightly around the dough and squeezed, forcing long thin strands of the mixture through the holes. The strands of dough are dropped into a pot of boiling water and instantly become cooked noodles. The noodles are removed with a bamboo strainer to a pot of cold water, then shaped by hand into tiny bundles, one fingerful at a time. Gently squeezed together to extract the water, the bundles of noodles are then twisted into figure-eight shapes. Some Thais believe that the process of making the noodles symbolizes the flow of merit from those making the noodles to those who have died. There is a superstitious belief that noodles shaped into smooth long strands bring good fortune to the noodle makers, while those with lumps or breaks foretell a troubling future. My elderly friend from Pitsanulok has never once made a bad batch of *kanum jean*.

Just when I was ready to accept the loss of this ancient tradition, I found noodle makers where I live in San Diego. April is when Buddhist Thais, Laotians, and Cambodians celebrate the New Year. In San Diego's Buddhist community, plates of *kanum jean* are offered to Buddha in temples all over the city. One day, while chatting with several elderly women, I learned that immigrant families have a New Year's tradition of making *kanum jean*. They shorten the work by using long-grain glutinous rice flour and a fermented paste mixed with water, which is then fermented. Each day, for a week, the water is drained from the wet dough and fresh water is added. Once the dough has fermented, the water is squeezed out and the dough is mixed with cornstarch. It's then kneaded and pressed through a brass strainer into a pot of boiling water. It is ironic that my nostalgic search for this ancient tradition ended in my own American town.

Today *kanum jean* is so popular in Thailand that it often replaces rice, and it is commonly served with *keang pet,* curry. Each region has its own *kanum jean* sauce recipe, but there are three nationally recognized favorites. *Sow namm* is a delicate dish with fresh pineapple slivers, salty dried shrimp, and a rich coconut cream sauce seasoned with galangal. *Namm ya* is a boldly flavored dish with a pungent creamy sauce seasoned with dried chiles, lemongrass, pureed dried fish, and coconut cream. *Namm prikk* is a full-flavored and rich sauce made with ground roasted mung beans, roasted chiles, pureed grilled fish, palm sugar, and thick coconut cream. A whole kaffir lime with its sour, acidic, and bitter taste is added to temper the sauce. These and other *kanum jean* dishes are often served as *aharn jarn deuw*, "one-dish meals," but they are also always included in elaborate menus for special occasions. The preparation of these dishes is part of the art and ceremonial ritual of Thai life.

For today's modern Thai families, a plate of *kanum jean* with sauce and a couple of accompaniments will suffice. If you wish to duplicate the authentic version of these recipes, do as Thais do—invite friends and family to participate in the cooking and preparation. Otherwise, reduce the number of accompaniments. One or two selections with *kanum jean* and sauce will still give you a magical Thai meal.

Kanum Jean with Somen Noodles

Makes 6 servings

3 bundles (9 ounces) somen noodles
Mint sprigs, for garnish
3 to 4 fresh red bird chiles or
   2 to 3 serrano chiles, for garnish

During my early years in America, I was unable to satisfy my craving for Thai rice noodles until I discovered somen, the Japanese dried wheat noodle, which has a similar taste and texture. Today, as a result of the migration of Southeast Asians to the United States, dried *kanum jean*, labeled rice vermicelli, is sold in most markets. It tastes even closer to the real thing than the somen noodles I have been using for years.

There are two kinds of dried somen noodles sold in supermarkets and Asian markets. One is white, made with wheat, and the other gray, made with buckwheat flour. For *kanum jean* noodles, use the white variety; the buckwheat noodles have a coarser texture. I prefer the Tomoshiraga brand, which comes in 16-ounce packages, each containing five individually wrapped bundles. One bundle weighs about 3 ounces and makes 2 to 3 servings of *kanum jean*. Uncooked somen noodles keep well for months in the freezer. They are delicious in noodle soups or salads.

In a 6-quart saucepan, bring 5 cups water to a boil. Drop the noodles into the boiling water and stir to separate the strands. When the water returns to a boil, add 1 to 2 tablespoons cold water to cool it slightly and prevent it from boiling over. Let the noodles boil vigorously for about 2 minutes, then drain and rinse with several changes of cold water. Fill the saucepan with cold water and return the noodles to the saucepan.

With your middle or index finger, scoop up a 1-inch bundle of noodles. Squeeze out the excess water with the other hand, or twist the noodles into a figure-eight bundle, or a circular nest, and place on a large serving platter. Repeat with the rest of the noodles. Decorate the platter with fresh mint leaves and red chiles. Cover with plastic wrap and set aside until ready to serve, or refrigerate. Bring to room temperature before serving.

Kanum Jean with Rice Vermicelli

Makes 6 servings

The noodle section in Asian supermarkets reminds me of the breakfast cereal section in American supermarkets, full of overwhelming and confusing choices. Asian noodle manufacturers seem to name almost every kind of noodle "vermicelli," without any sense or logic. Luckily, the rice vermicelli used for *kanum jean* noodles is called "Instant Rice Vermicelli." It's easy to recognize because the strands are not clumped together in one large mass like other noodles, but are packaged with the individual strands loosely separated, easy to slide back and forth in the cellophane package. The dull, translucent noodles are cut into 7- to 8-inch lengths. Wider ones are like fettuccine, and thinner noodles are the size of angel hair pasta—buy the wider ones. The best brand is manufactured by Caravelle. The package label is in four languages—English, Chinese, Lao, and Vietnamese—with the weight listed as 10.58 ounces.

Cook instant rice vermicelli the same way as somen noodles (see page 278), but for 5 minutes longer.

Kanum Jean Sow Namm
COOL NOODLES BATHED IN LIQUID

Makes 6 servings

For the sauce
(makes about 2½ cups)

2 cups Fresh Unsweetened Coconut
Cream (page 69)

½ cup dried shrimp, softened in
warm water and pureed (see
page 192)

3 bundles (9 ounces) somen noodles
or rice vermicelli, boiled and
shaped into nests as described on
page 278

For the garnishes and
accompaniments

3 cloves garlic, thinly sliced

1 small pineapple, peeled, eyes
removed (see page 28), and
slivered

7 fresh red bird chiles or 4 serrano
chiles, seeded and slivered
(or more or less, depending on
individual preference)

6 tablespoons sugar (optional)

6 tablespoons fish sauce (*namm pla*)

¼ cup fresh mint leaves, torn

The name *sow namm* describes cool noodle strands bathed in a thin delicate sauce. It is a simple, exquisite dish served during the hot season in Thailand, when the temperature on most days reaches over 100°F. The sweet juicy pineapple used in the dish renders a sharp contrast to the slightly fishy and salty minced dried shrimp. A rich creamy coconut sauce is ladled over the noodles. Crushed mint leaves are served as a garnish. To me, a bite of *kanum jean sow namm* is like a cooling balm.

In a 4-quart saucepan, bring the coconut cream to a boil over medium heat. Add the dried shrimp and cook, stirring, until the sauce thickens, about 2 minutes. Transfer to a serving bowl to cool. Cover and set aside.

Place the nests of noodles on a platter, with bowls of the garlic, pineapple, chiles, sugar, fish sauce, and mint leaves around them. Have each guest place 2 to 3 noodle nests on his or her plate and top with 3 to 4 garlic slices, 1 to 2 tablespoons pineapple slivers, several chile slivers, 1 tablespoon sugar, 1 tablespoon fish sauce, and a few mint leaves, then ladle several spoonfuls of the coconut sauce over the noodles, tossing the noodles to separate the strands so they absorb the sauce.

Cook's Note

The noodles, sauce, garnishes, and accompaniments can be prepared several hours ahead and stored separately in the refrigerator. An hour before serving, bring everything to room temperature, then arrange on the serving platter and in bowls.

Kanum Jean Goong Nang
COOL NOODLES WITH BABY SHRIMP

This dish makes a wonderful hors d'oeuvre. You can prepare the *kanum jean* noodle bundles, pineapple, and sauce several hours ahead. Before serving, warm the sauce.

In a 2-quart saucepan, bring the coconut cream to a boil over medium heat. Stir in the Big Four Paste and shrimp and cook until the shrimp turn slightly pink, 1 to 2 minutes. Add the sugar, fish sauce, and coconut milk, mix well, and cook for another 2 minutes. Transfer to a serving bowl to cool. Cover and set aside.

Cook the somen noodles according to the instructions on page 278, but shape the cooked noodles into small nests, about the size of silver dollars. Place a nest inside each leaf of Belgian endive and garnish with the pineapple slivers, red chile slivers, mint leaves, and lime wedges. Arrange them on a platter and serve the sauce on the side, either warm or at room temperature. Have each guest spoon some sauce over the noodles and loosen the noodle strands gently so they absorb the sauce.

For the sauce

⅓ cup Fresh Unsweetened Coconut Cream (page 69)

2 tablespoons Big Four Paste (page 86)

¼ pound medium shrimp, peeled, deveined, and coarsely chopped

1 tablespoon sugar

2 tablespoons fish sauce (*namm pla*)

1½ cups Fresh Unsweetened Coconut Milk (page 69)

1 bundle (3 ounces) somen noodles

2 heads Belgian endive, leaves separated

½ small pineapple, peeled, eyes removed (see page 28), and slivered

6 to 7 red bird chiles or 4 to 5 serrano chiles, seeded and slivered

10 to 12 sprigs mint, leaves only

1 lime, sliced into thin wedges

Kanum Jean Namm Ya

COOL NOODLES WITH HERBAL SAUCE

For the chile paste
(makes ¾ cup)

1 teaspoon sea salt

12 cloves garlic, minced

1 dried New Mexico (or California) chile, softened in warm water and seeded

10 dried de árbol or Japonés chiles, softened in warm water and seeded

4 fresh red bird chiles or 2 serrano chiles, minced

7 cilantro stems and roots, minced

2 stalks lemongrass, green parts and hard outer layers removed, minced

One ½-inch chunk galangal or ¾-inch chunk fresh ginger, peeled and minced

Minced zest of ½ lime

10 roots kra-chay (lesser galangal; see page 132), minced, or ½-inch chunk fresh ginger, peeled and minced

2 shallots, minced

1 teaspoon fermented shrimp paste or 1 tablespoon red miso

(continued)

Namm ya is a sauce so perfumed and seasoned with dried herbs and spices it resembles a curative tonic. The seasonings play against the strong briny aroma of the sauce's thickening ingredients—pureed dried fish and *pla-rah*, or fermented fish, for which I substitute salted anchovies. The mixture is sweetened with rich coconut cream. Accompaniments include parboiled bean sprouts, bitter greens, and pickled vegetables.

Using a mortar and pestle, pound the sea salt, minced garlic, and softened dried chiles together into a paste. One at a time, add the fresh chiles, cilantro, lemongrass, galangal, lime zest, *kra-chay*, shallots, and fermented shrimp paste in sequence, adding each new ingredient only after the previous one is pureed and incorporated into the paste. Set aside.

In a 4-quart saucepan, bring the water to a boil. Add the kaffir lime leaves, anchovies, catfish, shallots, garlic, and lemongrass and boil over medium-high heat for 15 minutes, or until the catfish is cooked through and beginning to fall apart. Turn off the heat and transfer the catfish to a platter to cool.

Strain the liquid into another saucepan, reserving the shallots, garlic cloves, and anchovies and discarding the rest. Bring the liquid to a boil over medium heat and cook for 5 minutes, or until it is reduced to 1 cup. Remove from the heat and set aside.

Fit a food processor with the steel blade and puree the shredded catfish with the reserved shallots, garlic, and anchovies for 20 seconds. Transfer to a bowl and set aside.

In a 4-quart saucepan, bring the fresh coconut milk to a boil over high heat and cook for 2 minutes, or until the cream separates and rises to the top. Reduce the heat to medium-high and skim off the cream into a 12-inch skillet. Reduce the heat under the coconut milk and leave at a simmer.

Add the fresh coconut cream to the skillet with the skimmed coconut cream, then add the chile paste and blend well. Heat the mixture over medium-high heat for 1 to 2 minutes, or until it begins to thicken, stirring occasionally to prevent sticking. When the oil begins to separate from the mixture and takes on the color of the chile paste, about 6 minutes, transfer the mixture to the saucepan with the simmering coconut milk. Stir well, add the catfish puree and the reduced liquid and increase the heat to medium. Cook, stirring, for 10 minutes, or until the sauce thickens. Transfer to a serving bowl.

Arrange the nests of noodles on a platter and garnish with the accompaniments. Put the bowl of the sauce nearby. Have each guest put 2 or 3 noodle nests on his or her plate, garnish them with the accompaniments, and ladle the sauce over the noodles, loosening the noodle strands so they absorb the sauce.

Cook's Notes

The chile paste can be made ahead and stored in the refrigerator for at least a month. The sauce keeps overnight in the refrigerator. Reheat before serving. If it has thickened, add 3 to 4 tablespoons of water, 1 tablespoon at a time, until its consistency resembles that of pancake batter.

For the sauce (makes 6 cups)

2 cups water

6 to 7 kaffir lime leaves, torn, or zest of 1 lime, removed with a peeler in strips and julienned

6 salt-packed anchovies, rinsed and dried

1 pound catfish fillets

3 shallots, peeled

6 cloves garlic, peeled

1 stalk lemongrass, green parts and hard outer layers removed, sliced into 2-inch lengths

4 cups Fresh Unsweetened Coconut Milk (page 69)

1 cup thick Fresh Unsweetened Coconut Cream (page 69)

3 bundles (9 ounces) somen noodles or rice vermicelli, boiled and shaped into nests as described on page 278

For the accompaniments

¼ pound fresh bean sprouts (1 cup), parboiled for 30 seconds and rinsed with cool water

10 arugula leaves

1 head radicchio, thinly sliced

½ cup pickled mustard greens (see page 142), rinsed, dried, and finely julienned, or 1 large kosher pickle, thinly sliced

2 hard-boiled eggs, peeled and quartered

3 fresh red bird chiles or 2 serrano chiles, thinly sliced

6 to 7 sprigs Thai basil or mint

Kanum Jean Namm Prikk
COOL NOODLES WITH CHILE SAUCE

For the chile paste
(makes ½ cup)

2 tablespoons red lentils
2 cups vegetable oil
¼ pound smoked tuna or halibut
12 dry-roasted chiles (see page 13)
3 tablespoons Crispy Shallots
  (page 138)
2 tablespoons Crispy Garlic
  (page 138)
One ¼-inch chunk galangal or
  ½-inch chunk fresh ginger,
  peeled and minced

For the sauce
(makes 5 cups)

¼ cup plus 3 tablespoons palm
  sugar or light brown sugar
3 tablespoons fish sauce (*namm pla*)
4 cups Fresh Unsweetened Coconut
  Milk (page 69)
1 cup Fresh Unsweetened Coconut
  Cream (page 69)
3 firm kiwi, peeled and slivered
1 kaffir lime or 1 regular lime,
  seeded and juiced, so you just
  have the rind left
¾ cup thick tamarind juice (see
  page 128)

(*continued*)

Namm prikk is a brilliant red chile sauce. In this dish, the chiles' heat is tempered with palm sugar and coconut cream. The secret ingredient is the rind of fresh kaffir lime, which adds a musty, citrus aroma and bitter, fruity flavors to the sauce. The accompaniments to "dress up" the dish are carefully selected and numerous.

Experienced Thai cooks love to display their artistry. Because of its complexity, the preparation of this dish should be broken down into several stages. I make the chile paste ahead and store it in the refrigerator, where it will keep for several weeks. The sauce can be made a day ahead, stored in the refrigerator, and reheated. If it thickens, add 3 to 4 tablespoons water to thin it. Selecting the accompaniments is fun. They, too, can be prepared ahead. For a sumptuous meal, I include at least ten accompaniments. This makes a striking variety of contrasting flavors and textures. For a simpler version, select two to three items from the list, such as stir-fried broccoli rabe or spinach with crispy fried dried chiles. One thing is for sure, you will have a feast worthy of your efforts.

For the chile paste, in a small mixing bowl, soak the lentils in 2 cups warm water for 30 minutes, or until softened. Drain and pat dry.

Line a platter with paper towels. In a 10-inch skillet, heat the oil for 2 minutes, or until it is hot, then add the lentils. Deep-fry for 10 to 12 seconds, or until they are crispy and golden. With a wire strainer, transfer to the lined platter to cool. Transfer the oil to a metal bowl and reserve it.

Fit a food processor with the steel blade. Process the crispy fried lentils for 30 seconds, or until the consistency resembles coarse cornmeal. Add the smoked fish and puree. With the motor running, add the chiles, shallots, garlic, and galangal through the feed tube and puree. Transfer the mixture to a mixing bowl and set aside.

For the sauce, in a small saucepan, heat the palm sugar and fish sauce over medium-high heat for 1 to 2 minutes, or until the sugar is dissolved. Remove from the heat and set aside.

In a 4-quart saucepan, heat the coconut milk over medium-high heat for 2 minutes, or until it boils and the cream rises to the surface. Lower the heat and skim the cream into a 12-inch skillet. Reduce the heat to low and leave the coconut milk at a simmer.

Add the fresh coconut cream and the chile paste to the skimmed coconut cream in the skillet and mix well. Cook over medium-high heat, stirring frequently to prevent sticking, until the mixture thickens and the oil rises to the surface, taking on the color of the paste, about 4 minutes. Transfer the chile paste mixture to the simmering coconut milk, mix well, and bring to a boil. Add the palm sugar mixture, kiwi slivers, and whole kaffir lime rind, reduce the heat to medium-low, and let the sauce simmer until thickened, 10 to 15 minutes. Add the tamarind juice and simmer for another 5 minutes. Taste for an even balance of salty, peppery, sweet, and fruity flavors. Remove the saucepan from the heat and cover. When ready to serve, remove the lime shell, if desired, and transfer to a serving bowl.

In a 12-inch skillet, heat 2 tablespoons of the reserved lentil-frying oil for 2 minutes, or until it begins to smoke. Add the broccoli rabe and cook, stirring, until the color brightens, 1 to 2 minutes. Transfer to a plate and set aside. In the same skillet, cook the spinach, stirring, until wilted, 1 to 2 minutes; set aside.

In a medium mixing bowl, combine the flour, baking powder, sea salt, white pepper, and water. Mix lightly until the batter is the consistency of thick cake batter; do not overmix. In a 12-inch skillet or wok, heat the remaining reserved lentil-frying oil over high heat to 350°F. Gently coat the zucchini blossoms one by one in the batter, slide into the hot oil, and deep-fry for 2 to 3 minutes, or until they are golden. With a strainer, transfer to a plate lined with paper towels.

To serve, arrange the cooked noodle nests on a large platter. Arrange a bowl of the sauce and individual bowls and plates of the garnishes and accompaniments: the zucchini blossoms, crispy garlic, roasted dried chiles, cilantro, arugula, papaya, banana blossom, broccoli rabe, and spinach. Have each guest put 3 or 4 noodle nests on a plate, garnish with broccoli rabe and the other garnishes, drizzle several spoonfuls of sauce over the noodles, and top with crispy garlic, then loosen and separate the noodle strands so they absorb the sauce.

For the garnishes and accompaniments

6 stalks broccoli rabe (rapini), parboiled for 1 minute in salted water and rinsed in cool water

1 bunch fresh spinach, rinsed and dried

1 cup unbleached all-purpose flour

1/2 teaspoon baking powder

1/2 teaspoon sea salt

1/4 teaspoon freshly ground Thai white peppercorns

1/3 cups water

7 to 10 zucchini blossoms, left whole, or 1 zucchini, thinly sliced lengthwise

2 tablespoons Crispy Garlic (page 138)

7 to 8 dry-roasted chiles (see page 13)

7 to 8 sprigs cilantro

12 arugula leaves

1 small papaya, peeled, seeded, and cut into long thin slices

1 banana blossom (see page 23) or 1 head Belgian endive, slivered

3 bundles (9 ounces) somen noodles or rice vermicelli, boiled and shaped into nests as described on page 278

Kanum Jean Namm Prikk Sodd

COOL NOODLES WITH FRESH CHILE SAUCE

**For the chile sauce
(makes 1 cup)**

1 teaspoon fermented shrimp paste
or 1 tablespoon red miso

3 dried corn husks, softened in
warm water and dried

6 tablespoons sugar

6 tablespoons fish sauce (*namm pla*)

7 cloves garlic, minced

10 to 12 (or more) fresh bird chiles,
6 to 7 minced, 4 to 5 left whole,
lightly pounded; or 6 to 7
(or more) serrano chiles,
3 to 4 minced, 3 to 4 left whole,
lightly pounded

½ cup fresh lime juice

2 tablespoons pureed dried shrimp
(see page 140; optional)

**For the shrimp and
coconut cream sauce
(makes 2 cups)**

2 cups Fresh Unsweetened Coconut
Cream (page 69)

½ pound small shrimp, peeled and
deveined

1 teaspoon sea salt

(continued)

Kanum jean namm prikk sodd is actually a dish with two sauces: a fresh chile sauce and a sauce made of fish patties and coconut cream. It is an ancient recipe with the same concept as *Kanum Jean Namm Prikk* (page 284), but lighter and easier to make. I substitute baby shrimp for the fish patties in the original recipe. The chile sauce can be made a day ahead without the optional pureed dried shrimp and refrigerated; just before serving, add the pureed dried shrimp to the sauce.

Heat the oven to 400°F. To prepare the chile sauce, wrap the fermented shrimp paste in the softened corn husks and roast for 20 to 25 minutes. Set aside to cool.

In a small saucepan, combine the sugar and fish sauce; cook over medium heat until the sugar is dissolved. Set aside to cool.

Using a mortar and pestle, pound the garlic and minced chiles into a paste. Blend in the roasted shrimp paste. Add the remaining whole chiles and pound lightly. Stir in the fish sauce mixture. Add the lime juice and taste for an even balance of peppery, salty, sweet, and sour. Set aside. Just before serving, mix in the dried shrimp, if using, and transfer to a serving bowl.

For the shrimp and coconut cream sauce, in a 4-quart saucepan bring the coconut cream to a boil over medium heat and boil for 2 minutes. Add the shrimp and sea salt and stir and cook for 1 minute, or until the shrimp turn pink and the liquid comes back to a boil. Transfer to a serving bowl, cover, and set aside to cool.

For the garnishes and accompaniments, combine the pork strips and Big Four Paste in a bowl; let sit for at least 20 minutes.

In a 12-inch skillet, heat 3 tablespoons of the vegetable oil over high heat until very hot, 1 to 2 minutes. Add the pork to the hot oil and stir-fry until the pork strips are cooked through, about 2 minutes. Add the sugar and fish sauce, stirring to coat the pork strips, and cook, stirring and tossing, until the liquid evaporates, 3 to 4 minutes. Transfer the pork to a mixing bowl to cool, then toss with the crispy shallots and set aside.

Add 1 tablespoon of the oil to the same skillet and cook the parboiled spinach, stirring, for 1 minute. Transfer to a platter and set aside. Add the remaining 1 tablespoon oil to the skillet and cook the parboiled green beans, stirring, for 1 minute. Transfer to the serving platter and set aside.

Light a grill fire or preheat the broiler. Spray the tuna steak with vegetable oil spray and grill it or broil for 4 minutes. Flip over and cook for another 4 to 5 minutes, or until completely cooked. Transfer to a platter to cool, then shred into bite-sized pieces and set aside.

To serve, put the nests of noodles in a large platter along with individual bowls or plates of all the accompaniments. Set the chile sauce and shrimp and coconut cream sauce near the platter. Have each guest put 3 or 4 nests of noodles on his or her plate and top with pork and grilled tuna, spinach, green beans, and bean sprouts, then ladle 2 to 3 tablespoons of each sauce on top, garnish with chopped arugula and dried shrimp, if using, and loosen and separate the noodle strands so they absorb the sauces.

For the garnishes and accompaniments

1 pound boneless pork loin, sliced into thin strips about 1 by 2 inches

2 tablespoons Big Four Paste (page 86)

5 tablespoons vegetable oil

¼ cup sugar

¼ cup fish sauce (*namm pla*)

2 tablespoons Crispy Shallots (page 138)

½ pound spinach with stems and leaves, parboiled in salted water for 1 minute, or just until the color brightens, rinsed in cool water, and squeezed dry

¼ pound green beans, parboiled in salted water for 1 minute, or just until the color brightens, rinsed in cool water, dried, and thinly sliced on the diagonal

½ pound tuna steak

Vegetable oil spray

¼ pound fresh bean sprouts (1 cup)

20 arugula leaves or watercress sprigs, coarsely chopped

½ cup pureed dried shrimp (see page 140; optional)

3 bundles (9 ounces) somen noodles or rice vermicelli, boiled and shaped into nests as directed on page 278

Kanum Jean Namm Ya Paa

COOL NOODLES WITH JUNGLE-STYLE SAUCE

Makes 6 servings

For the sauce
(makes 3 cups)

3 shallots, unpeeled

6 large cloves garlic, unpeeled

2 teaspoons vegetable oil

1 pound fresh center-cut halibut or
    red snapper fillet, cut into several
    large chunks

1 tablespoon sea salt

5 whole salt-packed anchovies,
    rinsed and dried

4 cups water

20 dried de árbol or Japonés chiles

2 stalks lemongrass, green parts and
    outer hard layers removed,
    minced

One ¼-inch chunk galangal or
    ½-inch chunk fresh ginger,
    peeled and slivered

5 kaffir lime leaves, torn, or zest of
    1 lime, removed with a peeler in
    thin strips and julienned

3 bundles (9 ounces) somen noodles
    or rice vermicelli, boiled and
    shaped into nests as directed on
    page 278

(continued)

This recipe is from the province of Nakorn Radchasema in northeastern Thailand. It's an area where poor country folks struggle to make ends meet, especially during the drought that the hot, dry season brings. They rely on two common staples, dried fish and *pla-rah,* or fermented fish, as seasonings and as a main source of nourishment. In this recipe, I substitute anchovies for fermented fish. I've also opted to use a food processor in lieu of the traditional technique of pounding the cooked ingredients by hand, which is more laborious.

Preheat the oven to 400°F. For the sauce, slice off the tops of the shallots and garlic and place them on two separate pieces of aluminum foil. Drizzle each with a teaspoon of the oil. Seal the packets and roast for 25 minutes, or until softened. Remove from the foil to cool, then squeeze to extract the soft garlic and shallots from the cloves and set aside.

In a colander in the sink, rub the fish with the sea salt. Let sit for 15 minutes, then rinse several times in cool water, pat dry, and set aside.

In a 4-quart saucepan, combine the anchovies and water, bring to a boil, and boil for 3 minutes. Reduce the heat to medium, add the dried chiles, lemongrass, galangal, and kaffir lime leaves, and boil for 15 minutes. Add the fish and cook for another 10 minutes. Remove from the heat and transfer the fish to a platter. When cool enough to handle, shred the fish by hand or flake it with a fork.

Pass the broth through a strainer into a saucepan and set aside. Fit a food processor with the steel blade and puree the chiles, lemongrass, galangal, and kaffir lime leaves with the shredded fish and roasted shallots and garlic. Add the mixture to the saucepan with the broth. Cook, stirring, over medium-low heat until the sauce thickens and is reduced to about 3 cups, about 30 minutes. Taste for an even balance of peppery and salty. Transfer to a serving bowl.

To serve, arrange the nests of noodles on a serving platter and garnish with the chopped scallions. Place the whole scallions, green beans, cucumber, hard-boiled eggs, chile slivers, cilantro sprigs, and beef jerky, if using, on the side. Serve with the sauce. Have each guest put 3 or 4 noodle bundles on his or her plate, top with green beans, cucumber slices, hard-boiled egg, and chile slivers, and ladle several tablespoons of the sauce over the noodles, separating and loosening the noodle strands so they absorb the sauce. The noodles should be eaten with cilantro sprigs, scallions, and beef jerky.

For the garnishes and accompaniments

5 to 6 whole scallions, 3 minced, 3 trimmed and left whole

20 to 24 tender green beans, parboiled in salted water for 1 minute, or just until the color brightens, and rinsed in cool water

1 cucumber, peeled, halved lengthwise, seeded, and thinly sliced on the diagonal

2 hard-boiled eggs, peeled and quartered

5 to 6 fresh bird chiles or 3 to 4 serrano chiles, seeded and slivered

7 to 8 sprigs cilantro

Beef jerky (page 208; optional)

Kanum Jean Namm Yeow

COOL NOODLES WITH SHAN-STYLE SAUCE

Makes 6 servings

For the beef broth
(makes 3 cups)

> 3 pounds beef bones
> 4 cups bottled or filtered water
> One 1-inch chunk fresh ginger,
>   unpeeled
> 1 scallion, sliced into 2-inch lengths
> 1 teaspoon sea salt
> 2 pieces star anise

For the chile paste
(makes ½ cup)

> 1 teaspoon fermented shrimp paste
>   or 1 tablespoon red miso
> 2 to 3 dried corn husks, softened in
>   warm water and patted dry
> 1 teaspoon sea salt
> 5 cloves garlic, minced
> 12 to 15 dried de árbol or Japonés
>   chiles (or less, for a milder paste)
>   softened in warm water, seeded,
>   dried, and minced
> One ½-inch chunk galangal or
>   1½-inch chunk fresh ginger,
>   peeled and minced
> 1 stalk lemongrass, green parts and
>   hard outer layers removed,
>   minced
> 2 to 3 sprigs cilantro with stems and
>   roots, minced
> One 1-inch chunk fresh turmeric,
>   minced, or 1 teaspoon turmeric
>   powder
> 3 shallots, minced

(continued)

The northern Thai version of *kanum jean* is called *kanum senn.* The recipe is believed to have come from the Shan, or Yeow people, a group of early settlers in northern Thailand and Burma. Today they are the major producers of opium, living in the hills in an area of Burma, Thailand, and Laos known as the Golden Triangle.

Kanum senn namm yeow is eaten for breakfast. Noodle stands selling *kanum senn* are set up in the morning markets, with bamboo tables on short stubby legs surrounded by short-legged stools that serve as a dining area for shoppers. Customers squat on the stools, gulping down the hot steaming meat broth and fishing out slippery strands of noodles with their chopsticks. They doctor their noodles, between slurps, with salt, soy sauce, fresh lime, and red chile powder.

Today, however, most noodle stalls have replaced *kanum senn* with rice noodles known as *senn chan.* They are the same rice noodles used for *padd Thai.* Instead of a broth, they are served with a sauce thickened with ground beef and pork and seasoned with fermented shrimp paste and cherry tomatoes. I have tried both kinds of noodles, and am partial to the traditional *kanum jean.*

Kanum jean namm yeow is served in single servings with the condiments in separate bowls. These include sea salt, soy sauce, fresh lime wedges, and red chile powder.

For the broth, in a 6-quart saucepan, cover the beef bones with tap water and bring to a vigorous boil over high heat. Drain the beef bones in a strainer and rinse several times with cool water. Rinse out the saucepan and return the bones to the pan. Add the bottled water and bring to a boil over high heat. Skim the film from the surface of the broth. Add the ginger, scallion, sea salt, and star anise, lower the heat to medium-low, cover the pan, and let the broth simmer for 1 hour.

Strain the broth into another saucepan, or a storage container. You should have about 3 cups. If not using immediately, cool completely before refrigerating.

Preheat the oven to 375°F. For the chile paste, wrap the fermented shrimp paste in the softened corn husks and roast for 25 minutes. Cool completely.

Using a mortar and pestle, pound the sea salt and garlic to a paste. One at a time, add the chiles, galangal, lemongrass, cilantro, turmeric, shallots, and roasted fermented shrimp paste, adding each new ingredient only after the previous one is pureed and incorporated into the paste. Pound and mix well, then transfer to a bowl. Cover and set aside, or refrigerate until ready to use.

In a 12-inch skillet, heat the oil over high heat for 1 to 2 minutes, or until very hot. Add the chile paste and cook, stirring, for 1 minute, or until fragrant. Add the ground pork and ground beef and stir and toss to coat with the chile paste. Cook, stirring, until the meat is cooked through and browned, 2 to 3 minutes. Add the spareribs and continue to stir and toss until the spareribs turn slightly brown, about 2 minutes. Add the bean sauce, then the reserved beef broth, and bring to a boil. Lower the heat to medium, cover, and boil for about 20 minutes, until the spareribs are tender. Uncover, add the cherry tomatoes, and cook over high heat for about 3 minutes, or until the tomatoes are softened. Transfer to a soup tureen.

Put the garnishes and condiments in small bowls and arrange them on the table. Prepare each bowl of noodles by putting some bean sprouts in a soup bowl, then topping with 3 to 4 nests of noodles. Ladle the meat broth, including pieces of the spareribs, over the top. Garnish with crispy garlic, scallions, and cilantro and serve hot, with bowls of the soy sauce, lime slices, and chile powder on the side.

Cook's Notes

The chile paste will keep for a month in the refrigerator. Both the beef broth and the finished sauce can be made ahead. If you prefer, instead of chopping the spareribs for the broth, have the butcher cut them into 1-inch cubes.

For the sauce

2 tablespoons vegetable oil
½ pound ground pork
¼ pound ground beef
1 pound country-style pork spareribs, chopped into bite-sized chunks
1 tablespoon bean sauce or bean paste
½ pound cherry tomatoes, halved

For the garnishes and condiments

1 pound fresh bean sprouts (4 cups)
¼ cup Crispy Garlic (page 138)
2 whole scallions, finely chopped
15 to 20 sprigs cilantro, coarsely chopped
¼ cup soy sauce
2 limes, sliced into wedges
2 tablespoons Roasted Dried Chile Powder (page 91)

3 bundles (9 ounces) somen noodles or rice vermicelli, boiled and shaped into nests as directed on page 278

Kanum Jean Yurn Song Kreang

COOL NOODLES WITH VIETNAMESE GARNISHES

Makes 6 servings

**For the sauce
(makes 1 cup)**

1 teaspoon sea salt
4 large cloves garlic, minced
9 to 10 fresh bird chiles or
    5 to 6 serrano chiles, minced
3 tablespoons granulated sugar
¼ cup palm sugar or packed light
    brown sugar
⅔ cup rice vinegar or cider vinegar
5 tablespoons fish sauce (*namm pla*)

For the turkey topping

3 tablespoons vegetable oil
¾ pound ground turkey
2 stalks lemongrass, green parts and
    hard outer layers removed,
    minced
1 teaspoon Madras curry powder
½ teaspoon sea salt

3 bundles (9 ounces) somen noodles
    or rice vermicelli, boiled and
    shaped into nests as directed on
    page 278

**For the garnishes and
accompaniments**

¼ pound fresh bean sprouts (1 cup)
¼ pound green beans, parboiled in
    salted water for 1 minute, or just
    until the color brightens, rinsed
    in cool water, and thinly sliced
1 small bulb fennel, thinly sliced
7 to 8 sprigs cilantro, coarsely
    chopped

The Vietnamese and Thai peoples have enjoyed a friendly relationship for centuries. In Bangkok, as well as in the central provinces and the border cities, there are large Vietnamese settlements. This recipe came from the Vietnamese community in Chai Phumi, a city in northeastern Thailand. During the summer at my restaurant, we serve this dish as a weekly special. I use ground turkey instead of the original ground beef because it's lighter.

The recipe uses Madras curry powder from India as a seasoning. In both Asian and American supermarkets, it is now sold as pure curry powder, pure hot curry powder, or Oriental curry powder, all packaged in 3- or 7-ounce tin cans. Some supermarkets carry the S&B brand in a bright red and yellow 3-ounce can, which is a good substitute.

For the sauce, in a mortar, with a pestle, pound the sea salt and garlic into a paste. Add the chiles and pound to a paste. Transfer the mixture to a small mixing bowl and set aside.

In a small saucepan, combine the granulated sugar, palm sugar, vinegar, and fish sauce and cook, stirring, over medium-low heat until the sugar is dissolved, about 2 minutes. Cool, then add to the pounded paste, mix well, and set aside.

In a 12-inch skillet, heat the oil over high heat for 1 to 2 minutes, or until very hot. Add the ground turkey. Cook, stirring to separate and crumble the meat, until evenly browned. Add the lemongrass, curry powder, and sea salt, mix well, and cook, stirring, for another 2 minutes. Transfer to a serving bowl and cover until ready to serve.

To serve, place a bowl of the chile sauce in the center of a large platter. Arrange the nests of noodles on one side and mounds of the bean sprouts, green beans, fennel, and cilantro on the other. Set a bowl of the turkey topping nearby. Have each guest put 3 or 4 noodle nests on his or her plate, top with a couple of spoonfuls of turkey meat, as well as bean sprouts, green beans, fennel, and cilantro, and drizzle several spoonfuls of the sauce over the noodles, separating and loosening the strands so the noodles absorb the sauce.

Noodles: Creative Thai Adaptations

In 1939, my father stepped off a boat from Shiang Hai, China, onto a dock in Bangkok. He was thirty-five years old. He paid an equivalent of 20 baht (less than one American penny in his time) in customs fees and for the next forty years lived in the country as if he were a Thai citizen. From the time he was nineteen years old, he had traveled all over Southeast Asia, selling embroidered goods from his hometown in Shantung Province while looking for a temporary place to settle. China had become uninhabitable because of the war with Japan.

Hearing that Thailand was friendly to Chinese immigrants and a good place for doing business, he made the journey that would totally change the life of our family. He did not speak the language and never really mastered it. During those first few years living in Thailand as a bachelor, he did not worry about cooking, because the streets abounded with food stalls and vendors open all hours of the day and night. Among them were southern Chinese from Hokkien, Touchew, and Canton selling noodles from their provinces. They were not like noodles from his northern hometown. Nevertheless, he thought they were good. They were also wholesome, simple, and cheap. To him, noodles were a comfort food, something familiar and reminiscent of home.

Eventually my father returned to China to bring my mother back to Thailand. They rented a house on Siphraya Road near the center of the shipping and banking district along the riverbank of Manam Chao Phraya. My mother worked as a seamstress. She would catch a riverboat for Sampeng or Chinatown, where she bought material to sew for her clients. My father walked the neighboring streets with a heavy pack, selling embroidered goods to the Europeans and wealthy Thais.

Near this bustling business center, Muslims, Indians, and Chinese immigrants crowded into their ethnic communities, sandwiched between the opulent estates of Europeans and Thais. Street vendors catered to their ethnic clientele with food stalls along the streets and in the alleys. My father was fastidious when it came to eating street foods and he was repelled by what he considered their unsanitary conditions. Occasionally, however, the aroma from the food stalls would stir his appetite and overtake his concerns about cleanliness. Giving in to his hunger, he would try something he considered to be safe and, like the time he ate southern Chinese noodles, would find them to be delicious.

While my father only ate from "tried and true" vendors, my mother was more adventurous. The more unfamiliar and exotic the noodles, the better she liked them. She was fascinated with how the Thais could take the same simple noodles she knew from home and cook them so many ways. The only thing familiar to her was the shape of the noodles, and she loved them all. My parents' tastes for street foods reflected the cosmopolitan taste of their fellow immigrants and native Thais, who are attracted to the convenience and variety, as well as the delicious taste, of noodles.

There are many kinds of noodles. Some are made with rice flour, others from wheat flour and eggs. Shapes vary from bite-sized triangles, tiny pellets, or long hair-thin strands to thick wide strands. The ways noodles are cooked are as numerous as the shapes. Some are stir-fried, boiled, or deep-fried and garnished only with meat and vegetable toppings, while others are served immersed in steaming-hot broth or rich, spicy, thick sauces.

Noodles were created by the Chinese, and quickly became a favorite ingredient of imaginative cooks, especially in Asia, who adapted and created their own noodle recipes. The Thais were not content just to cook their noodles differently, and began to invent their own methods of making noodles. The most famous are *send chan*, or rice noodles, from Chanburi, a province in Central Thailand. These are used exclusively to make *padd Thai*, Thai stir-fry noodles. Originally, *padd Thai* came from the Vietnamese. Thai cooks adapted and changed the recipe to make it their own and christened it with a name that identifies it as a Thai noodle dish. Another variation is *mee Pimand*, named after the city in the northeastern province where the noodles were first introduced by a Chinese noodle maker. The townfolk created their own recipes for stir-fried noodles, smothered with rich curry sauces. Other foreign settlers in Thailand, such as the Muslims, Indians, Laotians, and Vietnamese, also took to creating and naming their own noodle recipes.

During the 1940s, when my parents settled in Bangkok, it was a city full of marvelous and exotic noodles. By the time I was born, noodles from my parents' favorite vendors were a part of my everyday existence and as familiar as rice. Noodles are considered to be *aharn jarn deow*, or "one-dish meals." They are a staple eaten at all hours of the day or night. Street vendors often specialize in one or two kinds of noodles to create a loyal following of customers who can always count on consistency, regardless of how long they might have been away. It is almost like going home to mother's cooking.

When I came to America, noodle stalls and street foods were missing from my new life. I have made up for years of deprivation by returning to Thailand annually for a feasting ritual with my brother and friends. They stake out the best noodle stalls all over Thailand and when I arrive, the feeding frenzy begins. We attack hole-in-the-wall stands, famous for Hokkien-style rice noodle soup with crunchy fish balls. Another favorite of ours is *yen tho fho*, rice noodle soup seasoned with tomato paste, chiles in vinegar, and crispy fried garlic. We travel up and down the country to sample the best. We go north to Chiang Mai for *kao soy*, thin silky egg noodles topped with rich lamb or chicken curry sauce. We eat authentic *padd Thai* at a makeshift stand on the grounds of a Buddhist temple in the ancient city of Ayuthiya. We savor *mee krob*, crispy deep-fried rice noodles laced with sweet-and-sour sauce, which we buy from the descendants of the original recipe's creator, who still own a restaurant by the river Manam Chao Phraya, near the Royal Palace in Bangkok. Or even better, with a couple of hours of driving, we are in Petchburi for the night market and eat our fill from a pushcart vendor who makes the best *mee kati*, rice noodles bathed in rich coconut cream.

Kao Soy

Makes 6 servings

Most Thai believe this dish originated with Muslim immigrants, but it actually comes from the Tai people, an ethnic group living in southern China, who are the ancestors of the Thai people. *Kao soy,* in Tai, means "shredded rice." It describes the process of mixing rice flour with water to make rice sheets that are folded and cut by hand with a knife. The result is thin rice noodles resembling Chinese-style egg noodles. The sauce is made with beef or chicken, cooked in coconut cream and seasoned with a chile paste made from dried spices reflecting the Muslim influence, such as cumin, nutmeg, mace, and cardamom. *Kao soy* has multiple layers of tastes and textures.

There are many brands of egg noodles available in supermarkets and Asian markets. The Asian sections of many American supermarkets have Dragon Chuka Soba, a brand of Asian-style noodles from Taiwan. They come in an 8-ounce package, which is enough for 4 servings. In Asian markets, several brands of both fresh and dried egg noodles are available. I recommend Six Fortunes or Yu-Meng Noodles, made in Taiwan. They come in 12-ounce packages, containing 6 individual bundles. Each bundle is enough for a single serving. If none of these suggested brands is available, substitute fettuccine-style egg noodles.

For the chile paste, fit a food processor with the steel blade, add the crispy garlic, sea salt, dried chiles, galangal, coriander seeds, nutmeg, mace, cinnamon, cumin, cloves, cardamom, crispy shallots, and turmeric and puree into a paste. Transfer to a bowl and set aside, or store in a tightly sealed jar in the refrigerator until ready to use.

For the sauce, in a medium mixing bowl, combine the chicken and curry powder and toss to coat; let sit at room temperature for 20 minutes.

In a 4-quart saucepan, bring the coconut milk to a boil; lower the heat to simmer. Meanwhile, in a 12-inch skillet, bring the coconut cream to a

For the chile paste
(makes 1/2 cup)

3 tablespoons Crispy Garlic (page 138)

1 teaspoon sea salt

1 New Mexico (or California) chile, dry-roasted (see page 13)

12 de árbol or Japonés chiles, dry-roasted (see page 13)

One 1-inch chunk galangal or 2-inch chunk fresh ginger, roasted (see page 137), peeled, and minced

1 tablespoon coriander seeds, dry-roasted (see page 13) and finely ground

1/2 teaspoon freshly grated nutmeg

1/2 teaspoon ground mace

1/2 teaspoon ground cinnamon

1/2 teaspoon cumin seeds, dry-roasted (see page 13) and finely ground

1/2 teaspoon whole cloves, dry-roasted (see page 13) and finely ground

1/2 teaspoon cardamom seeds, dry-roasted (see page 13) and finely ground

2 tablespoons Crispy Shallots (page 138)

One 1-inch chunk turmeric, roasted (see page 134) and minced, or 1 teaspoon turmeric powder

(continued)

For the sauce
(makes 5 cups)

1½ pounds boneless, skinless
   chicken breasts, sliced across
   the grain on the diagonal into
   ¼-inch-wide slices
1 teaspoon Madras curry powder
3 cups Fresh Unsweetened Coconut
   Milk (page 69)
1 cup Fresh Unsweetened Coconut
   Cream (page 69)
5 tablespoons soy sauce
1 tablespoon light brown sugar
Sea salt to taste

For the noodles

Three 8-ounce packages dried
   Dragon Chuka Soba noodles (see
   headnote)
4 cups vegetable oil
Sea salt

For the accompaniments

7 sprigs cilantro, coarsely chopped
3 shallots, thinly sliced
One 8.8-ounce package pickled
   mustard greens (1 cup; see page
   142), rinsed, dried, and coarsely
   chopped, or 2 kosher pickles,
   chopped
2 tablespoons Roasted Dried Chile
   Powder (page 91)
2 limes, sliced into wedges

boil over high heat. Add the chile paste, stirring to blend well, lower the heat to medium-high, and cook and stir the mixture until the oil separates and takes on the color of the chiles, about 2 minutes.

Add the chicken and stir to coat it well with the mixture. Cook, stirring, until the chicken is partially cooked, about 2 minutes. Transfer the mixture to the saucepan with the simmering coconut milk, increase the heat to medium, and cook for about 10 minutes. Stir in the soy sauce, brown sugar, and sea salt, if needed, and cook until the broth thickens, about 15 minutes. Taste for an even balance of spicy, salty, and sweet flavors. Cover and set aside, or cool completely, transfer to a storage container, and refrigerate. Reheat before serving.

In a large mixing bowl, soak 1 package of the noodles in cool water until the strands are pliable, about 30 minutes. Drain the noodles, shaking the strainer to release the excess water, transfer to a large mixing bowl, and dry thoroughly with a dish towel. Wrap the noodles in the towel and set them near the stovetop, next to a platter lined with paper towels.

In a 12-inch skillet or flat-bottomed wok, heat the oil over high heat to 350°F. (You can also test the oil temperature by inserting the end of a wooden spoon in the oil; if bubbles form around it, the oil is ready for deep-frying.) Add a couple of pinches of sea salt and wait for a minute, then add a handful of softened noodles to the oil and deep-fry until the noodle strands are crispy, 2 to 3 minutes. Remove with a strainer to the plate lined with paper towels. Repeat with the remaining noodles. Set aside to cool completely before storing in a Ziploc bag.

Fill a 6-quart pot two-thirds full of water and bring to a vigorous boil. Drop the remaining 2 packages of dried noodles into the boiling water, stirring to separate the strands, and boil until the noodles are completely cooked, 2 to 3 minutes. Drain the noodles and rinse several times with cool water. Shake off the excess water, then transfer the noodles to a large mixing bowl. Cover and set aside.

To serve, put the cilantro, shallots, pickled mustard greens, chile powder, and lime wedges in individual bowls. Put the crispy fried noodles on a plate along with a bowl of the sauce. Place the boiled noodles in individual serving bowls and top each with several tablespoons of the sauce, 1 to 2 tablespoons crispy fried noodles, and 1 tablespoon coarsely chopped cilantro. Have each guest season with the remaining accompaniment, mixing and stirring the noodles to blend in the flavors.

Cook's Notes

The chile paste will keep for months in the refrigerator. The sauce can be made ahead and refrigerated overnight; reheat before serving. The softened noodles can be stored overnight in a Ziploc bag in the refrigerator. The crispy fried noodles will keep for several days in a Ziploc bag. Lastly, the roasted dried chile powder, which is considered the secret behind a good *kao soy,* can be stored for months.

Padd Thai

STIR-FRIED NOODLES THAI-STYLE

Padd Thai is perhaps the best-known Thai dish in America. It has taken on many variations, including some with tomato paste and even ketchup! After returning from Thailand, having learned the authentic version, I was excited to introduce the real thing to my customers. I almost had a revolt on my hands as they tasted a new *padd Thai* that they did not expect, or recognize. They wanted the old version, which we immediately brought back.

Over the past several years, I've learned to make *padd Thai* from vendors at different stalls all over Thailand and appreciate its versatility. Each version is slightly different, and each is wonderful. *Padd Thai* is a dish dictated solely by the wishes of the customers, but it depends on the expertise of the cooks, who know precisely how to regulate the heat with a quick stir-fry technique. Most *padd Thai* stalls sell only this one dish. Each serving is prepared individually, based on the customer's specific requests, and is usually eaten piping hot, immediately transferred from the wok to a plate. Traditionally *padd Thai* made for takeout was wrapped in a newspaper lined with fresh banana leaves and tied together with banana twine. Ayuthiya, the ancient capital, has a stall that still wraps it this way, which is the best way for keeping the noodles from drying out or getting soggy. But other Thai vendors have switched to modern packaging, either Styrofoam containers or plastic bags, which alters the taste somewhat. I encourage my customers to stay and eat their *padd Thai* fresh from the wok: otherwise, I must package it in Styrofoam. American health inspectors would never allow banana leaves and newspapers!

I have selected three *padd Thai* variations: the original from Ayuthiya; one from a famous stall in Bangkok; and another made with bean threads. The main ingredients for each recipe are portioned for a single generous serving, just as the street vendors do.

Guidelines for Making Padd Thai

It's best to make *padd Thai* one serving at a time, or two or three servings at the most. Have all ingredients prepared and arranged close at hand in bowls or plates in the sequence they are to be added to the pan.

Select a 12-inch flat-bottomed wok or skillet. The larger the cooking vessel, the easier it is to stir-fry the noodles and keep the heat evenly distributed throughout the cooking process.

Place the wok or skillet over the highest heat possible for 1 to 2 minutes, or until you can feel the heat when you hold your hand above the empty pan. Add the sauce or oil. When you add the noodles, lower the heat a bit. If the heat is too intense, the noodles will clump into one big lump. On the other hand, if it is too low, the noodles will get soggy. Use two large spatulas for stir-frying.

The amounts in these recipes are recommended as guidelines. In my versions, I use less oil than is traditional, which makes *padd Thai* less greasy; most street vendors opt for the sheen created from more oil. I also use water to loosen the noodle strands and to prevent them from sticking together. Experiment to find out what works best for you.

Common Padd Thai Ingredients

NOODLES

In California, I buy vacuum-packed fresh thin rice noodles. The 1-pound package will make 5 to 6 servings of *padd Thai*. If you can't find fresh noodles, dried rice noodles are readily available in Asian markets, as well as in most supermarkets. In Asian markets, look for Caravelle, a brand made in Thailand that comes in a 16-ounce package. This easily makes 5 to 6 servings. In American supermarkets, the Thai Kitchen brand is beautifully packaged in smaller 8-ounce portions. They are labeled "Jasmine Rice Stir-fry Noodles." Each package makes 2 to 3 servings. If you cannot find either of these brands, look for noodles that are a dull translucent white; the whiter the color, the better the quality of noodles. About ⅛ inch wide, these noodles resemble fettuccine and are quite brittle. The strands are bundled in one large mass and wrapped in cellophane. Dried noodles tend to shatter and scatter, so I like to unwrap them inside a paper bag.

Dried noodles need to be soaked in lukewarm water for 15 minutes, or until pliable and no longer brittle. Drain the noodles and wrap them in a kitchen towel until you are ready to stir-fry. This will keep them from drying out. Leftover cooked soaked noodles will keep in a plastic bag in the refrigerator for several days. Prior to stir-frying, bring them to room temperature.

TOFU

Fried tofu, which is also called "savory baked tofu" or "baked bean curd," is available in many health food stores and Asian markets. It's the color of coffee, approximately 2½ to 3 inches square, with 2 to 4 pieces packaged together. Each package weighs between 6 and 10 ounces.

If premade fried firm tofu is not available, make your own: Buy very firm fresh tofu packaged in water in a plastic tub. These weigh 14 to 19 ounces packaged, and after deep-frying will yield about 1 cup. Put the tofu in a pie plate and weight it down with a plate and a full soup can or a heavy bottle on top of the plate. Place the whole thing in the refrigerator. It takes a couple of hours to press out the excess liquid. Then slice the tofu into thin strips and deep-fry in 2 cups of hot oil (325°F) until golden, 4 to 5 minutes. Once the strips are nice and crispy, transfer them to a plate lined with paper towels. When completely cooled, store in a Ziploc bag at room temperature. It will keep for a couple of days.

Padd Thai Ayuthiya

PADD THAI FROM AYUTHIYA

Makes 1 generous serving

**For the sauce
(makes about 1¹⁄₂ cups,
enough for 6 servings)**

One 1¹⁄₂-inch chunk fresh tamarind
    or 1 cup pureed dried apricots
1¹⁄₂ cups boiling water (for tamarind)
    or 1 cup concentrated cherry juice
    (for apricot puree)
¹⁄₂ cup palm sugar or packed light
    brown sugar
¹⁄₄ cup granulated sugar
¹⁄₂ teaspoon sea salt
¹⁄₄ cup fish sauce (*namm pla*)

**For the noodles
(for 1 serving)**

¹⁄₄ cup sauce (above), plus 2 to 3
    tablespoons, if needed
2 to 3 ounces dried wide rice
    noodles, softened in warm water
    (see page 299) and loosely
    wrapped in a towel (about 2 cups)
1 tablespoon Crispy Garlic (page 138)
1 teaspoon salted Tien Jing cabbage
    (see page 143), rinsed, patted dry,
    and minced, or salt-packed
    capers, rinsed and dried
9 to 10 dried baby shrimp, softened
    in warm water and dried
¹⁄₄ pound fresh bean sprouts (1 cup)
10 to 12 blades Chinese chives or
    2 whole scallions, sliced into
    1-inch lengths
1 tablespoon unsalted peanuts, dry-
    roasted (see page 13) and ground
¹⁄₂ teaspoon Roasted Dried Chile
    Powder (page 91)

(continued)

Unlike the versions found in most Thai restaurants in America, this *padd Thai* uses oil only for scrambling the egg. The sauce, which is made with palm sugar, white sugar, thick tamarind juice, and fish sauce, can be made ahead and refrigerated for at least a week. The original recipe did not include an egg, but it is offered as one of today's popular options. A sour taste is necessary to balance the sweetness of the sauce, so slivers of sour fruits, such as star fruit, *mah kok* (hog plum), and *madan* (garcinia), are used to garnish the dish.

For the sauce, in a small bowl, combine the tamarind chunk with the boiling water; let sit until cool. Massage the tamarind to "milk" it and separate the pulp from the seeds. Spoon 1 cup of the thick tamarind juice into a small saucepan; refrigerate the rest for future use. (If using pureed apricots, combine with 1 cup concentrated cherry juice.)

Add the palm sugar, granulated sugar, salt, and fish sauce to the saucepan of tamarind juice and cook over medium heat for 1 to 2 minutes, to dissolve the sugar. Transfer the mixture to a bowl to cool. Set aside, or store in a plastic container in the refrigerator or until ready to use. It will keep for a week.

For the noodles, heat a 12-inch skillet or flat-bottomed wok for 1 to 2 minutes. Test for readiness by putting your hand 2 to 3 inches above the skillet: If you feel the heat, the skillet is ready. Add ¹⁄₄ cup of the sauce; it will begin to bubble immediately. Add the loosened noodles and cook, stirring, for 45 seconds. Lower the heat to medium-high—or, if the noodles begin to clump, lower the heat further, and sprinkle 2 to 3 tablespoons of sauce over them—and continue to cook, stirring, until the noodles are cooked, 1 to 2 minutes. Add the crispy garlic, salted cabbage, and dried shrimp and stir the noodles to mix and blend in the seasonings. Add the bean sprouts and Chinese chives and continue to cook, stirring, until the vegetables turn slightly limp, about 1 minute. Add the peanuts and chile powder, stir, and slide the noodles onto a

300

platter. Garnish the top with the peanuts, Chinese chives, and star fruit slivers. Decorate the side of the plate with the sprigs of pennywort and banana blossom wedges. Serve with the chile powder on the side.

Variation

If you choose to add an egg to the *padd Thai,* do so after seasoning it with the chile powder. Push the noodles to one side of the skillet. Add 1 tablespoon oil to the center of the skillet and crack the egg into it. After the egg begins to set, about 30 seconds, stir to scramble. Push the noodles over the egg and mix lightly.

For the garnishes and condiments

- 1 tablespoon unsalted peanuts, dry-roasted (see page 13) and ground
- 3 to 4 blades Chinese chives or 1 whole scallion, sliced into 1-inch lengths
- ¼ star fruit, slivered, or ¼ Granny Smith apple, slivered, soaked in fresh lemon juice and water, rinsed, and patted dry
- 10 to 15 sprigs pennywort or 2 to 3 arugula leaves
- ¼ banana blossom (see page 23) or ½ head Belgian endive, sliced into wedges
- 1 teaspoon Roasted Dried Chile Powder (page 91)

Padd Thai Bann Gog
BANGKOK-STYLE PADD THAI

Makes 1 generous serving

¼ cup vegetable oil

3 large cloves garlic, minced

2 to 3 ounces dried wide rice
noodles, softened in warm water
(see page 299) and loosely
packed (about 2 cups)

1 cup water (or as needed)

2 tablespoons rice vinegar or cider
vinegar

1 teaspoon fish sauce (*namm pla*)

⅓ cup diced fried tofu (see page
299)

1 tablespoon dried baby shrimp

1 tablespoon salted Tien Jing
cabbage (see page 143) or salt-
packed capers, rinsed and dried

2 tablespoons unsalted peanuts,
dry-roasted (see page 13) and
ground

½ teaspoon Roasted Dried Chile
Powder (page 91)

1 tablespoon sugar

¼ pound fresh bean sprouts (1 cup)

10 to 12 blades Chinese chives or
2 whole scallions, cut into 1-inch
lengths

1 large egg

**For the garnishes and
accompaniments**

2 ounces fresh bean sprouts (½ cup)

3 to 4 blades Chinese chives or
1 whole scallion

¼ young banana blossom (see page
23) or ½ head Belgian endive,
sliced into 2 to 3 wedges

1 lime, sliced into wedges

My cousin Susie has a friend who is a *padd Thai* vendor. For years her cart was in an alley close to Central Department Store in Bangkok's Silom area. She became so successful selling only *padd Thai* that she eventually rented a shop house in the alley and opened a restaurant. She continues to set up her cart every morning in front of the restaurant where she or her sister makes *padd Thai* for the long line of customers. Susie asked her friend to teach me to make *padd Thai*, and for the first week, she put me to work in the kitchen with the rest of the staff. The second week, I stood at the cart and watched with amazement as she or her sister made *padd Thai* one order after another while taking money, making change, and never once making a mistake. Each *padd Thai* order was perfect. One day, without any warning, I was asked to take her place. As regular customers formed a line and gave me their orders, I tried my best to cook each and every one without ruining it, or worse, having a nervous breakdown on the spot. Everyone had a good laugh when the owner told her customers that I was a Japanese tourist who wanted to learn to make *padd Thai*. After that, I understood why a proprietor selling *padd Thai* would make only this one dish. It takes a lot of practice to be good, and perseverance to be perfect.

Heat a 12-inch skillet or flat-bottomed wok over high heat for 1 to 2 minutes. To test for readiness, put your hand 2 to 3 inches above the skillet: If you can feel the heat, the skillet is hot enough. Add 3 tablespoons of the oil and the garlic and cook, stirring to prevent burning, until the garlic is golden. Lower the heat to medium, add the noodles, and cook, stirring with two spatulas to separate the noodles. If the noodles start to clump, lower the heat and add 1 tablespoon of water, stirring and tossing. Continuing to add water 1 tablespoon at a time if necessary, stir-fry until the noodles are cooked but not soggy. Add the vinegar, fish sauce, tofu, dried shrimp, and salted cabbage and continue to cook, stirring for 1 minute. Sprinkle the peanuts, chile powder, and sugar on top of the noodle mixture and stir to mix, then quickly mix in the bean sprouts and Chinese chives. Push the noodle mixture to one side of the skillet and add the remaining 1 tablespoon oil to the center of the skillet. Break the egg directly into the oil and scramble it lightly. When the egg begins to set, push the noodle mixture back on top of the egg, then slide the noodle mixture onto a serving platter. Garnish with the bean sprouts, Chinese chives, banana blossom, and lime wedges. Serve immediately.

Woon Senn Padd Thai

THAI-STYLE BEAN THREAD STIR-FRY

Makes 1 serving

¼ cup vegetable oil

2 tablespoons dried baby shrimp

3 large cloves garlic, minced

3 ounces bean threads (glass
noodles), softened in cool water
(2 cups)

2 to 5 tablespoons water

3 tablespoons thick tamarind juice
(see page 128), or 2 tablespoons
rice vinegar

1 tablespoon sugar

1 tablespoon fish sauce (*namm pla*)

1 tablespoon salted Tien Jing
cabbage (see page 143) or salt-
packed capers, rinsed and
thoroughly dried

2 ounces savory baked tofu (see
page 299), diced (⅓ cup)

½ teaspoon cayenne (optional)

2 tablespoons unsalted peanuts,
dry-roasted (see page 13) and
ground

¼ pound fresh bean sprouts (1 cup)

10 to 12 blades Chinese chives or
2 whole scallions, sliced into
1-inch lengths

1 large egg

**For the garnishes and
accompaniments**

2 ounces fresh bean sprouts (½ cup)

¼ young banana blossom (see page
23) or ½ head Belgian endive,
sliced into wedges

1 lime, sliced into wedges

1 tablespoon cayenne (optional)

During the early 1990s, *woon senn padd Thai* became the rage among Bangkokians, who found the soft and delicate texture of bean threads a refreshing change from the usual *senn chan,* or regular rice noodles.

Bean threads resemble angel hair pasta but are translucent white. The seemingly endless strands of noodles are packaged in cellophane, bunched tightly together in one large bundle, and tied with twine. In Asian markets, bean threads are labeled many ways: green bean thread, bean threads, vermicelli, glass noodles, or *sai fun*. The most reliable brand is from China, labeled Lung Kow vermicelli or green bean thread. Noodles or bean threads are sold in individual packages of 3.5 ounces, or sometimes with 12 individual small bundles packaged together.

In supermarkets here, China Sea, from Taiwan, is the most common brand. Labeled *sai fun*, it comes in 6-ounce packages, containing 3 individual bundles.

The smaller packages are easiest to work with, because each is enough for one serving. With the larger packages, open them inside a large shopping bag before separating the strands. This prevents the noodles, which are brittle, from scattering everywhere. Inside the bag, cut the noodles with a pair of sharp scissors into manageable lengths in the portions needed.

Soak bean threads in cool water until pliable (see page 299). Dry them thoroughly with a kitchen towel; wrap them in the towel until ready to use. After the noodles are softened, they will keep in a Ziploc bag for several days. Bring to room temperature before cooking. With a pair of scissors, cut the softened bean threads into 5- to 6-inch lengths for cooking.

Bean threads will congeal when you add them to the hot oil. It is important to regulate the heat, starting at medium, then slowly increasing it until the bean threads start to get sticky. If the bean threads clump during stir-frying, add several tablespoons of water and stir to separate the strands.

If you'd like to add meat, chicken, or seafood to this recipe, use 2 to 3 ounces per serving, thinly sliced into bite-sized pieces. Add it after stir-frying the minced garlic, and stir-fry until cooked through before adding the noodles.

In an 8-inch skillet, heat the oil over high heat to 325°F. (You can also test for readiness by dipping the tip of a wooden spoon into the oil; if bubbles form around the spoon, the oil is ready.) Add the dried shrimp and deep-fry until crispy, 10 to 15 seconds. Remove them from the oil with a slotted spoon and transfer to a plate lined with paper towels. Set aside. Transfer 3 tablespoons of the oil to a 12-inch skillet. Save the rest of the oil in a small metal bowl.

Heat the skillet over medium-high heat for 1 to 2 minutes. Lower the heat to medium and add the garlic, stirring to prevent burning. When the garlic turns golden, after 1 to 2 minutes, add the noodles and 2 tablespoons of the water. Continue to cook, stirring and tossing with two spatulas to separate the noodles, for 15 to 20 seconds. Add another 2 tablespoons of water if needed to prevent the noodles from bunching up. If the noodles start to clump, lower the heat and add another table-spoon of water. Add the tamarind juice, sugar, and fish sauce and con-tinue to cook, stirring, for 15 to 20 seconds. Add the salted cabbage and tofu, and stir to combine. Sprinkle the noodle mixture with the cayenne, if using, and the peanuts and continue to cook, stirring, for 1 to 2 minutes. Add the bean sprouts and Chinese chives, mixing and stirring. Push the noodle mixture to one side of the pan and add the remaining 1 tablespoon oil to the center of the pan. Break the egg directly into the oil and scramble lightly. When the egg begins to set, push the noodle mixture on top of the egg, then slide the noodles onto a serving platter. Garnish the top with the crispy fried dried shrimp and the bean sprouts. Arrange the banana blossom wedges, lime wedges, and a small bowl of cayenne on the side, if using. Serve immediately.

Mee Krob

CRISPY NOODLES

When King Chulalongkhorn returned from one of his trips on the royal barge, His Majesty noticed a group congregated opposite the boat landing of the royal palace. For the next several weeks, he noted that there was always a crowd at the same spot. When he inquired among his officers the reason for the crowd, he was told that it was a restaurant famous for *mee krob,* a new noodle dish invented by the owner. Being a food connoisseur, the King was intrigued and ordered one of his attendants to purchase some *mee krob* from the restaurant. After tasting the crispy fried noodles, laced with sweet and sour syrup and perfumed with bitter orange zest, His Majesty became enchanted and was a regular customer. That is, he was until the women in the Royal Court learned how it was made.

Mee krob is served as a snack or an accompaniment to curry. As a snack, it is like eating noodles spun with sugar. As an accompaniment, the intensely sweet taste and crispy texture make it a perfect foil for spicy curry. The original recipe included both cooked pork slices and whole shrimp.

Mee krob is made with rice noodles called *senn mee,* packaged as rice sticks, or *mai fun,* in Chinese. The strands are the same size as spaghetti but opaque white, and come in bundles often tied with twine. I like the Egret brand, which is made in China and comes in a 16-ounce package. Half of the package is enough for 6 servings. If this brand is not available, select noodles that are as white as possible. Avoid grayish noodles; they are poor quality. Store opened packages of rice sticks in Ziploc bags; they will keep for months. In some supermarkets, rice sticks are sold as "*mai fun*—rice stick." The China Sea brand from Taiwan, in a 6-ounce package, is available in some markets. One and a half packages (9 ounces) of this brand will easily make 6 servings. Unlike *padd Thai,* which needs to be made in individual servings, *mee krob* can be made several servings at a time.

Mee Krob Muu Gai Kub Goong

CRISPY RICE NOODLES WITH PORK, CHICKEN, AND SHRIMP

Makes 6 servings

Mee krob with meat and shrimp also includes deep-fried tofu or savory baked tofu, available in Asian supermarkets and health food stores. The sweet syrup will keep well at room temperature for a couple of days. Reheat in a double boiler until the syrup is the consistency of honey. *Mee krob* should be served immediately to prevent it from getting soggy.

In a large mixing bowl, soak the rice sticks in cool water for 15 minutes, or until they are pliable and separate easily. Dry on kitchen towels and set aside.

Heat the 6 cups oil in a large flat-bottomed wok or skillet over high heat to 350°F. (You can also test the oil by putting a couple of noodle strands in the hot oil; if they curl and puff up immediately, the oil is ready.) Carefully put a handful of noodles in the hot oil. As soon as they puff up, after about 2 seconds, flip them over to cook the other side, about 2 seconds more. Remove the noodles with a strainer and transfer to a large platter lined with paper towels. Deep-fry the remaining noodles a handful at a time. When the noodles are completely cool, cover with paper towels or transfer to a Ziploc bag and seal tightly to prevent them from getting soggy. The noodles will keep this way for a couple of days.

In the same skillet, deep-fry the dried baby shrimp until crispy, 7 to 10 seconds. Transfer to another plate lined with paper towels. Set aside or store them in a glass jar. Do the same with the firm tofu and set aside. It will take about the same time as the dried shrimp.

In a 12-inch skillet, combine the fish sauce, palm sugar, granulated sugar, and vinegar and cook over medium-low heat, swirling the mixture in a circular motion, until the sugar dissolves and caramelizes to the consistency of honey, 10 to 12 minutes. Do not stir, as this can cause the sugar to crystallize. Transfer to a bowl and let cool.

Meanwhile, add the remaining 2 tablespoons oil to another 12-inch skillet and set over high heat until quite hot. Add the garlic and a pinch of sea salt, stirring to prevent burning. When the garlic is golden, after

½ pound rice sticks

6 cups plus 2 tablespoons vegetable oil

2 tablespoons dried baby shrimp

½ cup savory baked tofu (see page 299), sliced into long thin strips and patted dry

3 to 4 tablespoons fish sauce (*namm pla*)

¾ cup palm sugar or packed light brown sugar

¼ cup granulated sugar

¾ cup rice vinegar or cider vinegar

3 large cloves garlic, minced

Sea salt

¼ pound pork loin, thinly sliced into thin 2-inch strips

½ pound boneless, skinless chicken breast, thinly sliced into 2-inch strips

½ pound large shrimp, peeled, deveined, and halved lengthwise

1 tablespoon bean sauce or bean paste

1 teaspoon Roasted Dried Chile Powder (page 91) or cayenne

Grated zest of 1 bitter orange, blood orange, or Valencia orange

3 to 4 blades Chinese chives or 1 whole scallion, sliced into 1-inch lengths

(continued)

For the garnish

1 head pickled garlic, cloves
   separated, or 5 pickled onions,
   minced
2 fresh red jalapeño chiles, seeded
   and slivered
4 to 5 sprigs cilantro, coarsely
   chopped
½ pound fresh bean sprouts
   (2 cups)
½ young banana blossom (see page
   23) or ½ head Belgian endive,
   sliced into wedges
1 lime, sliced into wedges

about 1 minute, add the pork and cook, stirring, until cooked through, 1 to 2 minutes. Add the chicken and cook, stirring, until cooked through, 1 to 2 minutes. Add the shrimp and continue to cook, stirring, until the shrimp turn pink, about 1 minute. Add the bean sauce and roasted chile powder and cook, stirring, for another 1 to 2 minutes, or until the liquid has evaporated. Add half of the syrupy sauce, stirring to coat the meat. Cook for another 1 to 2 minutes, or until the meat mixture is well coated with the sauce, then remove the pan from the heat.

Put the crispy noodles in a large mixing bowl, breaking them into bite-sized clumps. Sprinkle the orange zest over the noodles; toss gently. Coat your hands lightly with oil and drizzle one third of the remaining syrupy sauce over the noodles, mixing lightly with your hands to coat the noodles. Repeat until all the sauce is used and the noodle strands are coated. Add the Chinese chives and toss gently. Add half of the meat mixture and toss gently, then add the remaining meat mixture and toss gently.

Transfer the noodles to a serving platter. Sprinkle the top with the minced pickled garlic, jalapeño slivers, cilantro, and bean sprouts. Arrange the banana blossom and lime wedges on the side of the platter. Serve immediately.

Mee Kati

NOODLES WITH COCONUT CREAM

Makes 6 servings

Wattana, the Thai boarding school I attended for ten years, had a strange ritual. Every evening after we finished dinner, we were given a snack. Instead of being served dessert or fruit, we often had some kind of noodles or fried rice wrapped in banana leaves, clipped with a pin made from bamboo. We walked around the school grounds or sat on the grassy lawn, eating these snacks with our hands. This was my first introduction to *mee kati*. *Mee kati* is a rich and aromatic noodle dish served either warm or at room temperature.

Fill a 6-quart pot three-quarters full with water and bring it to a boil. Add the noodles, stirring to separate the strands, and cook for 2 to 3 minutes, or until softened. Drain and rinse several times with cool water. Shake the strainer to remove excess water before transferring to a bowl. Pat dry with a dish towel; cover and set aside.

In a 12-inch skillet, bring the coconut milk to a boil over high heat and cook for 2 minutes. Add the shallots, pork, shrimp, and tofu and cook, stirring, until the pork is cooked and the shrimp turn pink, 1 to 2 minutes. Add the bean sauce, palm sugar, granulated sugar, cayenne, and tamarind juice and cook, stirring, for 2 minutes more. With a strainer or slotted spoon, transfer the meat and shrimp to a bowl. Cover and set aside.

Cook the sauce for 7 to 8 minutes longer, until it is thickened. Reduce the heat to low and add the noodles to the sauce, mixing to coat the noodle strands. Add the preserved turnips, if using, and the bean sprouts and mix well. Remove from the heat and stir in the Chinese chives, mixing and tossing, then transfer to a serving platter.

Garnish with the reserved meat and shrimp, the cilantro, and chile slivers. Decorate the sides of the platter with the lime wedges, banana blossom wedges, and pennywort. Serve hot.

Cook's Notes

Mee kati can be made in stages. Cook the rice sticks ahead, cool them completely, and store them in a Ziploc bag in the refrigerator; they'll keep well overnight. Reheat by immersing them in boiling water for 10 seconds. The sauce can also be made ahead and refrigerated overnight; reheat gently before serving.

6 ounces rice sticks, soaked in cool water until pliable, drained, and dried on kitchen towels

2 cups Fresh Unsweetened Coconut Milk (page 69)

3 shallots, thinly sliced

1/4 pound ground pork

1/2 pound medium shrimp, peeled, deveined, and halved lengthwise

2 ounces savory baked tofu (see page 299), finely chopped (1/2 cup)

1 tablespoon bean sauce or bean paste

2 tablespoons palm sugar or light brown sugar

2 tablespoons granulated sugar

1 teaspoon cayenne

1/2 cup thick tamarind juice (see page 128)

2 tablespoons fish sauce (*namm pla*)

1/2 cup sweet preserved turnips or preserved radishes, sliced into long thin strands, rinsed, and dried (optional)

1/2 pound fresh bean sprouts (2 cups)

20 blades Chinese chives or 2 whole scallions, sliced into 1-inch lengths

For the garnishes and accompaniments

10 sprigs cilantro, coarsely chopped

2 fresh red bird chiles or serrano chiles, seeded and slivered

1 lime, sliced into wedges

1/2 young banana blossom (see page 23) or 1/2 head Belgian endive, sliced into wedges

20 sprigs pennywort, arugula leaves, or watercress sprigs

Mee Namm Bann Rad-Cha-Toud

NOODLE SOUP FROM THE HOUSE OF RAD-CHA-TOUD

Makes 6 servings

**For the chicken broth
(makes 6 cups)**

One 3-pound chicken, rinsed

1 tablespoon Scotch, bourbon, or
   Irish whiskey

One ¼-inch slice fresh ginger,
   lightly pounded

4 cloves garlic, unpeeled, lightly
   pounded

3 whole scallions, cut into 1-inch
   lengths

10 sprigs cilantro, coarsely chopped

2 tablespoons soy sauce

½ teaspoon dry-roasted Thai white
   peppercorn powder (see page 85)

½ teaspoon sesame oil

7 cups bottled or filtered water

(continued)

Than Phu Ying (Her Ladyship) Prann wrote the first Thai cookbook in the late 1800s, under the pen name of Mae Khloa Hoa Paa. Her husband served as a royal cadet to King Chulalongkhorn and one of her daughter's became the King's royal consort. Her ancestors, including the queen of King Rama III, were celebrated cooks. Her cookbook, an ambitious task, celebrated Thai culinary arts and recorded her family's and friends' recipes. The books were given away to her circle of friends and family in the Royal Court.

This recipe is her creation and her husband named it after their estate, Bann Rad-Cha-Toud. He also wrote a poem celebrating her creation.

Although the recipe serves six, each portion should be assembled individually. Besides being light and delicious, this is a gorgeous dish for a noodle party, where the guests can help themselves to the ingredients assembling their own dishes.

Put the chicken in a 6-quart stockpot with the whiskey and enough tap water to cover and bring to a boil. Remove the chicken, discard the water, and rinse out the stockpot. Return the chicken to the pot and add the ginger, garlic, scallions, cilantro, soy sauce, white peppercorn powder, sesame oil, and bottled water. Bring to a boil, then reduce the heat to medium-low and simmer, covered, for 1½ to 2 hours, or until the chicken meat falls easily off the bone. The broth will be a rich golden color. Strain the broth into a large saucepan and keep at a low simmer. If preparing ahead, cool completely before storing in the refrigerator. Save the chicken for another use, such as Stir-Fried Rice (page 48) or Grilled Chicken Salad (page 258).

For the meat topping, in a small saucepan, combine the bean sauce, soy sauce, molasses, fish sauce, sea salt, sugar, and vinegar and cook over medium heat for 2 minutes, or until the sugar is dissolved. Transfer the sauce to a bowl to cool.

In a 12-inch skillet, heat the oil over high heat until it is quite hot, about 2 minutes. Add the shallots and cook, stirring, for 10 to 15 seconds, or until softened. Add the sliced pork and cook, stirring, until browned, about 2 minutes. Add the chicken and cook, stirring, until cooked through, about 2 minutes more. Add the shrimp and cook, stirring, until they turn pink, 1 to 2 minutes. Add the sauce, mixing and stirring until it begins to boil. Transfer to a serving bowl, cover, and keep warm.

To assemble the dish, fill a 6-quart pot three-quarters full of water and bring to a boil. Put a handful of the softened rice sticks in a strainer and plunge the strainer of noodles into the boiling water for 20 seconds, or until the water returns to a boil. Remove the strainer of noodles from the boiling water and immediately plunge into a large bowl of cool water. Shake the noodles to discard the excess water and transfer them to an individual serving bowl. Use the strainer to blanch a handful of bean sprouts, drain well, and place on top of the noodles. Garnish with 3 to 4 tablespoons of the meat mixture and its sauce, about 1 tablespoon crabmeat, 1 teaspoon pickled garlic, a pinch or two of orange zest, 2 teaspoons orange juice, 1½ teaspoons fish sauce, 2 teaspoons lime juice, and a pinch or two of Chinese celery. Ladle enough chicken broth over the noodles to cover them, garnish with chile slivers and chopped cilantro, and taste for an even balance of salty, fruity, sweet, and peppery flavors. Serve hot, and repeat the same process for each guest.

For the meat topping

- 1 tablespoon bean sauce or bean paste
- 6 tablespoons soy sauce
- 2 tablespoons molasses
- 1 tablespoon fish sauce (*namm pla*)
- 1 teaspoon sea salt
- 1 tablespoon sugar
- 3 tablespoons rice vinegar or cider vinegar
- 2 tablespoons vegetable oil
- 2 shallots, minced
- ½ pound boneless pork loin, sliced into thin strips
- 1 pound boneless, skinless chicken breasts, sliced into thin strips
- ½ pound medium shrimp, peeled, deveined, and halved lengthwise
- ¾ pound rice sticks, soaked in cool water until pliable, drained, and dried on kitchen towels
- ½ pound fresh bean sprouts (2 cups)
- ½ pound cooked crabmeat, picked over for shells and cartilage
- 4 cloves pickled garlic or 4 pickled onions, minced
- Grated zest and juice of 2 blood oranges or Valencia oranges
- 3 tablespoons fish sauce (*namm pla*)
- Juice of 2 to 3 limes
- 4 stalks Chinese celery or 1 stalk regular celery, minced
- 7 to 8 fresh red bird chiles or 5 to 6 serrano chiles, seeded and slivered
- 12 sprigs cilantro, minced

Mail-Order Sources

Adriana's Caravan
409 Vanderbilt Street
Brooklyn, NY 11218
800-316-0820
Fax: 718-436-8565
adrianascaravan@aol.com

Aiko's Oriental Foods
781 Granada Center
Alamogordo, NM 88310
505-434-1040
www.neonwok.com

Bann Thai at Saffron
3735 India Street
San Diego, CA 92103
619-574-0048
Fax: 619-574-0322
www.sumeiyu.com

Kalustyan
123 Lexington Avenue
New York, NY 10016
212-685-3451
Fax: 212-683-8458
www.kalustyans.com

Kam Man Food Products
200 Canal Street
New York, NY 10013
212-571-0330
Fax: 212-766-9085

Oriental Pantry
423 Great Road (2A)
Acton, MA 01720
800-828-0368;
978-264-4576
Fax: 781-275-4506
oriental@orientalpantry.com

Rafal Spice Company
2521 Russell Street
Detroit, MI 48207
800-228-4276;
313-259-6373
Fax: 313-259-6220

South China Seas Trading
    Company
1689 Johnston Street
Granville Island Market
Vancouver, BC V6H 3R9
604-681-5402

Spice Merchant
P.O. Box 524
Jackson Hole, WY 83001
307-733-7811
Fax: 307-733-6343
stirfry@compuserve.com

ThaiGrocer/SEC
3161 North Cambridge
    Street
Suite 507
Chicago, IL 60657
Tel/fax: 773-477-6268
www.thaigrocer.com

Thai Grocery
5014 North Broadway
    Street
Chicago, IL 60640
773-561-5345
Fax: 733-561-5522

Uwajimaya
519 6th Avenue South
Seattle, WA 98104
800-889-1928;
206-624-6248
www.uwajimaya.com

Resources

Bremness, Lesley. *Herbs*. New York: Dorling Kindersley, 1994.

Chaichean, Ahnusonn. "Neang Nai Nyan Phraradchathanpraensoum Mom Luang Chaichean Kumphu Na Maeruwat Thepsirinthasawad." August 19, 1997.

H.R.H. Prince Chula Chakrabongse. *Lords of Life*. Bangkok: DD Books, 1960.

Hall, D.G.E. *A History of South-East Asia*. Fourth edition. New York: Macmillan, 1994.

De la Loubere, Simon. *The Kingdom of Siam*. Kuala Lumpur: Oxford University Press, 1969.

Jacquat, Christiane. *Plants from the Markets of Thailand*. Bangkok: Dorling Kindersley, 1990.

Kaosaodd, Amonrad. *Khloa Thai, Koun Thai*. Bangkok: Sang Daend, 1998.

Komodjiti, Jitsamunn. *Tum Ra Aharun Prajum Wun*. Bangkok: Kao Na, 1960.

Luce, Gordon H. "Rice and Religion." *Journal of the Siam Society*, July 1965.

Nitsarad, Nueng. *Chivit Nai Wung*. Krung Tepp, 1998.

O'Kane, John, trans. *The Ship of Sulaiman*. New York: Columbia University Press, 1972.

Padsagonevong, Prann. *Mae Khloa Hoa Paa*. Somdet Phranangchao Phrabarongradchaninadd Songphragunaproankhlao Hai Pimphraradchathan Nai Nyan Phraradchathan Praen Som, Chao Chom Phit, Nai Radchagan Thi Hha Nah Maeruprayuwongsagan, February 21, 1976.

Phillips, Roger, and Martyn Rix. *Vegetables*. New York: Random House, 1993.

Phupinyo, Watlaya. *Sarapan Kaeng Ret Sod*. Bangkok: Dudjara, 1997.

Radchani, Junjern. *Tum Ra Kubb Kao*. Bangkok: Sarimvitbunnakarn, 1949.

Rajadhan, Anuman, Phya. *The Life of the Farmer*. Bangkok: Thammasat University Press, 1949.

Reubreing, Kanyabadee. *Menu Prod Sadet Poh*. Bangkok: Bunteg Siam, 1997.

Sapa Sathri Hang Chadd (International Women's Club). *Tum Ra Yumm Rarh Kreang Jimm Thai*. 1966.

Smith, George Vinal. *The Dutch in Seventeenth-Century Thailand*. Center for Southeast Asian Studies, Special Report no. 16. Detroit: the Cellar Book Shop, 1977.

Smithies, Michael. *The Mons: Collected Articles from the Journal of the Siam Society*. Bangkok, 1986.

Sinthavalai, Sirilak. *Thai Snack Foods: Part I. Basic Information for Product Development*. Bangkok: Kasetsart University, 1990.

Sinthavalai, Sirilak. *Food Preservation in Thailand: Theory, Application, and Recipes*. Bangkok: Kasetsart University, 1990.

Sonakul, Sibpan. *Everyday Siamese Dishes*. Bangkok: Prachandra Press, 1969.

Teingbuntumm, Vit. *Samud Pai Thai*. Bangkok: Prachum Thong, 1996.

Trager, James. *The Food Chronology*. New York: Henry Holt & Company, 1995.

Index

daikon, 21
  salted, 143–44
deep-fried, deep-frying:
  big four paste in, 87
  chile powder, crispy, 92
  fire crackers, 102
  fish, 16, 183, 186
  fish patties, 148–49
  garlic, 138
  legumes, 23
  mackerel, 183, 186
  rice crackers, 6
  shallots, 138
  stuffed potatoes, 104–5
  vegetables, 183, 185
dok, 23
dok gulab, 135
dok jun tedd, 130
dok mali, 135
dok pratani, 23
drunken stir-fried beef, 175
dry-roasted:
  coconut flakes, 71
  garlic, 137
  ginger, 137
  ingredients, 10, 13, 94, 136–37
  peanuts, 136, 140
  peppercorns, 56, 85
  rice, 13, 32–33, 49, 136
duck, 15–16
  roast, *laab* with, 49, 250–51

egg(s):
  boiled, 186
  in fish custard in banana pouches,
    170–71
  in omelet with stir-fried chicken
    and bean threads, 116
  in open-faced spinach omelet, 187
  salted, 143, 186
  thousand-year-old, 143
eggplant(s), 24
  baby, 25, 181, 192–93
  green, 25
  grilled, chile sauce, 195
  Japanese, 25
  long purple, 25
  stuffed, 25

faithful See Da, the, 76
"fender bender" fried stuffed snow
    peas or squash blossoms,
    150–51
fire crackers, 102
fish, 62
  cleaning and scaling of, 16
  custard, steamed, in banana
    pouches, 170–71
  deep-fried, 16, 148–49, 183, 186
  dried salted, 46, 139, 143
  dried smoked, 46, 47, 73
  fermented, 82, 83, 96, 125
  fillets of, 16
  grilled, 16, 186
  patties, deep-fried, 148–49
  salad, grilled, 270
  soup, 62, 73
  steamed, 16
  yellow curry with pineapple and,
    227
fish sauce, 48, 62, 73, 81, 82, 83, 96
  fresh chiles with, 93
  in roasted chiles in oil, 94
flowers, 23, 27, 56, 135, 248
food processors, 5, 8, 9, 18, 68, 69,
    86–87
fresh chiles in vinegar, 93
fresh chiles with fish sauce, 93
fresh squid salad, 262
fruit(s), 27–29, 62, 63, 127–28
  accompaniments, 54
  in curry, 206
  as garnishes, 54
  salad, 271
fuk, 26–27
fuzzy melon, 26

gab glam, 144
gai, 15–16
gai lan, 19–20
gai yang, 162
galangal, 131–32
  chunk, 46, 73
  in coconut cream soup with dried
    fish, 73
  in curry, 205–6
  lesser, 112, 132, 206
galloping horse, 154–55
ga-pao, 134
garcinia, 127–28
garlic, 2, 7, 81, 83

  in big four paste, 86–87, 132
  in chicken coconut cream soup,
    74
  in chicken rice, 40–41
  crispy, 138
  in crying tiger, 114–15
  dry-roasted, 137
  pickled, 140
  preparation of, 12, 84–85
garnishes, 11, 14
  cilantro leaves, 40, 41, 48, 100,
    103, 104–5, 109, 116, 131
  coconut, 68
  cucumber, 40, 41, 48, 116
  fruit, 54
  ginger, 103
  mint leaves, 60, 76, 77
  scallion, 40, 41, 48, 116, 134
  vegetable, 24, 40, 41, 48, 100, 116
  Vietnamese, with cool noodles,
    292
ga-tiem, 132, 206
ga-tiem chew, 138
ga-tiem dorng, 140
ga-tiem pow, 137
geun chai, 20
ghin kao, 62
giem bouy, 144
ginger:
  in coconut cream soup with dried
    fish, 73
  dry-roasted, 137
  fresh, 46, 48, 49, 132, 184
  as garnish, 103
  sweet pickled, 44, 45, 56, 103,
    140–41, 184
  in vinegar, young, 141
glurh, 82, 83, 84, 86–87
glurh, ka-tiem, prikk Thai, rugg pakk
    chee, 86–87
goong, 16
goong heang, 140
granita, Lois Stanton's coconut, 79
green curry, sweet, 205, 220
  with meatballs, 222–23
grilled, grilling:
  Anaheim chiles with minced pork
    and minced shrimp, 243
  big four paste in, 87
  chicken, 39, 162
  chicken salad, 258
  Chinese sausage salad, 156–57